Attract Mode

ALSO BY
JAMIE LENDINO

Breakout: How Atari 8-Bit Computers Defined a Generation

Adventure: The Atari 2600 at the Dawn of Console Gaming

Faster Than Light: The Atari ST and the 16-Bit Revolution

Attract Mode

The Rise and Fall of Coin-Op Arcade Games

Jamie Lendino

Steel Gear Press
Audubon, NJ

Steel Gear Press
PO Box 459
Audubon, NJ 08106

Printed and bound in the United States of America.

Edited by Matthew Murray.
Cover photo by Dean Notarnicola.

While every precaution has been taken in the preparation of this book, the publisher and author assume no responsibility for errors or omissions, or for damages resulting from the use of the information contained herein.

Hardcover edition, October 2020.
ISBN: 978-1-7323552-3-1
Library of Congress Control Number: 2020917411

To Mom and Dad

> Contents

> Introduction

In the Golden Age of arcades, video games were more than pop culture—they were portals to the future. Shooting galleries and claw machines seemed archaic next to the video arcade's sizzling colors and animated attract mode screens. Subdued room ambience accentuated bright, backlit marquees, displays, and coin boxes. Buttons with flashing red LEDs looked like rocket ship controls. The sharp, neon lines of vector graphics drafted a perfect, minimalist design language.

More distinct than the visuals were the sounds. Video game coin-ops together formed this dissonant mashup of explosions, laser blasts, computer music, and synthesized speech. The ominous, walking bass lines of *Asteroids* and *Space Invaders* stood out the most. You could feel the pulsing in your gut as you scanned the floor to see which games were in the room, and which of those were unoccupied, waiting for the next quarter. Play a game and the feel of the vibrating cabinets and custom controls—different from game to game—made for a new kind of amusement park ride.

Even finding just a couple of new arcade games was terrific. I grew up in Brooklyn, and for a time it seemed as if cabinets were everywhere: crammed into the local pizza place or bodega, tucked inside a bowling alley, adjacent to a miniature golf course, or underneath an elevated subway station, one of many "street spots." Sometimes one or two new coin-ops would surprise you in a store you hadn't been to recently.

The rest of the country saw a wider variety of locales, including college campuses, airports, and bus depots. Hotels kept them in recreation rooms off the lobby, sometimes with a pool table or next to the gym. Indoor malls included larger, independent arcades along with chain locations such as Time-Out. The biggest were housed in their own buildings, destinations all their own.

Real arcades were the most fun because they had dozens of machines. They were always crowded, usually with a lopsided mix of teens and adults. Often one person played a game as a few others watched, sometimes to crib strategies, sometimes with a quarter on the lower-left corner of the screen to show they had the next game. To a 9-year-old in 1982, this was all amazing—and maybe a little overwhelming. But the more I played, the more I thought that this, the arcade, was where everything was going.

I wasn't alone. Amusement industry pundits marveled at the rapid rise of video games. At the height of the arcade's popularity in the early 1980s, the average coin-op raked in thousands of dollars per year for the operator and store proprietor, both of whom shared in the profits 50-50—much more than a jukebox, pool table, or pinball machine would earn.[1] But to a kid already dreaming of video games and science fiction worlds, arcades weren't just the sensation of the moment. It was easy to see where this was going, in my not-yet-mature brain: lifelike graphics, three-dimensional holograms—maybe even on actual spaceships. This was the age of the Space Shuttle, after all, where dreams of exploring the moon gave rise to possibly visiting other planets—even other worlds! Somehow, I figured, arcade games would be part of all of this.

Or so I thought. As we all know, that's not what happened. Instead of arcades becoming society's premiere form of entertainment, the entire phenomenon came and went. One day, video arcades just disappeared from the collective consciousness. Sure, they existed after the market crash and are still around, sort of, as family establishments, retro-themed bars and taverns, and fixtures in some collectors' basements. But the heyday of the video arcade ended suddenly and irrevocably. Decades later, I'm still stunned at the way things turned out.

What the Heck Happened?

From their inception in the early 1970s, video games transformed the arcade and amusement industry. The video game explosion occurred in many forms simultaneously, from university mainframe systems to home consoles and personal computers. But it was the arcade that led the way, thanks to massive hits such as *Pong*, *Space Invaders*, *Asteroids*, and *Pac-*

Man.[2] Coin-op manufacturers such as Atari, Midway, Exidy, and Centuri marketed their new machines not to gamers, but to the proprietors of these establishments. The brochures promised operators the games were reliable and would increase revenue. Vendors touted self-test modes, difficulty tuning, and maintenance and repair options. The ads were much less about the games themselves.

But the arcade made the games what they were. The environment, the cabinet designs, the control panels—all were hugely important and are not easily modeled in an emulator setup. Today it takes only seconds to fire up an "arcade-perfect" game of *Asteroids* on your home computer—an incredible development, and one we only dreamed of during the Golden Age! But the way you rotated your ship with two buttons instead of a joystick, the cabinet vibrations from the sounds, and the faint trails of the afterglow from the vector graphics all made a real difference in how you played the game. The same went for the variously sized and calibrated trackballs in *Missile Command* versus *Centipede*; the specific wheel, pedal, and stick shift configurations found in *Pole Position* or *Turbo*; and the sophisticated flight yoke in *Star Wars: The Arcade Game*, a controller that also found its way onto *Paperboy* cabinets for a different purpose. The video arcade environment, including its social and public aspects, often made the biggest difference of all.

In short order, arcade machines migrated out of bars and found their way into all manner of locations large and small. They became fixtures in local restaurants, office lobbies, and corner delis. And then, after an explosive period of growth right up until 1982, and even more quickly than they had risen, the coin-op as cultural zeitgeist disappeared. Sure, arcades have stuck around in one form or another ever since, and the early 1990s saw a brief resurgence in popularity. But the glory days of arcades ended fast and hard in 1984. They never returned.

To take the 10,000-foot view, what happened seems simple in hindsight: Video games came home. Cartridge-based consoles such as the Atari Video Computer System (2600) gave way to increasingly impressive systems closer to arcade cabinets in graphics, sound, and gameplay, if not controls and the overall visceral and social experience of being in the arcade. It wasn't just newer game systems such as the ColecoVision and the Atari 5200 SuperSystem, but it was also home computers that offered increasingly sophisticated, deeper titles, plus a dizzying array of other software, often for not much more money than a console. Arcade games remained a step ahead in graphics and sound quality for several decades, but as new generations of home systems appeared, the gap narrowed and narrowed until it no longer mattered. Video games were still as popular as ever, but there was little reason to venture out to an arcade with a pocket full of quarters that would only amount to an hour or two of playtime.

Why You Should Read This Book

The home video game revolution is one obvious explanation for what happened to arcades. But there's much more to the story. What made the video arcade first appear? How did the games capture players' imaginations? How did they evolve? What about all of those late-1980s and early-1990s games that originated in the arcade, supposedly after its heyday? And what did it take to seal the video arcade's ultimate doom? There had to be more to it than an industry crash and new generations of consoles such as the Nintendo Entertainment System (NES) and the Sony PlayStation—and there was. This book tells that story.

Attract Mode covers the Bronze Age (1971–1977), the Golden Age (1978–1984), the Platinum Age (1985-1991), and the Renaissance (1991–1994). Both arcades and video games have a bit of earlier history, and we'll sprint through that B.C. period (Before *Computer Space*, naturally)—just a few pages, to get us as fast as possible to the good stuff. Then the narrative will progress game by game in an approximate chronological order, because the games are what tell the history of this loosely correlated, hugely important period of time. The treatment for each game will focus on its significance in the context of the video arcade, even in cases where it seemed derivative. For example, *Galaxian* was much more than a clone of *Space Invaders*, and not just because some of the aliens broke away.

Throughout, I'll maintain a near-relentless focus on the video arcade and the games themselves. You're here because playing *Defender* and *Space Fury* is awesome—not because you want to read four pages about some executive's childhood years. I'll cover how the largest companies started, of course, but only briefly. As is probably obvious by now, I'll target coin-op games—not arcade-like games played on home systems, and not conversions of arcade games. I'll briefly touch on home conversions only to note something significant, such as an indicator of the coin-op's popularity.

I'll cover every major arcade development as we go through the timeline, both with "firsts" and "first popular" examples of key milestones as well as how they changed arcade gaming for the better. Bonus rounds, continues, high score initials, AI behaviors, cooperative play—all of it had to come from somewhere. Arcade games were defined by their simplicity, intuitive and customized controls, addictiveness, and sheer difficulty. The average game lasted two minutes, more or less. If you had never played one before, you'd be lucky if you got 30 seconds out of it. They could be brutal. Most arcade cabinets included hidden adjustments, such as toggles for the number of lives you received on a single quarter and at what score you would earn a bonus life. But these were for the operator and under lock and key, used to tune the game's difficulty to maximize revenue in specific locations as locals became better at the game.

Conventions

Each game's subhead will include the name of the game, who developed it, who distributed it in the U.S., and the year it was released. As with many things about the old days of video games (and computing in general), the exact date something was released isn't always known, and often several sources from the time period disagree with each other. Sometimes it was by region (e.g. the American version arriving several months later than in Japan, and from a different manufacturer), and sometimes it was a difference between the introduction at an industry event and its appearance in local arcades. For our purposes, it doesn't matter if a certain coin-op hit the market two weeks before or two weeks after another one did, given the vagaries of distribution, delivery, and someone plugging in the thing and bringing it up. In the cases where it does matter, such as when the "first" of something appeared, I'll clarify or condition it in the text.

As with all discussions of the past that can also apply to the present, tense can be a difficult subject. In this book, I'll keep just about everything in the past tense, including when discussing how a game was played, even though you could walk up to a surviving or restored example of that machine and play it today. I'll only shift when it's natural to do so, such as things we've learned since and in retrospect.

Looking back at what now seems a fleeting moment in time, the 270-pound arcade machines were everywhere. When the local bodega or pizza shop switched out an older game for a brand new one, it was an event. This book is about both the arcade games themselves and the arcade phenomenon as it rose and fell.

1 > Press Start

The video arcade of the late 20th century seemed like a modern evolution of the amusement park. But the concept was much older, and the coin-ops that went into arcades were older still. A popular pastime in late-18th century Europe was bagatelle, a wooden countertop game that resembled pool. Unlike outdoor sports of the time such as ground billiards or bowling, people could play bagatelle even when it was raining. Players began fixing the "pins" to the table so it was easier to start new games, eliminating the need to walk around the table and clean up all of the knocked-over targets and obstacles each time. A later variant called *Billard japonais*, or Japanese Billiards, swapped the cue stick for a plunger and a spring. And in 1871, a British inventor named Montague Redgrave patented the spring launcher and pioneered the use of a marble for the ball.[1] Soon, coin-operated versions of bagatelle tables covered in glass joined other amusement and slot machines in retail and restaurant locations across America.

The newfound success of the coin-op industry could be attributed to the Great Depression. Worsening economic conditions made it difficult for most Americans to spend money on leisure activities. But these machines were affordable, costing just a nickel or even a penny per play.[2] Arthur Paulin and Earl Froom began selling *Whiffle*, the first coin-operated pinball game, in 1931. You used a plunger to launch the balls one at a time onto a glass-covered sloped surface, which contained several dozen pins arranged in three concentric circles and scoring pockets.[3] *Whiffle*'s popularity led others to try their hand at making machines, but David Gottlieb nailed the formula later that year with *Baffle Ball*, the first "hit" coin-op-erated game. One penny gave you either seven or 10 balls, depending on the model; the scoring pockets were arranged as a baseball diamond. You could also bump the table in order to nudge the ball where you wanted it to go.[4] There were still no flippers or bumpers, and you kept track of the score yourself. But people loved playing it nonetheless, and the machines were reliable enough to stand up to daily abuse. Gottlieb manufactured the machines on an assembly line, an industry first. At one point, Gottlieb was shipping 400 *Baffle Ball* cabinets per day and is rumored to have sold some 50,000 units.[5]

Other individuals and companies furthered the pinball art. In 1932, an entrepreneur named Harry Williams began buying used pinball games and redesigning the playfields. He developed a mechanism to cause the machine to end the game when it was "tilted" too much, and later refined its design to an internal pendulum device.[6] The next year, Williams unveiled *Contact*, the first electric pinball machine. It had scoring pockets that would knock the ball back into the playfield. Ray Maloney made a table called *Ballyhoo*, and soon renamed his company Bally after that machine became a huge seller. Chicago Coin released *Beam-Lite*, a 1935 table that was the first to use colored light bulb covers. The table saw sales of more than 5,000 units.[7] Before becoming a jukebox giant, David Rockola also made his own pinball games.

These and other developments in the 1930s soon resulted in an arcade industry boom. The Great Depression led to several innovations in low-cost amusement devices that could earn their owners significant revenue. People down on their luck could buy a few machines at a price of $20 each (or even less, in some cases), become entrepreneurs, and get a decent return on their investments from the coin boxes.[8]

But penny arcades never shook the seedy image of peep shows and the kinds of clientele they would attract. By default, pinball was associated with that sort of thing, just thanks to its proximity to slot machines on the arcade floor. The biggest threats to pinball's reputation, though, were shady slot machine manufacturers that built pinball-like gambling machines called "pay-outs." These reeked of organized crime. To combat it, states passed laws outlawing not just those machines but all kinds of pinball games to protect "impressionable" women, children, and minorities.[9] After a six-year fight, New York City mayor Fiorello La Guardia banned pinball in 1942. In short order, he had 2,000 pinball machines confiscated and destroyed, and he donated the metal scraps to the war effort. La Guardia made a big PR spectacle out of the ban and even demolished several confiscated machines himself for the cameras.

Figure 1.1: Early pinball tables, such as this 1933 Bally *Rocket* payout table, were constructed of wood and metal, with fixed pockets, a plunger, and a metal ball. Note the lack of flippers.

The shadow of organized crime would hang over pinball for decades to come, but the industry managed to absorb the blow of the bans. First, legit manufacturers Gottlieb and Bally joined the war effort by manufacturing airplane parts and munitions for the Armed Forces.[10] After 1945, they soldiered on along with Williams Electronics in an amusement market diminished by the war. In 1947, Gottlieb's *Humpty Dumpty* table introduced the flipper, which added an element of skill much more consequential than the plunger. This new play mechanic let manufacturers demonstrate to authorities and politicians the games weren't about gambling. Operators began affixing "For Amusement Only" stickers to machines to indicate the premises were clean. In 1956, a federal court distinguished between games of chance, such as bingo, and skill-based flipper games, which were not regulated as gambling machines.[11] Pinball manufacturers, preferring the flipper design and its non-gambling connotations, were able to convince politicians to lift the bans on a state-by-state basis throughout the next two decades.

In the 1960s, pinball enjoyed a surge in popularity that resulted in the opening of new arcades both inside major cities and in suburban sprawl. Pinball machines became common on college campuses. Giant shopping centers and malls arose with game rooms and family entertainment centers. These helped shed some of the arcades' negative connotations.[12] More than anything, the emerging industry struggled for legitimacy, just as earlier carnivals and turn-of-the-century penny arcades had.[13] Pinball games had become an important part of popular culture, as encapsulated in The Who's 1969 hit "Pinball Wizard."

Electromechanical Games

Evolving alongside pinball was the electromechanical game, which fused mechanical games with electronics. This allowed for the introduction of such components as motors, switches, resistors, solenoids, relays, bells, buzzers, and lights for a more immersive experience. One example of what could be achieved with an electromechanical design was the earliest arcade racing game. *Drive Mobile*, which International Mutoscope Reel Company released in 1941, put you on a "road" affixed to a rotating cylinder in the console. The upright design, already looking like a video game cabinet would later on, displayed a giant static map above the road and a steering wheel below. You had to race from New York to Los Angeles in 60 seconds without going off-road. Each time you reached a new city, the corresponding location on the map lit up, a bell rang, and your score increased. A two-player version was released in 1948, and a sit-down cabinet followed in 1954.[14]

Between the 1940s and the 1960s, other manufacturers joined in with their own electromechanical creations, spanning diverse genres such as shooting, baseball, pool, and bowling. In 1966, Sega introduced the surprise hit *Periscope*. This giant shooting-gallery contraption combined plexiglass waves and ships, lights and sounds, and electronic controls that resembled those of a submarine. Like *Drive Mobile*, the game was designed as an upright cabinet, in this case with a steerable periscope in the center of the view. Soon, some operators raised the price of the game from 10 to 25 cents, making *Periscope* the first coin-op to cost one quarter per play.[15] Taito Trading Company countered *Periscope* in 1967 with *Crown Soccer Special*, a two-player table game that used pinball flippers and electronically controlled players.

More sophisticated racing games soon followed. In Chicago Coin's *Speedway*, released in 1969, players controlled a race car and had to avoid opponent cars projected onto a screen displaying a road background. *Speedway* looked a lot like a prototype video arcade coin-op, with its upright cabinet, yellow marquee, three-digit scoring, coin box, steering wheel, and accelerator pedal. Allied Leisure's 1970 release *Wild Cycle*, a daredevil motorcycle game, may have been the first coin-op to feature background music, in this case via an embedded eight-track player inside the cabinet. In 1972, Bally unveiled *Hill Climb*, which put you in control of a motorcycle climbing a steep and rugged hillside. The terrain was depicted with a miniature model bike "riding" on the surface of a rotating drum painted in greens, tans, and browns. The controls consisted of handlebars with a twist control on the right side to govern your speed.

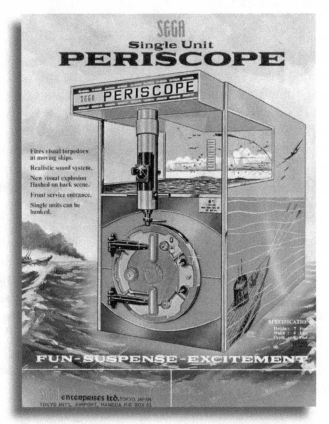

Figure 1.2: *Periscope* marked a turning point in the development of electromechanical games that began to resemble what we now call an arcade coin-op.

Like pinball games, electromechanical games were profitable for operators, if somewhat unreliable thanks to all of their moving parts. Nonetheless, entrepreneurs strove to make the most of the available space in their arcades. They arranged the machines in rows or clusters, ensuring there was plenty of extra room for customers to walk around or observe games in progress. Even with new machines such as the above, an arcade in the early 1970s would still look the same as it did years earlier: stocked with pinball machines and electromechanical games. You could try your hand at becoming a pinball wizard, race a car around a track, shoot at wooden ducks, and more. This coincided with the arrival of the air hockey table, patented in 1969 by three employees of Brunswick Billiards. The pool table manufacturer installed the addictive game in arcades, pizza places, and other establishments, and within five years the sport had its own first championship tournament in New York City.[16]

Arcade Origins

Pinball machines were not the first coin-ops, and the rooms that housed them were not the first arcades. So-called novelty machines were popular as far back as in the late 19th century, mechanical pastimes that included fortune tellers, vending machines, and slot and dice games. Inventions also included some seedier ideas such as the "love tester," which would measure one's sex appeal or abilities in the sack, and the mutoscope, a mechanical peep show.[17] Some delivered electric shocks to participants, supposedly as a health benefit. (It's safe to assume they may have caused a few problems as well.)

Entrepreneurs in North America and Europe began to establish large venues as a kind of evolution of the traveling carnival, fixed locations where they could display many machines together and attract more customers for higher profits. In cities, shopping arcades emerged, enclosed passageways between buildings lined with plate glass store windows that displayed the latest consumer goods produced as a result of industrialization.[18] These developments dovetailed with the invention of the phonograph that served as a jukebox, and the kinetoscope, which let a single person at a time view a short film, or "motion picture."[19] Shop owners played musical recordings in store windows and added novelty machines to draw in customers. Soon, thousands of people would visit inexpensive amusement centers that popped up in cities around the country.[20] Between 1905 and 1910, the centers became known as penny arcades, reflecting the price of most of the attractions.[21] Later additions included coin-operated small shooting games, automatic scales, and punching bags.[22]

Interest in arcades began to soften after the development of projected film and the rise of movie theaters with large screens. When penny arcades flourished, a few key people such as Marcus Loew built fortunes that they later used in the film industry, while others competed with vaudeville houses and burlesque theaters.[23] Slot machines were in high demand in bars and stores. As automobiles became more common in the 1920s, a new kind of operator emerged who would maintain a truck delivery route to install and service machines in small-town restaurants, bars, and other retail locations.[24] Novelty game manufacturers developed new coin-operated attractions, from Gottlieb's Husky Grip, which tested a player's strength, to games such as mechanical horse racing, hunting, baseball, hockey, soccer, gun fighting, and larger shooting galleries.[25] These skill-based games led to a new kind of 1930s arcade, such as the Sportland franchise in New York City.

Adjacent to games and the biggest earner in the 1940s and 1950s was the jukebox, found in restaurants, diners, malt shops, and even bus stations. Operators paid store owners a portion of the proceeds to keep their equipment there, maintain it, empty the coin boxes, and put new records in the jukeboxes to keep people interested and keep earning money for the owners.[26] Some of the machines were called wall boxes, often seen in restaurants when patrons sat in a booth, browsing and choosing some music to listen to while they ate.[27] The jukebox industry dovetailed nicely with electromechanical games and pinball, and by extension, the modern concept of the arcade.

Video Game Origins

The video game age began in 1958 with a bored nuclear physicist. William Higinbotham, of Brookhaven National Laboratory on Long Island, New York, decided to create a game to liven up the dull presentations the lab offered on public visitor days.[28] He repurposed the lab's Donner Model 30 analog computer to plot the trajectory of a tennis ball instead of missiles; interfaced the computer with an transistor-based oscilloscope to use as a display;[29] and added two lines, to depict the ground and the net, and a dot to represent the ball.

Higinbotham unveiled the game to the public in October 1958 at the lab's annual open house. Two lab visitors at a time could play each other using small boxes wired to the computer. Each box had a knob to control the angle of the shot and a button to hit the ball.[30] People loved it. It was the first computer game made to entertain, instead of to educate or demonstrate some technology.

Inklings of video games had appeared earlier than Higinbotham's creation, though none had the real-time control of a picture. During the

1940s, academic researchers and engineering students first began fiddling with new ways of interacting with electronics and computers, hulking, room-filling machines found in just a few colleges lucky enough to afford one. This occurred in tandem with the advent of operations research, a new field dedicated to running war simulations on computers. These programs weren't fully realized video games—most surviving nonmilitary examples were ways to play chess using the computer. In 1947, Thomas T. Goldsmith Jr. and Estle Ray Mann, two employees at DuMont Laboratories in Passaic, New Jersey, filed U.S. Patent 2455992 for a "Cathode-Ray Tube Amusement Device." The invention simulated an artillery shell arcing toward targets on a cathode-ray tube (CRT) screen, and that could be controlled with knobs to change the shell's trajectory.[31] No actual prototype was ever built,[32] though, and the concept languished.

In 1950, Canadian engineer Josef Kates designed a tic-tac-toe game called *Bertie the Brain*. It used a keypad and nine light bulbs that would light up panels for the Xs and Os, and the computer opponent used AI to make its moves. The next year, Ferranti unveiled the Nimrod Digital Computer as part of the Festival of Britain, a 1951 World's Fair–type national celebration. It was a giant contraption that played an ancient strategy game called Nim to teach people about how computers worked. It also used light bulbs as a display, in this case to simulate the play pieces. That year also saw the introduction of Oliver Aberth's bouncing ball program on MIT's Whirlwind, possibly the first example of real-time graphics. In 1952, a Cambridge PhD student named A.S. Douglas programmed Noughts and Crosses (tic-tac-toe) on the EDSAC, a British mainframe, as part of a thesis on human-computer interaction. This one displayed graphics, but they didn't move. William George Brown and Ted Lewis developed a pool game at the University of Michigan in 1954 on the MIDSAC, a unique mainframe. The program simulated the movement of balls on a pool table when struck with a cue stick.[33] It may have been the first computer software that could track the movements of multiple objects. It's possible other examples of video-game-like programs existed as well, and that were lost to time.

Some dispute Higinbotham's game, later dubbed *Tennis for Two*, as the first video game. It lacked scoring and a timer; the game just went on until the next two lab visitors wanted to play. And it didn't use a real video signal from a television set—something even Higinbotham's son has argued.[34] Various factions point to this or that example as the true "first." But *Tennis for Two* was nonetheless the first video game you could play in real time, or at least the start of one.

Later, Higinbotham set up the game on a larger display. In 1959, he added some astronomy demonstrations that also proved popular with visitors. His creation never made it out of the lab, and the various components of *Tennis for Two* were dismantled and used for other things—the same fate that befell most early examples of video games.[35] Higinbotham later wrote that he considered the game he created a "minor" achievement. He said he wanted to be remembered as someone who fought the spread of nuclear weapons rather than the inventor of a computer game. Besides, no scientist or engineer worth their salt thought a multimillion-dollar computer should be used for entertainment.[36]

Figure 1.3: The video game age began in 1958 with *Tennis for Two*, an oscilloscope-based game two players could control in real time. Credit: Brookhaven National Laboratory

It was because of *Tennis for Two*, though, that the simple, human act of recreation would never be the same.

Spacewar!

At MIT in the late 1950s, the denizens of the Tech Model Railroad Club tinkered with the underside electronics of the club's railroad table with reckless abandon. They hacked in new routes, lights, and wiring to run the trains different ways. Soon the appeal of the university's homegrown TX-0 computer beckoned, and they began hacking that instead—and later, a Digital Equipment Corporation PDP-1, which MIT installed in September 1961.[37]

Both computers were next-generation, transistor-based systems that didn't quite take up an entire room the way earlier vacuum-tubed models had, even if they were still tremendous by today's standards. Because they no longer required punch cards, the TX-0 and DEC PDP-1 meant users didn't have to navigate the bureaucracy of self-appointed guardians that restricted access to the university's IBM systems[38], and could instead program their own tools and algorithms. This hacking included more pedestrian uses, such as a program called "Expensive Desk Calculator."[39] The DEC PDP-1 also tempted with its Type 30 Visual Cathode-Ray Tube monitor that could display detailed vector graphics.

An MIT student programmer named Steve Russell had already established himself coding the first implementations of the recursive LISP computer language that kickstarted the field of artificial intelligence. He soon found himself working on what would become the greatest known hack—an actual game two people could play using the computer. Soon, other programmers chimed in, as was customary for any good hack. They added a star at the center with its own gravity pull, and they cobbled together some rudimentary control boxes to make it easier to play.

Russell and a team of other MIT and Harvard programmers debuted *Spacewar!* at MIT's Science Open House in May 1962. It pitted two spaceships against each other until one vanquished the other with missiles. Each player controlled a ship using four flip switches on the PDP-1: rotate left, rotate right, thrust, and fire torpedoes. The missiles and ships left beautiful glowing trails as they moved, an artifact of the CRT's design. The tube was designed for radar scopes and employed a coating with two layers of phosphor, a bright blue one for freshly activated blips and a dimmer, greenish one for decaying blips in a faded afterglow.[40]

Spacewar! was the world's first complete video game, and the first one where the players' skill and reflexes mattered. It ate up countless hours of computer time—still shared, and still something you signed up for on a scheduling sheet. Students played the game at all hours of the day and night. Soon DEC, appreciative of quality free code and impressed with what the MIT students had made, began shipping the *Spacewar!* program with its PDP-1 models. Field engineers used it as a test whenever they set up a new installation in universities and corporations around the country.

Students at other universities began to play the game in their own college labs as well.

In 1969, PLATO programmer Rick Blomme created a text-based *Space-war!* running on top of a Seymour Cray–designed CDC 1604, a miraculous accomplishment given the system's antiquated storage and time-sharing OS. The game used *X* and *O* characters for the ships and included a fuel mechanic, if not much else. The code had to run within the limits of the hardware and the phone lines and depended on PLATO's Fast Round Trip algorithm for responsive keyboard input.[41] Many rudimentary computer games, all text based, had also appeared by this point. But Blomme's dedication to porting the world's first skill-based video game to a system that had no business running one illustrated the power of this new medium.

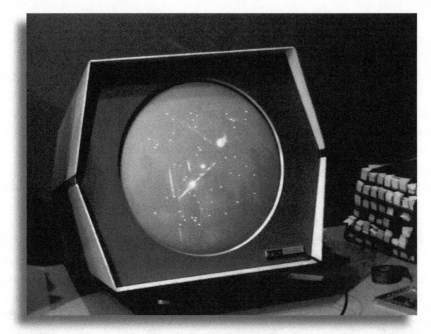

Figure 1.4: *Spacewar!* **running on a DEC PDP-1 in 1965. Credit: Kenneth Lu, licensed under CC BY 2.0.**

It was just a couple of years later when video games made a giant leap from the research lab to the arcade, laying the groundwork for a new industry and a new way of life. The arcade would fast become the way most people were exposed to video games. Relays and solenoids would give way to circuit boards and phosphors.[42] And these video games would set standards and establish conventions still used to this day.

Syzygy

Nolan Bushnell was born in 1945 near Salt Lake City. A natural tinkerer even when young, he fell in with a local ham radio operator who taught him all about how the radios worked. He became the youngest ham radio operator in Utah. When Bushnell was 15, his father died, and Bushnell took over his cement business—quite a job for a teenager.[43] In college, he worked part-time at an amusement park, learned all about the business, and became a manager. In his college computer lab at the University of Utah, he played *Spacewar!* on the mainframe. He realized it would make the perfect amusement park game if he could figure out how to build one for less than the price of a current-model DEC PDP-8, which cost upwards of $120,000 in the mid 1960s.[44]

Bachelor's degree in electrical engineering in hand, Bushnell went to work for Ampex, the original videotape company, in Sunnyvale, California. By 1970, he started to design a *Spacewar!*-like game.[45] He tried numerous ideas, including incorporating a minicomputer with terminals for a multiplayer game, but all were too expensive. Instead, Bushnell and his friend and Ampex coworker Ted Dabney developed a prototype arcade game using on the cheap using transistor-to-transistor logic (TTL), sometimes called discrete logic.[46] The two designed and hand-soldered a circuit board that generated a playfield and enemy saucers using raster graphics, which divided up the screen into a grid of pixels and was less expensive to produce than vector graphics on an inexpensive black-and-white television.

"100 percent of the video games up until 1977 used my discreet logic technology…that I had a patent on," Bushnell said.[47]

The resulting game was so compelling, Bushnell saw his techie friends camping out in his yard for a chance to play.[48] To formalize their new business venture, in October 1970 Bushnell, Dabney, and fellow Ampex engineer Larry Bryan started an outfit called Syzygy.[49] The name came from the word for three celestial bodies in the sky lining up, such as when the moon, the sun, and Earth are in eclipse.

"People would look at you like you had three heads," Bushnell said of describing the game. "'You mean you're going to put the TV set in a box with a coin slot and play games on it?'"[50]

They shopped their game to various investors to no avail. So to build the product, they met with Dave Nutting, who ran a local novelty and quiz coin-op game manufacturer. Soon, the first electronic video arcade game in history entered production, kicking off the Bronze Age in our timeline.

Computer Space (Syzygy/Nutting Associates, 1971)

Your goal in *Computer Space* was to destroy two enemy flying saucers before they destroyed you or the clock ran out. The 13-inch black-and-white television monitor depicted a star field, with three two-digit numbers on the right for the rocket score (the player); the saucer score (the computer); and the elapsed timer. You could see the individual points of light that made up the rocket and saucers, with a tiny bit of space surrounding each one. The saucers were quite good at chasing you, so it took considerable practice to avoid their shots and fire off some of your own. When the timer hit 99, if you had more points than the saucers, you'd start again on a reversed playfield where the sky was white and the star points were black.

Figure 1.5: An early brochure advertising *Computer Space*.

The game's curvaceous, lightweight fiberglass cabinet was finished in attention-grabbing, metal-flake paint that could be ordered in blue, yellow, white, or red. The silver control panel had four square, black, spring-loaded buttons for rotating the rocket left and right, thrusting, and firing torpedoes. Colorful lights above the buttons indicated what each one did. The control panel also held a coin slot, a coin-return plunger, and a white button to start the game. One quarter was required, a price that soon became the standard for arcade games.

Computer Space didn't ignite the industry on its own. Nutting Associates churned out some 1,500 examples, some of which brought in good revenue. But the company couldn't convince enough bar and tavern owners and operators to take a chance on it. *Computer Space* was a complex game with difficult controls, and it didn't help when many of the cabinets landed in establishments where patrons weren't used to seeing such complicated nonsense while inebriated. The screeching alarm sound that played whenever bullets were fired couldn't have done it many favors, either.

Computer Space doesn't hold up well on its own today; it's kind of a stiff-feeling combination of *Asteroids* and *Spacewar!*. But few games were more influential. Aside from being the first video arcade coin-op, *Computer Space* set the template for most games to come, from the upright design of its cabinet to the position of the monitor and controls, the backlit marquee, the power supply, and the audio speaker.[51] And the cabinet was just stunning, with its shimmering metallic-flake paint. Even powered off, it was so pretty. It looked so much like it belonged in a science fiction film that it appeared in one in short order: 1973's *Soylent Green* starring Charlton Heston.

Galaxy Game (Computer Recreations, 1971)

Right around the time Bushnell and Dabney were finishing and releasing the first *Computer Space* cabinets, Stanford student Bill Pitts and his friend Hugh Tuck, a student at California Polytechnic State University, were hard at work on their own coin-op *Spacewar!* that they hoped would not just match but improve on *Computer Space*. Like Bushnell, Pitts had marveled at *Spacewar!* in the mid 1960s and thought a coin-op model would do well if it could be mass-produced. Pitts knew the finished machine would have to come in around $20,000 to be viable as a product for arcades.[52] Arriving in late 1970 at a cost of just $14,000 in a usable configuration, DEC's new PDP-10 was inexpensive enough that they could work up a prototype.

In June 1971, the two formed a company called Computer Recreations and went to work.[53] Pitts handled the programming and engineering; Tuck designed a walnut-veneer enclosure with the display, game controls, and a coin box. They settled on final prototype hardware consisting of a DEC PDP-11/20 minicomputer with 8KB of memory and an optional hardware multiply/divide card, along with a point-plotting display interface and an HP 1300A Electrostatic Display with vector graphics, just like the original. They even fitted two seats to accommodate both players. With the PDP-11/20, the display, and the related peripherals, wood, and cabinet parts, the total bill of materials was $20,000—right on target.

Galaxy Game was closer to the original *Spacewar!* than *Computer Space*. It depicted the MIT game's "needle" and "wedge" spaceships and modeled the sun's gravity. It also offered ways to tweak the gameplay, such as speeding up the ships or torpedoes, removing the "wrap-around" effect at the edges of the screen, and making the sun disappear.[54] Playing the game cost a modest 10 cents; a quarter would allow three plays, and if someone did well enough, they'd get a free game. Pitts and Tuck installed the *Galaxy Game* cabinet on campus and set it up. Once word got around, small crowds would form around the machine every night.

Figure 1.6: *Galaxy Game*, the second of two machines built, in the Computer History Museum in San Jose, CA, in October 2008. Photo by the author.

Pitts and Tuck built a second, more elegant prototype that consisted of two blue fiberglass enclosures. Each contained a recessed display inside a black shroud, two improved joysticks, and a row of control buttons on the front panel. Hidden inside one of the two consoles was the requisite PDP-11/20, although it controlled games on both, and it could support up to eight connected consoles playing separate games. In June 1972, the pair installed the second prototype in Stanford's student union cafe. They moved the first model to a different location on campus.[55] After spending somewhere north of $60,000 and making precious little revenue in return, and with no investors biting, Pitts and Tuck gave up on their enterprise.

There has been some debate about whether *Galaxy Game* beat *Computer Space* in becoming the world's first coin-operated video game. As of late, evidence has tilted toward this not being the case. According to a 2016 interview with Tuck, the game wasn't put on location for testing until late November 1971; by that point, *Computer Space* was already in testing itself.[56] The second prototype became a fixture at Stanford, and was played continually through 1979 before being taken out of service once the display assembly became unreliable.[57] The game was then restored in the mid 1990s and found a permanent home in the Computer History Museum in San Jose, California, where it remains to this day.

Atari

The story of arcade video games followed two tracks: arcade coin-ops and home game consoles, with the former having a couple of years lead time on the latter. One company was at the forefront of both: Atari. And key to its contributions was someone who never worked there.

Ralph Baer, an electronics engineer who defected from Germany just before World War II to serve on the American side, realized that a television set could be used for purposes other than broadcasting a signal. He prototyped the world's first-ever video game system in 1966, and by 1967 had playable video ping-pong and hockey games displaying on a 17-inch RCA console. Baer iterated the design several times before shopping it around. Thanks to an employee who had seen an early demonstration of Baer's invention, Magnavox signed on to manufacture and distribute it.

By May 1972, Magnavox began to show the prototype Odyssey, now encased in a sleek white-and-black plastic housing, to dealers around the country. It played 12 games; players would insert small circuit boards into a slot on the console to activate tennis, ping-pong, handball, and some other games contained in the core hardware. They also had to place a translucent plastic overlay on the TV set for each game; it would define the game board and add an appropriate backdrop, such as a skiing course for Ski and a haunted house cutaway for, well, Haunted House.

Meanwhile, for his second act, Nolan Bushnell wanted a simpler game than *Computer Space*. One day, he attended one of Magnavox's dealer demonstrations in California and the Odyssey's table tennis and handball games. Although he found some of their mechanics difficult (an extra knob on top was required to determine the angle of the rebound, aka add English to the shot), and the Odyssey's system architecture precluded the inclusion of scoring and sound effects, Bushnell saw that with some tweaks, a two-player tennis game had the potential to make money. He decided to manufacture his own coin-op.

At the time, Bushnell was under contract with Bally for a new driving game. He needed another engineer, so he hired Al Alcorn, whom he had met during a work-study program while at Ampex. Ostensibly to acquaint him with the new job, Bushnell gave Alcorn a training exercise first: Design a video game with two paddles, one ball, and a way to keep score. The score was important, Bushnell felt; it established a marker for how well you did when you played the game. Alcorn went to work, and soon realized Bushnell's schematics for *Computer Space* were indecipherable.[58] He scrapped those and created a new TTL design. He added a mode where the ball's speed (and thus the game's difficulty) increased after you'd been playing for a while.[59] Bushnell also wanted sound, so Alcorn figured out an ingenious way to amplify audible frequencies from the display's vertical sync circuit to play some effects for the ball.[60] Bushnell liked the sounds so much he named the game after them.[61]

The final design was made up of three circuit boards: one for the paddles, one for the ball, and one for the scoring. Alcorn bought a $75 Hitachi black-and-white TV from a local electronics store, stuck it in a four-foot-tall wooden cabinet, and soldered wires into the boards to connect everything together.[62] Alcorn thought the game would be too expensive to build, but Bushnell and Dabney liked it so much, they decided to test it out in public as-is.[63] In August 1972, Bushnell and Alcorn installed the first machine, an orange and wood-paneled tabletop unit, at Andy Capp's Tavern in Sunnyvale to see how it would do. After a couple of weeks, Alcorn received a call to come check out the machine; the bar manager, Bill Gattis, said that it had stopped working. When Alcorn arrived, he opened it up only to find out that the machine had jammed because the coin box was overflowing.

"[Andy] said to me, 'Al, this is the weirdest thing. When I opened the bar this morning, there were two or three people at the door waiting to get in. They walked in and played that machine. They didn't buy anything. I've never seen anything like this before.' I opened the coin box to give myself a free game and lo and behold, this money gushed out."[64] Needless to say, that was all the confirmation Alcorn and Bushnell needed that they had a hit.

Soon after, Bushnell, Dabney, and Alcorn hand-built 12 upright units. Bushnell tried to convince Bally to accept *Pong* as the game he owed them instead of the driving game, but they weren't interested. Bushnell had them sign a letter saying they didn't want *Pong*, and then he owned the game free and clear.[65] On June 27, 1972, Nolan Bushnell and Ted Dabney founded Atari, Incorporated in Sunnyvale, California. The new firm would manufacture, sell, and distribute *Pong* machines.

Securing capital and employees became a problem. The specter of pinball's past continued to haunt the amusement business, and that wouldn't change overnight just because television monitors were added to the machines. In a later interview, Alcorn said, "Banks wouldn't talk to us because we were obviously in the Mafia if we were in coin-op." For a time, Bushnell hired just about anyone he could to build the cabinets, from the unemployment office to motorcycle gangs. This meant he had to fire a lot of people along the way too.[66] Nonetheless, Atari Inc. was up and running, building and selling its first hit game.

Pong (Atari, 1972)

Pong kicked off the video arcade revolution. It showed people would gather around a video game machine, wait their turn, and fill it with quarters to play again and again—much to the delight of establishment owners and proprietors. (All the better to sell more beer.) And for a public accustomed to pinball machines, pool tables, and dart boards, the video game was new and exciting, even if it was just table tennis on a screen. In contrast to *Computer Space*, *Pong* was the most minimalist of game designs. The playfield consisted of a black screen with a simple, dotted white line running down the center depicting the net. To either side, two thin rectangular lines represented the paddles. A lone dot depicted the ball, while two large numbers across the top of the screen displayed the current score for each player. As it was a two-player game, there was no simulated AI for computer-controlled opponents. The near cacophony of *Computer Space*'s piercing alerts and bombastic explosions gave way to simple bleeps. The rules of the game, inscribed on the front panel of the machine, totaled six words: "Avoid missing ball for high score."

**A *Pong* machine in all its wood-paneled glory. Credit: Rob Boudon, licensed
under CC BY 2.0.**

Its score display and sound effects weren't the only innovations compared with the Odyssey's game. Rather than using a separate English knob, Alcorn added the ball's deflection angles to different areas of the paddle. To do this, he segmented the on-screen paddle into several areas. Hit the ball close to the center of the paddle, and it would fly straighter. Hit it off to the side, and it would bounce off at a sharper angle. The segments weren't visible to the player; the paddle appeared on screen as a solid rectangle. This method gave the game an element of strategy on top of the skill necessary to manipulate the spinner control, but without the unintuitive complexity of twisting two separate knobs. Overall, the game just played "right," and really felt like table tennis.

Atari's production model consisted of a wooden cabinet with an attention-getting yellow marquee and control panel. The simplicity of the gameplay enticed people to try it out, and the two-player requirement hardly dampened enthusiasm. Inside the company, though, things were already going south. Dabney soon tired of Bushnell's self-promotional behavior, which was already seeming to overshadow his efforts to promote Atari. Dabney sold Bushnell his half of the company and, after a brief stint overseeing production and on the board of directors, exited a year later.[67]

Within a few months, Atari debuted *Pong* nationwide, and had manufactured and sold some 6,000 cabinets by the end of the year—a nice hit for a brand-new industry. But Atari couldn't keep up with demand. At the start of 1973, Atari still had just six employees. Capitalism being what it is, other companies soon started building clones, such as *Paddle Ball* from Williams Electronics, *TV Ping Pong* from Chicago Coin, and *Paddle Battle* from Allied Leisure (which sold 17,000 units by itself).[68] Atari also released its own iterations, such as the four-player *Pong Doubles*, which was also soon copied. Other manufacturers tried their hand at Pong variations, such as Midway's *TV Flipper* and Chicago Coin's *TV Pinball*. Clones from more than a dozen manufacturers accounted for another 65,000 to 70,000 sales.[69] None of the profit from those went to Atari. Detailing all of the clones is beyond the scope of this book. But the collective effect was that it became the first widespread instance of bootlegging, a phenomenon that would plague the video arcade for more than a decade.[70] Some of these manufacturers had an existing business, such as pinball, and just wanted in on the new craze. Nonetheless, several important players in the history of the video arcade got their start doing this. For most of 1973, video games looked, sounded, and played like *Pong*. The coin-op made its own movie debut in 1974's *The Parallax View*.

For many years, people often called *Pong* the first arcade game, or even the first video game. It was neither, but it might as well have been.

Space Race (Atari, 1973)

The hysteria around *Pong* would fade. Bushnell and Dabney knew they could stay one step ahead of the clones and make more money selling new kinds of video games. And as Bushnell the former carnival barker understood, the public was fickle and always wanted something different. Soon, Atari was hard at work on what it hoped would become the next big thing.

Space Race, the company's next coin-op, seemed like the right idea on paper. It was mostly designed by Dabney, with Bushnell and Alcorn providing input. Alcorn engineered and prototyped the game. In it, two players moved joysticks up and down to control the speed of their spaceships as they raced across the galaxy (up the screen) while dodging meteoroids and asteroids (a collection of simple dashes moving back and forth). Whoever reached the top first would receive one point, and the race would start again from the bottom. A ship that collided with an asteroid would disappear with a short "bloop" sound and then reappear at the bottom of the screen. A single player could also race against the clock while the other side sat idle. The time limit for the game was represented by a vertical line in the center of the screen that also served as a lane divider. It shrank as the game progressed; when it was all gone, the game ended.

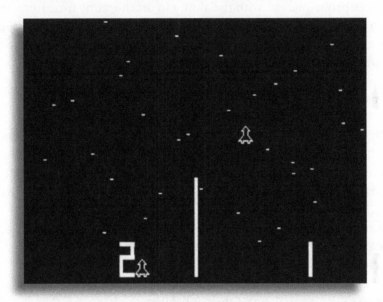

Figure 1.8: Atari's *Space Race*, introduced in 1973, was an unsuccessful attempt to develop a competitive two-player space video game.

Atari manufactured the first 50 *Space Race* cabinets with a detailed, asymmetric fiberglass enclosure, similar to the one for *Computer Space* but more alienlike details: creases, cut lines, edges, and a hexagonal hood on top that surrounded the display.[71] Bushnell said in an interview that the cabinet was too expensive and difficult to produce, costing upwards of $2,000 per unit and only one could be made in a day.[72] Atari soon switched to the nondescript black cabinet seen in advertisements and photos. It measured 58 inches high by 25 inches deep and 29 inches wide, and it weighed 217 pounds. It featured a marquee on top—still not backlit—along with a black paint job on all sides and a small 13-inch monitor surrounded by wide bezels. Inside was the motherboard, which contained all discrete chips, and an amplified mono speaker—*Pong*'s design, but simplified.

Space Race was one of the first games to demonstrate itself with an animated display and sound effects. This soon became known as an attract mode.[73] Just about every arcade game would include an attract mode in one form or another to help boost collections. One advertisement for *Space Race* promised operators easy access to the components and the locked cash box. It said the clean lines meant the cabinet was suitable for placement "anywhere and everywhere," including "fine shops, restaurants, waiting rooms, recreation areas, reception lobbies, and offices." It also promised the game was a "fast profit-maker," with the ability to set the game time from 45 seconds to three minutes, or to enable two plays for a quarter instead of one.

Space Race didn't catch on. Some 1,500 cabinets were produced, but most were scrapped after the game flopped.[74]

Midway

The Chicago-based Midway opened in 1958 selling amusement park equipment. It produced electromechanical games of various kinds, from shuffle alleys to pinball tables. Bally acquired the company in 1969, and as a Bally subsidiary Midway began to release arcade video games in 1973. Its first was *Winner*, another clone of Atari's *Pong* and unremarkable save for one innovation: a glass screen that covered the TV monitor. This useful upgrade protected the TV tube and would appear on every arcade game cabinet thereafter.

Thanks to Bally's prior contract with Atari, Midway company executives knew Bushnell still owed them a driving game. Bushnell offered *Space Race* instead, they accepted it, and soon Midway sold its own model under the name *Asteroid*. But Atari continued to sell *Space Race*, which Midway said violated the contract. Atari ended up agreeing to forfeit the royalties to Midway.[75]

Asteroid played identically to *Space Race*, but its striking cabinet design was something else. It was the first mass-produced game with side art. *Asteroid* included full color images of rockets, asteroids, and stars covering the sides, the front panel around the coin box, and the bezel surrounding the black-and-white monitor.[76] Side art was attractive and inviting, but more than that, it conveyed all of the imaginative details coin-op games couldn't with their primitive on-screen graphics. Depending on the game, it was either applied as colorful decals or hand-screened onto the cabinet.

(A few electromechanical games had side art before the video game age, and some say For-Play's *Star Trek*, a late 1972 bootleg of *Computer Space* except with a joystick instead of buttons, beat *Asteroid* to the punch. Little is known about *Star Trek*, and For-Play disappeared after producing a few *Pong* clones in 1973.[77])

Midway's next few arcade games also did well, if not overwhelmingly so. Its *TV Basketball*, introduced in 1974 as an American release of Taito's *Basketball*, was the first arcade game to depict humans with graphics and the first Japanese game distributed in America. Midway didn't have a hit yet. But it would have one soon enough.

Atari Branches Out

Pinball remained far and away the number one type of machine found in taverns, restaurants, and other off-street locations, according to a November 10, 1973, *Cashbox* survey. But something new was happening. "TV Ping Pong Games" became the top-earning category of amusement machine at an average of $38 per week, more than pinball machines and pool tables. It marked the first time 25 cents became the most common price per play across the industry, rather than two-for-a-quarter, as had been the standard with pinball machines.[78] Video games were proving less prone to breakdowns than electromechanical machines, and they didn't carry the gambling stigma still stuck to pinball. Video games were clearly skill-based and evoked the Space Age and other futuristic imagery.[79]

Atari continued releasing new coin-ops, fresh off the success of *Pong* and undaunted by the middling performance of *Space Race*. It took some time to get the formula right. Some engineers at Atari thought the phallic-looking joysticks of their games contributed to the mostly male clientele. So, in an "effort" to bring in more female gamers, they designed a new maze-chase game called *Gotcha*, with controllers that looked like…breasts. After plenty of blowback, Atari switched gears and fitted the final production unit with joysticks. In 1974, the company unveiled *Touch-Me*, an electronic game that used four flashing lights instead of a computer monitor. You had to remember the sequence of the lights and then duplicate them from memory by pushing four huge buttons in the same order. *Gotcha* and *Touch-Me* both flopped. Atari also released more *Pong* iterations to help keep the lights on, including *Super Pong*, the volleyball-like *Rebound*, and *Quadrapong*. None of these broke through. But a different kind of Atari video game did.

Gran Trak 10 (Atari/Cyan Engineering, 1974)

Atari's *Gran Trak 10* was the first video game about driving and the first to feature a steering wheel, as well as an accelerator pedal, brake pedal, and gear shift. *Gran Trak 10* was developed by Larry Emmons and Steve Mayer of Atari's new subsidiary Cyan Engineering, and it was completed by Al Alcorn. You raced a single car along a fixed-screen racetrack with an overhead view. Two red strip overlays marked the finish line; four green overlay lines denoted checkpoints. You had to avoid the rows of pylons marking the track edges and drive through as many checkpoints as you could before you ran out of time. If you hit a pylon, the car would spin out. You'd get two points each time you crossed a checkpoint or the finish line, for a total of 10 points per lap. The engine roared and whined as you played, and the pixel squares that represented pylons made for a challenging course on screen. Although the time counter started at 78 on-screen, the game was set to a default of 105 actual seconds; the owner and operator could adjust the speed of the counter and crash duration.

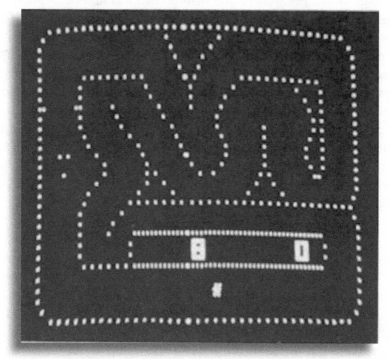

Figure 1.9: *Gran Trak 10* **was Atari's foray into driving video games—the first of its kind—and conveyed a genuine sense of speed from its top-down view.**

The gear shift offered first, second, third, and reverse options, and the sound of the engine would change with each of these. The pedals were on-off affairs, though with no intermediate points to offer a lower level of braking or acceleration, and the steering wheel would spin freely with no center point stop. This meant whenever you were steering, the car changed direction, but otherwise it went straight the moment you let go of the wheel. Atari did model gradual braking, though, and the car would skid if you tried to steer at the same time (remember, this was before antilock brakes were invented!). The owner and operator could adjust the length of time each game lasted, as well as the volume level of the sound effects.

The game included the first example of integrated-circuit-based read-only memory, a huge leap over the diodes used in *Computer Space*, to store the car, track, and scoring information.[80] Atari advertised *Gran Trak 10* as "completely solid state," and IC ROM chips soon became the standard in coin-op machines.[81] The game was also the first to use a dedicated monitor rather than a television set, and it employed interlaced graphics for higher resolution and smoother race car animation.[82] This meant the CRT drew the screen in two top-to-bottom passes, first with the odd-numbered lines and then with the even. In addition, *Gran Trak 10* emitted synthesized audio of the engine roar, squealing tires, and crash sound effects. Alcorn even took steps to ensure no one bootlegged the game, as he recounted in 2017:

> *The board used a ROM chip that had the images of the cars at various rotations and it was a custom part. I chose the part number to be SN74816 which was a TTL part that was the same package as my custom part. When the copiers plugged in the standard TTL part it burnt out. We learned who was copying our boards because they would call our customer service and complain.*[83]

Gran Trak 10 became a success in the arcades and spawned a number of variations from Atari, including the two-player *Gran Trak 20* (complete with two sets of driving controls); the smaller *Trak 10*; and the six-track iteration *LeMans*. It was where the rubber began to meet the road for Atari not just as the *Pong* company, but as a full-fledged arcade coin-op juggernaut. In a big blow, the company lost a lot money on *Gran Trak 10* because of an accounting error. Atari sold each unit for $995 even though it cost Atari $1,095 to produce one, thanks to a miscalculation of parts costs between departments. Despite a course correction, this led to more than half a million dollars in losses for the fiscal year 1974.[84] Fortunately for the company, more revenue was just around the corner.

Kee Games

As Atari created and sold more games, Bushnell pushed hard to get the company's coin-ops into as many arcades and other event spaces as possible. To do that, he needed to sign on with more distributors, but there was a problem. Often a territory had a single distributor, but in larger territories, there could be two. And thanks to older exclusivity practices dating back to pinball, those two distributors couldn't represent the same coin-op manufacturer. If owners and operators of bars and other establishments wanted an Atari game, but did business with the other distributor instead, that customer would just buy a clone or bootleg. Each time this happened, Atari didn't collect any revenue.[85]

So, in one of the more twisted stories of video arcade game history, to get around the problem Bushnell founded Kee Games as a fake competitor. He installed his friend Joe Keenan at the helm and even maintained separate research departments for the two companies. Kee Games would market and sell clones of Atari games to customers and give the illusion of a competitive marketplace, letting Atari skirt some industry regulations in the process.[86] For a time, this strategy worked and created a narrative where Atari and Kee Games battled for the same customers with different games. Behind the scenes, they were one and the same, as every Kee Games coin-op was a minor variation of an Atari coin-op. For example, *Formula K* was a clone of *Gran Trak 10*.

Kee Games developed just one original title that wasn't a clone of an Atari property. It turned out to be one of the most important of the Bronze Age of video arcades and soon posed a problem for Bushnell.

Tank (Kee Games, 1974)

Tank was one of the first games to have solid, contiguous shapes and characters, made possible by the inclusion of ROM chips to store the graphics data, the same as in *Gran Trak 10*.[87] This meant that the game wasn't restricted to dots and lines as with earlier ball-and-paddle games. *Tank* was designed by Steve Bristow, who had moved from Atari to Kee Games, and programmed by Lyle Rains. The fixed playfield consisted of a series of walls in different shapes, with a solid wall around the entire screen. Each player controlled a small tank, with one white and one black. Scattered about the playfield were mines, depicted as small black Xs. You had to destroy your opponent's tank as many times as possible before the timer ran out. The game began with one tank at the upper-left corner and the other tank in the lower right. The cabinet played rumbling engine sounds that increased in pitch whenever the tanks were on the move and decreased to indicate they were idling. A clanking tread sound could also be heard.

Figure 1.10: *Tank*, **shown here in a later cocktail model, gave each player a pair of joysticks to control their on-screen tank and shoot at their opponent.**

On top of the wood-paneled cabinet's control panel were four oversize, four-way joystick handles, with two for the left player and two for the right. To move a tank forward, you pushed both handles forward; to move it back, you pulled both of them back. Turning was accomplished by pulling one stick back and pushing the other forward; to turn right, you pulled the right stick back and pushed the left forward. The reverse pattern would turn the tank left. To shoot shells, you pressed the red button on top of the right handle.

Each time you shot the other tank, you'd receive one point. If you ran into a mine, your opponent would score a point. Otherwise, shells would explode upon hitting a nearby wall or in midair after traveling a few inches across the screen. Whenever a tank exploded, it would flash for a few moments and you would hear an appropriate sound effect. During this period, the other tank couldn't fire. When there were just 20 seconds left, the timer would begin to flash, warning the game was about to end.

The mechanics were simple, but the effect was profound. Despite *Tank*'s still-blocky graphics and lack of color, the game conveyed serious realism.

Both *Tank* and *Gran Trak 10* were new evolutions of existing electromechanical shooting and driving games, proving that although *Pong* and related games may have been a fad, video arcade games in general certainly weren't.[88]

When *Tank* became successful, Atari realized it had to find a way to also sell it without looking as if it were copying Kee Games, even though they were both the same company. In September 1974, Atari and Kee Games merged, ending the scheme and installing Joe Keenan as president of Atari. *Tank* went on to sell an impressive 10,000 cabinets—much more than *Computer Space*, and more than each of its various *Pong* iterations. The revenue stabilized the company and improved its financial position. Atari also released a cocktail model. Two people would sit on opposing sides, each with the requisite two sticks and Fire button on the right handle, and then gaze at the center of the table, where the black-and-white monitor was mounted facing upward. (It wasn't the first cocktail cabinet, as Kee Games and Meadows Games also released four-player variants of *Pong* called, respectively, *Elimination* and *Flim Flam*.) Atari released numerous *Tank* sequels throughout the rest of the decade, culminating in 1978's *Ultra Tank*. Other manufacturers also iterated on the concept, such as Fun Games with *BiPlane*, a two-player airplane combat game with the same twin-stick controls. But at the time of *Tank*'s release, nothing could top grabbing the two big handles and driving the tank as if it were real.

For video arcades, it was the slightest hint of what was to come.

Taito

Taito Trading Company launched in Japan in 1953, the brainchild of Michael Kogan, a Ukrainian Jewish businessman. The company spent its first years importing and distributing vending machines, and it was also known to be the first to distill and sell vodka in Japan. Later, it branched out into jukeboxes and electromechanical amusement games such as Pachinko, first as a distributor and then by manufacturing its own machines in the 1960s. Taito also built novelty arcade games such as Cannon Ball and Fantasy.

In 1972, the company changed its name to Taito Corporation, and the next year it launched *Astro Race*, a *Space Race* clone that employed four-way joysticks for horizontal as well as vertical movement. After several additional popular if derivative coin-ops, including *Pong* clones such as *Pro Hockey* and *Basketball* and a space shooter called *Attack UFO*, Taito landed its first hit.

Speed Race/Wheels (Taito/Midway, 1974)

At first glance, Taito's *Speed Race* seemed derivative of both Astro Race and Atari's *Gran Trak 10*. But *Speed Race* racked up numerous "firsts" of its own in coin-op history. It was the first arcade game with vertical scrolling. It was also the first true racing game, with its depiction of several cars on screen. You competed against computer-controlled cars and the clock; the farther you drove, the more points you would score.

Figure 1.11: Midway's *Wheels* brought Taito's first car racing game to America. It was the first to feature racing against computer-controlled opponents.

The attract mode showed cars driving by the player's larger vehicle near the bottom of the screen. The game scrolled vertically, with moving pylons on the sides of the road to convey a sense of movement. Insert a quarter and nothing would happen on screen; the game would just enter play mode and the accelerator pedal would be enabled. To start racing, you accelerated through low gear up to redline before shifting into high. The faster you went, the higher up the screen your car would move, meaning that you had even less time to react to the appearing computer-controlled cars. During play, the engine note idled and rose in pitch with its rotational speed, and a crash "pop" sounded when you collided with another car. When this happened, you shifted back down into low to get rolling again. In the meantime, computer-controlled cars would whiz by.

Built on Taito's discrete logic hardware, *Speed Race* was designed by Tomohiro Nishikado. Taito had also established an American presence that could license the company's video games for distribution stateside. *Speed Race* marked the first time a Japanese arcade game was released in America—in this case, via Midway Games with the title *Wheels*, which appeared a few months later in 1975.

The Taito console contained an instructions panel on the left, a racing steering wheel in the center, and a two-position gear shift with a horizontal bar on top. Two red numerical LED displays to the right of the screen showed your current score and time remaining. To the left of the monitor was an analog tachometer gauge. Midway's *Wheels* cabinet had a different color scheme and graphics, and the monophonic speaker grill was visible to the left of the coin box. It also didn't have the instructions panel on the console and the red LED displays to the right of the monitor. Instead, the game displayed the score and time remaining as graphical numbers in the upper-left and upper-right corners of the screen, respectively. Otherwise, the gameplay between the two titles was identical.

Wheels went on to sell 7,000 cabinets in North America, making it a serious hit and helping to put Midway on the map after the *Asteroid* debacle. Sales numbers weren't made available for Japan, but *Speed Race* was reportedly popular there as well. After the initial fun wore off, and without anything but a straight road to drive on and identical computer cars, the game had little enduring appeal. As a stepping-stone in arcade game history, though, it could hardly have been more significant.

Indy 800 (Atari, 1975)

One of the coolest arcade games to come out in the Bronze Age, Atari's massive *Indy 800* was a top-down racing game with support for up to eight players. It was the first arcade game to do so, coming after Atari's horse-racing game Steeplechase, the first six-player coin-op. *Indy 800*'s layout was that of a massive cocktail cabinet, like a park fountain where you'd look in over the edge and see fish swimming. Atari fitted an expensive color monitor, a 25-inch GE CRT mounted facing upward, so there was no need for overlays.

The controls were arranged two to a side. Each player had his or her own steering wheel, accelerator pedal, and brake pedal, and controlled a differently colored IndyCar. The eight two-digit scores on screen matched the colors of the player cars, and each driver also had a horn button just for kicks. The graphics consisted of dots for pylons and little rectangular lines with four square "wheels" for each race car. Drivers scored two points for passing a checkpoint. To get ahead of the others, you'd have to drive the shortest line between the turns, clip the "apex" of each turn, and avoid crashing into the other cars or the walls. The cars oversteered, meaning that you could get them to skid and spin out (rather than understeer, which would send them wide of a turn). The game played simultaneous engine roars and skid-out sounds. When the timer ran down to zero, the highest score would begin flashing to indicate the winning player.

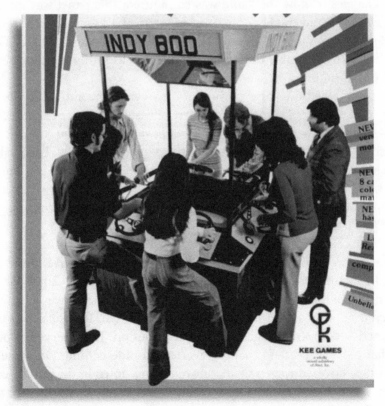

Figure 1.12: Atari's gargantuan _Indy 800_ cost a whopping $9,000, thanks to its extensive hardware loadout, color screen, and eight sets of controls.

Atari's discrete logic hardware underneath contained a card rack system with eight separate motherboards and sound circuits, plus three processing boards for synchronization, coin collection, and scoring.[89] Operators loved the game because they'd collect up to eight quarters per game, and the giant cabinet was hard to miss on the arcade floor. The 16-square-foot-system measured 87 inches high, 50 inches wide, and 50 inches deep. The four sides were paneled in wood-look vinyl over a plywood cabinet construction, with a piece of plexiglass on top covering the monitor. An optional overhead canopy featured marquees on all four sides, plus two wide, slanted mirrors so spectators could see what was happening on screen. The game also came with a "remote start" option, letting operators stage tournaments.[90]

Included with *Indy 800* was a "complete set of back-up components" for easier repairs, according to the marketing brochure. The set included two spare car motherboards and two card extender boards. A small remote control panel containing a number of switches let the attending operator make changes to how the game was configured; this panel was intended to be worn around the neck, as if it were part of a keychain to access the amusement park's merry-go-round and haunted house attractions.[91] Operators had to disassemble the cabinet to move it, as lifting it intact was out of the question.

Atari released the game both under its own name and under its subsidiary Kee Games. The next year, Atari released a smaller cabinet called *Indy 4*. *Indy 800* was a strong hit and the most profitable the company had seen since *Pong*, thanks in part to its sticker price of $9,000. Each cabinet had a long shelf life, and it tended to occupy the central space of an arcade or game room.[92]

Gun Fight (Midway, 1975)

In *Gun Fight*, two players took on the roles of cowboys in a classic Old West, high-noon shootout. As with earlier arcade games, *Gun Fight* took place on a fixed-screen playfield. Whoever shot the other player most in the allotted time won. The game had several different backdrops, such as those with cacti and covered wagons you could shoot up. These served as obstacles that blocked fire and that a player could hide behind. On some levels, a single covered wagon would move up and down in the middle of the screen; this one was impervious to shots. When a player was hit, he would fall down and text reading "Got me!" would appear over the body. Each gun only held six bullets; when both players exhausted their ammo, the round would end. A player could also use the screen boundaries to ricochet shots, which could catch the other player unaware. The sound effects consisted of gunfire, a hit-and-fall sound, and a short one-voice "Death March" music phrase that sounded whenever a player died.

The standard upright cabinet consisted of a control panel with a 23-inch black-and-white monitor, which itself was covered with a yellow translucent overlay. Each player had an eight-position joystick for the left hand and a two-position revolver handle for the right hand; the gun could move up and down, and it had a trigger on it for firing bullets. The top of the screen displayed a timer in the center with the players' scores on either side. Two speakers sat near the bottom of the front panel, adjacent to the coin box. The cabinet graphics played up the Western theme, with appropriate drawings and even "cowboy position" labels beneath each of the movement joysticks.

Figure 1.13: Dave Nutting's adaptation of Taito's *Gun Fight* for America included the first instance of a microprocessor in an arcade video game.

Taito's Tomohiro Nishikado, of *Speed Race* fame, developed the game for release in Japan. Midway wanted to distribute it in the U.S., but the company found it somewhat lacking. So Midway hired Dave Nutting, the brother of Nutting Associates' founder Bill Nutting and someone who had already designed hardware for pinball machine concepts. Nutting knew how to incorporate a microprocessor into the design to enhance the graphics and gameplay.[93] Midway's version of *Gun Fight* became the first arcade coin-op based around a CPU, an 8080 running at 2MHz. The architecture included a Fujitsu MB14241, which may have been the first instance of a graphics processor unit (GPU) inside a video game.[94] It included a 7KB frame buffer for producing bitmapped black-and-white graphics, animating the characters, and displaying text.[95] The printed circuit board (PCB) also included a barrel shifter circuit, built from multiple discrete chips, that enabled fast and smooth animation. *Gun Fight*'s production run used $3 million worth of RAM, which was estimated to be 60 percent of the world's supply.[96]

CPU-based coin-ops not only looked and sounded better, but they could track more objects on the screen at once. With fewer chips necessary for hardcoding game elements, microprocessor-based games could transfer much of the load to software, simplifying game boards in the process.[97] Microprocessors even changed the way sound worked. In discrete logic games, the audio design was linked to the hardware; a shooting game would require a different circuit design than a driving game.[98]

Gun Fight became Midway's biggest hit to date, with the company selling some 8,000 cabinets. The Intel 8080 and Midway's hardware platform would go on to power all of the company's hit games for the next five years. In 1976, Atari unveiled a similar title called *Outlaw*. "As a game, I thought our version of *Western Gun* [its original name in Japan] was more fun," Taito's Nishikado said in a 2004 interview. "But just from using a microprocessor, the walking animation became much smoother and prettier in Midway's version."[99] Nishikado would soon have far greater success of his own.

Arcade Cabinet Design

By the mid 1970s, arcade games converged on several cabinet form factors. The average coin-op consisted of a shell constructed of wood and some metal. Most cabinets featured some kind of side art, though some were blank. The front presented a monitor in either horizontal or vertical orientation; the decision made here would inform or reflect everything from the playfield and level design to the control calibration. The marquee or sign was backlit and displayed the game's title. A bezel surrounding the monitor contained more artwork, sometimes with game instructions. Speakers could be found just about anywhere on the front panel, depending on the game.

The heart of an arcade game was at least one PCB containing the main hardware such as the CPU and other processors and the memory chips. This board would be connected to a power supply that also drove the monitor, speakers, and cabinet lighting. The front control panel included the game's controls and one- or two-player start buttons, and sometimes the game instructions were located there instead. Some type of tough coating, be it a laminated panel or plexiglass overlay, protected the control panel from wear. The game's industrial-grade primary controls were designed to survive abuse day in and day out. Below the control panel was a coin box with coin slots and returns mounted in front. Pressing the translucent red plastic buttons returned a coin, in case a player changed their mind, or if the credit didn't register because of a technical problem.

Standard upright cabinets were the most common. They were roughly six feet tall, 26 inches wide, and 34 inches deep, and weighed 250 to 280 pounds, with a control panel about 35 inches off the floor and the monitor set into the cabinet and titled back. The monitor would be either 19 or 25 inches in diameter. The marquee was situated on an overhang, useful for shielding the display from reflections or sunlight, though some games kept the marquee flush and instead relied on more of a tunnellike setup for the monitor. A later sibling design was called the cabaret or mini, a smaller upright about five feet tall and with a smaller 13- or 15-inch monitor. It weighed less (maybe 200 to 220 pounds) and younger players could reach the controls without standing on something.

Cocktail cabinets looked like small, rectangular tables. Two control panels were set on two opposite sides, with the CRT in the center inside the table and facing upwards. The top was covered in tempered glass to protect the screen and also give the players a place to put drinks. The design worked fine in two-player mode because the cocktail model was programmed to flip the screen 180 degrees for whomever was playing. Cocktail games fell out of favor because they required more overall floor space in an arcade, even if they looked smaller. But collectors often prefer them for their decor-friendly look and the ability to sit on a regular chair while playing.

There were plenty of variations on these themes, including standard uprights with a seat attached, or "candy" cabinets with easy-to-clean, plastic-looking finishes, large CRTs, and lower control panels that worked better for seated players. As a quick look at an arcade photo from the 1970s or 1980s would indicate, these descriptions and dimensions are all only rough approximations. Veteran arcade gamers know coin-ops varied not just by cabinet type, but by manufacturer and often even from one coin-op to the next.

Look and Feel

An important part of the cabinet design process was the look and feel, which comprised the construction materials, the artwork, the presentation, and for owners and operators deciding what machines to put on the floor, the advertising materials. For example, Atari developed a visual language for the company's entire range of coin-op and consumer products.[100] The task fell to Atari's art director George Opperman, who commanded a team of artists and industrial designers. The cabinets had to be attractive to owners and operators visualizing them on location as potential income generators, as well as entice arcade gamers in loud, busy environments enough that they'd walk over, see the attract screen, and put in a quarter.[101] This called for bright colors, silkscreened art, and attention-grabbing designs.

"Part of what established a business style were the pre-existing pinball machine companies," said Roger Hector, part of Atari coin-op and later head of R&D, "and it's a very big process to create a set of pinball artwork. The backglass and all the pieces, the playfield...you can't really shop that out if you're Gottlieb or Bally. You build an in-house group. And Nolan and the gang—the executives at the time—they found that out."[102]

As the 1970s wore on, coin-op art at Atari began to affect how the company was presenting its consumer products. Hector said in the early days, coin-op was "the premier group, because you had dedicated hardware—a lot bigger proportional investment in creating a coin-op game than you did a consumer game. But [later] that flip-flopped." The design cues necessary for cartridge boxes and printed manuals differed from those for coin-op machines destined for an arcade floor. Coin-op design evolved as cabinets changed shape, and as arcade owners and operators packed more machines into a space, butting them up against each other and therefore hiding all of that carefully designed artwork on the sides.[103] But that didn't happen until later, and there was still plenty of room for artistic expression.

An Industry Is Born

The low-cost microprocessor, like the one used in *Gun Fight*, heralded not just better arcade games, but a giant expansion of the tech industry. It enabled the 1975 introduction of the Altair 8800, a $399 kit that made it possible for just about anyone to put a real computer on their desk at home for the first time. Soon, multiple manufacturers would release their own kits, and within two years, the first fully assembled personal computers would arrive.

That same year, Atari broke open the console market with *Home Pong*, which marked the first time you could play an existing arcade game on a television screen. Competing models from dozens of copycat manufacturers emerged such as Coleco, locking Atari in a brand-new race for the living room. Magnavox sued Atari for copying its table tennis game from Ralph Baer's Odyssey console system. The two companies settled out of court in 1976 for $800,000, clearing the way forward for Atari but also allowing Magnavox to continue suing Atari's competitors such as Midway and Seeburg, much to Bushnell's delight. Ultimately, the others lost and had to pay far greater fines.[104]

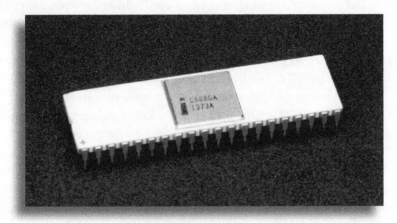

Figure 1.14: A variant of the Intel 8080 microprocessor. Credit: Konstantin Lanzet, licensed under CC BY-SA 3.0.

Some bizarre coin-op games came out during this period as manufacturers learned what worked and what didn't. For example, Nutting Associates released a successful *Pong* clone called *Table Tennis* and a shooting game called *Missile Radar*. But it also sold *Watergate Caper*, a video game version of the…Watergate break-in. "You Watched It On TV / You Read About It In Papers / Now—Discover the Secret Combination and Break Into Watergate Yourself." The game promised to simulate the "larceny in us all to see if we can break in and not get caught." This went right along with Atari's Kee Games scheme, the rumors of Atari employees doing cocaine on company premises, and the taint of organized crime on pinball games. In 1975, a new company named Project Support Engineering (PSE) released *Maneater*, a game designed to capitalize on the release of the 1975 blockbuster film *Jaws*. Today, *Maneater* is remembered not for its gameplay but for its cabinet, which was shaped like a giant shark's open mouth. You reached inside the mouth to control the game. None of PSE's coin-ops caught on and it shut down three years later.[105] Atari tried a similar game with an unlicensed coin-op called *Shark Jaws*, sizing up the letters so that the word "jaws" was much larger than "shark" but without triggering a lawsuit.[106]

Two trade magazines for the coin-op industry also launched around this time: *Play Meter* (initially *Coin Industry Play Meter*), founded by Ralph C. Lally II in December 1974, and *RePlay*, founded by Eddie Adlum in 1975 after he left the music-and-coin-focused *Cashbox* (founded in 1942). In 1976, Atari started its own corporate newsletter for coin-ops called *Atari Coin Connection*. These three joined existing industry publications such as *Cashbox* and *Vending Times* (founded in 1961). In short order after their debut, *RePlay* and *Play Meter* began tracking the performance of coin-op machines and surfaced some surprising trends. In 1975, video games still didn't earn as much as pool tables or pinball, but they recovered a bit from a noticeable dip in 1974. The big hits of the year for earnings per machine were Atari's *Indy 800* and *Tank*, and Midway's *Wheels*. In total, Atari sold 25,000 coin-ops in 1975, with Midway and Allied Leisure bringing up second and third with 10,000 and 7,500, respectively; these accounted for more than 75 percent of coin-op video game sales for the year.

Video games were an addicting new attraction that kept people coming back and inserting more quarters. Their moneymaking potential was obvious, and with relevant editorial coverage in place, the stage was set. Now the industry just needed a breakout hit.

2 > Breakout

The circumstances surrounding this next game's development are legendary. Atari had yet to embrace microprocessors, but it did want to reduce costs and stop using expensive arrays of 150 chips or more to build its arcade games. Bushnell assigned its next game to Steve Jobs, Atari's 40th employee. In turn, Jobs recruited his close friend and HP employee Steve Wozniak to help him with the project. Wozniak would design a circuit, and then go play *Gran Trak 10* on the production floor while Jobs breadboarded the design.[1] As the now-infamous story goes, Jobs told Wozniak Atari would give them $700 if they could bring the new game in under 50 chips and $1,000 if they could do it under 40. Wozniak was able to cut the design down to just 45 chips, and Jobs gave Wozniak his "half" of the bonus, or $350. It turned out Atari gave Steve Jobs a $5,000 bonus, and Jobs kept almost all of it for himself.

In the end, Atari couldn't figure out how to manufacture Wozniak's tight design. The company ended up using about 100 chips for the final machine. It launched a genre of video games that persists to this day.

Breakout (Atari, 1976)

The concept of *Breakout* was simple and only a slight variation on *Pong*. Instead of hitting a ball at an opponent, you fired it at a wall at the top of the screen, trying to break it apart brick by brick. Thin, translucent cellophane overlays covered the wall's eight rows so that each of four pairs was colored (from top to bottom) red, orange, yellow, and green. The bricks of each color were respectively worth seven, five, three, and one point each. Blue cellophane overlaid the bottom of the screen to give the paddle its own color. As the rows of bricks were stationary, the illusion of color worked, and the only giveaways were that the ball changed color when traveling through the bands and that the colors bled into the side walls.

Figure 2.1: This 1976 arcade game by Steve Wozniak broke open an entirely new genre of video game.

The ball would speed up after your fourth and 12th successful hits, and whenever you first hit one of the orange and red bricks. Once you broke through the wall and the ball hit the top of the screen, it would bounce along the top and knock out lots of bricks. At this point, the paddle would shrink by half and the game would get even tougher. The key was mastering how to hit the ball such that it shot back up near the top of the screen at the angle you wanted. The closer to the edge of the paddle the ball hit, the sharper the angle would be, just as it was in *Pong*.

Significantly, the game lacked a timer; if you missed the ball three times, the game would end. This small change meant that skill, not the clock, determined how long you played, at least until a certain point. If you cleared all 112 bricks, the game would start again with a second wall. Clear that one and you'd max out the game with a total score of 896 points. The game still limited how long you could play, but the length of a play per quarter wasn't as predetermined as it was with other games.

Breakout led to big sales for Atari, with more than 10,000 cabinets sold in the U.S. It also spawned a tremendous piracy effort in Japan, with thousands of bootleg cabinets installed around the country. When Bushnell couldn't deliver enough legitimate cabinets to Namco for Japanese distribution, several Yakuza clans stepped in. They were organized crime syndicates that ran much of the country's underground markets. One clan approached Namco CEO Masaya Nakamura and tried to get cut in on the deal, causing Nakamura to redouble his efforts to secure more cabinets from Bushnell, to no avail. In the end, Namco broke its contract with Atari and started to build its own PCBs for *Breakout*, at which point Namco entered the video game manufacturing business.[2]

The next year, after Wozniak built the Apple I, he based his second personal computer design in large part on a machine that could play *Breakout* at home. Jobs and Wozniak introduced the Apple II in 1977 with color graphics, sound capability, and support for two paddle controllers. A home conversion of *Breakout* for the Atari 2600 became notable for its rainbow wall, with bricks that blended into solid bands of color. *Breakout* went on to define an entire genre of video games, from high-powered derivatives such as *Arkanoid* and Atari's own *Super Breakout* variant to the *Brick Breaker* game that came built into BlackBerry smartphones.

Much of this later significance has come to smother the original game's popularity in the arcades. But it's because of its minimalist design and refined concept that the rest followed. *Breakout* wasn't quite as simple as "avoid missing ball for high score," but it proved far more enduring.

Night Driver (Atari, 1976)

The original first-person driving game, *Night Driver* delivered smoothly animated black-and-white graphics. It was Atari's first game to feature a microprocessor, in this case a MOS 6502, the same chip that would power the Apple II and Atari's own 400 and 800 home computers a couple of years later. In *Night Driver*, you earned points by driving as far as you could in the time allotted. As you kept the accelerator pedal depressed and shifted gears, from first through fourth, the car went faster and faster. The game delivered a three-dimensional sensation by rendering the edges of the road with vertical white rectangles ostensibly representing roadside reflectors. These fell to the bottom of the screen at an increasingly fast rate and then shifted to the left and right as the road began to curve. When the player steered the car, it would also shift the falling rectangles to the left or right, either keeping the car on the road or crashing into one of the reflectors. If you crashed, you'd come to a halt and would have to accelerate from a stop again. Atari sold the illusion of racing by animating the rectangles at a high rate of speed. Setting the game in the nighttime made it easier to develop, as the programmer didn't have to worry about depicting trees, buildings, or other obstacles that were just assumed to be in the dark and impossible to see.

Figure 2.2: *Night Driver* **was the first driving game to feature a first-person perspective, a trick of animating the roadside pylons at high speed.**

The upright cabinet included a steering wheel, an accelerator pedal, and a four-speed gear shift lever that moved in an *N* pattern. A black light above the monitor lit up the bezel, while an amplified monophonic speaker provided the rumbling engine, skidding, and crash sounds. A color overlay on the screen depicted the front of the Sebring race car you drove, and a piece of plexiglass covered that and the 23-inch monitor, protecting them both from damage. A rocker switch offered the player three difficulty options at the start of each game: Novice, Pro, and Expert, with increasingly difficult curves to navigate. Regardless of which setting you chose, as the game progressed, the road became narrower and curvier. Operators could configure multiple aspects of the game, including the length (from 50 to 125 seconds, with a default setting of 100), an extended play mode that kicked in after the player achieved a score of 350, and two different sets of three courses (the same courses reversed, to save memory) so that regular patrons wouldn't get too used to the way the game worked. A later sit-down model kept track of the highest speed and score for each of the three difficulty levels. Later games would eclipse what *Night Driver* achieved, relegating it to the back shelves of game history, but it's a mistake to understate its initial impact in video arcades.

F-1 (Namco/Atari, 1976)

In contrast to the future that was *Night Driver*, Namco's *F-1* game served as a look at the past. One of the last electromechanical arcade machines, *F-1* seemed to bridge the divide between the mechanical world and video game graphics. It had no graphics of its own; instead, it generated images via a spinning carousel projected onto a plastic translucent screen, a technique used in early animation.

You raced against two computer-controlled opponents on a circular track until you ran out of time. It was *F-1*'s presentation that grabbed people, with its sit-in-a-race-car design and giant projection screen that made it impossible to miss in arcades. The game had a racing steering wheel, a two-position gas pedal, a brake pedal that slowed the rotational speed of the track cylinder, a low/high gear shift, and some fake circular gauges in its dashboard. Two small plastic cars, just two inches across, were attached to linkages on a round, translucent racetrack 20 inches in diameter, which rotated depending on how fast you were driving. A lamp then projected this setup onto the screen.[3] Across the top of the cabinet were a couple of small LED displays for the current and high score, along with backlit *F-1* and Atari logos and a fake fuel gauge. During play, the cabinet's speaker emitted a loud engine whine, and the sense of speed was palpable and gripping. The brake triggered a skidding-out sound. If you crashed, it played the sound of an explosion, and the screen displayed frightening (to a kid) orange and yellow explosion graphics. In 1976, nothing else played like it or had such a big, imposing display.

Figure 2.3: *F-1* was one of the last great electromechanical arcade games, putting on an imposing and even scary light and sound show for each player.

F-1 was designed by Namco engineer Sho Osugi, who based it on his earlier games *Racer* (1973) and *Formula-X* (1975) but built it to a smaller size so that it could be located in stores. "*F-1* not only was smaller, but had better effects that were more realistic," Osugi said in a 2019 interview. "We'd project the course using a magic lantern, but that had a modified light bulb. Thanks to that, even when clones popped up, they weren't able to replicate the lighting effects."[4] The basic game layout dated to Auto Test, a 1959 simulator that taught driving skills to students.[5]

The package for *F-1* came with a lot of parts and had to be assembled in place. Then you went through an operator checklist and tested out each of the controls to make sure that they responded correctly and the game was working as intended. In daily operation, the game proved reliable, with the only simple (if common) repairs being needed for blown light bulbs and sticking linkages for the cars.[6] If an operator replaced a part, such as the racetrack motor or the control board, they had to recalibrate the score, main car, and two competition cars for the game to work correctly again.

F-1 was Namco's first major hit and is considered the first Formula One arcade racing game, even if it wasn't a pure video game with pixels. In this case, pixels weren't necessary. Appropriately enough, an *F-1* coin-op showed up in the arcade scene of George Romero's 1978 zombie film *Dawn of the Dead*. In the early 1980s, Tomy made a toy called the Turnin' Turbo Dash that adopted the same technique on a miniature scale. And of course, people have recently taken to modding that thing to play an actual arcade game of Sega *Out Run* with an LCD and a Raspberry Pi, because people are awesome.[7] Fun projects aside, most electromechanical games have fallen into disrepair over the years, as their complex assemblies of moving parts didn't last.[8]

Stunt Cycle (Atari, 1976)

In his day, Evel Knievel was the world's most famous daredevil stunt performer, and his steed of choice was the motorcycle. A video game based on this idea made sense. Atari's *Stunt Cycle* was the first motorcycle video game and the first coin-op with handlebar controls. You had to jump over an increasing number of buses without crashing, Evel Knievel–style. The cabinet contained a 19-inch black-and-white monitor and illuminated marquee on top. A large handlebar dominated the control panel. You couldn't steer, though; the right handgrip acted as your throttle control.

The stunt course was presented in a three-level side view. The first player rode a white motorcycle; the second, if present, rode a black one. The edges of the screen showed a silkscreened U-shaped pipe on the top right and a second one on the bottom left. You navigated the pipes, switching between sides of the screen, until you reached the ramp for the bus jump. The reality was the game code was just wrapping the playfield around and shifting the vertical position of the motorcycle each time. On the top two levels, you couldn't drive too fast or your cycle would pop a wheelie or even flip over backwards.

When it was time to jump on the bottom level, you approached the ramp and revved the engine such that you launched at just the right speed. Too slow and you'd end up on top of the buses; too fast and you wouldn't be able to land. The idea was to land in a specific area beyond the second ramp but not too far beyond. Each time you jumped the buses without crashing, you would then loop back to the start of the course at the top left. The number of buses would increase by one, shifting the rightmost ramp over a bit more to accommodate the extra bus. Your score was equal to the number of buses you successfully jumped, starting at eight. An amplified mono speaker situated to the left of the coin mechanism played simulated sounds of the motorcycle accelerating through different gears. It also played crowd cheering sounds after each successful jump, a skidding sound for flipped-over wheelies, and multiple bounces followed by a crash when you wiped out.

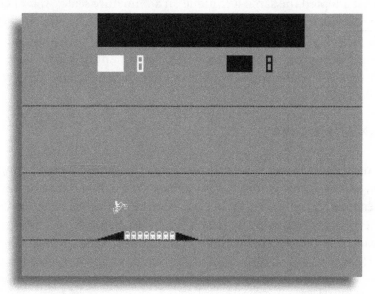

Figure 2.4: *Stunt Cycle* **paved the way for a subgenre of 2D motorcycle stunt racing games such as** *Excitebike* **and the BMX portion of** *California Games.*

Operators could set options so that 25 cents bought either one or two games, or that it cost 25 cents per player, or that a free play mode unlocked whenever the player reached the selected number of buses. As with *Breakout*, *Stunt Cycle* came from the factory set to "three misses," and there was no timer; it would end whenever you wiped out three times or if you made it to the maximum number of buses (27). The next year, Atari released two home console versions of the game. The first was shaped like a handlebar control on top of a platform; it played *Stunt Cycle* and three other variants called Motocross, DragRace, and Enduro. The second, a Sears Tele-Games variant, included the same four games plus 16 versions of *Pong*, along with detachable paddle controllers for those. *Stunt Cycle*'s influence carried through the 1980s to games such as Nintendo's colorful *Excitebike* and *California Games* from Epyx.

Sea Wolf (Dave Nutting Associates/Midway, 1976)

Sea Wolf was conceived as an update to Midway's earlier electromechanical coin-op Sea Devil. Dave Nutting and Tom McHugh, inspired by Sega's *Periscope*, designed and programmed the game. The result was a new kind of coin-op all its own. *Sea Wolf* was an imposing presence, and looked nothing like the standard upright cabinet design of most arcade games. A large bulge in its marquee housed the mount for a metal sighting device. Players used the periscope to aim torpedoes at submarines and ships. A mono speaker was positioned to the left of the bulge in the marquee. The cabinet was covered in eye-catching under-the-sea graphics, with submarines and deep-sea wildlife. Inside was a large 23-inch black-and-white monitor mounted flat and facing upwards. The image displayed on the monitor was reversed; an angled mirror in turn reflected the image toward the player.

The attract mode showed the name of the game, an "Insert Coin" message, and the current three-digit high score. Look through the periscope and you'd see the reflected image through its own series of mirrors, along with a firing crosshair line and orange indicator lights, thanks to another translucent overlay. A side benefit of the design: Bystanders could look around the sides of the periscope and still see the correct image. Someone would have to stick their head in farther and look down to see the reversed image on the monitor. The fixed playfield showed a side view of an underwater ocean, with the sea level near the top as a horizon line. A blue overlay on the monitor tinted the view an appropriate shade. Start a game and one at a time, ships would begin to sail back and forth across the top of the screen. You had to sink as many ships as possible with torpedoes within the allotted time. You used the periscope handles to aim your shots; a button under your thumb on the right handle fired the torpedoes. Different ships were worth different amounts of points, with the PT Boat being the most valuable. Numerous mines floated by in the water, and if a torpedo hit one, the mine would block it from traveling further. If you reached a high enough score before the time ran out, you'd earn bonus time and could keep playing.

Showing the game's electromechanical roots, a series of lights sat behind the mirror in the cabinet. Torpedo a ship and the nearest light would flash orange to simulate an explosion while the ship tilted over and sank. The game's sonic palette included sonar pings, radar warnings, hissing torpedo shots, and of course, full-bodied explosion sounds. The orange indicator lights inside the periscope consisted of "Ready," "Reload," and numbers denoting your four torpedo slots. Every time you shot your last torpedo, the "Reload" indicator in the periscope view would light for a second or two; during this time, you couldn't shoot. Then it would go back to "Ready" and all four numbers would relight, indicating that the torpedoes were reloaded.

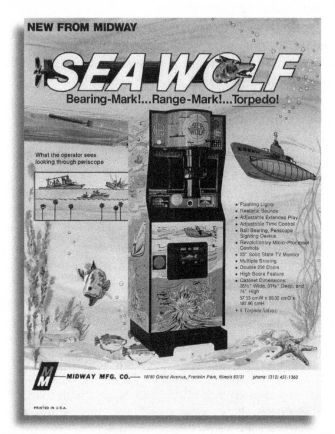

Figure 2.5: Midway's *Sea Wolf*, conceived as a video game update to Sega's *Periscope*, incorporated electromechanical features into its cabinet to enhance the black-and-white graphics and synthesized sound effects.

Sea Wolf was popular in its day, and Midway went on to sell a significant 10,000 cabinets over the next several years. Later, Midway released *Sea Wolf II*, which supported two players and employed a color monitor. It was impressive how convincing the overall effect was of the various video and mechanical parts, between the periscope view, the controls, the audio, the blue and orange overlays, and the multiple mirrors generating the two views. *Sea Wolf* is often credited as the game that brought electromechanical games into the video game age.

Exidy

Exidy was founded in late 1973 by Pete Kauffman and Samuel Hawes, former Ramtek and Ampex engineers. They had both played *Pong* in Andy Kapp's Tavern and knew video games would become a major enterprise.[9] Exidy, a portmanteau of "Excellence in Dynamics," started off with its own *Pong* clone called *TV Pinball*, which included an attract mode similar to *Space Race*'s.

The company stretched its design chops in 1975 with *Destruction Derby*, which came equipped with two steering wheels, gear shifts, and accelerator pedals. The game presented the cars in a fixed playfield; you had to smash into the other one as many times as you could. It was an enjoyable game and a hit. Exidy found itself incapable of producing enough cabinets to meet demand, so it licensed the game to Chicago Coin, which released its own iteration called *Demolition Derby*.[10]

The agreement didn't work out as planned. Exidy's take proved smaller than expected, and Chicago Coin ran into financial trouble and couldn't pay the licensing fees anyway. Exidy found itself in dire straits. To stay afloat, it needed a second hit game—fast. Instead of starting from scratch, the company modified *Destruction Derby*'s existing discrete logic design and code to create a new game.[11] In the process, Exidy kicked off the video game industry's first moral panic.

Death Race (Exidy, 1976)

Aside from the general seediness of hanging out in a low-rent, smoky bar, there wasn't much negative publicity around video games. The same went for Dungeons & Dragons, introduced in 1974; stuffed shirts hadn't yet latched on to either hobby as something that could be a bad influence the way they had with, say, marijuana. Even *Gun Fight*, the first video game to depict one human inflicting violence on another, didn't seem to register. That changed with *Death Race*. Hitting arcades the year after the sci-fi movie *Death Race 2000* was unleashed in theaters, *Death Race* grabbed attention with its skeleton-infused artwork and a cross standing in for the *T* in the first word of the name. The game's screen and console were angled almost cocktail style, propping up two steering wheels that looked straight out of a pair of Camaros. A three-position gear shift sat next to each wheel, for low gear, high gear, and reverse. The cars accelerated on their own; there were no pedals.

In *Death Race*, you played the Grim Reaper. You drove around the playfield running over "gremlins" (as per the manual; a brochure called them "monsters" instead). The playfield was divided into three areas; cars could only drive in the large area in the center. At any one time, two gremlins ran amok, although the manual hinted that there was some artificial intelligence behind their movements. The gremlins were safe from you in the other two portions of the playfield. Each kill was worth one point. The gremlins turned into cross-shaped tombstones whenever they were killed. The more gremlins you ran over, the more tombstones would appear. This would create a new game mechanic, as the tombstones would clutter up the playfield and make it difficult to drive around. Part of the appeal was the way this would generate a pseudorandom maze each time you played. You could also drive off the edge of the screen and reappear at the other side. If you were playing against a second person, you could ram their car to prevent them from gaining a point.

Figure 2.6: Exidy brought the video arcade industry its first moral reckoning—and bought itself some early publicity in the process. Credit: Piotr Konieczny, licensed under CC BY-SA 3.0

The game's black-and-white graphics were still simple, with the cars and gremlins maybe one step above stick figures. The synthesized sounds were closer to what you'd hear when tuning an old radio than actual screams. Regardless, it looked a lot like you were running over pedestrians, and anyone with half a brain would see the title of Exidy's game and connect it with the movie. Reverse gear even let you back up over the dead body just to make sure. The killing-people premise and the satanic look of the cabinet graphics made *Death Race* a different proposition than the familiar paddleball, driving, and shotgun video games on the market. Once word got out that the game's internal code name during development was Pedestrian, the media jumped; stories soon appeared on *60 Minutes* and NBC's *Weekend Show*.[12] The National Safety Council called the game "sick and morbid."[13] One safety authority denounced the game in a newspaper article on Dec. 29, 1976, writing, "One of [the game's] most insidious and probably unrecognized characteristics is its shift from imaginary visual behavioral actions taken by the player. The person is no longer just a spectator, but now an actor in the process of creating violence."[14] A safety consultant for the Automobile Club of Southern California called the game "sick, sick, sick."[15]

The added notoriety made the game more desirable to play (the "Streisand Effect," albeit years before the term was coined). All told, *Death Race* wasn't a tremendous success. Reportedly, Exidy only sold about 500 cabinets,[16] though other sources put the number closer to 1,000. Nonetheless, lots of people ended up learning about the game, and by extension Exidy. *Death Race* became popular and well remembered enough that it saw a re-release more than two decades later on the PC and the Nintendo Entertainment System. In the age of Grand Theft Auto, and untold numbers of first-person shooters with graphic depictions of blood-soaked displays of violence, a bunch of stick figures turning into crosses seems quaint.

Sprint 2 (Atari, 1976)

Atari's next hit racing game was *Sprint 2*, a top-down competition with two steering wheels. *Sprint 2* was also designed around a microprocessor and improved on *Gran Trak 10*, with its additional tracks, computer-controlled race cars, and sharper graphics. At just under 67 inches, *Sprint 2*'s cabinet wasn't too high, but its 36-inch width allowed for two separate steering wheels, four-speed gear shifts, and accelerator pedals so that two players could race side by side. Three backlit buttons on the control panel started one- and two-player games and also let you select a track. A 23-inch monitor displayed black-and-white graphics and was tilted back and covered in plexiglass.

The object was to complete as many laps as possible before the timer ran out. One player controlled the white car and the other drove the black one. Two gray computer-controlled cars raced along in each game, and if you were playing by yourself, the computer would also assume control of the black car. To start the game, you put in a quarter, and then pressed the Track Select button until you arrived at the track you wanted to race on. Each of the 12 tracks were progressively more difficult. Then you had to press either of the two Start buttons, depending on how many quarters you inserted, and the game would begin with the timer set to 100 and counting down. Once the timer ran out, each player would get a rating: Granny, Rookie, or Pro, in what we should see now as an insult to cool grandmothers everywhere.

Figure 2.7: Atari's *Sprint 2* updated *Gran Trak 10* with computer opponents, an interlaced monitor, microprocessor-based hardware, and the industry's first on-screen font. Credit: Piotr Konieczny, licensed under CC BY-SA 3.0

The cars drove well given the 1976 release date and top-down graphics. You couldn't accelerate from a stop fast enough unless you were in first gear. You would then shift through the other three gears as you kept accelerating while turning the steering wheel with your left hand. The game lacked brake pedals, unlike *Gran Trak 10*, but it didn't matter much in gameplay, and you could still trigger oversteer by swinging the steering wheel abruptly. If you drove into any of the other three cars or ran over an oil slick, you'd skid out, and if you hit the side of the road you would crash, and the car would stop. The speaker played the various engine sounds as well as skidding and crashing sound effects.

Each time you passed a checkpoint area, your score at the top of the screen would increase, for a total of 10 points per lap. Unlike in *Gran Trak 10*, the checkpoints weren't visible on screen; as there were 12 tracks, a plexiglass overlay denoting the checkpoints wouldn't have worked. In a fun bit of history, *Sprint 2* was the first popular arcade game to display the "arcade font" in use throughout the late 1970s and for decades beyond.[17] Originally used earlier in the year on Atari's *Quiz Show* as well as in Kee Games' *Cannonball*, a new monospace font in *Sprint 2* at the top of the screen showed the black car's score, the white car's score, and the time remaining. These three games were Atari's first coin-ops to use its new microprocessor-based hardware, so it's possible the digital logic just wasn't there for a full readable font prior to this.[18]

Designed by Dennis Koble and Lyle Rains of Kee Games, *Sprint 2* became Atari's second-biggest hit of the year, accounting for some 8,200 units sold. As had become standard, the operator could adjust how much each play cost (from 25 cents for both players to 50 cents each) and how long each game was (from 60 to 150 seconds), as well as whether extended play was allowed for the best players and whether there were oil slicks in the game. In 1977, Atari released *Sprint 4* and *Sprint 8*, both of which offered full-color raster graphics and support for either four or eight players, and the next year Atari released *Sprint 1*, neatly capping its foray into the Backwards Land of sequels. (The odd naming scheme referred to the number of players each model supported.)

Arcades Hit a Speed Bump

In the mid 1970s, Atari dominated the video arcade industry it had created. Now just a few years old, the only real competition was from Taito and Midway, even though dozens of manufacturers threw in with *Pong* clones. Some had already given up by 1975, dejected by the quick rise and fall of the ball-and-paddle game's popularity, though Allied Leisure, Exidy, and Atari were still releasing new ones that year.

By the end of 1976, the video arcade industry was in full swing, although sales of new cabinets began to stagnate. The public shifted from playing *Pong* clones to newer driving and racing games. Some of the Bronze Age's titles proved more popular than others, but all were enticing curiosities for new gamers, and some proved deep enough for repeated and more rewarding play. Coin-ops such as *Breakout*, *Sprint 2*, *Sea Wolf*, and *Night Driver* began to capture a distinct "feel," a potent combination of graphics, sound effects, and more polished gameplay that would start to increase in difficulty the longer you played. They were mostly timer based but gave the player something significant for each quarter, often a more cerebral experience with a one-player mode than in two-player-only games. Even if the 1976 releases looked somewhat primitive compared with what was to come, many of these newer games were eminently playable then and remain so today.

It was also clear video games had changed the amusement industry. "Electro-mechanical games, with some exceptions, are becoming pretty rare offerings," said Joe Robbins, a vice president of Empire Entertainment, in a 1976 interview with *RePlay* magazine. "The cost of making them has forced most manufacturers to cancel most production plans. This includes the once-popular gun types and baseball games, to name a few."[19] And although arcade video games had hit a speed bump in sales this year, solid-state pinball games had just debuted and were doing strong business, more than making up the shortfall to owners and operators. The new pinball games remembered the state of the playfield as each player took a turn, thanks to their scoring memory.[20]

Nonetheless, aside from *Breakout* and *Sprint 2*, *Sea Wolf* was the only other game of 1976 to crack 5,000 units sold. Meanwhile, the shakeout of lesser arcade coin-op manufacturers would continue. PSE produced half a dozen coin-ops between 1975 and 1977 before calling it quits. Electra Games produced a few paddle-style games in 1975 and 1976, including *Eliminator IV*. Many others disappeared without a trace.

Atari Launches the 2600

Much of the new action in video games around this period was in the nascent home market. With the success of *Home Pong*, Coleco, Bandai, Nintendo, and RCA all released consoles of their own; in response, Atari converted some of its other arcade releases into nifty new television games, such as *Stunt Cycle* and *Video Pinball*. Soon, the public tired of these, and in the first half of 1977 console sales fell. The market had become saturated. Some wondered if video games were just another passing fad.

But several developments changed the industry's trajectory. Electronic handheld games from Nintendo, Mattel, and others began to appear in earnest. These products modeled arcadelike play with buttons and sliders, but created "displays" out of red LEDs instead of using screens. Fairchild unveiled the Video Entertainment System, the first programmable home console that let you play different games by inserting plastic "Videocarts," with the promise of new ones being introduced in the future. It eliminated the problem of becoming bored with a console, because there would always be new games to buy. This would soon become the model for the home game industry. It laid down the outline for the biggest challenge arcades would someday face.

Figure 2.8: The Atari 2600, shown here with an *Adventure* cartridge. Photo by the author.

Atari engineers had built their own prototype of a programmable, cartridge-based game console, something that could reinvigorate the stagnant market. The issue was securing enough capital to finish, manufacture, and distribute the retail product. In October 1976, Bushnell solved the problem by selling Atari to Warner Communications for $28 million. Development continued, and in October 1977, Atari unveiled the 2600, a $199 console that came with two joysticks, two paddles, and a pack-in cartridge called

Combat. The game was a straight-up home conversion of the two-player *Tank*, with some added variations and a couple of *Jet Fighter*–like side games thrown in for good measure—27 games in all, in one cartridge. To this end, Atari also sold eight other boxed cartridges separately. One was called *Indy 500*, a two-player conversion of Atari's *Indy 800* arcade game and the only one to come with its own controllers—in this case Driving paddles, which spun around without a stop, unlike the standard Paddle controllers.

None of the launch titles matched the quality of the latest arcade games, but that didn't matter—you could play them at home, and there was unlimited potential for new games. And unlike arcade coin-op cabinets, which remained prohibitively costly, cartridges were inexpensive enough to buy and even collect, with average prices hovering around $20 and $30 apiece. Soon, Atari built out the 2600's catalog by converting its other coin-op games, such as the Wild West–themed *Outlaw*. Rob Fulop's home conversion of *Night Driver* gave the game a second life, adding color graphics, a genuine on-screen car depiction, and more to the original formula. I remember playing the arcade game incessantly at a hotel my family stayed at, in a recreation room with a pool table. I liked playing pool with my dad, but I was obsessed and kept returning to *Night Driver*—especially because I had the 2600 cartridge at home and was dying to play the original. Comparing arcade coin-ops with home conversions soon became a prime topic of discussion between gamers. Within the span of a year, stand-alone home consoles without cartridge slots all but disappeared off the market. Atari's latest consumer product had rendered them obsolete. And arcades had a new threat to contend with, in addition to rampant bootlegging and a fickle public looking for the next big thing.

Cinematronics and the Rise of Vector Graphics

In 1977, a certain major motion picture opened in theaters nationwide. A space opera set a long time ago in a galaxy far, far away, *Star Wars* soon came to dominate the cultural landscape. Around the same time, an MIT grad had developed a system for a new kind of arcade graphics that would put all existing raster-scan efforts to shame. It would make possible in a video game some of the same cutting-edge visuals seen in that movie. The MIT grad, Larry Rosenthal, loved *Spacewar!*, the game Steve Russell programmed there some 15 years earlier. On his own, Rosenthal designed a discrete logic board that could run the game, and yet was inexpensive enough to manufacture at scale for arcades.

Rosenthal's board could also handle graphics the way *Spacewar!* was meant to be played. Up until this point, manufacturers were designing and releasing arcade games using raster graphics. Each game displayed images on a CRT coated in phosphors and covered with glass. A gun in the back fired electrons that lit up the phosphors horizontally across the screen 60 times per second. Raster graphics had plenty of potential and had proven to be reliable in the field. The gun had to scan the entire screen on every pass and could only move so fast, so to represent objects game designers used pixels, chunks of phosphors that looked like illuminated blocks. This was fine for paddle games, and Bushnell, Dabney, and Alcorn had used pixels for *Computer Space*. But the technique was proving too blocky looking for anything else.[21]

Instead of raster graphics, MIT's original *Spacewar!* and Stanford's *Galaxy Game* had both employed vector graphics (sometimes called X-Y graphics). With that technology, first introduced in the 1950s, the electron gun moved between specific coordinates on the screen and lit up only the phosphors in between, leaving the rest of the screen black. Vector graphics drew clean, sharp lines and depicted movement especially well, making it look dramatic and distinctive. But it couldn't handle filled-in shapes or detailed bitmap-style designs, and vector graphics had been far too expensive to build into a mass-produced coin-op.

Rosenthal's vector graphics technology, which he dubbed Vectorbeam, would be affordable to produce. It would deliver clean rotations and a frame rate higher than the flicker fusion rate, or the speed at which we can perceive a moving image to be continuous. Cinema had standardized on 24 frames per second (fps). Broadcast television used 30fps and also interlaced frames, which doubled the perceived frame rate by displaying alternating sets of lines; the resulting phosphor glow lent a more realistic-looking picture. Vectorbeam managed 30fps.[22] Rosenthal also employed a "watchdog" circuit that ensured the electron beam stayed within the confines of the safe area of the CRT, because if the beam ever pointed away from the face of the tube, the system could burn up or even explode.[23]

Around the same time Rosenthal began his project, Dennis Partee and Gary Garrison, two football players for the San Diego Chargers, founded a coin-op video game company named Cinematronics in El Cajon, California. Its first two years were unremarkable; neither of its two releases—*Flipper Ball*, a *Pong* clone, and an original game called *Embargo*—did all that well.

The company may well have faded into obscurity, but its fortunes changed in 1976. Rosenthal's design was ready; he secured a license from

MIT to produce a commercial *Spacewar!* and began shopping for a manu-facturer. He tried to license the game to Atari and others without success, mainly because he was demanding a then-unheard-of 50 percent royalty on every game sold—and he also wanted to retain his patents on the hardware. He finally landed a bite at Cinematronics, where Jim Pierce, whom Partee and Garrison had brought in to manage operations, agreed to license the technology at a lower rate and distribute Rosenthal's game as a coin-op.

Cinematronics unveiled the game, now called *Space Wars*, at the annual trade show of the Amusement and Music Operators of America (AMOA) in October 1977. It was an immediate hit; having a name similar to *Star Wars* helped. But Cinematronics had to secure funding. Pierce connected with Tom Stroud, a veteran amusement industry operator, to mass-produce the game.

Figure 2.8: Cinematronics broke open arcade vector graphics with *Space Wars*, an updated take on MIT's *Spacewar!* that any operator could afford.

Space Wars (Cinematronics, 1977)

The final cabinet came in white, with blue, black, and purple decals on the sides and a black front panel with a white strip across the center. At 72 inches high, 32 inches wide, and 30 inches deep, and with its squares-in-side-a-rectangle design, *Space Wars* was an imposing presence on the ar-cade floor. Extra weight on the back of the cabinet was reportedly required so it didn't fall over onto players.

The control panel was daunting at first impression, with 11 square buttons and a two-row numeric keypad in the center. But the controls were simpler than they looked. There were five buttons for each player: Left and Right (to rotate the ship), Forward (for thrust), Fire, and Hyperspace. The keypad in the center let the player choose from 10 options before starting a game. These options, grouped into Beginning, Intermediate, and Expert categories, included games with or without the sun and its gravitational pull, or a wraparound screen, as well as ship and missile speed settings. A Reset button sat below the numeric keypad.

Space Wars depicted a star field, two ships, and the sun at the center. Occasionally, an asteroid would float by. One of the two player ships resembled the Enterprise from *Star Trek*. Each player had 18 missiles and 250 units of fuel to use to destroy their competitor. The company advertised the display as capable of 1,024 horizontal positions and 768 vertical positions, a crisp resolution that wouldn't become commonplace on raster displays until the early 1990s. The game resembled nothing else in the arcades.

Rosenthal added some new features to the *Spacewar!* concept. An indirect hit would cause your ship to become visibly damaged; fragments would break off and float away, and from then on, your ship wouldn't fly or maneuver as easily. And you could extend the 90-second time limit by pumping in more quarters, one for each additional minute and a half, thanks to the cabinet's new coin accumulator.

Reports differed on whether *Space Wars* was a hit for Cinematronics, though according to *RePlay*, it remained in the top-10-earning arcade games for several years.[24] Each *Space Wars* cost Cinematronics about $1,000 to manufacture and distributors $2,000 to buy. This worked out to $500 in profit per unit for Rosenthal, plus $50 per unit for the licensing bonus, earning him an unconfirmed $15 million from the game.[25] *Space Wars* also quickly developed a reputation for unreliability, as the company hadn't gotten the kinks out of the vector graphics system yet. According to various reports from the time, dead screens were a pervasive issue.

Vectorbeam

Pierce and Stroud were pleased with Cinematronics' newfound success, but they didn't like their arrangement with Rosenthal, and Rosenthal thought he wasn't getting his fair share either. After a dispute, Rosenthal left Cinematronics along with some colleagues and formed a separate company called Vectorbeam, after his graphics system. Meanwhile, Cinematronics continued making new games using the same technology, all thanks to a single entry-level employee.

Tim Skelly, an engineer who interviewed with Rosenthal, scored the job, and arrived at the office four days later to find Rosenthal and all of the development hardware and documentation gone.[26] Now the only programmer left at Cinematronics, and a novice at that, Skelly began designing his first video game. Meanwhile, company technicians were busy rebuilding the Vectorbeam development system using a copy of the documentation that they were lucky to find after Rosenthal left. Skelly created *Starhawk*, a cool 1979 game that modeled the trench sequence from *Star Wars*. The game included a nifty feature unheard of before or since: Some of the attacking ships, if not stopped, would attack the digits of the player's score, dropping it by 800.[27] Next, Skelly developed *Sundance*, a game where you caught balls of light, again using fancy vector graphics that no other coin-op manufacturer had access to.[28]

Over at Vectorbeam, Rosenthal and Craven decided to move the company to Union City, California, and manufacture and sell *Space Wars* machines themselves. To differentiate their model, they dropped the plural *s* from the title and fashioned the control panel edge in black. Next, Rosenthal designed *Speed Freak*, a Vectorbeam release remembered for its first-person-view vector graphics and sense of speed; some have called it "the best driving game of its day."[29] Vectorbeam's Dan Sunday designed *Tail Gunner*, a space combat coin-op that put you in control of a gunning station on a large spaceship. It was the first to feature three-dimensional animated polygons on screen.[30] Cinematronics, still working with Rosenthal on licensing deals despite the somewhat acrimonious departure, decided to purchase Vectorbeam outright, dissolving it in 1979 while letting Rosenthal retain his patents.

Super Breakout (Atari, 1978)

Super Breakout was more than just a sequel to *Breakout* with some superficial tweaks. The graphics were attractive; although the game still had a 19-inch black-and-white monitor, it now included color overlays to delineate different sections of the walls. The console contained a Serve button, the main spinner control in the center, a second spinner, and two buttons to start one- and two-player games along the front edge. The white, red, and yellow cabinet displayed broken brick wall graphics this time, instead of just the name of the game.

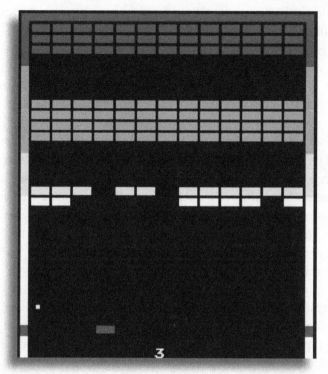

Figure 2.9: *Super Breakout* **updated the original with three levels, including a shifting, double-wall mode and one with two extra balls on screen at once.**

Super Breakout introduced an unusual play mechanic: After inserting a quarter, the player could choose from one of three game variations. In Double Breakout, you controlled two paddles in tandem, with one positioned above the other with a good amount of space between them. The game then served two balls at once, with each brick counting for double points as long as two balls were in play. Cavity Breakout included two holes in the wall that held extra balls in captivity. You freed them to enable up to three in play at once. Scoring doubled with two balls active and tripled with three. Progressive Breakout, the most interesting game option, split the large eight-row wall into two smaller ones of four rows each with some space between them, allowing for interesting "break-through" physics when a ball would be caught in between the two walls as well as on top of the upper one. As you played, new rows of bricks would appear at the top and the existing rows would shift down. This allowed you to break through multiple times during the game, and the longer you played, the faster the bricks fell. The operator could choose when a player would earn a free game, with different settings for the three variations ranging from 200 to 2,000 points.

Each variation played similarly to *Breakout* otherwise, with a side wall, top wall, and similar physics that decided how and where to aim the ball depending on where along the paddle's edge you hit it. The cabinet's attract mode stepped through short demonstrations of each of the three game options, albeit without the paddle visible. After each person played, the board would freeze, and the attract mode adopted the remaining pattern of bricks from the last game. *Super Breakout* also displayed the high score for each of the three games. The operator could set the PCB so that you started with either three or five balls per game, and whether a quarter earned you two games or one game, or whether you needed 50 cents to play once.

Super Breakout saw numerous ports, most notably to the Atari 2600 that same year, albeit with full color, improved sound effects, and two children's versions that were simpler to play. It also showed up as an Atari 8-bit home computer cartridge, with support for up to eight players thanks to the four joystick ports on the 800 and Atari's Paddle Controllers that came two to a connector. Finally, Atari made it the pack-in cartridge for the 5200 SuperSystem released in 1982; at the time, this was criticized because a four-year-old game wasn't the most compelling choice to bundle with a brand-new console.

Football (Atari, 1978)

Atari's *Football*, designed by engineers Dave Stubben and Steve Bristow, had two important distinctions: It was the first popular arcade game of American football, and it was the first to popularize the trackball as an input device. Billed as "a chalktalk that moves," the black-and-white *Football* was a cocktail game, with both two- and (later) four-player versions available. As you played the game, the sides with the X and O letters would switch depending on who had the ball. The cocktail design included a spacing module that would position the height at 40 inches for standing or, when removed, 31 inches for sitting.

The player on offense (shown with O letters), in possession of the ball, had to score a touchdown over the goal line in the end zone by spinning the trackball as fast as possible; the playfield scrolled in tandem. The defense (X) had to prevent the opposing player from reaching the end zone by choosing from two pass plays and two running plays, also with the object of repossessing the ball. The idea was to use the plays to plan a strategy and outguess the opposing side by anticipating what they might do and then outmaneuvering them. Each game started with a huddle; there was a scoreboard, timer, the down number, and the number of yards to go.

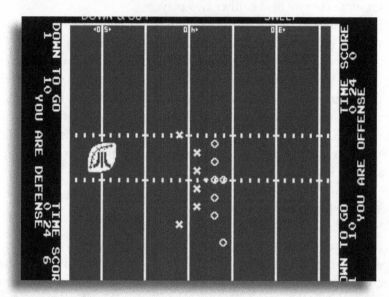

Figure 2.10: The coin-op that gave many players their first video game blisters, Atari's *Football* delivered a surprisingly realistic interpretation of the American sport.

The two control panels, one on each side, were identical. Each contained a large trackball, an LED-lit button, and a Play Select board. The button would either select the play or pass the ball; during play selection, the LED flashed. The Play Select board contained four offensive and four defensive plays, for Sweep, Keeper, Bomb, and Down and Out.

There were two seven-man teams, but the player controlled just one person. On offense, you'd want to run wherever there was a hole in the defense, or if you were on defense, you ran to tackle the ball carrier. The rest of the team would move as designated by the play chosen. The trackball was a 360-degree control; spin it faster, and the player ran faster. During the game, the trackball either moved the quarterback or pass receiver on offense, or the safety if you were on defense. Scoring was seven points for a touchdown run, six points for a touchdown pass, and two points for a safety. There were no kicking plays, such as field goals.

The four-player model introduced cooperative play, with two players on each side controlling two of the seven men on each team. On offense, the two players controlled the quarterback and wide receiver, and could pass to either the wide receiver or tight end. On defense, the two players controlled the two defensive backs. The four-player cocktail cabinet could still accommodate just two players, with one on each side; in this case, the computer would resume control of the other two players.

This was a tough game in a physical sense. That may sound silly about a video game versus the real sport. Nonetheless, be it on offense or defense, many players spun the trackball so fast that their hands would blister. To mitigate this, wearing gloves during play was a common strategy. *Football* was a big hit for Atari, and reportedly made plenty of money during the first three months of its release.[31] I spend a good portion of this book focusing on the hardware controls of each coin-op and how they made the game special. Suffice to say this is one of the few times I would trade the real arcade controls for a joystick.

Sunset of the Bronze Age

As market leader, Atari continued to churn out games at a fast pace. Take 1977 alone. *Starship 1* put you in defense of the Federation against alien spacecraft, in an obvious nod to *Star Trek*; the game employed an analog control yoke with two potentiometers and a throttle control. *Canyon Bomber* put the player in control of aircraft bombing rocks in a kind of reverse-*Breakout* scenario, later reimagined with colorful bricks as an Atari 2600 cartridge. *Drag Race* pitted two players against each other in short bursts of blinding speed; you modulated the throttle and shifted just right to earn a good time without blowing the engine. Exidy countered the onslaught with the microprocessor-based *Circus*, a more humorous take on *Breakout* where you controlled a seesaw and propelled a clown up into the tent to pop rows of moving balloons.

Atari's *Subs* was the first arcade coin-op to employ two monitors, one for each player's view. It was also the first game to process action that wasn't visible on the screen. You had to torpedo the opposing sub, but you couldn't see it except for a fraction of a second when hit; all you had to guide you the rest of the time was sonar. In addition, *Subs* was the first game to let you add extra time by putting in another coin as you played. Atari's 1978 release *Sky Raider* simulated flight; you had to destroy as many targets as you could scattered about flyover terrain within the allocated time, using a yoke similar to the one in *Starship 1*. The wacky *Fire Truck,* also released in 1978, introduced cooperative play to the arcades with separate driving controls for the fire engine's front tractor and the rear tiller.

At this point, and despite the above innovation, pinball machines remained the top earners in arcades. This was fresh off of the introduction of solid-state tables in 1976 that included electronic scoring, sounds, and more sophisticated play, and the legalization of pinball in New York City and Chicago. Operators said in a 1977 survey that if they could choose only one kind of amusement machine, it would be pinball, followed by pool, jukeboxes, soccer tables, and only then video games.[32] Video game coin-op sales were steady, which was another word for stagnant. Hits such as *Breakout*, *Sea Wolf*, *Gun Fight*, and *Sprint 2* remained on the popularity charts in *RePlay* and *Play Meter* month after month in 1977 despite their relative age.[33] The next couple of years, though, would prove pivotal—not just for video arcade coin-ops, but for the amusement industry across the board.

3 > Invasion

Video arcade games attracted a sophisticated and intellectual clientele to bars and restaurants, boosting their image. But many establishment owners were still reluctant. In 1978, *RePlay* magazine surveyed operators about what they referred to as "TV games," and learned that the primary concerns were that they needed to be moved and repaired frequently.[1] Pinball emerged as the clear preference for reliability, thanks to the new solid-state machines, and for revenue collection.[2] This ran counter to what was expected, as arcade games were mechanically simpler. But most operators at the time were still more familiar with pinball machines.

It didn't matter. Aside from some occasional newer hits such as *Breakout* and *Night Driver*, no new video games were sticking. Would they just be a fad after all? Soon, all concerns within the industry were put to rest. One new game ignited the Golden Age of arcades, and it made just about every existing coin-op from the Bronze Age look old. It came from a company still best known for its Pachinko machines. Considering its impact, it may as well have come from outer space.

Space Invaders (Taito/Midway, 1978)

With moviegoers captivated by blockbusters such as *Star Wars* and *Close Encounters of the Third Kind*, space aliens were on everyone's mind—including that of one Tomohiro Nishikado, a Taito engineer who worked on some earlier games for the company's home market in Japan. Nishikado was also inspired by H.G. Wells's *The War of the Worlds*. With this backdrop, he designed a new space shoot-'em-up game where the aliens returned fire and there was no time limit. He did everything by himself—the concept, programming code, graphics, sound, and hardware. He built his own microcomputer with new chips from the United States: an Intel 8080 microprocessor, a Texas Instruments SN76477 sound processor, and 16 Intel 2708 RAM chips.[3] The hardware still lacked sprites, so the code had to draw and erase sprites in frame buffer RAM using bitmaps.[4]

Taito launched Nishikado's creation, *Space Invaders*, in Japan in July 1978. Within months, the country's largest competing Pachinko manufacturer shut down from the sudden loss of business. By the end of the first year, Taito had already sold 100,000 *Space Invaders* machines for $600 million.[5] The Bank of Japan reportedly had to triple its production of 100-yen coins for addicted gamers, although an oft-told story that the government declared a shortage of those coins on account of *Space Invaders* is probably not true.[6] Nonetheless, within a matter of months, you could find entire arcades populated only with *Space Invaders* cabinets. Still, Taito thought the game wouldn't do well overseas because it was so different. Taito of America disagreed, and approached Bally's Midway division.[7] Midway licensed *Space Invaders* for U.S. distribution and began selling it in America in October 1978. The aliens invaded not just Earth but American pop culture.

The object of the game, if it somehow still needs explaining, was to blast apart wave after wave of approaching aliens using a laser turret that moved back and forth across the bottom of the screen—all while dodging the aliens' missiles. If one hit you, or if the alien armada managed to land, you'd lose a life. Clear all 55 aliens on the screen and you'd progress to the next, more difficult wave.

The control panel contained five buttons: two to move your laser base left or right and one to fire, and then two more to start either a one- or two-player game. Today we play emulated games with joysticks and gamepads, so it's important to note just how different it felt in an arcade to move your ship using buttons instead of a stick. The black-and-white graphics consisted of 256 horizontal lines and 224 blocks per line in a vertical orientation—nothing special, but some visual tricks boosted the presentation. A yellow moon and dark blue sky sat behind the graphics; this was accomplished by lighting a plastic overlay with a black light bulb. Additional color strips allowed for red UFOs to fly over and green bunkers along the bottom of the screen. The layered effect was thanks to a mirror that reflected the screen upwards.

Not only was there no time limit, but there was also no artificial end to the game, such as the two walls in *Breakout* or the maximum number of buses to jump in *Stunt Cycle*. The better you became at *Space Invaders*, the longer you could play—a mechanic that would soon become standard in arcade coin-op design. You received anywhere from three to six lives, and as an extra way to draw you in, you would win one bonus life at either 1,000 or 1,500 points depending on how the game was configured. The three main alien types were worth 10, 20, and 30 points, respectively. Every 25 seconds, a UFO flew across the top of the screen; if you nabbed it, you'd earn a random amount of bonus points. As you blasted the aliens, the remaining ones would begin to speed up—another mechanic Nishikado discovered quite by accident, as it turned out the Intel 8080 processor could render frames faster when there were fewer aliens on screen.[8]

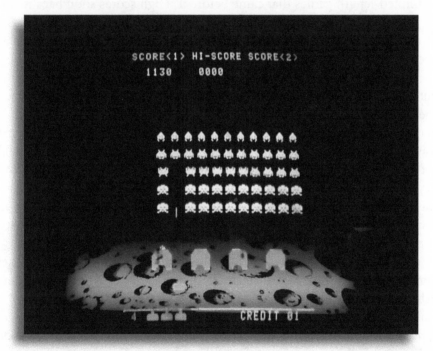

Figure 3.1: Aliens descended on Japan and America in *Space Invaders*, the coin-op that ignited the Golden Age of arcade video games. Credit: Joe Lyons

The audio consisted of sound effects for your laser cannon, blasting the aliens, and the laserlike warble of the UFO flying overhead. But the most significant sound, and possibly the most memorable thing about the game, was the steady, repeating bass pattern in the background. It signaled the relentless onslaught as the aliens moved across the screen and made their way toward your laser base. You felt the low end in your chest as it shook the cabinet, adding to the tension. As the aliens descended further and you blasted more of them, the four-note loop would speed up until it became a continuous machine-gun-fire rumble. However simple it was, *Space Invaders* was the first video game to have continuous background music.[9]

Space Invaders also had the distinction of popularizing the high score concept previously seen in *Sea Wolf* and the sit-down *Night Driver*. Tracking and displaying the high score was all it did—entering initials would come later, and it would reset whenever the machine was powered down or unplugged. But players noticed whenever their handiwork was preserved for the next player to try and beat. Achieving a high score in *Space Invaders* meant staying alive as long as possible, in stark contrast to all the timed or limited-length games that came before it. High scores soon became local competitions for bragging rights and respect among your peers. In the arcades, your score would soon become paramount, and you were only as good as your last attempt.

Those attempts kept coming. *Space Invaders* was not just challenging, but addictive—the hypnotic march of the aliens across the screen, which sped up as each board progressed, captivated players. You could sweat while playing it. Gamers popped in quarter after quarter to try to reach the next wave; it never mattered that it was impossible to finish as long as you could get a higher score than before. You'd begin to learn the game's quirks and develop strategies. For example, although the lone remaining alien was always the fastest, it moved faster in one direction than in the other. Or you learned you could vaporize alien missiles if you hit them just right and happened to have a shot in reserve.

Within one year, Midway sold 40,000 machines in the U.S.[10] The cabinet graphics depicted monsters instead of alien spaceships; Nishikado said he believes this was because the artist based the design on the original concept, which was a new video game in the vein of Taito's 1972 electromechanical *Space Monsters*, instead of the resulting alien invasion.[11] The attract mode did some fun things to draw in gamers, such as sending out an alien to fix an upside-down *Y* in "Play Space Invaders," or to shoot away an extra *C* in "Insert Coin" on screen. In addition to the upright model, Midway also made a 19-inch cocktail table where one or two people could play while seated. A joystick replaced the move buttons, but this model didn't have the room necessary to generate the backlit yellow moon backdrop.

Space Invaders laid down the template for the fixed shooter. By April 1979, it had created demand never seen before and was the "world's hottest game."[12] One year later, Taito introduced a 64-page, $1.95 book called *How to Play Space Invaders: Secrets From an Expert,* anonymously written and believed to be the first-ever arcade video game strategy guide.[13] Establishments that were used to carrying one or two coin-ops found themselves needing multiple *Space Invaders* machines next to each other, and the game rewarded skilled players with longer durations. Midway's parent company Bally made a pinball table based on the game. In short order, *Space Invaders* took over both Japan and America, with some 300,000 cabinets sold in Japan and 60,000 in America by 1980.[14] It kept going. By 1982, the game had grossed $2 billion and $450 million in net profit—much more than the highest grossing film of the time, *Star Wars*, which had brought in a paltry $486 million gross revenue and $175 million profit.[15] The game's success led to a large number of knockoffs and bootleg versions, often with slight tweaks to the name or gameplay, as others rushed to cash in on the craze.

Even more than *Computer Space* and *Pong, Space Invaders* broke coin-op games out of dive bars. After *Space Invaders,* "video games would never again be thought of as filler games or relegated to the back corners of game rooms."[16] Soon, you could find versions of the game not just as cartridges for home consoles, but as handhelds, tabletop games, computer games, and even watches and pocket calculators. *Electronic Games* magazine awarded the game a place in its hall of fame in 1983. It said *Space Invaders* had "penetrated the fabric of our society."[17]

Star Fire (Exidy, 1978)

Exidy's *Star Fire* wasn't the first sit-down video game—that distinction went to Atari's 1975 release *Hi-Way,* which offered a seat as part of a red fiberglass cabinet to go with its steering wheel and pedals, and *Night Driver* also came in a sit-down model. But *Star Fire* was the first "environmental" or cockpit game. These were sit-down models that were enclosed, perfect for flight simulators and driving games, or any game where the designers wanted to convey a sense of total immersion. The trade-off was that they needed a certain amount of floor space, something many retail shops and small venues couldn't afford to sacrifice.

Star Fire put you in control of a space fighter ship; you had to destroy as many enemies as possible in dogfights before the clock ran out. The entire game resembled *Star Wars* on purpose; Exidy hoped to pick up the license, but could change some of the game elements to avoid being sued if that didn't happen.[18] This began with the attract screen, which displayed the title in a design that mimicked the *Star Wars* logo.

The control panel consisted of a two-handed flight yoke with a Fire button on the top left. A red Game Start button sat to the left, while a metal handle on the right controlled thrust. The screen displayed a crosshair gunsight at the center, floating over a background star field. The first-person view meant as you piloted the ship, the crosshairs stayed in the center; the yoke let you climb, descend, and bank left or right. A long-range scanner let you view the positions of enemy ships in the sector. The game displayed the current speed and direction, along with the score and fuel remaining. Enemy ships could be seen flying around in the view out; most looked like TIE fighters, and your own ship was basically an X-wing. The game would display when you were locked on target and ready to fire the laser cannon, which triggered an array of four beams that converged in an *X* pattern. Fire it too much and it would overheat for a few moments. Shoot an enemy fighter and it would explode into many pieces; the resulting shockwave would temporarily slow down your ship. You could also avoid the explosion by throwing the thrusters into reverse. Sometimes you'd come across a large, sleek mothership with "Exidy" inscribed on the tail; it resembled an Imperial light cruiser. This ship was worth a lot of points, and the game prevented you from locking your laser system onto it. The enemy base, which you couldn't attack, resembled the Death Star.

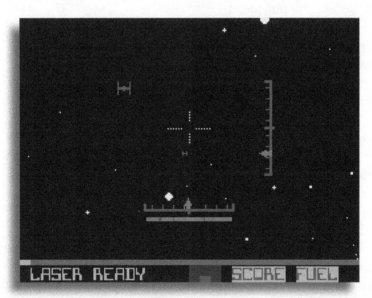

Figure 3.2: Exidy's *Star Fire* introduced the environmental cabinet to arcades and brought *Star Wars* to the video game five years before Atari did—and without an official license.

Star Fire was programmed by David Rolfe, and the impressive graphics, which were in full color without the use of overlays, were by Ted Michon and Sun Ogg. The animation was smooth enough for a realistic dogfight feel. Each time you exceeded a certain score, you'd earn bonus time. But, if you were willing, you also could pop in additional quarters to extend your time. *Star Fire* was notable for being the first game to let you enter your initials for a high score, instead of just displaying the score itself. It kept track of the top 10 scores and displayed them in a table. Soon, every game would do this. The deliberate pace of the game—lasers would take a few seconds to reach their target, for example—led to a more cerebral feeling than most action games provided. Rick Pearl, writing for *Electronic Games,* said *Star Fire* was a "closet classic…deserving of a better fate," and that it was "ahead of its time and unable to find a market."[19] Exidy also released a smaller (60-inch-tall) upright that it positioned as "ideal for street locations." The expected *Star Wars* license never materialized. Neither did a lawsuit.

Bushnell Leaves Atari

Despite Atari's good performance in the arcades and the Warner Communications buyout, early 1978 marked a tumultuous time at the top levels of the company. Poor initial 1977 holiday sales of the 2600 left Atari in a vulnerable position. Its founder was also having second thoughts. Nolan Bushnell's interest in the establishment side of the business dated back to his amusement park roots. Around the time Warner acquired the company, Bushnell had begun planning a new franchise where families could dine in a safe environment and play arcade games as they waited for their food, in contrast to the dim lighting and implied seedier adult elements found in bars. The restaurant concept was perfect for landing arcade games in malls, something the industry had struggled with. Bushnell opened the first one, called Chuck E. Cheese's Pizza Time Theatre and named after an animatronic rat Bushell had Atari engineers develop.[20]

"What food are people used to waiting a long time to eat? Pizza," Alcorn said in 2000. "While they wait, we'll give them tokens to play games, so they don't mind waiting half an hour for the pizza. We'll use these animatronic robots that Grass Valley engineered."[21]

Warner management thought little of this concept, however, and didn't want to pursue it despite owning it. Warner executives had also begun hiring employees with business backgrounds, whereas Bushnell focused on hiring engineers. Warner hired a textile business executive named Ray

Kassar to run Atari's consumer division. Bushnell soon clashed with both Kassar and Warner's Manny Gerard, both of whom were angling for the company to get into home computers. Bushnell was against the idea and preferred to begin work on an immediate successor to the 2600. In November 1978, Warner Communications terminated Bushnell's position at Atari. Unable to compete for five years thanks to his contract, Bushnell nonetheless secured the rights to his new Chuck E. Cheese franchise and bought the sole restaurant for $500,000 from Warner, which was glad to be rid of it. Bushnell's restaurant venture flourished, thanks to *Space Invaders* and other hot games. By the end of 1982, there were 200 Pizza Time Theatres in operation.[22]

Over the years, Bushnell has expressed some regret about the 1976 sale to Warner, saying that if he had thought about it for a couple of weeks he may not have done it. But Gerard remembered it differently, recalling that the day they signed the papers to close the deal, Nolan had said, "I've been telling people I'm a millionaire for years, and at last I am."[23]

Sega/Gremlin

Sega was founded in 1960 by two American businessmen, Martin Bromley and Richard Stewart. The company soon acquired the assets of Service Games of Japan, which had sold amusement machines to overseas American military bases for the prior 20 years. Sega began selling coin-op games in 1966, beginning with the launch of the electromechanical light-and-sound game *Periscope*. The giant (7-by-9-foot) game sold well in Japan, Europe, and the U.S., and is credited with establishing the 25-cent standard cost for a single play. Sega began to produce more games, but rampant bootlegs soured the company on the business.[24]

Sega pivoted to video arcade games and tried again in 1973 with *Pong-Tron*, one of the many *Pong* clones released that year, and then stuck with it developing new versions of tennis, hockey, and gun games common to the period. In 1976, Sega released four similar coin-ops: Road Race, a car-racing game; *Moto-Cross* and *Man T.T.*, two motorbike variants; and *Fonz*, a rebranded *Moto-Cross* for the *Happy Days* television show. *Fonz* included handlebar motorcycle controls and is credited with the introduction of haptic feedback; the handlebars vibrated whenever the player crashed the on-screen bike. These four coin-ops also featured a quasi-three-dimensional, third-person perspective, where objects near the top of the screen appeared small on the road and then became larger as they approached your bike.

Sega acquired Gremlin Industries, another unsuccessful American arcade company, in 1978 to serve as its coin-op manufacturer in America. In short order, the combined company began to figure out the formula for successful video game coin-ops. To start with, Gremlin made a dot-eating game. No, not that one.

Head-On (Gremlin/Sega, 1979)

Head-On combined elements of top-down racing coin-ops such as *Gran Trak 10* and *Sprint 2* with a new gameplay mechanic. Although not well remembered today, *Head-On* was the first dot-eating game. You had to race your white car around the rectangular maze "track" and clear all of the dots in the five concentric sets of lanes. The points you earned would go up as you raced. Sometimes the dots would turn to diamonds, which were worth more points.

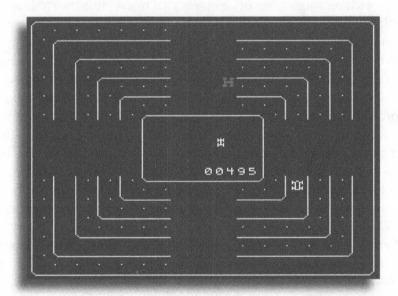

Figure 3.3: *Head-On* was the world's first dot-eating video game. In it, you controlled…a car.

Inside the white and orange cabinet was Sega's tile-based VIC Dual arcade board, which was capable of both black-and-white and color graphics and would soon drive some of the first RGB color games of the era.[25] The control panel consisted of a single four-way joystick and an accelerator button. During the game, you had to avoid one or more red computer-controlled cars that were trying to crash into you head-on. You'd start the game with your car at the bottom of the screen. There were four locations for changing lanes. To do so, you pushed and held the joystick just long enough to complete the lane change, or otherwise the car would snap back into its current lane and miss the change. If you were driving slowly, you could change two lanes at once, but not if you were speeding.

The computer cars moved just one lane over at a time, and they were generally much slower (except near the end of the level). All cars could only move forward through the track; you always drove counterclockwise, while the rival cars drove clockwise. If you collided head-on with a computer car, you'd see a smoke-filled, animated explosion and hear the crash. Clear all the dots and you'd score bonus points and move on to the next board. The second level introduced a sped-up rival car. Levels three and four alternated between two slow and fast rival cars. Level five added a third car, and from level six on, there were always three fast rival cars. Strategically clearing just parts of each rectangular set of lanes was vital to avoiding the rival cars and completing each level. As with *Space Invaders*, *Head-On* wasn't timed, so you could clear each board without feeling rushed.

No official sales records seem to exist, but the general wisdom was that Sega didn't sell many examples. Sega nonetheless iterated on the design; *Head-On 2* added color graphics, but little else. The similar *Car Hunt* had a more intricate course design. Sega also licensed *Head-On* to other manufacturers. Irem's version displayed a black screen, green walls, and some other minor changes, including the letters *I*, *R*, *E*, and *M* in the lanes. These letters changed color when you ran over them, and if you could match up the color as you finished the board, you would get extra bonus points.

Head-On saw some clones appear on the home systems of the day as well. *Dodge 'Em*, released in 1980, was Atari's 2600 conversion, albeit with a different name to skirt trouble with Sega. Other similar games included *Tunnels of Farhad* for the TRS-80 and *Car Wars* for the Texas Instruments TI-99/4A. *Head-On* is mostly forgotten today, but it helped establish Sega as a force to be reckoned with.[26]

Warrior (Vectorbeam, 1979)

Warrior depicted a top-down battle between two armored fighters with swords in a medieval dungeon. The arena contained several staircases you could force the opposing player up or down and pits you could push them into. *Warrior* was designed by Tim Skelly, and was his only game marketed under the Vectorbeam brand before Cinematronics acquired and dissolved the company. The cabinet had white sides and a black front panel and included fantasy artwork by Frank Brunner. Bat-handle joysticks controlled the two warriors, and each had a small black button on top. Pushing the joystick in a direction without the button depressed moved the warrior around; pushing and holding the button while moving the stick aimed the sword in the same direction.

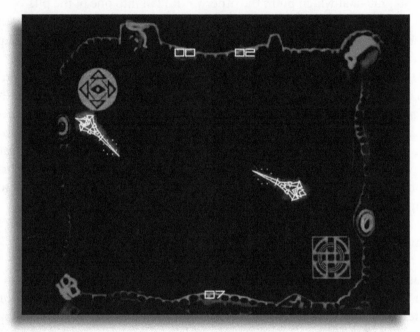

Figure 3.4: *Warrior* **was an early video game with one-on-one fighting—in this case, via two medieval knights with swords.**

The game successfully modeled swordfighting, with forward and backhand swings all the way around and the clash of two swords hitting each other (albeit without much of a "clank" sound effect). You could score points either by hitting your opponent's center with the tip of your sword or by forcing him into one of the pits. Each player's two-digit score was displayed on top. The timer at the bottom of the screen slowly counted down; a quarter was good for 10 time units, which meant anywhere from 30 to 120 seconds as per the operator's choice. Destroy the other player and he would disintegrate into a cloud of sparkles to the sound of an explosion. Whoever had the higher score at the end of the game won, and that person's score pulsed in brightness.

The 19-inch black-and-white X-Y monitor included a detailed overlay of the fixed-screen playfield, complete with a beautifully drawn stone floor and curved staircases. The monitor was mounted below, facing up, and the image reflected off of a silver mirror lit by a backlight.[27] The combination looked as if the vector graphics and the overlay were sharing the same surface.[28] The attract mode showed the two warriors appear in their safe zones, walk up the stairway toward the center of the screen, and fight until one disintegrated, at which point the other would fall into one of the pits.

Warrior wasn't *the* first one-on-one fighting game, though it was the first one many people played. Sega's *Heavyweight Boxing* and Project Support Engineering's *Knights in Armor* both preceded it, though aside from a 1987 remake, the former does not survive, and the latter is difficult to find. It's doubtful Vectorbeam employees had seen either game when designing *Warrior*. "Brilliant vector graphics and [an] incredibly beautiful backdrop and internal cabinet artwork made the game enthralling to watch, producing more complex images than Atari's vector hardware was capable of," said The Electronics Conservatory's *Videotopia*. "Unfortunately, the Cinematronics vector system was also far less reliable. Most Cinematronics vector games are rare, and *Warrior* is rare among them."[29]

Namco

Masaya Nakamura launched Namco in Ōta, Tokyo, in 1955 as Nakamura Seisakusho, a manufacturer of coin-operated amusement rides. Nakamura entered the video arcade industry in 1974, when he purchased Atari's Japanese division from Nolan Bushnell and began releasing Atari coin-ops in Japan. Beginning in 1978, the newly renamed Namco began releasing its own games, starting with *Gee Bee*, a hybrid of video pinball and *Breakout* designed by then-new-hire Toru Iwatani. Namco's next game would harness a new Zilog CPU called the Z80, which had been designed by former Intel employee Federico Faggin. The Z80 improved on the Intel 8080 and was more powerful than the inexpensive MOS 6502. The resulting game landed Namco at the top of the sales charts, and the hardware would soon drive more of the company's most popular arcade games from this period.[30]

Galaxian (Midway, 1979)

Namco released *Galaxian* in Japan in November 1979, and the company tapped Midway for distribution in North America in the first half of 1980.

Midway was thrilled with this arrangement, as it had lost its license with Taito following the success of *Space Invaders*, after which Taito decided to distribute games in the United States.[31] *Galaxian* improved on *Space Invaders* in a number of ways—most notably in its use of color. Up until this point, nearly all arcade games included a black-and-white monitor, sometimes with translucent color overlays. Inside the monitor, an electron gun fired a beam of electrons at the screen. A layer of phosphor dots coated the inside of the screen; the dots glowed briefly when the beam hit. Monochrome monitors had just one color, whereas color monitors had three different phosphor dots arranged in groups coating the screen: red, green, and blue, for RGB.[32]

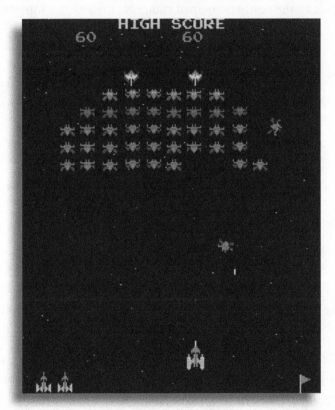

Figure 3.5: With *Galaxian*, Namco updated *Space Invaders* by adding RGB color graphics and more sophisticated game mechanics.

It's not that RGB displays didn't exist, or even that they hadn't been used in video games; a Nutting Associates *Pong* clone released in 1974 called *Wimbledon* employed a color monitor to present a green lawn, white ball, and different color paddles for the various players, for example. Most manufacturers found color way too expensive to incorporate. *Indy 800* had a color screen, but the cabinet was obscenely expensive, and all of the objects were of a single color each; the same was true of *Star Fire*. *Galaxian* was the first true color arcade coin-op, thanks not only to its RGB screen, but also to its multicolor sprites that represented the player's ship and the aliens. It was a leap beyond anything seen before, and it made black-and-white games look old. *Galaxian* also displayed smoothly animated aliens and a scrolling background complete with twinkling stars, both significant improvements over *Space Invaders*. It started with a short theme song and played detailed, musical sound effects on top of a pulsing background drone. The remarkable advance in the aesthetic helped catapult video games into the 1980s.

Figure 3.6: Arcade games consisted of at least one printed circuit board (PCB). Shown here is the board for Namco's *Galaxian*. Credit: Dennis van Zuijlekom, CC BY-SA 2.0

In *Galaxian*, you controlled the defender Galax starship, which traversed the galaxy in search of buglike aliens to destroy. It moved horizontally across the bottom of the screen. You could only fire one shot on screen at a time and had to wait until it hit a target or the top of the screen before you could fire again. But unlike in *Space Invaders*, where the aliens marched across the screen in lockstep as they descended on Earth, in *Galaxian* the alien convoy itself never descended. Instead, the force sent out squadrons to attack the defender Galax. One, two, or three aliens together would repeatedly dive down, a descending musical pitch indicating that they were swarming the bottom of the screen. There were four kinds of aliens in the convoy: green, purple, and red, worth 30, 40, and 50 points each, respectively, and two red-and-yellow flagships on top worth 60 points. But each alien was worth at least double the points when it was in attack formation, either by itself or in a squadron. If you picked off lesser aliens in a squadron before shooting the flagship, you'd get from 150 to 800 bonus points.

Another difference from *Space Invaders*: There were no barricades for your ship to hide behind. Thanks to the breakout attack formations, aliens came at you from multiple directions instead of just moving horizontally and vertically. Each time you cleared a wave, you'd earn another red flag in the bottom-right corner of the screen. The action was also faster than *Space Invaders* and with additional frames of animation for your ship and the aliens. Play *Galaxian* first and *Space Invaders* after, and the latter felt more deliberate and plodding. The jump in processing speed showed.

Galaxian's white, blue, and green cabinet eschewed the misaligned space-monster theme found on *Space Invaders* machines, instead depicting a green dragonfly-like alien targeted by a spaceship. Midway sold more than 45,000 *Galaxian* machines in North America, including both upright and cocktail table models. *Pac-Man*, *Gorf*, and *Galaga* resurfaced the red-and-yellow Galaxian flagship as bonus awards, and we later saw variations on the *Galaxian* theme in *Phoenix*, *Radar Scope*, and Namco's own sequel *Galaga*. But with the release of *Galaxian*, there was no going back to monochrome raster graphics.

Lunar Lander (Atari, 1979)

From the darkest corner of a smoky bar or tucked into a spot near the front of a pizza shop, anyone could land on the moon. This was the promise of *Lunar Lander*, Atari's first game to employ vector graphics, which the company called Quadrascan—so named because Atari's system broke the screen into four quadrants to speed up processing. The object of the game, which Howard Delman and Rich Moore based on a 1969 Apollo 11 simulation by Jim Storer, was to land a manned spaceship on the moon's mountainous surface. You burned off fuel to rotate the module and fired the thruster to balance the craft against the gravitational pull of the moon.

Getting into such a complex-seeming game was easier than it appeared. The control panel consisted of Select and Start buttons for the missions, Left and Right buttons for rotating your ship, and an Abort button to end your mission. A large handle on the right controlled the throttle. Six fields at the top of the screen displayed your score, remaining time, remaining fuel, current altitude, horizontal speed, and vertical speed.

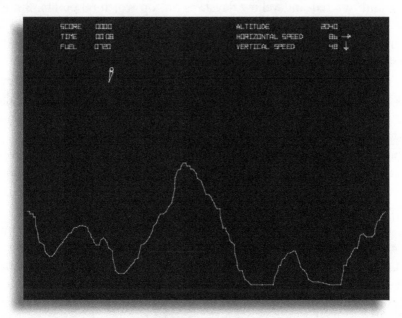

Figure 3.7: Atari brought a taste of NASA moon missions to every arcade gamer with the sophisticated *Lunar Lander*.

A game began with the sound of the engine and the lander drifting toward the bottom-right corner of the display. As the lander flew, it approached the mountains and a prospective landing site. Soon, the display zoomed in and showed you a close-up of the imminent landing attempt. *Lunar Lander* was the first video game with multiple perspective views. Land the craft well, and you'd get 50 points plus 50 extra fuel units. Land it hard, and you'd only earn 15 points. A crash still gave you five points for some reason; it would occur whenever you tried to land at speeds faster than 15 vertically and 31 horizontally (no units were indicated). Bonus multipliers would give you two or five times the score for landing on increasingly narrow areas. If you were in for a crash landing, pressing the Abort button would fire the thruster at maximum speed at a cost of 120 to 180 fuel units. If you weren't too late, you'd save the ship and could try again. Each time you landed, the game started over and randomized the mountainous terrain and landing area location. The game ended when you ran out of fuel, though you could add more by inserting another coin—as with Cinematronics's *Space Wars*, a clever move that helped increase revenue for the operator. The cabinet emitted engine rumbling and crash sounds, plus a beep warning to signal that your fuel was almost depleted.

Across the top of *Lunar Lander*'s control panel were five squares, one with instructions for the game and the others for describing the four available missions: Training, Cadet, Prime, and Command. The Training mission consisted of light gravity, atmospheric friction, and smooth rotation. Cadet increased the gravity and removed the friction, and Prime boosted gravity further. The Command mission also included moderate gravity and no friction, but this time it modeled rotational momentum, which meant you had to allow for additional time when altering the craft's rotation. You could change the mission difficulty during the game as well as before you started.

Atari's *Lunar Lander* coin-op did well, with 4,830 units sold.[33] Various clones of the concept appeared on home computers and consoles throughout the decades that followed. Some gamers felt *Lunar Lander* didn't have tremendous replay value, but no other arcade game delivered such a combination of realism, strategy, and action. *Lunar Lander* would have had even more lasting impact if Atari hadn't released another vector graphics game just a few months later.

Asteroids (Atari, 1979)

The iconic *Asteroids* looked impossibly refined and futuristic in 1979. Your triangular ship was lost in distant outer space, mired in an asteroid field. To survive, you had to obliterate as many asteroids as you could, as well as two varieties of flying saucer. Whenever you collided with an asteroid or saucer, or were shot by one of the saucer's missiles, you'd lose a ship. Two-dimensional black-and-white vector graphics rendered the playfield, which wrapped around at the edges of the screen. *Asteroids* was one of the purest and most minimalist of video arcade presentations and remains captivating to this day.

It also wouldn't have been possible without vector graphics. Lyle Rains, Atari's vice president of coin-op, asked Ed Logg to design a game where you shoot asteroids with something that kept players from doing nothing (because there wouldn't be a timer, similar to *Space Invaders*). Logg had the idea of occasional flying saucers to keep the player alert.[34] He also knew he would need some kind of high-resolution display, which Atari had already developed for *Lunar Lander*.

"If you tried to put a little ship like the ship in *Asteroids* up on standard resolution, it would look like garbage; you couldn't tell what it was," Logg said. "Part of the deal I had with Lyle was that I'd go vector because, at the time, its high resolution was 1024 by 768, and at that resolution, the game would look nice."[35] Quadrascan was "capable of rendering a solid line of unbroken brightness," wrote *Electronic Games* magazine. "The difference between Quadrascan and the earlier raster scan method is like the difference between a connect-the-dots puzzle and the smooth lines of an etch-a-sketch." It also meant objects could drift onto the screen from any direction and at any speed.

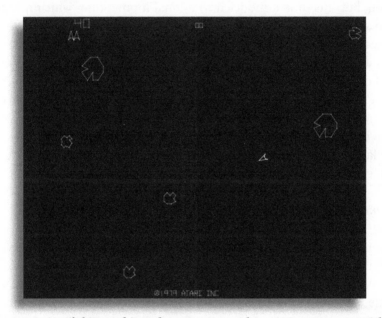

Figure 3.8: Atari's biggest hit to date was *Asteroids*, a 1979 space game with the satisfying premise of blasting asteroids to smithereens.

A game of *Asteroids* began with the player's ship in the center of the screen. Four large asteroids appeared at the edges and drifted toward the player. Shooting a large asteroid netted 20 points and broke it into two medium-size pieces that moved faster. Blasting one of those would accrue 50 points and break it into two small pieces (worth 100 points) that moved faster still. Once you cleared the board of asteroids, you'd move on to the next wave, which consisted of six asteroids instead of four. The third wave contained eight, and the fourth and all successive waves started with 10 asteroids each.

Five buttons controlled your ship. Two buttons labeled Left Rotate and Right Rotate let you turn the ship, and by holding one down you could spin the ship all the way around. The Thrust button powered the ship's movements, and the Fire button shot torpedoes. The Hyperspace button made your ship disappear and then reappear in a random spot on the board. Sometimes, it was just what you needed to get out of a jam; other times, it dropped you right on top of an asteroid, or in the immediate path of one, dooming your ship. Sometimes your ship exploded on re-entry just for the heck of it, which added to the fun.

Once your score reached 1,500 points, a large flying saucer would begin to appear on occasion; it moved slowly and was a bad shot, with maybe one out of four or five shots aimed at your ship. A small saucer appeared beginning at 6,000 points; that one was faster, and 80 percent of its shots targeted your ship. The large saucer was worth 200 points, while the small one was worth 1,000. Once you reached 40,000 points, assuming you were good enough, only the small saucer would appear from then on out. The game could be configured to start you with three, four, or five ships, and you earned an extra ship every 10,000 points. This led to the only problem with *Asteroids*, at least from an operator's point of view: After a while, it no longer became more difficult. Once you were good enough, you could keep playing and playing on a single quarter, and the machine wouldn't earn any money during this period.

Atari sold more than 70,000 *Asteroids* cabinets in both upright and cocktail models, some of which had to be equipped with larger coin boxes to hold all the additional income operators earned.[36] In an era where a successful game spent six months at or near the top of the sales chart, *Asteroids* was into its third year running in that position by 1981, and it led all coin-ops in gross revenue in 1980 with up to 10 million quarters pumped into machines per day.[37] *Asteroids* inspired a tremendous number of imitators and downright clones, as well as the first Atari 2600 home conversion to employ bank switching to access additional memory stored in the cartridge. Some three million copies were sold.

Although *Asteroids*'s 6502-based graphics and sound design were exceptional, the physics modeling sold the game. The way the ship drifted whenever the rumbling thrust was applied and then released conveyed the vastness, silence, and loneliness of free space. Optimizing the ship's aim, placement, and speed to destroy the asteroids and saucers posed a satisfying challenge.[38] Heartbeat-like alternating bass notes provided a lone sonic accompaniment. The notes would speed up throughout each board, and then "reset" in tempo once the next wave of asteroids appeared—a fitting metaphor for the quickening pulse of the arcade game industry.

Monaco GP (Gremlin/Sega, 1979)

Gremlin's second arcade hit demonstrated how electromechanical components and systems could be adapted to a video context. As with *Head-On*, *Monaco GP* is not well remembered today. But it was the first full-color driving game and included separate LEDs on the screen for the score, high score, and timer. Even the instrument panel gauges worked, a rarity in an industry where they were usually just decals or painted onto the cabinet. The cabinet also included a padded steering wheel, accelerator pedal, and two-position gear shift.

This was still a beat-the-clock game in the style of earlier 1970s coin-ops. You had to drive the small red car as fast as you could, racing other cars while avoiding collisions with them. You had 90 seconds to reach a score of 2,000 points, and you had as many extra cars as you needed (though crashes would of course slow you down). You earned about eight points per second in low gear and 25 in high gear.[39] If you made it to 2,000, gameplay would be extended, and you would get an extra car. Extra cars would continue to be awarded every 2,000 points thereafter. The game sped up at 6,000 points and got faster still at 8,000 points. The roads featured hazards such as ice patches, gravel roads, narrow bridges with two-way traffic, and ambulances with their sirens blaring. Driving through any skid zone or bridge would double your points for the duration. The game offered operators a dual-play option for a single quarter.

Sega produced *Monaco GP* in four cabinet styles, with the most dramatic being the attractive cockpit model, complete with a racing seat and the gear shift lever moved to its side. It was the most realistic driving available in a video arcade at the time. The other three cabinets were the expected standard upright, cabaret, and cocktail versions.

Monaco GP debuted to a stunned crowd in November 1979 in Japan and went on to become one of the highest-grossing games of 1981. The game appeared on *RePlay*'s monthly sales charts a record 71 times.[40] Notably, and despite how technologically advanced it was, *Monaco GP* was one of the last TTL-based games without a microprocessor and the last successful one. Two circuit boards containing more than 100 chips ran the game, while ROM chips stored images for the cars and the "game over" message.[41] Operational amplifiers and analog circuits generated sound effects for the engine, the ambulance siren, and skidding wheels. It turned out you could still get a lot of flash and bang out of an arcade cabinet—and an adrenaline-soaked driving game—with tried-and-true technology.

Figure 3.9: Sega's *Monaco GP* was the last great TTL game, and thanks to its color graphics and decked-out deluxe cabinet, you wouldn't know it lacked a microprocessor. Credit: 空練 - 撮影者提供 CC BY-SA 3.0

Space Invaders Deluxe (Taito/Midway, 1979)

Perhaps the most obvious business move in the history of everything was for Taito to create a sequel to *Space Invaders*. Gamers didn't have to wait long for *Space Invaders Part II*, released in the U.S. as *Space Invaders Deluxe*, though it also read as "*Deluxe Space Invaders*" from the way the marquee was designed. Basic gameplay remained similar to the original, down to the sound effects and pulsing four-note bass line in the background that sped up as you shot more aliens. A new, colorful overlay for the monitor improved the three-dimensional effect, and the score contained five digits instead of four. High scorers could put in their initials or even spell out a name (up to 10 characters), unlike with the original game, and you could "rub" (out) a letter if you made a mistake. Start a game and there would first be a moment where the new aliens appeared at the top of the screen before marching down into attack position. *Space Invaders Deluxe* was one of the first games with short, humorous intermissions between waves. They showed the last alien zigzagging up the screen saying "SOS," or the Mystery Ship running into "Engine Trouble."

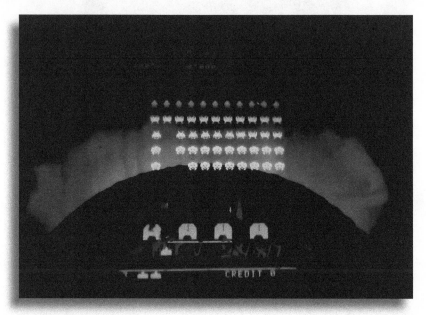

Figure 3.10: *Space Invaders Deluxe* **added some new game mechanics and the first intermissions ever found in a video game to the otherwise tried-and-true alien invasion formula. Credit: Joe Lyons**

There were also some gameplay differences. Beginning with the second wave, the UFO at the top of the screen randomly dropped invaders. In the third wave, when you shot invaders, they split into two smaller ones, and in the fourth wave aliens fired more missiles at you. Sometimes a "Flasher" ship appeared instead of the UFO, so you'd have to not only maneuver into position to hit it but also hit it when it was visible. The Flasher was worth 200 points. The aliens also switched up their appearances in later waves, with skulls and pointy-headed ones appearing, sometimes being different even within rows instead of one type running through a single row. The last alien was always fast, just like in the original, and left a trail if it was one from the bottom two rows. But when you shot it, the game displayed a rainbow cascade and awarded you 500 bonus points.

Space Invaders Deluxe made it to number four in *RePlay*'s April 1980 earnings chart.[42] It was successful by any measure other than in comparison with the original. The gameplay advances and improved overlay made *Space*

Invaders Deluxe seem more advanced, even if the hardware, audio, and basic play mechanics remained the same. Manufacturers were still figuring out what it meant to release a sequel, and a lot of new games were barely veiled copies of originals (see: Atari's iterations on *Pong* and *Gran Trak 10*, or Midway's *Sea Wolf II*, which was *Sea Wolf* with a color monitor, a faster CPU to drive it, and a larger power supply.) Today, *Space Invaders Deluxe* would be considered too cautious for a sequel. But there were enough new gameplay elements and visual changes to make playing it feel worthwhile.

Rip Off (Cinematronics, 1980)

This multidirectional shooter was notable for its innovative, cooperative gameplay, a first for the genre. Each game began with a group of pulsating, triangular fuel cells in the center of the playfield. Your land cruiser could turn left or right, accelerate forward, and shoot energy bolts. Alien vehicles appeared in waves, starting from the edges of the screen and heading toward the fuel cells. When a craft reached one, it dragged it away to restock its own fuel supply. The enemies also exhibited "flocking behavior," meaning that they grouped together on their own and attacked the player. *Rip Off* was the first arcade coin-op with this gameplay mechanic.

As you played, several alien craft would gang up on you, with one shooting at you as a distraction as another one ripped off a fuel cell. You'd score anywhere from 10 to 60 points when shooting one of six different kinds of enemy. Each time your cruiser was destroyed, you'd get another one. Unlike most games, you had an infinite supply, and there was no in-game timer. As long as there were still fuel cells remaining on the screen, you could keep playing. Once the enemy craft dragged the last fuel cell away, the game would end.

The vector graphics were perfect for depicting several fast-moving ships and the triangular fuel cells, which would have looked terrible with low-resolution pixels. The starting low-frequency tone changed in pitch and tempo as the game progressed, becoming more urgent and ominous. Occasionally a player would reach a bonus level, where three enemies would appear at once and be worth more points. In two-player cooperative mode, each player appeared on opposite sides of the screen, and the game defaulted to grouping enemies three at a time instead of two. The two players would then work together to protect the singular fuel supply and share a combined score. If the operator set *Rip Off* to Opponent mode, each player had their own score, but you'd both still work together.

Tim Skelly said *Rip Off* was his favorite of all the games he programmed for Cinematronics—even despite more well-known titles he designed. "[*Rip Off*] was not only the most fun to play and the most successful, but I've always been proud of being the first to try two-player cooperative gameplay," he said in a 1997 interview.[43] Skelly added that the idea for cooperative gameplay came in part from financial considerations. Even though he began *Rip Off* as a one-player game, or a game where you'd trade off with another player, Cinematronics brass felt that two-player simultaneous games such as *Space Wars* and *Warrior* generated more income. This jibed with Skelly's memories as well.

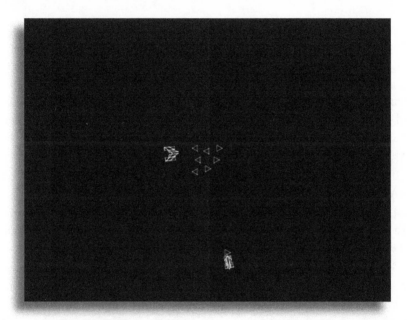

**Figure 3.11: Tim Skelly's masterpiece of resource defense disguised as a shooter,
Rip Off displayed sharp vector graphics and innovative enemy AI.**

"At the time, I was in a relationship with a disc jockey in Kansas City," Skelly said. "The station she worked for was part of a large chain that issued huge market research papers for the affiliates. Someone writing one of these papers had inexplicably determined that young people at that time were interested in 'cooperation rather than competition.' I always take market research with a ton of salt, but it did spark the idea of having the two players work toward the same goal."[44] *Rip Off* only saw a home conversion on the Vectrex, as no other system at the time could pull off the game's complex vector graphics, object rotation, and speed.

Missile Command (Atari, 1980)

Plenty of movies and TV shows had depicted the horror of nuclear war. *Missile Command*, designed by Dave Theurer, was the first video game to tackle the issue head-on. Incoming intercontinental ballistic missiles (ICBMs) rained down from the sky in an Armageddon-style war. You had to intercept and destroy all of them using antiballistic missiles (ABMs) before they hit your six vulnerable cities. The game continued until all of your cities were destroyed.

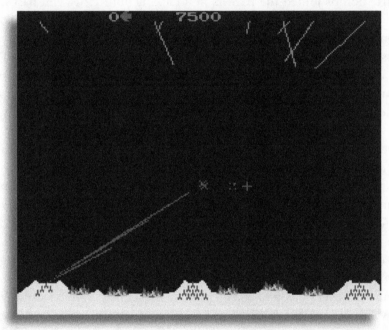

Figure 3.12: Dave Theurer packaged up the Cold War into a brilliant arcade game with *Missile Command*.

Each game began with ICBMs heading straight for your cities and missile bases. Some branched off into multiple directions. The coin-op's grapefruit-size black trackball controlled a small crosshair target indicator on screen. Three buttons to the left, lit up with red LEDs, fired missiles from each of your three bases—Alpha, Delta, and Omega—at the bottom of the playfield. Whenever you pressed one of the Fire buttons, a missile from the appropriate base would launch toward the crosshair and explode there. Because the explosion lingered for a couple of seconds, if the body of an incoming ICBM was caught up in the ensuing explosion, it would also be destroyed. Each ICBM that reached the bottom of the screen obliterated one of your cities or missile bases.

At the start of every wave, the three bases were replenished with 10 missiles each. The Delta (center) base shot ABMs faster than the other two bases flanking it. Successive waves became tougher, and were numbered in pairs (1-1, 1-2, 2-1, 2-2, 3-1, and so on). Notably, the color scheme changed with every new pair of waves, with the yellow ground becoming green and the black sky turning blue and then white. The second set of waves introduced killer satellites and bombers. Beginning with wave 3-2, "smart" bombs joined the ICBMs in attacking your cities and bases. The diamond-shaped bombs emitted high-pitched sounds and were capable of evading exploding missiles on their way down to destroy one of your assets. The way to nab these was to fire faster ABMs from the center Delta base and to target the missile so that it exploded on top of the invading smart bomb before it could perform an evasive maneuver. Players learned it was better to target incoming ICBMs as soon as possible, when they were still near the top of the screen. Another common strategy, useful beginning in wave 2-1 with the killer satellites and bombers, was to "spread" or "spray" a horizontal line of missiles to form a temporary wall of explosions that caught multiple incoming ICBMs released from the enemy craft.

Atari sold the game in upright, environmental, cabaret, and cocktail table versions, with a 19-inch color monitor in the first two models and 14-inch color monitors in the other two. The operator could set the game to start the player with four to seven cities (the default was six) and award a bonus city every 8,000 to 20,000 points. The game played beautifully and was well balanced, but getting there required some trial and error. Theurer said in 2000 that at various points during development, the team added vulnerable railroad tracks between the cities for manufacturing and transporting missiles; an option to set the game in the east, west, or middle portions of America with labeled cities; and even submarines. All of these ideas were discarded as either too confusing or complicated.[45] One idea from project lead Steve Calfee made it in: When you lost all of your cities, Theurer had programmed it so the screen would display a huge explosion. Calfee suggested that the game display "THE END" as part of the explosion; dozens of missiles then took away large chunks of the letters.[46] This became an enduring image of the game, if not the Cold War.

Atari sold some 20,000 *Missile Command* cabinets, making it one of the most successful games of the Golden Age of video arcades. Some of the developers working on the project said that they often had nightmares about nuclear war. The potential for a real one would go on to define the rest of the Cold War, thanks to such films as 1983's *The Day After*, a made-for-TV movie that became a national event seen by 100 million, and 1991's *Terminator 2: Judgment Day* evoking the horror. (*Terminator 2* is notable here, as the explosion at the end of *Missile Command* made it into the movie.) Rob Fulop programmed the Atari 2600 home conversion of the game, which went on to sell a stunning 2.5 million copies. Home computers would later see more sophisticated and nuanced strategy games about nuclear annihilation, such as *Balance of Power*, *Wasteland*, and the *Fallout* series. *Missile Command* was at once brilliantly designed and reflective of its moment in a way few others have managed.

Star Castle (Cinematronics, 1980)

In *Star Castle*, you piloted a spaceship in a fixed playfield, with a view similar to that of Space War and *Asteroids*. Here, you had to destroy an Energy Cannon (alternately called the Star Castle in Cinematronics literature) by blasting through its three concentric ringed defenses. In an eerie detail, the cannon tracked your ship's location throughout the game. It spawned three spark mines, which would emerge through the rings and chase your ship's position like heat-seeking missiles. If you collided with one, your ship would be destroyed.

Each time you started with a new ship, it appeared near the top-right corner of the screen with the Star Castle in the center. The ringed defenses consisted of 12 sections, each of which took two shots to eliminate. As you took out sections of the rotating rings, the next one below would be exposed to your shots. Outer, center, and inner ring sections were worth 10, 20, and 30 points each. Expose the Star Castle itself by penetrating all three rings and it would begin shooting fast, hissing, and difficult-to-avoid projectiles. If you destroyed the Star Castle, it would explode all remaining ring sections, earning you 1,440 points and another ship for the next go-around.

You couldn't just shoot all of the rings away first, either. If you destroyed all 12 sections of a ring, the cannon regenerated its defenses. The two inner rings moved outward, and a new, smaller ring emerged at the center. You could destroy the mines, although they were hard to shoot and not worth any points. And depending on how the game was set up, they'd either regenerate instantly or when you cleared out a ring. The operator could set the game to give you anywhere from three to six ships per game. There was no time limit, but the spark mines and the Star Castle's ability to shoot you lent plenty of urgency to the proceedings.

Figure 3.13: *Star Castle* **mixed tense gameplay with a sense of foreboding, thanks to the way the central Energy Cannon always watched you.**

Unlike previous vector graphics games, *Star Castle* looked as if it was in color. It wasn't; the game included a black-and-white Vectorbeam monitor, plus a translucent overlay for the backdrop and several in the center for the various turret rings. As such, the game was a natural for a home Vectrex conversion a couple of years later, as the Vectrex employed a screen overlay system to provide the same false color. *Star Castle* also served as the inspiration for *Yars' Revenge* on the Atari 2600. In fact, the cartridge was supposed to be a home conversion of *Star Castle*, but programmer Howard Scott Warshaw realized it would be impossible and convinced Atari to do an original interpretation—a risk considering the built-in customer base of fans of the arcade cabinet. The gamble worked; Yars' Revenge, based on a mutant space fly that had to destroy a monster behind an orange shield, was a tremendous hit.

Star Castle was a challenging game—more difficult than *Asteroids* or *Space Invaders* and a bit repetitive, but with a look and feel all its own.

The Rise of Real Arcades

The video game industry continued to grow. Atari revenue soared, thanks to *Asteroids* and other innovative cartridge releases for the 2600 leading up to the 1978 holiday season, where it became a must-have gift. Some of the cartridges were conversions of Atari coin-ops such as *Breakout* and *Canyon Bomber*, while others were original and not suited for arcade play, such as *Video Chess* and *Superman*, the first non-linear console adventure game. But arcades still ruled the video game industry. For the first time, revenues exceeded $1 billion that year and then rose to $1.5 billion in 1979. Industry profit would skyrocket from there. Coin-op trade publications were already covering the new video arcade games from an amusement industry perspective, but in 1979, *Video* magazine launched a new column by Bill Kunkel and Arnie Katz called "Arcade Alley." This marked the first critical coverage of video arcades intended for consumers to read.

The image of arcade gamers playing coin-op machines began to become a regular thing—even a creative influence. William Gibson, the novelist known for coining the term "cyberspace," said he began his writing career not by imagining the future but by engaging deeply with the present. He said he had his first ideas for science fiction stories in the late 1970s by watching kids playing games in video arcades and "noticing how they ducked and twisted, as though they were on the other side of the screen."[47] Another sign of the times: Atari closed its pinball division. Granted, it took Atari four months to produce a game Bally could make in two weeks.[48] But the greater trend was clear: Video games made pinball seem dated. Revenue numbers reflected this trend, as operator and amusement park dollars began to shift in earnest from pinball to the video arcade.

People couldn't get enough of video games. Beginning with *Space Invaders*, arcade machines started appearing in supermarkets, restaurants, liquor stores, gas stations, and many other retail establishments.[49] With the advent of high scores, the industry began to track world records and would soon stage national tournaments. Gamers could gain fame and fortune for seemingly impossible feats that could only be tracked in real time with some titles, as there weren't enough digits displayed to total up the achievements. Video games would only get bigger still.

4 > Fever

With the arcade craze in full swing, gamers across the globe hacked away at space shoot-'em-up, driving, and war-themed games. The new sights and sounds of the arcade began to surpass the black-and-white graphics and audible bleeps and bloops, with colorful sprites dotting the otherwise dimly lit landscapes of backlit marquees and grungy floors and short musical themes sounding out. But one game, unveiled in October 1980, became the biggest-selling arcade coin-op ever. For several years, it dominated American culture. And for many people, it became synonymous with video games.

Pac-Man (Namco/Midway, 1980)

More than any other single coin-op in history, *Pac-Man* became a cultural phenomenon. And it all started over lunch—or so everyone thought. Designer Toru Iwatani said the famous story about him getting the idea for *Pac-Man* when he served himself pizza and saw the pie missing a slice wasn't accurate. "Well, it's half true," Iwatani said. "In Japanese the character for mouth (kuchi) is a square shape. It's not circular like the pizza, but I decided to round it out."[1]

Iwatani designed the game while working for Namco in Japan. The working title was Paku-Paku, for the sound the character made when eating dots, and then later Namco released it in late 1979 as *Puck-Man*. After the game saw decent success, Midway agreed to bring the game to America as *Pac-Man*, as Namco CEO Nakamura was concerned vandals would change the *P* to an *F*. No one knew if the game would find takers, given the predominantly male U.S. audience playing space and war games. There was also some concern that *Pac-Man*'s state-of-the-art hardware and high $2,450 price tag could prove a problem.

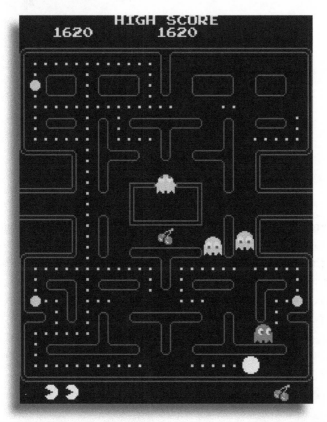

Figure 4.1: The arcade video game that became a phenomenon. The industry and gaming public alike were never the same after the launch of *Pac-Man*.

There was no need to worry. Over the course of its production run, Namco manufactured and sold some 400,000 machines. To this day, *Pac-Man* remains perhaps *the* most recognized video game ever made by the widest swath of the human population. It was the game spawned a thousand clones, in arcades and on home computers and video game consoles alike.

The concept was as simple as it was brilliant. The original *Pac-Man* included a lone joystick with a hard red plastic ball and took place in a single maze. You had to eat all 240 dots (each worth 10 points) and four power pellets (each worth 50 points) on each board. Eating a bonus fruit that periodically appeared at the center of the maze would get you extra points.

Each time you cleared a maze, you advanced a level, indicated by the bonus fruit icons at the bottom-right corner of the maze. Four ghosts chased you around the board, each with a distinct personality that the programmers spent a tremendous amount of time honing and perfecting for just the right game balance. The red Shadow, nicknamed "Blinky," was the smartest and most difficult to outmaneuver. The pink Speedy ("Pinky") was the fastest. The blue Bashful, also known as "Inky," followed the others and was otherwise not aggressive. And the orange Pokey, nicknamed "Clyde," was the slowest, but could surprise you by getting unexpectedly close after some sneaky maneuvering. Before *Pac-Man*, games didn't have mascots or even characters. *Pac-Man* was the first.

The power pellets were the key game mechanic. Each time you ate one, the ghosts turned blue and ran away. If you were fast enough, you could catch them for 200, 400, 800, and 1,600 points, respectively. Eat one and its eyes would travel back to the center of the board to regenerate the original ghost. Once the power pellet ran out, the remaining blue ghosts returned to their original colors and again became dangerous. Sometimes it made sense to use the time the ghosts were blue in order to eat more dots, especially on later levels, and with a few exceptions that amount of time became shorter and shorter. *Pac-Man* cornered faster than the ghosts, but slowed down when eating, and the two eating and not-eating speeds changed relative to ghost speed from board to board.

The above combination of rules was straightforward for a newcomer, and if you played the game before, you memorized most if not all of them. This game personified arcades, with their communal and competitive aspects and the desire to play as long as possible on one quarter. Dozens of strategy books began to appear on store shelves, revealing the tips, secrets, and even the exact patterns to memorize in order to beat each screen of the arcade game. *Pac-Man* attracted gamers of all ages, male and female. Some arcades purchased entire rows worth of *Pac-Man* cabinets. Soon, there were reports of "Pac-Man elbow" from moving the joystick too much without a break, similar to "Space Invaders Thumb."[2] Local news stations covered how kids would play the same video game for hours and hours each day and stunt their social skills. (It's a law of nature: Whenever something becomes popular enough, there's always a backlash.)

Pac-Man spent its first six months in 1981 at the top of *Play Meter*'s popularity chart and the rest of the summer in the number two position. Most video games earned about $150 per week in quarters, but *Pac-Man* was averaging $200 to $240, with some locations reporting as much as $800 per machine.[3] The game spawned national tournaments, a Saturday morning cartoon, bumper stickers ("I Brake for *Pac-Man*"), sleeping bags, tablecloths, a *Time* magazine cover, a series of collectable Fleer stickers, and famously, a hit single by Bruckner & Garcia called "Pac-Man Fever" that together with a later 1982 album of video game songs sold more than 2.5 million copies. I used to collect the stickers; there was a run of 54 different stickers you could get in packs, featuring characters from the game and silly slogans such as "Pac-Man for President." They also came with scratch-off mazes you could play…once.

Plenty of bootlegs soon appeared, some with obvious titles such as *Gobbleman* and *Hangly-Man*. Other unscrupulous operators imported existing Namco boards from Japan and installed them in U.S. cabinets, which grabbed the attention of Midway's lawyers.[4] The bootleg machines often contained tweaks to the built-in rules that made the ghosts unpredictable, and therefore immune to memorized patterns.

Perhaps the craziest thing was, as with other successful coin-op designers, Iwatani never earned royalties as an employee of Namco. He only received a small bonus (less than $3,500) at the end of the year, though his career with the company soon flourished.[5] A running theme throughout the evolution of the video game industry would be how to handle royalties, with the general consensus being that there couldn't be any, as companies claimed they needed to own the assets created for their games. This often meant game developers, artists, sound designers, composers, and other people would gain tons of fame but little fortune, unless they owned a piece of the company and could share in the bounty from a giant acquisition. Some exceptions were the royalties Atari paid to 2600 cartridge programmers after losing top employees over the lack of name recognition—a development that led to its own problems, such as the creator of 2600 *Pac-Man* Todd Frye becoming a millionaire from sales of a poor conversion (thanks to cynical management, not anything Frye did). Perhaps with Iwatani more than anyone else, it just seemed wrong to not reward him with a giant payday.

Williams Electronics

Williams Manufacturing Company, founded by Henry Williams, launched in 1943 and produced a variety of types of amusement park machines, from pinball to novelty games. Its first title was *Selector Scope*, a fortune-telling coin-op released in 1944. In 1973, after the success of *Pong*, the company started to produce arcade games, beginning with a customary *Pong* clone called *Paddle-Ball*. Williams Electronics still focused primarily on pinball during the rest of the 1970s, and along with former Atari pinball veteran Steven Ritchie it produced several important tables. This later run included *Gorgar*, the first with a speech synthesizer; even if you're not a pinball veteran, you may know the table, because it's the one with the giant red demon on the backglass.

Williams' first major video game hit, unveiled in October 1980 alongside *Pac-Man*, became another one of the biggest titles of the Golden Age of arcade coin-ops.

Defender (Williams, 1980)

Defender was not just the quintessential horizontal-scrolling arcade shooter—it was also one of the top coin-ops of the Golden Age of arcade games and an important milestone in game development. Upon its release (Europe in December 1980 and the United States in February 1981),[6] it rendered earlier space games simplistic in comparison. You defended helpless humanoid astronauts, stuck on an unnamed planet's mountainous surface, against invading aliens that wanted to abduct them and turn them into mutants. If you destroyed all of the aliens in a given wave, you'd progress to the next. But if all of the astronauts were kidnapped and turned into mutants, the planet would explode. For the rest of the level, you'd be stuck in free space, blasting aliens to smithereens before the planet reappeared for the next board.

If the concept was simple, the implementation was anything but, with designer-programmer Eugene Jarvis using advanced hardware (a Motorola 6809 CPU, a generous 36KB frame buffer,[7] custom GPU chips,[8] and a 6800) to achieve a variety of immersive effects. The 16-color, 320-by-256-pixel resolution allowed for crisp, beautiful visuals, such as your lasers arcing across the screen. The sprites drew fast enough to never slow you down, no matter how quickly you flew from one area to the next. A scanner at the top of the playfield showed where you were in relation to the rest of the board, as well as the locations of the aliens and astronauts. The scanner was important because it also indicated another technological advance: Much of the action was taking place off screen. The chilling sound ranged from low, throbbing synths when you added a quarter and vocoder-like tones when you pressed Start to pulsating death rattles that echoed to oblivion when you shot an alien.

The control scheme was an unintuitive hybrid, occupying an awkward place between a four-way joystick and an all-button layout. A joystick with a red ball moved your ship up and down on the playfield. The Reverse button flipped your ship to fly in the opposite direction. The Hyperspace button launched you out of a jam quickly, or possibly sent you to certain death. A Smart Bomb button blew up everything on the screen; you received three to start with. To the right sat the Thrust and Fire buttons, perhaps the two most important in the game.

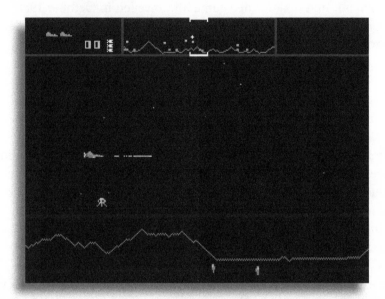

Figure 4.2: The intense, difficult *Defender* put the horizontal-scrolling shooter on the map and rocketed Williams to the top tier of the industry.

An experienced player could keep a game going for several minutes, but it was quite tricky for the newcomer. A 1983 article in *Softline* said *Defender* "remains one of the hardest arcade games ever developed. Initial attempts lasting less than 10 seconds are not uncommon for novices."[9] Soon players would devise different strategies; some preferred shooting the aliens after they captured the astronauts, while others chased higher scores by ignoring the astronauts and instead blasting as many aliens as they could.[10]

Larry DeMar, another game designer at Williams, called it a "hell of a game:"

I came into an arcade on a Friday night and there was a crowd of people four deep around this game, putting in their quarters and lasting maybe 35, 40 seconds. Defender was a very ferocious game—very difficult controls. They were seeing the special effects in the game and they just, they wanted to do it.

And one after the other, they were throwing quarters in. Defender made $700 its first week. I have never seen a quarter-a-play video game make money like that—not before or after Defender. It was the most phenomenal collection anyone had ever seen.[11]

Williams put a lot of work into the game's management software. A company brochure proclaimed it was "proud to bring you the most complete system of diagnostics ever programmed into an electronic video game." The company included tests for the *Defender* system's ROM, RAM, CMOS, color video memory, audio, switches and buttons, monitor, and internal bookkeeping system, the last of which kept track of the total money earned, minutes played, ships used, and extra ships won. There were also internal adjustments for starting and progressive wave difficulty that were invisible to the player.

Defender became one of the most popular arcade games of the Golden Age, with sales of 55,000 units and revenue exceeding $1 billion.[12] Williams made the coin-op in standard cabinet and later cocktail versions. All kinds of clones and iterations soon appeared, including *Planetoid* for the BBC Micro, *Dropzone* for the Atari 8-bit platform, and Activision's desert-themed *Chopper Command* for the 2600.

Defender also became another target for clones and iterations on its concept. For example, *Space Odyssey* was a horizontal-scrolling shooter that added alternating vertical boards (similar to *Vanguard*), unarmed flights through meteor showers, and a wider 256-color palette. Midway jumped on the vector graphics bandwagon with *Omega Race*, a space shooter that had the distinction of being the only game released in all four major form factors: upright, mini, cocktail, and cockpit. It was popular, too, with reports of more than 35,000 cabinets being produced and an average take per machine of $181 per week as of April 1, 1982.[13]

Battlezone (Atari, 1980)

The original first-person shooter and the first game to be set in a three-dimensional environment realized with computation, Atari's *Battlezone* put you in control of a tank with a view from the cockpit. The game was set in a large valley. You attacked other tanks and defended yourself from intelligent heat-seeking missiles. With a green-and-red color overlay, the game looked suitably futuristic, with its wireframe depiction of a mountainous horizon, crescent moon in the sky, and even an erupting volcano. The barren landscape was scattered with various pyramids and blocks, serving as both indestructible obstacles for the player and places to hide behind during a heated battle.

The game started with a single slow tank ahead. Most opposing tanks were slow moving and worth 1,000 points each. Faster "supertanks" proved challenging to dispatch and were worth 3,000 points. As the strategy pointers on the cabinet indicated, you couldn't just stay in place and spin around shooting opposing tanks; you had to move continuously to avoid being hit. Taking out a missile directed toward you earned 2,000 points; sometimes you'd hear one being fired before you could see where it was coming from, so the audio cue could save you. Sometimes a flying saucer appeared, accompanied by its own pulsing audio; these didn't attack, but were worth 5,000 points. When you shot a tank, it would explode and burst into several pieces. If you were hit, the display would "crack" to show that your tank was destroyed, and you'd lose one.

The controls consisted of two large joysticks that were derived from Atari's earlier gear shifter design but strengthened with additional ribs and rubber centering bellows. You would move both sticks to control the tank; pushing both up moved the tank forward, while pulling one down and pushing one up would turn the tank. Reverse engaged when you pulled both sticks back, and as the sticks only moved on the Y-axis, you could also move forward and to the right simultaneously, for example. An LED-lit button on top of the right stick fired missiles, and there was also a raised LED Start button. The top-left portion of the screen displayed messages indicating where the next enemy was located, and a circular overhead radar screen in the center would confirm the approximate positions of the opposing computer-controlled tanks. The rightmost display showed your current score and the high score. All three of these were in separate LED displays above the main CRT.

Ed Rotberg led the design, but a small team of people worked on it, including Morgan Hoff, Jed Margolin, Roger Hector, and Owen Rubin. They used Howie Delman's existing vector-graphics engine.[14] As with *Defender*, much of the action occurred off screen. Enemy tanks moved around to different positions regardless of whether they were visible in the player's view ahead. The radar would let you know if another tank was maneuvering into position behind you, as well as showing you where to go to find tanks to shoot. This was still a brand-new idea, with only *Subs* and *Star Fire* as earlier significant releases doing the same thing.

Battlezone's cabinet design is worth special mention. The white cabinet contained beautiful blue side art depicting a futuristic tank battle underneath the night sky. The player viewed the actual game graphics through a periscope, similar to that of *Sea Wolf*, but one that stayed in place instead of pivoting. The cabinet contained a 19-inch CRT and two speakers, one mounted above the screen and another below. Two windows sat to either side of the periscope so that others could watch you play and still see what was happening. Atari also made a conversion kit that would remove the periscope and mirror setup and prop up the monitor to a vertical position so you could play it like a standard upright cabinet. This had the practical effect of letting smaller kids play the game, instead of straining to reach the high-mounted periscope.

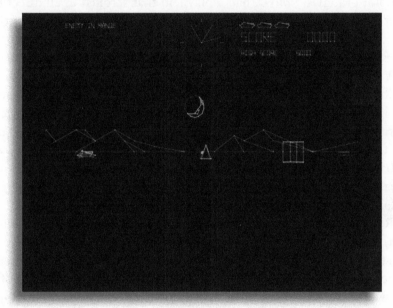

Figure 4.3: *Battlezone* **was a three-dimensional, first-person shooter that was equal parts tense and cerebral. It also looked amazing.**

Atari sold 13,000 *Battlezone* upright cabinets in the early 1980s, and the company soon reused the hardware for *Red Baron*, a first-person flight simulator game that made you a World War I flying ace (Snoopy was nowhere to be found). *Battlezone* also offered a first taste of VR gaming, thanks to the immersive, three-dimensional view through the periscope, complete with projected screen image. The game even made it to the military. A consultant group, made up of retired generals, modified the design so that they could offer targeting trainers for gunners on the Bradley Fighting Vehicle. Rothberg was asked (against his wishes) to implement the prototype; he modeled the vehicle's independent turret rotation, multiple guns, all the new weapons ballistics, and new training targets that included friendly and enemy vehicles.[15] The resultant product was called the *Bradley Trainer*. Only two were made, and the modified control yoke was later put into good use, as we'll soon see.

Rally-X (Namco/Midway Games, 1980)

This top-down racing game from Namco was a huge leap over single-screen racers such as *Sprint 2* and *Indy 800*. Aside from its detailed, full-color graphics, *Rally-X* had a playfield that scrolled in all directions, and it was much larger than what was shown on screen at any one time. The controls consisted of a four-way joystick and smoke screen buttons to either side. You drove the blue car and had to clear the 10 yellow checkpoint flags scattered about the mazelike city streets using as little fuel as possible. You drove by pushing the joystick in the appropriate direction; the playfield scrolled around it while the car stayed put in the center. If you ran into a wall, the car would turn automatically. As you cleared each flag, the points awarded increased, starting with 100 and ending with 1,000 for the last flag. A "special" flag (marked with a red S) would double the value of the remaining flags. You started the game with three cars, and the cabinet defaulted to awarding a bonus car at 20,000 points.

Red cars chased you around as you cleared the flags. To defend against them, you could put up a smoke screen that would spin them out and cause them to stall, at the cost of three liters of fuel. A *Battlezone*-like radar screen on the right-hand side of the monitor showed the relative positions of the cars, with a fuel gauge above. You also had to avoid rocks that didn't appear on the radar, so you looked out for them as you drove, and more would fill the roads on later levels. If you wrecked your car, you started over with 100 points for the next flag. Finish a board and the fuel remaining would dictate the size of the bonus you received.

Later "Challenging Stages" gave you a set time limit to clear 10 flags, with eight red cars waiting to give chase until you were just about out of fuel. This made *Rally-X* the first game to offer a bonus round. The first Challenging Stage occurred at round three, and then every four rounds thereafter. Available in standard upright, cocktail, and cabaret models, the cabinet was finished in a cream color, with orange edges and a green control panel. In the attract mode, it displayed the instructions on screen, similar to Namco's *Pac-Man*, instead of in a panel affixed to the cabinet itself.

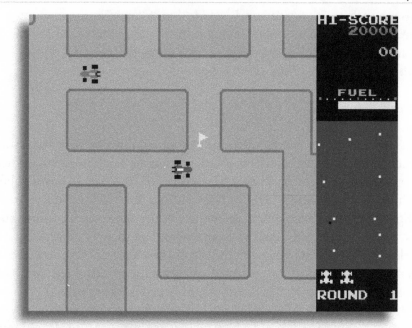

Figure 4.4: *Rally-X* expanded on the typical fixed-playfield racer with its radar screen and multiple boards, but it was really a flag capture game at heart.

In industry circles, *Rally-X* became infamous for a certain distinction it received. At the Amusement Machine Operators of America (AMOA)'s annual gathering in late 1980, *Rally-X* was shown alongside *Pac-Man*, *Defender*, and *Battlezone*. It was believed that of those games, *Rally-X* would earn the most revenue in arcades. In reality, although *Rally-X* became a hit, it performed the *least* well of those four games and saw no conversions to home consoles or computers sold in the U.S.—only the MSX overseas. It was no surprise to Midway that show attendees made a bad call on *Rally-X* over *Pac-Man*, not that it mattered because Midway was behind both games. "[We] had been through this kind of thing before," recalled Stan Jarocki, Midway's marketing director, in a later interview. "If you remember, *Space Invaders* also got the old ho-hum at the 1978 AMOA. From then on we just decided, 'Don't tell me it's bad until the players see the game.'"[16]

Stern Electronics

Stern Electronics was founded in 1977, sprung from the assets of the floundering Chicago Coin in a bankruptcy sale to the Stern family. Its first video arcade games were simple rebrandings of existing Chicago Coin arcade coin-ops such as *Stampede* and *Rawhide*, but its main business continued to be a range of popular pinball tables. It wasn't until 1980 that Stern saw its first major video game hit, one that became a generator of catchphrases and a cultural touchstone of the Golden Age.

Berzerk (Stern, 1980)

In *Berzerk*, you were a lone green humanoid who had to clear rooms full of enemy robots. Each board consisted of a simple, randomized maze with electrified walls, an entrance, and at least one exit. You could destroy robots either by shooting them with your laser pistol or by tricking them into colliding with walls or each other. The first wave of yellow robots didn't shoot back, but you could still die if you ran into one of them or touched one of the electrified walls. Starting with the second wave, red enemy robots began to return fire. Successive waves pitted you against ever-faster robots in other colors that could fire off increasing numbers of shots at a time.

If you've played this game, you can already hear the voices in your head. Clear a board of robots and exit, and you'd hear "The humanoid must not escape." Leave some of the robots alive and exit anyway, and you'd be subjected to "Chicken! Fight like a robot!" *Berzerk* may not have been the first talking arcade game—that was probably Taito's *Stratovox*, a full-color space shooter released in early 1980—but it was the first popular one. If you took just a few extra seconds on any one board, the evil Otto made an appearance. His unmistakable synthesized narration was guaranteed to raise your pulse: "Intruder alert! Intruder alert!" This hideous smiley-face ball bounced his way toward you undeterred, not just through walls but even by killing off other robots he touched. Your only recourse was to run away and escape. If Otto touched you, you'd lose a life: "Got the humanoid—got the intruder!" with the latter phrase three half-steps higher. Or worse, if you had run away in the previous room, you'd again get called a chicken instead of an intruder.

The raster game's spartan aesthetic added to the spare atmosphere. At the beginning of each level, the electric blue walls took a few seconds to appear as the game painted them onto the screen; a lightning-charge sound effect signaled the start of the action. The level designs were created using a pseudorandom number generator, but with internal consistency in each game. "I used the X-Y coordinate of the room as a 16-bit number to seed my random number generator," said programmer Alan McNeil. "That way you could exit, run back, and see the same room."

Berzerk was already one of the most popular games of the Golden Age of arcades, but its place in gaming history was cemented in part thanks to two disturbing urban legends. In one, a 19-year-old player died of a massive heart attack right after playing the game, with a devilish score of 16,660. In the second, an 18-year-old gamer landed on the high score board twice in 15 minutes, only to collapse and die of a heart attack.[17] Bloggers Charlie Grammer in 2013[18] and Cat Despira in 2015[19] put both rumors to rest with some investigation, finding that the first gamer died in a car accident earlier in 1981 and that the second player was already ill before entering the arcade. An autopsy revealed a congenital heart defect.

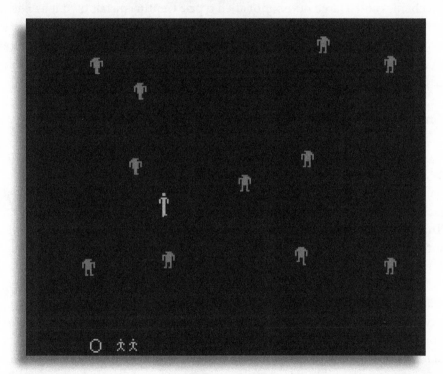

Figure 4.5: In *Berzerk*, you spent the game running and shooting enemy robots in a series of mazes, only to be called a chicken when you tried to escape.

Most of *Berzerk*'s home conversions lacked the synthesized voices. The cost of memory was still precious in 1980. Even the original arcade *Berzerk* contained only enough memory for a 30-word vocabulary, at a whopping $1,000 in development costs per synthesized word spoken.[20] Perhaps it was fitting that the game's most notable phrase was the one it spoke to potential players in attract mode: "Coin detected in pocket."

Nichibutsu

Nichibutsu was founded in 1970 by Sueharu Torii in Kita-ku, Osaka, as Nihon Bussan. For years, the company sold arcade machines from other companies. Nichibutsu's first true video game of its own (and this is stretching the term) was a 1978 *Breakout* clone called *Table Attacker*. The company soon found itself in legal entanglements with both Taito and Namco over its clones of *Space Invaders* (*Moon Base*) and *Galaxian* (*Moon Alien*). After releasing a number of such games, the company's outlook improved with *Moon Cresta*, a hit 1980 shooter that took *Galaxian* and added multiple-ship mechanics and a large number of alien types; Centuri distributed it as *Eagle* in the U.S. The company's single most influential coin-op didn't seem as exciting as a space game. Big in its day, today it's barely remembered except in coin-op collecting circles. It was a game about a guy climbing the outside of a skyscraper.

Crazy Climber (Nichibutsu/Taito, 1980)

Here's a tale of a game that, looking back on it now, was more than it appeared. Although *Crazy Climber* came out later than many vector graphics games such as *Asteroids* as well as newer shoot-'em-ups such as *Galaxian*, it lacked the former's minimalist-future design and the latter's overall polish. The graphics were pedestrian, and it played a bit stiffly. But it was notable for numerous reasons, most importantly that it was the first genuine platform climbing game—predating even *Donkey Kong*.

The goal in this two-dimensional game, designed by Shigeki Fujiwara, was simple: As "Crazy," a green-suited weirdo, you climbed four different skyscrapers. Each had 200 floors and was tougher than the last. The way you did this was novel. You controlled the climber with two joysticks that acted as the "hands," and were positioned as far apart on the console as an average person's real hands are. It took plenty of practice to do it smoothly, so there was a bit of a learning curve—which, being an arcade game, meant becoming proficient at it cost you money.

You gained points ascending from story to story on the skyscraper, using the open windows as grip points. Each building would get slimmer as you climbed farther up it, just like in real life. Along the way, tenants opened and closed windows, which made you lose your grip. To avoid this, when a window was closing, you grabbed the sill with both hands and then moved to the side before it closed. For added fun, building tenants would also drop flowerpots and other items out of the windows to knock you off the building. A condor dropped eggs and (no joke) excrement, and there was a giant ape (what else?) to contend with, along with hazards such as falling girders, dumbbells, signs, and live electrical wires. Once in a while, a desirable pink balloon appeared that carried you up eight stories. Get to the top of a skyscraper and a helicopter would carry you away to the next, more difficult one. You were awarded bonus points based on how quickly you completed your climb.

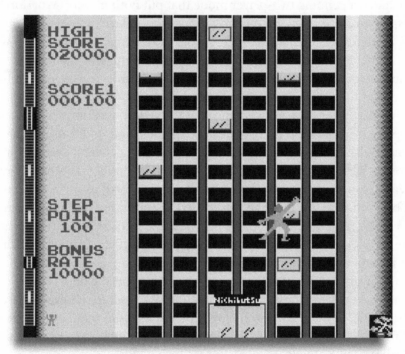

Figure 4.6: The original platformer, *Crazy Climber* made you a daredevil climbing skyscrapers. At least it wasn't as dangerous as the real thing.

During the game, several recognizable tunes played, such as "The Pink Panther Theme" and "The Entertainer." The U.S. model included voice synthesis. The game shouted "Go for it!" if you were stuck, or, worse, "Ouch!" when you were hit in the head. There were five machine styles, according to the International Arcade Museum. These included the Nichibutsu model, which was white and had a colorful cartoon of the climber grabbing at the two sticks with its hands, and an orange Taito cabinet with a cleaner, if less distinctive, control panel design that also moved the one- and two-player buttons from the left side to in between the two sticks.[21] The Taito cabinet was the most common, with the Nichibutsu model being much harder to find.[22] *Crazy Climber* was Nichibutsu's most popular coin-op and a significant milestone in the development of arcade games.

Wizard of Wor (Midway, 1980)

Wizard of Wor was set in a series of medieval dungeons and enclosed in a cabinet that evoked an overgrown Ozzy Osbourne album cover. This shooter included a genuine two-player mode that put both players (Worriors) in the same maze at once. In *Wizard of Wor*, you'd clear each maze of monsters by shooting them all. Worriors wore space suits and shot lasers with "unified field disturbance rifles," which didn't fit with the medieval theme, but just work with me here. The controls were simple, consisting of a ball-topped joystick and a Fire button for each player.

In one-player games, you controlled the yellow Worrior while the blue computer player assisted. In two-player games, you could team up with someone else to destroy monsters together, or compete and even shoot the opposing Worrior, causing them to lose a life. At all times, another Worrior for each player was cued up and ready to go in a box, as if it was on deck in a baseball game. When one player died, they'd have 10 seconds to move the next Worrior out of the box before the game forced their entrance. Each maze took place in the same-size rectangular playfield, but with different wall layouts and corridors. Doors on the left and right sides connected, letting players warp across the screen, at which point the doors closed for a few moments. A radar display at the bottom of the screen showed where all of the monsters were. There were five different monsters, and they appeared in different patterns based on the current board. A synthesized voice spoke periodically as ambient music played in the background.

The first maze began with six Blue Burwors worth 100 points each. When you killed the last one, a yellow Garwor worth 200 points would appear. Both the Garwor and the red Thorwor (worth 500 points) could turn invisible; you needed the radar to find them, and when you closed in on one in the same corridor it became visible. The monsters sped up until you could pick off the Thorwor. The second dungeon also began with six Burwors, but additional Garwors and Thorwors appeared later, followed by a blue Worluk with yellow wings. Nabbing him before he escaped through one of the side doors would net you 1,000 points and double the point values of everything in the next round. Sometimes, after killing the Worluk, the blue Wizard of Wor would make an appearance. This most fearsome enemy teleported around the board shooting lightning bolts at you until he either killed you and the opposing player, or was shot to death himself for 2,500 points.

Wizard of Wor had the feel of a competition, thanks to the appearance of two squadrons of Worriors on either side and the playfield acting as a sort of arena—which it was, on the fourth maze at least. And after the seventh maze, you'd graduate from Worrior to Worlord. You'd get a bonus worrior after level three or four (depending on the machine configuration) and again after level 13, at which point you enter the dreaded final Pit. Home conversions of *Wizard of Wor* appeared on several Atari systems, the Bally Astrocade (as "The Incredible Wizard"), and the Commodore 64. The game did well in arcades, and thanks to its successful home conversions, went on to develop a genuine fan base.

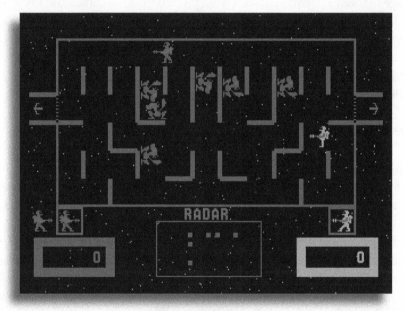

Figure 4.7: *Wizard of Wor* brought a touch of arena-battle competition to a game that was a mix of medieval fantasy and science fiction.

"I really believe we're in the movie business," designer Dave Nutting said in a 1981 interview. After *Computer Space*, Nutting had gone on to work on hits such as *Sea Wolf*, *Gorf*, and then *Wizard of Wor*. "Real-time graphics are making people participants in video games, like becoming a character in a movie. This is a far cry from the electromechanical film projection games I started out manufacturing in Milwaukee in the late '60s."[23] Indeed it was.

Centuri

Allied Leisure, founded in Hialeah, Florida, began releasing electromechanical games in 1967 and continued throughout the first half of the 1970s. It broke into the arcade video game scene in 1973 with some *Pong* clones such as *Paddle Ball* and *Tennis Tourney*. A massive fire devastated the company's manufacturing plant and headquarters in 1974, but the company survived the hit and continued operations, producing pinball tables and home video game consoles that played variants of *Pong*.[24] As late as 1979, Allied Leisure was still introducing new coin-ops at that year's AMOA show. Ed Miller, the former president of Taito of America, and his partner Bill Olliges took over the struggling company's assets, and in July 1980 renamed it Centuri.[25] The change marked a permanent shift from pinball to video games and jukeboxes.

With the new name and a massive loss on the books for 1980, the company's revenue outlook improved as it created new games and distributed others in the U.S. Centuri's first big hit was a game that added several new ingredients to the *Galaxian* formula—including a play mechanic that would soon become standard in video games.

Phoenix (Amstar/Centuri, 1980)

In this vertical raster shooter set in outer space, you had to clear four stages of enemy war birds before confronting the alien Phoenix mothership. You controlled your spaceship by moving it along the bottom of the screen with the Left and Right buttons. The Fire button launched missiles at the attacking birds, and the Force Field button froze your ship, enveloping it in a shield that lasted for a few seconds. You then had to wait at least 5 seconds before using it again.

The first stage began with 16 eggs that hatched into birds, which dropped missiles and dived to attack your ship. You earned more points by attacking birds closer to you, and waiting until they were attacking instead of just hovering. Destroy the first wave of birds and a second, similar wave appeared. The third stage featured eight eggs that hatched into larger, blue Phoenix birds that were tougher. You had to shoot them in the stomach; if you were off to the left or right, you'd clip off a wing, which regenerated a few moments later. If you shot off both wings and then killed the bird, you'd get the most points. Freakishly, sometimes the birds transformed back into eggs. Destroy all eight and a fourth stage with eight more eggs appeared; these hatched into pink Phoenix birds that you eliminated in the same manner.

The fifth stage made history. *Phoenix* was the first popular video game with an end boss, a large, hard-to-kill enemy presented as a separate challenge. In this case, it was an alien creature ensconced in an orange and green mothership. Small groups of birds swooped down from it to attack, and the mothership itself also dropped missiles. As you shot the mothership, pieces of it would chip away. Once you penetrated its rotating purple barrier in the center, you could take a clear shot at the alien creature. Score a direct hit and the game awarded you from 400 to 8,200 points. Then it started over at a harder difficulty level.

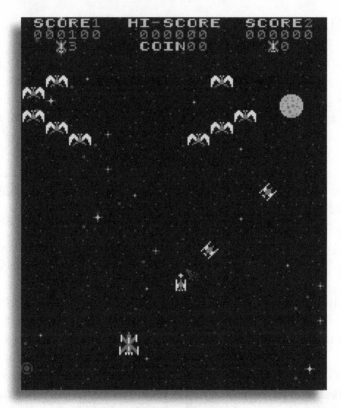

Figure 4.8: *Phoenix*'s wistful, musical sound effects and phrases contrasted nicely with its bird-alien shoot-'em-up premise.

Perhaps most distinctive was the audio, with its eerie bird calls and shrieks, garbled musical kill effects, and lone siren in the background, making it one of the earliest examples of disturbing sounds in a video game.[26] The game also played Beethoven's "Für Elise" and "Romance de Amor," a 19th-century Spanish guitar piece of unknown authorship.

The operator could adjust the machine so that you earned two bonus spaceships in a range from 3,000 and 30,000 points to 6,000 and 60,000 points. Amstar Electronics developed the game, Centuri licensed it for U.S. distribution, and Taito picked it up for Japan. The game's distinctive cabinet graphics and blue-and-green marquee were easy to spot in an arcade. The end boss concept would soon show up in more games, but on its own, *Phoenix* was a distinctive and impressive game that saw huge popularity and nearly a dozen clones and bootlegs. Then, aside from an excellent 1983 Atari 2600 port, the game disappeared from pop culture.

Gorf (Midway, 1981)

In *Gorf*, you were part of an Interstellar Space Force tasked with repelling the invasion of the evil Gorfian Empire. The game was one of the first to feature multiple screens and also offered voice synthesis, as had just become in vogue, thanks to a Votrax SC-01 chip. *Gorf* taunted you with phrases such as "Prepare yourself for annihilation" and "Some galactic defender you are," the latter punctuated with an evil laugh. *Gorf* was conceived as a *Star Trek* game. There's some disagreement about why the tie-in concept fell through; one reason cited was that the developers thought *Star Trek: The Motion Picture* would be tough to convert into a game.[27] Regardless, it's why your ship looks just like the Enterprise.[28]

The game took place across five stages. The first, Astro Battles, set up a *Space Invaders*–like screen of marching aliens that dropped bombs to destroy you, although a parabolic force field protected your ship. Then Laser Attack pitted you against two antiparticle laser ships, each surrounded by an array of supporting fighters. Next up was Galaxians, a clone of Namco's *Galaxian* with an armada of aliens that broke off in squadrons to dive bomb your ship. The fourth stage, Space Warp, saw aliens emerging from the center vortex of an "eerie web" of photons, as if it were a permanent warp drive. Finally, Flag Ship pitted you against a giant spacecraft protected by its own force field; you needed to blast a space in the shield before you could get a shot off at the flagship. Complete all five stages and you'd start again with a new ranking, which served as bragging rights (but wasn't that everything?).

The one-handed control scheme consisted of a simple flight stick with a trigger that fired your ship's missiles. This made *Gorf* feel different from, say, several of the arcade games *Gorf* simulated (meaning "ripped off"). Although you could fire one missile at a time in both *Gorf* and *Space Invaders*, in *Gorf* you could stop a missile in midair. Let's say you took a shot, but it missed the aliens and there was no UFO at the top of the stage. You just had to press the button again; that missile would disappear, and your ship would fire a new one. *Gorf* also gave you the option of putting in a single quarter for three lives, or additional quarters for six lives (or two and four, respectively, depending on how the machine was configured). It was a primitive form of a Continue, even though it wasn't called that at the time.

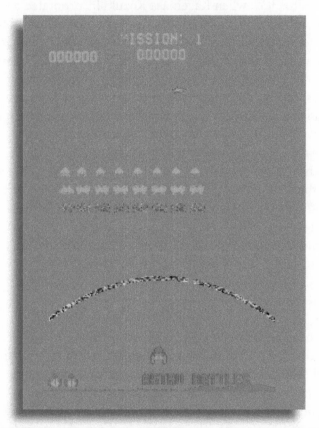

Figure 4.9: With five games in one, *Gorf* delivered plenty of bang for your quarter-buck, even if some of the minigames were clear infringements of existing coin-ops.

Gorf was available in standard cabinet, cabaret, and cocktail versions, the last of which was available with optional legs to bring the table up to the same height as the standard upright cabinet's control panel. The game's attract mode relayed the storyline in two short paragraphs and then walked potential players through all five stages. In a period print advertisement, Midway played up the standard model's "lighted header and front panel" and colorful cabinet-side graphics. Ports appeared on many platforms of the day, but only the Commodore 64 retained the game's synthesized speech. The home conversions were also missing the Galaxians stage, presumably over copyright concerns.

Konami

Konami dates to 1969, when Kagemasa Kōzuki incorporated a business for renting out and repairing jukeboxes in Toyonaka, Osaka. Soon his company pivoted to amusement machines for video arcades. It released its first three coin-ops in 1978 and 1979, one of which was a virtual clone of *Space Invaders* (*Space King*). Konami soon got going in earnest, though. The company was responsible for three 1981 hit coin-ops. The first, *Amidar*, introduced what soon became a popular subgenre called the grid-capture game. You maneuvered your player around a mazelike grid in order to enclose and capture the squares while avoiding several enemies at once. Later titles such as Exidy's *Pepper II* expanded on the concept. These games saw decent take-up in the arcades and proved successful at home, with conversions of those and iterative computer games such as *Kid Grid* and *Jeepers Kreepers* on the Atari 400 and 800.

A second Konami game didn't introduce a genre, but it cemented its popularity and was far more successful than *Amidar*.

Scramble (Konami, 1981)

Developed more or less at the same time as Williams' *Defender*, *Scramble* was one of the first horizontal space shooters. It was the first arcade game with forced X-axis scrolling (from left to right) and the first game with multiple levels. "*Scramble* was the first arcade game to send you on a mission and quickly earned a big following," *Computer and Video Games* said in its February 1982 issue.[29] The mission was straightforward: Shoot your way through five Scramble Defense Systems in order to reach and destroy the enemy base station, with each requiring a different strategy. The slower pace, the forced scrolling, and the wide trajectory of your ship's bombs made *Scramble* more deliberate and less stressful than *Defender*, even if it was still hard.

The joystick moved the ship up and down, and accelerated and decelerated. One button shot forward-firing lasers; a second released bombs out of the bottom of the ship. The bombs formed an arc as they dropped before reaching the ground. During gameplay, you had to destroy all manner of enemy rockets, "mystery targets," and UFOs to score points. Enemies were worth 50 to 100 points each, and mystery targets netted 100 to 300 points. The bases at the end of each play-through were worth 800 points. You also accrued 10 points per second simply by remaining alive. An important game mechanic was keeping your ship full of fuel. Shooting or bombing the fuel tanks that appeared bumped up your fuel stores and awarded 150 points. The operator could set the game so that you began with three, four, or five aircraft, and you earned one bonus ship at 10,000 points. Two players could also start a game, but you took turns.

Figure 4.10: *Scramble* was Konami's first big success, adding forced scrolling to the horizontal shooter template *Defender* defined.

The game started in a roomy mountainous region, but navigating the scenery became tougher as you progressed, and the colors of the mountains and background changed accordingly. Of note was a stage that was a maze in motion; to stay alive and not collide with the walls, you had to move your ship all around the screen, decelerating and accelerating to take advantage of the extra bit of horizontal room you'd get. Even though your ship was a bit slower than in *Defender*, it still moved at a good clip, enough so that there wasn't much time to react to what was coming. Repeat players would begin to memorize the boards so that they had additional time to plan their moves. If you reached the final stage and destroyed the enemy base, you'd start the game again, with an extra flag added to the bottom of the screen.

Stern manufactured and distributed *Scramble* in North America and managed to sell more than 15,000 cabinets. In America, only the Vectrex received an official home conversion, and it became one of the vector-graphics-based system's most popular cartridges.

Warlords (Atari, 1981)

Warlords was four-player *Breakout* with a medieval theme and Atari's best multiplayer game since *Indy 800*. The object was twofold: Defend your home castle from the other players launching fireballs and break through your opponents' walls and destroy their warlords by catching and launching fireballs by using your power stone. The game started with four different-colored L-shaped castles, one in each of the four corners of the playfield. The computer AI would assume control of any of the opposing castles that were missing a human player, up to three of them. Black knight faces in armor depicted the computer-controlled warlords, and human players were shown as crowns.

The massive cocktail cabinet supported four players (who could compete against each other or in teams of two) and included a 14-inch display and simple color overlay. Two players could battle on the standard upright, which included a larger 23-inch monitor and a more detailed background overlay with a mirrored three-dimensional playfield projection. Regardless of the cabinet, each player had a spinner control and a flashing red LED button that let them either join the game as that player or activate the power stone during play.

At the start, an animated dragon breathed a spinning fireball at one of the human players. The spinner controlled your shield, which acted as a paddle to deflect the fireball à la *Pong* or *Breakout*. Keeping the button depressed let you catch the fireball, hold on to it for a moment, and then shoot it at one of the opposing castles at a higher rate of speed. Each time you destroyed an opponent through a wall, the resulting death would spawn another fireball in the opposite direction. New fireballs also appeared during each game at periodic intervals. The game's AI would sense how well the player(s) were doing and adjust to compensate for an equivalent amount of playtime. Beginning players would get 30 seconds to catch a fireball before another was released. Skilled players would just get 8 seconds to not just catch the ball but hit an opposing castle wall. Each brick was worth 125 points, each warlord was worth 1,000, and the mystical Black Knight was worth 2,500. You'd also be awarded a bonus game for destroying the Black Knight's castle. The game would get quite hectic and was fun and challenging with three or four human players. Once all home castles were destroyed for all participating players, the game ended and the high score table appeared.

Figure 4.11: Describing *Warlords* as four-player Breakout misses the incredible competitive dynamic that became more than the sum of its parts.

Most people remember *Warlords* more for the Atari 2600 cartridge designed by Carla Meninsky. That conversion displayed native, if simpler, color graphics that made it look more like a *Breakout* variant. Atari's coin-op department, which remained separate from consumer, developed *Warlords* in tandem using the same castle-and-kings design. *Video* magazine's "Arcade Alley" column awarded *Warlords* "Best Pong Variant" in its third year running, writing that *Warlords* was "something really new and different in 'Pong'-style designs," and that it delivered "plenty of on-screen excitement."

Asteroids Deluxe (Atari, 1981)

Atari felt pressure to follow its *Asteroids* with a sequel, not just because it was a major hit, but also because some gamers had figured out how to play it for long periods of time. Many things about *Asteroids Deluxe* were the same: the basic premise; the hardware (a 1.5MHz MOS 6502 CPU and Atari's Quadrascan vector graphics); and the playfield wrapped at the edges of the screen, so if you flew off one of the edges, your ship would appear on the other side and continue in the same direction.

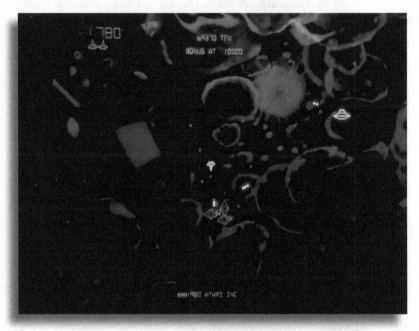

Figure 4.12: Atari fixed Asteroids's prime weakness—unlimited play, once you figured out the strategy—with *Asteroids Deluxe*, an otherwise lightly updated game with new physics and a shield mechanic. Credit: Joe Lyons

But some differences were apparent, starting with the white cabinet, bolder side art, and new marquee and control panel designs. A translucent color overlay with a mirror and backlight formed a backdrop of asteroids in space, adding a sense of a third dimension and making it a tiny bit tougher to see the vector graphics. The ship looked different with its new side-mounted fins, and its thrust came on faster, making tighter maneuvers possible. Flying saucers appeared immediately instead of after 1,500 points. The asteroids themselves were more detailed, with more fixed points making up the shapes, and they rotated as they drifted. The game replaced the unpredictable Hyperspace with a shield that depleted during use. The large flying saucer was more accurate, with one-quarter of its shots heading straight for you instead of one-fifth. As the game progressed, Killer Satellites appeared: These hexagonal enemies broke apart into diamonds and wedges and chased your spaceship with increasing accuracy.

Most importantly, *Asteroids Deluxe* nixed a strategy that worked in the original game, where you would repeatedly hunt flying saucers for extra points and therefore play forever on a single quarter. Despite having the same wraparound playfield, in *Asteroids Deluxe* the flying saucers knew how to target you from the opposite side of the screen. They could shoot so that the bullets wrapped around and hit you on the other side. You were no longer safe lurking at the side of the screen, away from saucers, and just watching out for asteroids, making it more profitable for owners and operators.[30] And instead of having to press the Fire button once for each shot, you could hold it down to shoot up to four bullets on the screen at any one time.

The original *Asteroids* employed discrete chips for sound effects, whereas *Asteroids Deluxe* was one of the first Atari arcade games to include the four-voice POKEY chip first developed for the 400 and 800 home computers. The *Jaws*-like bass note pulse in the background was higher pitched, and the sound effects were clearer and crisper, with more midrange. *Asteroids Deluxe* didn't do as well on the market as the original game, but many players preferred the new ship's faster acceleration, automatic firing, and more predictable shield mechanic.

Pleiades (Tekhan/Centuri, 1981)

Another fixed shooter, *Pleiades* picked up where *Phoenix* left off. It consisted of four phases that were more distinctive than the original game's five waves. In the first stage of *Pleiades*, you protected Earth City from 16 Martians that could fly, walk, or transform into UFOs. When on the ground, the Martians built up a barrier around Earth City, so you had to shoot away those pieces as well. You could move left or right, as well as "warp," which would randomly deposit you somewhere else to the left or right. As you reached the end of the board, the sky darkened, and then you'd blast off from the surface.

The next two stages took place in space. The first one pitted you against eight Space Monsters that you needed to shoot in the center. The next brought you to the Martian Space Battleship, which hovered at the top of the screen and consisted of five chambers defended by flaming rockets, and a squadron of 16 Martians defending the ship. Destroy it and you'd reach the fourth and final stage, where Mission Control ordered you to return to Earth and to your home base, collecting flags and avoiding other spacecraft. Some of the points awarded were dependent on actions taken earlier, such as the value of the center of a flying Space Monster (from 50 to 400 points) and stage completion bonuses.

Figure 4.13: Centuri's *Pleiades* added four different boards and new kinds of enemies to a vertical shooter that otherwise looked and sounded like *Phoenix*.

The control panel was embellished with fake extra buttons and red digital LED readouts, and the marquee and sides of the cabinet faithfully executed a "1980 space age" motif. Buried in the graphics were game instructions and six buttons: Left, Right, Warp, Fire, and one- and two-player game start. The lone difference between its controls and those on *Phoenix* was the Warp button replacing Shield, something multiple manufacturers seemed to go back and forth on for a few years. (Random hyperspace and warp lost out to shields over time.) In other markets the game was known as Pleiads without the *e* at the end, and some variations included a two-way joystick with a red ball in place of the two "left" and "right" buttons.

Pleaides used the same hardware as *Phoenix*, down to the Intel 8085A CPU—a budget variant of the 8080 that remained compatible with its instruction set. *Pleiades* didn't receive any notable conversions for home systems—a planned 2600 cartridge was canned as the video game industry crash loomed. In Greek mythology, the name *Pleiades* referred to the seven daughters of Atlas and Pleione, all born on Mount Cyllene. It's known today as a beautiful and distinctive star cluster in the night sky *and* a fun Golden Age arcade coin-op.

Centipede (Atari, 1981)

Centipede, an intense vertical shooter with a black playfield and bright, colorful raster graphics, was distinguished by its premise and the prominent pearl-colored trackball at the center of the machine's control panel. The trackball was small, about the size of a pool cue ball, and easier to maneuver than the larger models found on Atari's *Missile Command* and *Football*. In *Centipede*, you needed to clear a mushroom garden full of pests. You used the trackball to control a shooter in the lower fifth of the screen and the Fire button to shoot off a fast dart. (You could hold it down to shoot repeatedly, though only one dart could be in motion at a time.) The mushrooms were obstacles you either steered around or destroy with four shots; they even showed visible damage.

At the start of each level, a segmented centipede began to move back and forth at the top of the screen, descending one row and changing direction each time it collided with a mushroom. Shoot the centipede somewhere in its middle and it would break into two smaller centipedes; the segment you shot turned into a mushroom. Whenever a part of the centipede reached the bottom of the screen, it would begin to move just within the player's area. Meanwhile, new heads would appear at the sides of the screen and further clog up the playfield. Destroy all segments of a centipede and you'd move on to the next level.

Aside from the centipede, the spider was the biggest annoyance. It appeared with its own little soundtrack, a series of repeating tones, and flitted about in your part of the screen. If it crashed into you, you'd lose a life. It also erased any mushrooms it flew over. Shoot the spider and you'd earn either 300, 600, or 900 points, depending on how close you were to it. Beginning with the second wave, fleas descended on the player whenever a specific number of mushrooms remained in the bottom of the screen. Fleas left new mushrooms in their wake. Shoot a flea once and it would speed up; a second shot took it out. Beginning at 6,000 points, the scorpion started to appear with its own distinctive music pattern. It crawled across the screen and poisoned any mushrooms it passed over. When a centipede segment touched a poisoned mushroom, it began to wiggle and made a beeline for the bottom of the screen. When you cleared a board of centipede segments, all of the damaged and/or poisoned mushrooms would be restored in rapid-fire succession, earning the player five bonus points each.

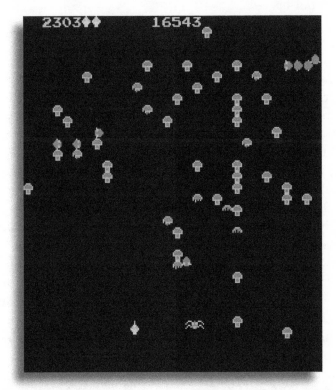

Figure 4.14: Dona Bailey's masterpiece, *Centipede* turned the vertical shooter on its head by sticking it in a bug-infested magic garden and giving the player a trackball.

Centipede was simple, streamlined, and unbearably addictive. The novel control scheme only made it more desirable to play. *Centipede* was the first arcade video game designed by a woman, Dona Bailey, along with Ed Logg. Unfortunately, Atari never let developers credit themselves in the games for fear of other companies poaching its employees. In his 1982 book

Video Invaders, author Steve Bloom had to disguise the names of the creators of *Centipede* in order to print their interview quotes about their time at Atari and how the game was programmed. (Meanwhile, Atari executives received all the praise by name, as only they were allowed to talk to the media.[31]) Nonetheless, *Centipede* helped bring more women into arcades, and along with *Pac-Man* was one of the first coin-ops to do so.

Figure 4.15: *Super Cobra* was an easy lift for Konami, as it played and ran a lot like *Scramble* with a helicopter, but its new boards and more varied enemies made it a compelling game all its own.

Super Cobra (Konami/Stern, 1981)

Scramble earned its place in history, but its sequel also saw plenty of recognition. In *Super Cobra*, you had to traverse 10,000 miles of open battle terrain and enclosed mine catacombs in your special attack helicopter. The game consisted of 10 stages; at the end, you needed to pick up a cache of gold and escape. There were no breaks or intermissions—you just flew from one area to the next. During the game, you faced Sidewinder missiles, roving tanks, gun turrets, rockets, satellites, and flying saucers. The color scheme of the boards shifted as you flew between stages. Occasionally, you'd have to navigate around meteor fields and tall space skyscrapers, and "mystery tanks" would show up that gave you a random score award when destroyed.

Super Cobra's playfield was similar to *Scramble*'s, with forced X-axis scrolling to the right at all times, your score on top, and a fuel gauge on the bottom. The eight-way joystick maneuvered your ship. The Fire button launched bullets, and the Bomb button dropped munitions on ground or air targets below you. Bombing or shooting fuel canisters replenished some of your missing fuel. You'd receive a bonus aircraft every 10,000 points, and when you ran out, the game ended. Players learned to keep an eye out for fuel canisters as well as to pay extra attention in the tough meteor stage. In a first for Konami, after the game was over it let you continue from the stage where you left off by inserting another quarter, with the only difference being that your score was wiped out. Continues were favored by arcade operators because of their increased revenue potential, but as the arcade age wore on they became the default and also expected even on home consoles.

Despite its similarity to *Scramble*, *Super Cobra* sold 12,300 cabinets, not far off from *Scramble*'s 15,100 total.[32] *Super Cobra* was tougher, but players liked it just the same and appreciated its increased number of stages and enemies to fight as well as the ability to continue with another quarter. Unlike its predecessor, it saw plenty of home conversions.

Venture (Exidy, 1981)

Space games full of aliens and UFOs had begun to saturate arcades, so it was time for something different. Enter *Venture*, Exidy's attempt at a fantasy action adventure game—just in time to capitalize on the surge in interest in role-playing games, along with movies such as *Excalibur*, *Dragonslayer*, *Knightriders*, and the biggest of them all, *Raiders of the Lost Ark*.[33] *Venture* conveyed a cool atmosphere, right down to the font for the in-game text and scores. The control panel consisted of an eight-way joystick and Fire buttons on either side for left- or right-handed use.

As Winky, you entered a mazelike dungeon, explored its four levels, and collected treasure while staying alive as long as possible. The game started with the Treasures screen, which was filled with rows of question marks indicating that you hadn't found any yet. Your character would descend a staircase to a zoomed-out overhead floor plan view of the first level of the dungeon. It contained four rooms of varying shapes and sizes. Invulnerable green Hallmonsters prowled the passageways; you were a tiny dot and had to select one of the chambers without colliding with a Hallmonster.

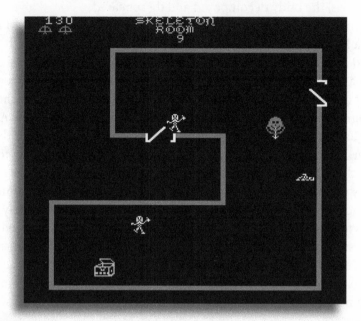

Figure 4.16: Universal's *Venture* was the first popular coin-op with a fantasy role-playing-game veneer, although it was still a maze shooter underneath the simple graphics.

Once you entered a room through one of the white doorways, the camera zoomed in and you'd see a much larger view of the inside, including where the treasure was located, and (most of the time) the monsters you would face. The treasure could be a chest, a diamond, a pot of gold, or even the occasional damsel in distress. Each time you collected the treasure and made it out of a room alive, you scored bonus points and the room filled in on the floor plan and was no longer open for exploration. The next time you saw the Treasures screen, you'd see the treasure you collected fill in one of the question-mark boxes.

The various rooms each had different names and themes. Names often reflected the meanies inside, such as Goblin Room, Skeleton Room, Troll Room, or Serpent Room. Sometimes a room had special features. For example, the Wall Room had four moving walls that would expand and contract, with treasure in the center of the screen. The Two-Headed Room started empty, but when you collected the treasure, a trap would spring, and four two-headed crabs appeared blocking the exits. The game's AI enabled enemies to evade your shots. When you shot a monster with an arrow, it would die. You still couldn't touch its carcass, or you'd lose a life. After several seconds, the body decomposed and disappeared.

If you took too long in any one chamber, a Hallmonster would find its way in à la Evil Otto from *Berzerk*. The Hallmonsters looked much scarier enlarged in the zoomed-in view. The game was littered with special details, such as a magic bow upgrade and secret rooms. Complete a full level and the next one would be tougher, with a different layout and color scheme.

Venture was the first game to introduce a bonus multiplier. A timer would slowly count down how long it took for you to collect all of the treasures on one level of the dungeon. Whatever the multiplier was set to when you finished the last room would determine the bonus score. The game's graphics were simplistic even for the time. Winky basically amounted to a happy face with a bow, and the rest of the game consisted of crudely drawn outlines for the boxy rooms, enemies, and treasures. The audio fared better, with persistent background music throughout the game, a still-unusual feature in 1981. *Venture* was notable as much for its complexity in the arcade as its near-perfect conversion for the ColecoVision—which, admittedly, wasn't a high bar to clear.

Personal Arcades

Coin-op fans of some means began exploring buying their own games to evoke the feeling of being in an arcade at home, the same way people coveted pinball machines. Especially desirable were cocktail models, thanks to their decor-friendly form factors, as well as newer cabaret cabinets that allowed for stand-up play in a smaller, more manageable enclosure than a standard upright. Either would fit into a living room or den, though regardless of the type, new coin-op machines cost between $2,000 and $3,000 each in 1981. But for the first time, it had become more affordable to purchase games that were then several years old, and such a used market existed. *Electronic Games* magazine advised prospective buyers to check out "classic" (already?) video game coin-op rentals that had outlived their short life expectancy on the arcade floor. These were returned, and instead of being cannibalized for parts or converted to a newer game, distributors sold into smaller markets such as hotel resorts and private clubs.

In late 1981, the magazine suggested Cinematronics' *Star Hawk* ($725, as valued then by the magazine), as well as Atari's *Night Driver* ($400), *Football* ($475), and *Breakout* ($300). On the high end, it suggested new games such as *Battlezone* ($2,000) and Exidy's *Targ* ($1,275),[34] a hit grid shooter with a blue-and-white playfield and a vehicular combat theme. Speaking of *Targ*, it was the first game licensed from a U.S. manufacturer to a Japanese one (in this case, Sega) and the first licensed from one U.S. manufacturer to another (Centuri, for the cocktail model). I will forever associate *Targ* with a pizza place in Brooklyn on Avenue U and West 9th Street. As places and smells are tightly woven into memories, we often remember specific coin-ops as much for where we played them as anything else.

5 > Fireball

In 1980, the video game industry was already on a huge upswing, bringing $2.8 billion in revenue—still nearly all of it from coin-op as opposed to home consoles. Atari raked in $415 million that year, and its competitors were also doing well.[1] Then the release of *Pac-Man* shook the world. As with all arcade coin-ops, distribution was uneven, so it wasn't like today where everyone could download the same game on launch day, or even in the 1990s and 2000s when large video game store chains would all stock the same cartridges, and only supply issues would delay some gamers from getting a hold of the latest title. But by late 1980 and early 1981 standards *Pac-Man* spread faster than any game before it. That same year, *Space Invaders* debuted on the 2600. Atari sold 1.25 million copies of the cartridge in its first year on the market, comprising a full 50 percent of existing 2600 owners and driving an untold number of new console purchases.

Video games had become an international craze. Arcade machines could be found in fast food restaurants, ice cream shops, convenience stores, laundromats, and train stations. Players intending to spend just a few quarters would spend five bucks before they knew it, and leave only because they ran out of quarters or were risking their job by taking too long a lunch break.[2] Articles about arcade games appeared in newspapers such as the *Wall Street Journal, Newsweek*, and the *San Francisco Chronicle*; in magazines such as *Sports Illustrated, Playboy, Fortune*, and *Forbes*; and on TV news programs including *60 Minutes* and *20/20*.[3] These sources and others also showed celebrities as diverse as Burt Reynolds, Farah Fawcett, Dustin Hoffman, Barbra Streisand, Alice Cooper, Ringo Starr, and Isaac Hayes playing coin-ops.[4]

People were amazed at the phenomenon, but it made plenty of sense in retrospect. In an uneasy and uncertain world, with the Cold War's threat of nuclear annihilation, video games offered a respite. They promised not just escapism, but also a sense of control and even mastery over something, an outlet for aggression, a break from the rat race, and a chance to concentrate intensely on something else for a few minutes or an hour. For dedicated fans, topping the list was the glory of running up a high score with a small audience fawning over your skills.[5]

Nintendo

Nintendo's impact on the game industry far exceeded what it accomplished during the Golden Age of video arcades. Most of it isn't relevant for our purposes here. But despite the company's never-ending battle for consumer dollars in in the console wars, against Sega and then Sony and Microsoft, Nintendo first had an outsize effect on the video arcade. And the arcade saw the birth of some of Nintendo's most famous characters.

Founded by Fusajiro Yamauchi in 1889, Nintendo produced hand-made playing cards for decades before branching out into numerous un-related businesses, such as taxi services, a TV network, instant rice, and even a chain of "love hotels" for short sexual encounters. It had more success with toys and electronic games, and in 1974 Nintendo joined the video game industry when it licensed the Magnavox Odyssey game console for Japanese distribution. Its first arcade coin-op was 1975's *EVR Race*, and Nintendo went on to develop many machines as well as hand-held electronic games, most notably the Game & Watch series beginning in 1980.

A college graduate with a degree in industrial engineering named Shigeru Miyamoto joined Nintendo 1977 as its first artist. He worked on the company's Color TV-Game console and coin-op titles such as the West-ern-themed *Sheriff* and the space shooter *Radar Scope*. These games did lucrative business in Japan but stalled in the North American market. Ya-mauchi put Miyamoto in charge of converting a large lot of unused *Radar Scope* machines—some 2,000 sitting in a New Jersey warehouse—into something new.[6] Miyamoto had no programming skills, so he began de-signing a game first and formulated a storyline. This marked the first time an arcade game's storyline informed the programming instead of the other way around. The resulting coin-op vaulted Nintendo to the top of the in-dustry's revenue charts.

Donkey Kong (Nintendo, 1981)

The name "Donkey Kong" means "crazy" or "stupid" in Japanese, and Nintendo's breakthrough coin-op hit was an obvious spin-off of the 1933 classic movie *King Kong*. At the start of the game, one of the first-ever examples of the "platform" genre and the first to include a jumping mechanic, the giant ape Donkey Kong kidnapped the maiden Pauline and climbed a series of structural beams to the top of a construction site. The ape then jumped several times, causing the girders to fall and become crooked, and finally, he grunted three times to show he meant business.

Your job as Jumpman was to rescue Pauline by climbing the structure using a series of ladders. Along the way, you needed to avoid a series of exploding barrels that Donkey Kong would fling at you, along with fireball creatures, a flaming oil drum, and other obstacles, all by either dodging or jumping over them as appropriate. Grab a hammer and you'd become invincible for several seconds, destroying enemies left and right, although you couldn't climb up or down when you had the hammer. If you reached the top, Donkey Kong would pick up Pauline again and climb to the next level, causing the heart that appeared above both of you to break in half.

There were four different stages, which you would reach in a certain order under the guise of the question, "How high can you go?" In addition to the first stage described above, there's a rivet level (2), an elevator-and-spring board (3), and a conveyer belt board with cement pans (4), which I've numbered here according to the first time you encounter them. The actual pattern of boards was 1+2 for the first level, 1+3+2 for the second, and 1+4+3+2 for the third. Each time you completed a board, you'd reunite with Pauline only to be torn away once more—with the exception of stage two, where you were reunited permanently and the story supposedly ended. As the game repeated boards, Donkey Kong would throw barrels faster and at diagonal trajectories, and the fireball monsters moved more quickly.

Designed by the legendary Miyamoto, *Donkey Kong* was responsible for other firsts in video games. It contained a full narrative story that unfolded as you played—unlike *Pac-Man*, which told something of a story in its cutscenes but otherwise lacked a complete plot. It displayed smooth, cartoonlike animation for the characters, something that would fast become a Nintendo hallmark. Bill Kunkel, writing in *Electronic Games*, praised the game's "marvelous visuals," and said the "animation of Kong, Mario, and the girl takes this video game as close to the realm of film animation as anything else in today's arcades."[7]

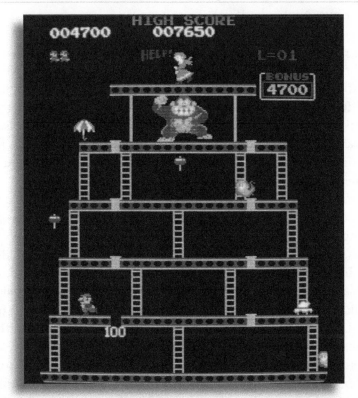

**Figure 5.1: The game that put Shigeru Miyamoto on the map, *Donkey Kong*
proved that a former trading card and novelty machine company could, in fact, go
very high indeed.**

Donkey Kong was difficult, more so than it appeared with its friendly
graphics; even completing the first board could take a new player many
tries, thanks to unforgiving collision detection when jumping over fireballs,
or worse, dodging barrels that would abruptly descend a ladder as Mario
walked beneath it. *Donkey Kong* also marked a leap forward for in-game
music. The game played different phrases for each stage, the stage intro,
and losing a life. And it played occasional bonus themes for things such as
grabbing the magic hammer or rescuing Pauline.[8] Some were monophonic,
but it was still new and exciting.

Donkey Kong spawned more than a dozen home conversions, plus
handhelds, miniature desktop games, and more. Everyone with home versions of *Donkey Kong* obsessed over this or that detail that their conversion
was lacking compared with the original coin-op. None of the consoles available in the second half 1981 could pull it off, but it would take just a year for

that to change dramatically. Nintendo released numerous coin-op sequels, two of which we'll get to later, in addition to some home-only games. Starting with the first sequel, Nintendo renamed the Jumpman character Mario—alternately described as a carpenter at first, then a plumber, and then just himself. Mario would go on to become one of the most famous mascots in video game history. How high can you go, indeed.

Space Fury (Sega/Gremlin, 1981)

You couldn't miss *Space Fury* in the arcade, even despite its 1970s-look wood veneer paneling and lack of cabinet graphics on the sides and front panel. The marquee read *Space Fury* in a vaguely horror-themed font, and to the right was a giant, green cyclops-brain head. The control panel presented a green hand imprint in the center, with two buttons to either side (Left and Right rotation on the left, and Thrust and Fire on the right). The overall effect was a distinctive, bio-space-alien motif that gained much more ground in the mid-to-late 1980s.

Space Fury displayed breathtaking color vector graphics, an industry first, using Sega-Gremlin's new ColorBeam X-Y system and companion G80 arcade board. It drew sharp, perfect lines of red, yellow, purple, blue, and green against a deep black background. Moreover, the synthesized speech in the game was front and center—literally, you saw it right in the beginning speaking to you with moving lips—and sounded clear and humanlike in its diction and rhythm. The sound chip, a General Instrument SP0250, modeled the human vocal tract and its various intonations in synthesis, which meant that the game didn't require the still-expensive ROM chips necessary to contain and play back digital speech samples as in games such as *Berzerk* and *Gorf*.

Space Fury consisted of five rounds of play that comprised battle with four different enemy ships. The first wave introduced scouts, the second cruisers, the third destroyers, and the fourth warships. The fifth round included the entire fleet. Scoring increased throughout, and you'd get extra points for shooting off parts of certain ships and fireballs. You had to destroy all alien ships in each wave without colliding with one or getting shot with a fireball. The Thrust button accelerated and decelerated the ship quickly, in contrast to *Asteroids*. The alien commander became annoyed and taunted you with verbal phrases throughout the game.

At the end of each round, you had a choice of docking with one of three motherships arranged in an upside-down U shape. Each time you docked, a weapons upgrade let you shoot in three directions simultaneously on the next board. Lose a ship and you'd lose the three-way cannon until the next time you docked with one of the remaining motherships. At the end of the game, the alien commander rated your skill, and said out loud whether you were an easy, adequate, amusing, stimulating, or outstanding opponent. Operators could set the game to give you anywhere from two to five ships per play, as well as choose from four difficulty levels and whether you'd get a free ship at 10,000 to 40,000 points. Most importantly for the operator, they could set the game to speak in attract mode or remain silent. With the speech being as good as it was for 1981, wanting the game to speak at all times was understandable.

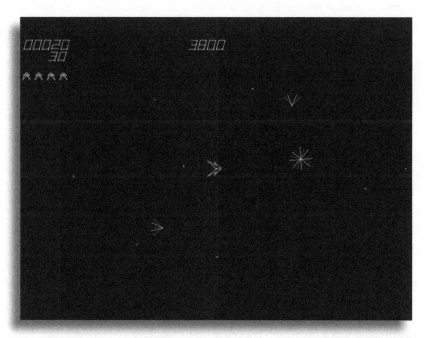

Figure 5.2: *Space Fury* **was a sight-and-sound extravaganza of a space shooter, capped off with the clearest speech synthesis in the industry.**

In an era already overloaded with space shoot-'em-up games, *Space Fury* stood out for its brand-new color vector graphics and high-fidelity speech synthesis. Today, the game is a wonderful throwback to the days when "talking" gadgets were considered state of the art, such as video games, car dashboards, alarm clocks, and the Speak & Spell. The alien commander even liked it when you played, saying at the start of the game: "So…a creature for my amusement."

Qix (Taito, 1981)

Qix (pronounced "kicks") was a unique, colorful game and maybe a touch too difficult for mainstream success. Start a game and the machine deposited you onto an empty black playfield. You were represented by a small marker. The Qix was a smoothly animated stick with colorful trails that moved erratically around the board. In one sense, all you did in *Qix* was draw. The control panel consisted of a four-way joystick and two buttons: "Fast Draw" and "Slow Draw." You used this ability to fence off at least a majority, if not a supermajority, of the playfield by drawing "Stix" using one of the two buttons.

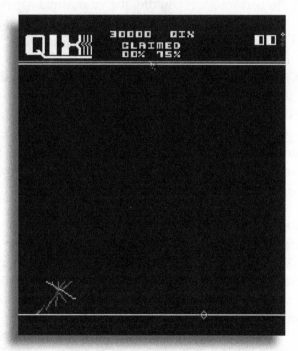

Figure 5.3: The thinking player's action game, *Qix* barely gave you enough time to plan your next space capture before the Qix put an end to it.

The Fast Draw button was the easiest to use; when you pressed it, you'd begin to draw blue Stix. Close up a shape and it would fill in with a solid blue color, and you'd earn points. You'd lose a life whenever the Qix touched one of the Stix you were currently drawing or if you touched one of the free-roaming Sparx that traversed various lines on the board. When you drew the red Stix using the Slow Draw button, you'd spend that much time at risk of getting caught out, but you'd earn double points for completing a red shape with it.

Complete 75 percent of the board (the default; sometimes operators switched it to as little as 50 or as high as 90) and you would win bonus points and move on to the next, tougher level. As you played, you'd create increasingly intricate designs containing dozens of rectangles in two different colors. Combined with the fluttery Qix and the roaming Sparx, the board resembled a futuristic digital quilt, which combined well with the chorused square-wave sound effects. Later levels added more Sparx and even multiple Qix, which afforded you a new way to finish a board: split it so that two Qix ended up in different sections. You also couldn't stop drawing a shape halfway through; if you did, the Fuse would appear and eat up the Stix you had laid down. If you ever drew a spiral, there would be no way out and you'd have to double back on yourself and lose a life.

A counter at the top portion of the screen let you know when the next Sparx would appear, as well as when they'd all mutate into deadly, faster Super Sparx. A big part of the strategy was to gradually build your shapes from the outskirts of the playfield toward the center of the screen, taking advantage of slow drawing when you could to earn more points but ultimately focusing on staying alive and completing levels. It was also important to know when to abandon a box you were drawing, if your marker was at too much risk of getting nabbed, or if the Qix was too close to your shape for comfort.

Qix excited players at first with its unique gameplay, and then struggled to maintain fans. It was "the territorial imperative in game form," Bill Kunkel and Arnie Katz wrote.[9] "*Qix* was conceptually too mystifying for gamers...It was impossible to master[,] and once the novelty wore off, the game faded," said Taito's Keith Egging in 1983.[10] Nonetheless, the game was ported to many different home systems, and it retained a cult following over the years. Call it the thinking player's action game—although no amount of thinking compensated for poor reflexes with Qix.

Frogger (Konami, 1981)

Why did the frog cross the road? Clearly because the chicken was unavailable, but who needs all that clucking anyway? In what soon became an industry-wide attempt to figure it all out, Konami's *Frogger* became its own arcade phenomenon. As with *Pac-Man*, *Frogger* was a refreshing, nonviolent alternative to the countless shooting and space games normally found in arcades. The playfield was divided into two main areas: a two-way, multi-lane road full of cars, trucks, and bulldozers, and a river stocked with floating logs, alligators, turtles, and other hazards. You helped your frog across the road and river, guiding it into one of the five empty homes at the top. You started the game on the sidewalk at the bottom; another sidewalk in the center gave you a moment's respite between the road and the river. When you filled up all of the available homes with frogs, you'd start again on a more difficult level.

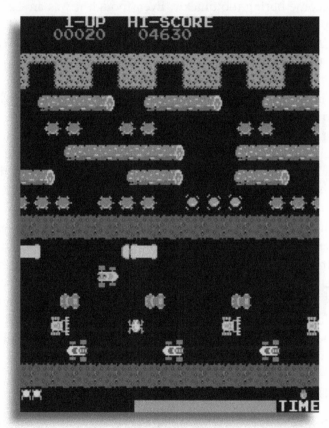

Figure 5.4: *Frogger* was, in video game form, the same game we all play when crossing busy city streets.

The game's control scheme consisted of a single four-way joystick that moved the frog with each tap in the appropriate direction. You couldn't hold the stick in one position; you needed to tap it repeatedly to move the frog multiple times. In the river, some of the logs would sink and reappear, so you'd have to time your jumps just right. The same went for some of the turtles and alligators, with the added challenge that you could only safely jump on the alligator heads near the eyes, not their gaping mouths. Sometimes, a "lady frog" would appear on one of the logs, which you could nab for bonus points.

Frogger was one of the earliest games to feature a full, multivoice soundtrack.[11] It played catchy renditions of popular Japanese songs and Americana such as "Yankee Doodle" and "Camptown Races" that became impossible to separate from the gameplay. The variety of tunes ensured that it didn't become boring too quickly. Even though it was an easy game to learn and play, it soon became difficult, with *Softline* magazine declaring in 1982 that "*Frogger* has earned the ominous distinction of being 'the arcade game with the most ways to die.'"[12] Whenever that happened to you, a skull and crossbones would appear where the frog once was.

In an interesting switch-up, *Frogger* may have been inspired by Freeway, David Crane's Atari 2600 cartridge. In that game, you were a chicken that had to cross a busy highway while avoiding speeding cars and trucks. Bill Kunkel called the bottom half of *Frogger*'s board a "straight knockoff of Freeway's traffic-jammed roadway," but nonetheless praised the game's more interesting second half of the journey for each frog.[13] *Frogger* had plenty of staying power in the arcades, at a time when many owners and operators had already begun cycling out older machines for newer ones.

Frogger was also ported to all major game consoles and home computers of the time. This became another point of contention for owners of certain systems to debate which one played the game best and whether the music was retained, because people love arguing. *Frogger* even found its way into pop culture, with appearances in a television cartoon in another song on the same album as "Pac-Man Fever," and even as a plot point on *Seinfeld* many years later.

Galaga (Namco, 1981)

Namco's *Galaga* took *Galaxian*'s dive-bomb attack, sped up the gameplay, and added new game mechanics, such as doubling up your ship for extra firepower. The game started with a trademark multivoice theme song—a concept *Pac-Man* debuted. The basic layout of the game was similar to *Space Invaders*: Convoys of invading space aliens filled the top of the screen, and you controlled a spaceship that had to eliminate all of the aliens in a convoy to move on to the next round. If one of them shot you, you'd lose a ship, and the game ended when you had none left.

Past the above, though, there were many differences. The convoys were made up of three kinds of aliens: Galaga command ships, red Galagas, and blue Galagas. When the game started, the aliens flew in, spun around, and arranged themselves in formation at the top of the screen. You could pick off some of them during this process, especially as they swooped close to you (although in later stages they would also try to bomb you simultaneously). Once all of the aliens arrived in place, they began dive-bombing attacks in squadrons of up to three. Meanwhile, the rest of the convoy would expand and contract, almost as if it was a single collective unit breathing instead of a group of individual aliens. You could fire up to two shots at any one time, but you needed to wait for at least one to reach the top or hit an alien before you could shoot again.

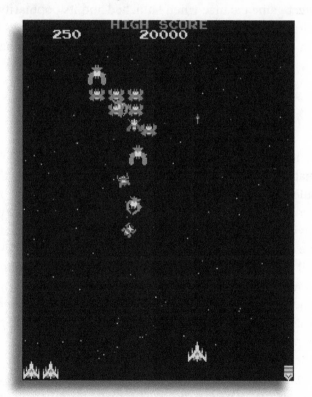

Figure 5.5: A high-water mark for vertical space shooters, *Galaga* polished and refined the mechanics to a slick sheen.

You could destroy red and blue Galagas with single shots. A Galaga command ship took two shots to eliminate; the first shot changed its color from green to blue. Sometimes the command ship would descend and emit a tractor beam to capture your fighter. If that happened, your fighter changed from white to red and stayed with that command ship, and you would then assume control of one of your reserve fighters and attempt to free the captured one. If you shot the captured fighter by accident, it would be destroyed. Clear a stage and you'd begin the next, more difficult one, with an extra flag shown in the bottom-right corner of the screen to indicate the current stage. The game awarded a free ship at 20,000 points, 70,000 points, and then every 70,000 points thereafter. Unlike most arcade games, it told you this in ready-to-play mode after a quarter was inserted. At the end of the game, it displayed a "Results" statistics page that listed the number of shots fired, the number of hits, and your hit-or-miss ratio.

Designed by Shigeru Yokoyama, *Galaga* received critical acclaim for its near-perfect game balance when launched and its popularity only grew over the years. Perhaps more than any other shooter, *Galaga* is often remembered as a peak Golden Age arcade game, even more so than *Space Invaders*. Many consider it the ideal space shoot-'em-up coin-op. The appeal of *Galaga* seems eternal, attracting plenty of fans to this day.

Tose

Tose was founded in 1979 in Kyoto as a video game company, but not one in the traditional sense. It was primarily a behind-the-scenes "ghost" developer, one that made games for other, more established brands. "Our policy is not to have a vision. Instead, we follow our customers' visions," vice president of Tose's U.S. division Masa Agarida said in 2006. "Most of the time we refuse to put our name on the games, not even staff names. We're ninja developers!"[14]

Tose still exists today and has developed about 1,000 games, mostly uncredited for its work. It developed some popular Nintendo products, including Game Boy Gallery and Game & Watch Gallery, original NES cartridges such as the Bases Loaded series, and many Dragon Ball games. Tose is only known for a single popular arcade game—and "known" is a stretch, given that the name Tose is nowhere to be found on the cabinet. Instead, Centuri licensed the coin-op for U.S. distribution, SNK distributed the coin-op overseas, and Cinematronics later made it into a cocktail model.

Vanguard (Tose/Centuri, 1981)

Defender pioneered the horizontal-scrolling shooter, but *Vanguard* turned it into an adventure. You flew the Vanguard spacecraft to save space colonies under attack from the Gond by navigating several tunnels, each with a varying number of stages and enemy alien invaders. A barometer at the top-right corner of the screen let you monitor your progress. In the first tunnel, there were eight stages: the Mountain Zone, the Stick Zone, the Stripe Zone filled with enemy bases, the Bleak Zone, and three Rainbow Zone stages interspersed between them. Each zone consisted of two sections, with the second being a bit tougher. If you reached the eighth and final Mystery City Zone, you had to destroy the Gond by shooting him between two moving barriers. This accomplishment would net a random bonus of 1,000 to 8,000 points. The next tunnel included the stages in a different order and only one Rainbow Zone.

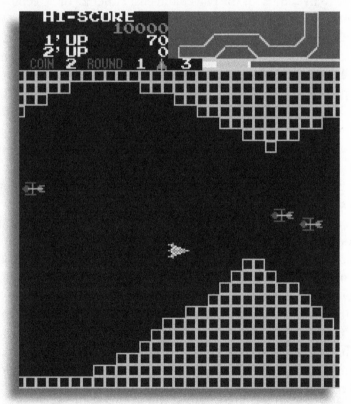

Figure 5.6: *Vanguard* **turned** *Scramble* **into an adventure, complete with multiple stages and several scrolling directions.**

Vanguard was primarily a horizontal scrolling shooter, but also moved diagonally in Rainbow Zones and vertically in the last zone. An eight-way joystick controlled the spaceship's movements, and an array of four Fire buttons shot up, down, left, and right. This dual-control method let you shoot in different directions independent of how the ship was moving and foreshadowed later games with dual joysticks for movement and firing weapons.

Technically, your ship consumed fuel. But as shooting each enemy refueled your ship a bit, this dynamic didn't affect gameplay much. More challenging was the environment. You'd lose a life not only whenever you collided with an enemy invader or one of its missiles, but also with any of the terrain. Scattered throughout the zones were energy pods; passing your ship through one temporarily made it invulnerable and let you crash into rockets and bases to destroy them. You'd earn bonus ships at 10,000 and 50,000 points, and the machine could be configured to provide anywhere from three to five ships for the player and cost either 25 or 50 cents per play.

Of note were the sampled voices, a first for Centuri and an attention-grabbing novelty. The game announced "Bon Voyage" at the beginning and called out the various Zone names as your ship reached them. It also warned "Be Careful" whenever an energy pod protection was about to wear off. The game even laughed at you during the Bleak Zone stage. *Star Trek* fans would pick out the musical theme, which was lifted from *Star Trek: The Motion Picture* (and later used as the title theme to *Star Trek: The Next Generation*), and *Flash Gordon* fans recognized the Energy Zone power-up music as "Volton's Theme" from the 1980 movie. *Vanguard* also offered a continuous play feature so that you didn't have to become an expert to see the later stages.

Vanguard's technical advances, string of "firsts," and balanced gameplay made it the perfect space shooter, and it received well-done home conversions on the Atari 2600 and 5200. One of my formative nerd experiences was playing this game out at an arcade near a Ramada Inn on Long Island, getting both home versions, and then going back to Long Island with my parents the next time in part to see the differences (of which there were many, in the case of the still-good 2600 game, and still some with the 5200). Despite having both cartridges, I was always thrilled to play the real thing in the arcade and loved the voice enhancements, additional colors, and physical controls.

Turbo (Sega, 1981)

In *Turbo*, you raced a Formula 1 car cross-country on a variety of roads, at all times of the day, and had to pass as many cars as possible. Designed by Steve Hanawa, the game took place across bridges, tunnels, crowded cities, and out on open country roads, with nightfall, snow, emergency vehicles, and hills and dips in the road that reduced visibility. To complete each phase, you needed to pass 30 cars within the allotted time, earning more points the farther you drove. Crashing into another car would send you back down to the bottom of the screen in a zigzag pattern. If you crashed within the first round, it didn't matter, but after that point, you could collide with another vehicle only three times before the game ended. You'd earn a bonus life each time you completed a round.

Figure 5.7: *Turbo* amped up the vertical-scrolling car race game with accurate controls and multiple scenes to race in, from cities to seaside and rural areas.

Turbo was the game industry's first color game with sprite scaling, a graphics animation technique that changed the size of the sprites to reflect the distance they were from the player, and that Sega would go on to perfect in the years to come. As you played, it felt as if you were really driving through various road conditions and scenarios, some of which changed within stages and not just at the start of the next one. The sense of speed was palpable, if not realistic given how much slower the computer cars were. The game was well received, with positive reviews in *Computer and Video Games* and *Video*'s "Arcade Alley" column. The former said *Turbo* "bears more resemblance to the real thing than it does to the arcade industry's first primitive attempts to provide Grand Prix thrills," with the main improvement being the "marvelous graphics capabilities which put a whole variety of backgrounds and racing conditions on the screen."

Topping the model lineup was a seated environmental cockpit with a 20-inch vertically oriented monitor, and an LED-based instrument panel that displayed your score and recent high scores, similar to Sega's earlier *Monaco GP*. The control panel consisted of a smaller-diameter racing steering wheel, a two-position gear shift lever, an accelerator pedal, plus backlit oil and temperature gauges. A standard upright unit retained the same controls, gauges, and displays. Sega later made available a mini-upright that ditched the LED readouts and employed a smaller monitor, with the whole cabinet taking up just 3.4 square feet of floor space and weighing 190 pounds: "The perfect earner for space-conscious street locations as well as arcades."

Turbo was ported to several home systems including the Commodore 64 (as *Death Race 64*) and the Mattel Intellivision. But far and away the most significant port went to the ColecoVision. The game was sold in a large box that also came complete with a plastic steering wheel controller and a wired gas pedal that would sit on the floor, a combination ColecoVision packaged and sold as "Expansion Module #2" with *Turbo* as the bundled cartridge. The brilliance of the wheel design was that you could insert one of the ColecoVision controllers in a space next to the wheel so that you had full control of the game. The gas pedal was a simple on-off affair, but the steering wheel offered several levels of control in each direction. No home conversion would be "just like the arcade" for years, and the ColecoVision version still lacked graphical detail, but it was a towering achievement.

Hanawa said that developing *Turbo* was his worst time at Sega. The stress of the intense time he spent coding and debugging the game led him to a collapsed lung and a monthlong hospital stay.[15] Nonetheless, Hanawa stayed on to help develop the Sega Master System.

Tempest (Atari, 1981)

One of the most groundbreaking and significant coin-op games of the era, *Tempest* was both ingenious and devilishly hard. Designed by Dave Theurer, it's best known for its stunning color vector graphics, a first for Atari and branded Quadrascan Color. The display employed the same technology as Atari's black-and-white X-Y monitors, but it now included three color guns and higher voltage. Describing *Tempest* as a "space shooter" understates its innovation and influence. It let the player start a game at the same level as what had been previously achieved, provided that a coin was inserted within 30 seconds. Later games absorbed this into regular "continues," but here it was a novel concept.

Saying something looked as if it were from the future was already overused by 1981, but if you could say it about anything, it was *Tempest*. You controlled a yellow, claw-shaped blaster inside 16 different three-dimensional playfields designed like tubes, viewed from the top and with a vanishing point in the center, as if you were looking down into a well. Each playfield consisted of 16 connected blue rails that converged on the farthest edge. Enemies appeared at the far end and began climbing toward you. You would destroy as many as possible by rotating around the closest rim of the tube and shooting down at them before any arrived at your side and collided with you. The spinner knob on the control panel rotated the blaster around the edge of the playfield. The edges of your ship always touched two rails, which formed a lane; those rails would change color to yellow, like a flashlight that would light up the tube so you could see which lane you were shooting down. The Fire button shot up to eight bullets at once in rapid-fire sequence, depending on how long you held it. Each time you hit an enemy, that enemy would vaporize; otherwise, the shot would reach the far end of the tube and disappear. In addition to shooting enemies, you could also trigger a superzap, which flashed the playfield and destroyed all the enemies on it. You also had a second superzap per level, but the second one would only destroy one random enemy, and it did nothing for flying enemy shots or spikes.

Destroy all the enemies on the board and you'd warp through the tube, fly through space, and come in for a landing on the edge of the next playfield. Each warp restored your superzaps; the game displayed "Superzapper Recharge" over the board during each transition sequence. If you were good enough to complete all 16 playfields, the next 16 changed color to red; then yellow, then cyan, then (frighteningly) invisible, and then green after level 81.

Six kinds of enemies stalked you. Flippers appeared at the far end on the playfield, slid toward your side, and would then begin flipping their way toward you on the edge. If you couldn't eliminate a flipper before it arrived, you still had one last chance to destroy it by sneaking under it and shooting it right before it landed on you with the last flip. Tankers rode between rails and carried one or two other enemies. Fuseballs hopped from rim to rim trying to land on you. Pulsars could ride in both directions as well as do the flip thing on your edge of the board. The dreaded Spikers rode the rails and grew spikes, which originated at the rim and built up toward you; get impaled and you'd lose a ship. The spikes also became a devious threat when you finished the level, at which point you would warp to the center at high speed while having to avoid the spikes. You could shoot the spikes away bit by bit, which became necessary the further you progressed in the game. Colliding with any enemy, bullet, or spike destroyed your ship.

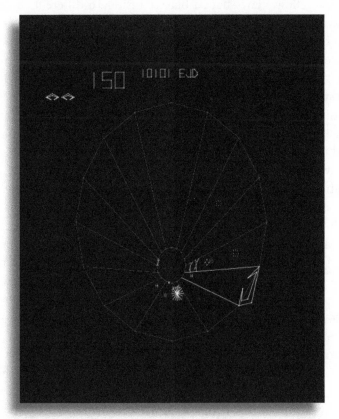

Figure 5.8: *Tempest's* **color vector graphics and 16 different levels were at once unique and brilliantly designed.**

Veteran game designer Chris Crawford praised *Tempest*, writing in *Byte*, "[*Tempest*] intimidates many beginners because it appears to be unwinnable," but noted that its smoothly increasing difficulty encouraged gamers to continue playing.[16] The game went on to influence such talents as Jeff Minter, who created the impressive *Tempest 2000* and *Tempest X* sequels for the Atari Jaguar and Sony PlayStation. It proved tough to convert for home use, with the only passable versions appearing in the late 1980s and early 1990s on more powerful platforms such as the 16-bit Atari ST and an unofficial clone called *Arashi* for the Mac. *Tempest* also showed up in the music video for Rush's "Subdivisions" and became a plot point in Ernest Cline's 2011 book *Ready Player One*.

Tempest wasn't the biggest hit for Atari, but it developed a devoted following. It was a new idea, a game that was impossible to make earlier and impossible to simulate in real life. Much like the wireframe playfields in the game, *Tempest* seemed to exist in another dimension.

Bosconian (Namco/Midway, 1981)

In this multidirectional-scrolling space shooter, you fought various incoming enemies from Bosconian space stations against an interstellar backdrop. *Bosconian* had the telltale polished graphics and audio of a Namco game, especially the sound effects and the main theme song. But *Bosconian* was most notable for its voice commands, such as "blast off!", "battle stations!", and "alive! alive!" (Various sources say the last one was supposed to be either alert" or "alarm" said twice, but I heard "alive" in my head.)

The main control stick moved in eight directions and was capped by a red ball. Push the stick and your ship would turn and fly in the appropriate direction. The Fire button shot unlimited rounds out of the ship's fore and aft sides. The playfield took up most of the screen, but a column on the right displayed the current score, high score, the "condition" of the stage (green, yellow, or red), a long-range scanner showing the locations of enemy bases in green and flashing red attack formations, the number of ships you had left, and the current round. If you scored 20,000 points, you'd get a bonus ship, and you'd get another every 70,000 points thereafter. You could also continue where you left off by inserting another quarter before a short timer ran out.

During gameplay, your ship stayed at the center of the screen. A round consisted of a group of green enemy space stations, each with six cannons around the edges; you could destroy those, or just skip them and shoot the station's core to destroy it and earn 1,500 points. As you did this, you needed to avoid or eliminate numerous kinds of enemy ships and missiles, including squadrons in formation. Stationary asteroids and cosmo-mines also littered the path; you could destroy them, but collide with one and you'd lose a ship. The game started in condition green, where it would say "blast off." Once you neared a station with enemy activity, it would change to condition yellow and shout "alive! alive!" As the attacks wore on, it would go to condition red and the game would get faster and deadlier. Sometimes the voice would say "spy ship sighted," and you had to act fast. Spy ships were worth a mystery number of points, but if you weren't fast enough, it would send the round into condition red immediately, regardless of its earlier state.

Electronic Games called out *Bosconian*'s robust instructions, in that Midway "actually [provided] players with hints on how to score higher and play longer." The company provided a booklet with each cabinet in a slot on the side of the machine, but if a gamer wanted their own copy, they could write a letter to Midway's Illinois address re: "Bosconian Scoring Tips."[17]

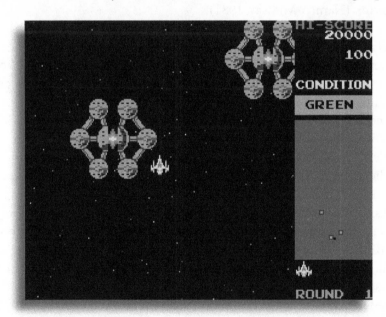

Figure 5.9: This four-way space shooter wasn't a huge sales success, but *Bosconian* was certainly fun to play and downright intense in a Condition Red.

For whatever reason, *Bosconian* was unsuccessful as an arcade machine and has been left to history, with no conversions on any popular consoles or computers at the time aside from the MSX in Japan. There have also no recent reboots, conversions, or even appearances in most of the Namco collections aside from a 1990s one for the first Sony PlayStation. Even so, *Bosconian* won *Electronic Games'* 1983 Arcade Award for "Best Science Fiction/Fantasy Coin-Op Game," with the magazine saying it "had the kind of action that is guaranteed to keep you glued to the controls," and highlighting the ship's fore-and-aft firing and secondary radar display.[18] *Bosconian* may not have the instant and near-unlimited appeal of *Galaxian* or *Galaga*. But for the few who remember it or find it for the first time—perhaps by reading this book!—*Bosconian* was plenty enjoyable.

Stargate (Williams, 1981)

Shortly after the release of *Defender*, Eugene Jarvis and Larry DeMar left Williams to form their own company called Vid Kidz. The two continued to develop games for Williams, starting with a sequel to *Defender*. *Stargate* arrived just eight months after *Defender* was released. Numerous differences marked *Stargate's* gameplay. First up were new enemies, which included Space Guppies (seriously), Dynamos, Space Hums, Phreds, Big Reds, Firebombers, and Munchies. Each humanoid you rescued in a wave would be worth more points: 500 for the first, 1,000 for the second, and so on. *Stargate* equipped your ship with a new Inviso feature, a cloaking device that made you both invisible and invulnerable for a brief period of time. Every 10,000 points, you'd earn another ship, smart bomb, and extra Inviso time, a bounty that helped make up for *Stargate's* insane level of difficulty. The rest of the controls remained the same, with a two-way joystick for maneuvering up and down, plus buttons for Reverse, Thrust, Fire, Hyperspace, and Smart Bomb.

Periodically, you'd come across a Stargate, represented with three concentric rectangles of different colors. Fly through it and you'd immediately warp to a portion of the board where some type of abduction activity was occurring, be it a straight abduction, more than one, or a falling humanoid. Otherwise, the gate would just take you to the opposite side of the planet. The Stargates also acted as a bonus warp. If you rescued at least four humanoids and then flew through a Stargate, you'd warp three levels ahead and gain an appropriate number of points, extra lives, bombs, and Inviso time—unless you flew into the gate in reverse, which would keep you on the same board.

As with *Defender*, if all 10 humanoids in a wave were abducted, the planet would explode, and you'd be thrown into a deep space battle with Mutants. The difference here was that if you made it to wave five, the game restored the planet, but all of the enemies became stronger and targeted you instead of the humanoids. Two special stages included the Yllabian Dog-fight, which first appeared at wave five and recurred every 10 waves, and the Firebomber Showdown, which first appeared at wave 10. And unlike *Defender*, *Stargate* kept track of 40 all-time high scorers and six daily high scorers, something we'd soon begin to see with other Williams games.

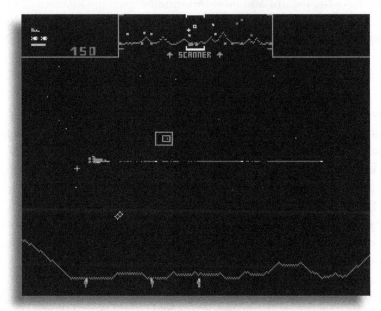

Figure 5.10: In *Stargate*, Williams updated *Defender* with new enemies, warp portals, and an even higher level of difficulty.

These were all small differences; despite the name change, *Stargate* was very much *Defender* with some gameplay tweaks. But perhaps most importantly, many of the strategies skilled *Defender* players developed didn't work in *Stargate*—making the new game difficult even for those with plenty of practice. No official sales figures were made available. But an interoffice memo where Atari estimated the sales of machines from competing companies pegged *Stargate* at some 15,000 units by the end of 1983, a good number for a sequel.[19] Other sources put the number much lower.

Video Games Go Mainstream

By 1982, video games were beginning to show up in mainstream culture—and unfortunately for arcade fans, more and more gamers were playing at home. Consumers would buy four million systems and 50 million cartridges in that year alone, and by the end of the year, 16 percent of homes would have at least one console. One survey showed the Atari 2600 was the most popular with 55 percent share, followed by the Odyssey 2 and Intellivision with 18 percent each. On the home computer front, the Atari 400/800 and the Apple II Plus were the most popular systems for gaming.[20]

Nonetheless, the video arcade still led the industry. "Coin-ops will still strongly influence home arcading this year," the editors of *Electronic Games* wrote in the May 1982 issue. "Companies are reluctant to put production money behind titles that haven't compiled a solid track record in the amusement centers. So, if you've played a game in an arcade last year, chances are good that you'll be able to buy a home version sometime in the next 12 months." The story noted a number of new entries would be games uniquely suited for the home, as they would be either too complicated or too long to be successful or profitable in arcades. These included "quest"- or "adventure"-type cartridges.[21] They would soon span movie tie-ins for blockbusters such as *The Empire Strikes Back* and *Raiders of the Lost Ark*.

In 1981, arcade gamers popped in between $5 billion and $9 billion in quarters and tokens—$200 million of which was for *Pac-Man*. By 1982, Atari made up 70 percent of Warner's revenue, more than its music and film businesses combined, and much more than it did back when Warner first bought Atari.[22] Arcades and amusement centers seemed to be everywhere, with coin-ops finding their way into airports, train stations, and movie theater lobbies.[23] Some arcades began to switch from quarters to tokens, with the rationale being that if you exchanged a dollar at the arcade for four quarters, you may decide not to use them all and save some. But if you're handed four tokens, you could only use them at the arcade. It also made it easier for the arcade to keep its books and track theft.[24]

With their increased memory and screen resolution, new coin-op games began to improve on the scant instructions shown for each game. *Electronic Games* pointed out that the "traditional joke among coin-op players has always been that game instructions generally consist of three words: Insert coin here." The latest arcade machines included some form of game instruction, either printed on the cabinet or as part of the attract mode. It was high time, too, because arcade games were also becoming more difficult. Coin-ops such as *Defender* and *Tempest* seemed unforgiving, and deliberately so. Since their inception, arcade machines had short shelf lives for two main reasons: The novelty wore off with market saturation (space games, maze games), and gamers began to get really good at them, which meant they'd last longer and longer on a single quarter. Both resulted in declining revenue, which would prompt operators to switch out the machines for new ones. Even *Space Invaders* wasn't immune; Bally Midway stopped producing it by 1981.

One way around the problem was to fiddle with the DIP switches inside the existing machine; most coin-ops offered higher difficulty options and lower numbers of lives, which operators could adjust toward the tougher end of the spectrum as gamers became too good at the games (though some took advantage of this and made the games too hard, too quickly, which discouraged players). Another way around the problem was for manufacturers to design brand-new games that were harder to get good at on purpose. Our next game is in the latter camp.

Zaxxon (Sega, 1982)

The shooter that put isometric gameplay on the map, *Zaxxon* used a groundbreaking three-quarter perspective view that foreshadowed the industry's quest for realistic three-dimensional gameplay. *Zaxxon* put you in control of a shuttle aircraft on a three-part space war mission. You needed to destroy various targets in an enemy fortress as you flew overhead, shooting and bombing enemy fighters, fuel tanks, satellites, radar towers, stationary guns, and more, all before taking on the boss robot at the end. Your ship's fuel tank slowly depleted; destroying a fuel depot would replenish some of it. Run out and your ship would crash.

Zaxxon displayed axonometric projection, which delivered a three-dimensional look from a third-person viewpoint and also lent the game part of its name. An important mechanic was the altimeter, which showed you how high or low you were and gave you a reference point more reliable than just eyeballing the colorful, but still low-resolution graphics. You needed that gauge, too, not just in the beginning when you first flew over the wall, but when you needed to avoid electric barriers and dodge enemy fire. Another assist in playing was the ship's shadow, the first time that effect had been used, along with a crosshair that showed where your fire would land once you pulled the trigger. Get through the entire first segment of the fortress and you'd then find yourself in deep space attacking squadrons of enemy fighters. During the space sequence, the shadow would disappear as there was nothing to project it onto, in which case the altimeter became the primary means of determining your ship's altitude. Once you destroyed enough ships, you'd fly back into the second half of the fortress. Reach the end and the boss war robot would appear and shoot heat-seeking missiles at you. You needed to shoot the missile launcher six times to destroy the robot and progress to the next round.

Zaxxon's primary control was an eight-way flight stick with smooth, accurate movements and well-balanced weighting, along with a trigger for firing weapons. The manual took pains to point out that the Zilog Z80A was necessary for operation, as the original Z80 wasn't "fast enough to run the programs." Like many of the arcade games to appear in the latter portion of the Golden Age, *Zaxxon* was known for its high difficulty, thanks to its relentless pace and unforgiving collision detection. Video magazine noted, "many players felt they needed flying lessons to have even a ghost of a chance of performing well."[25]

Figure 5.11: The game that put isometric graphics on the map, *Zaxxon* was an exceptionally tough scrolling shooter.

Ports quickly appeared on all the major systems of the day. The Atari 2600 and Intellivision weren't powerful enough to render the game in its proper three-quarter perspective, so those versions shifted to a behind-the-ship view. Other versions, including the ColecoVision and Atari 800 ports, came in for higher praise. Milton Bradley even adapted *Zaxxon* into a board game in 1983, the same way it had somehow managed to do with *Berzerk*, *Pac-Man*, and *Frogger*, all of which were short-lived.[26]

Although many home consoles had been advertised heavily on television, *Zaxxon* was the first arcade game to get its own commercial.[27] This was a smart play by Sega, as 1982 was right around the turning point where home console and computer sales began to compete with the coin-op versions. Getting players either back into the arcade or into one for the first time would juice revenue, and the technically advanced *Zaxxon* was the kind of game to pull it off. The flight stick control was also a novelty.

In addition to various clones, Sega released an official sequel called *Super Zaxxon*. Despite the name, the game was similar to *Zaxxon*, albeit with a new color scheme, different board layouts, a couple of extra enemies, a dragon end boss instead of a robot, and an overall higher speed of play that made the game even tougher, although it no longer had an interim deep-space stage. The game sold poorly as it was so close to the original model, although some existing *Zaxxon* cabinets were converted. Other games soon adopted the isometric concept, such as Sega's safari-themed platformer *Congo Bongo*, which somehow saw three million home conversions despite being a failure in arcades.

Robotron: 2084 (Williams, 1982)

One of the best games of the Golden Age of arcades, Williams' *Robotron: 2084* defined the dual-joystick shooter. The game was envisioned as third in a series, with *Defender* first, *Stargate* second, and *Robotron: 2084* third. In this last installment, as commander of the last spaceship, you were now stuck on the planet on your own and surrounded. Robots turned on humanity and began attacking everyone. Your job was to "save the last human family." (There were many such families in the game, with lots of "Mommy," "Daddy," and "Mikey" characters, but this was never explained.) You shot wave after wave of enemy robots, saving whatever human family members you could. Designers Eugene Jarvis and Larry DeMar said they were inspired by such games as *Berzerk*, where you ran through a maze shooting slow robots, and George Orwell's *Nineteen Eighty-Four*, which hadn't proved true yet, hence the jump 100 years forward in the game's title.[28]

Atari's *Space Dungeon*, released a month earlier, was probably the first game with twin eight-way stick controls. But *Robotron: 2084* is credited with popularizing the concept. Jarvis had the idea for the famed dual-joystick setup while lying in a hospital bed, after he broke his hand in a car accident. He loved *Berzerk*, but he hated the control scheme, where you used the same joystick to run as you did to aim and shoot, along with the Fire button. When Jarvis returned to work, he mocked up the dual-joystick concept by attaching two eight-way Atari 2600 joysticks to a panel. The left one moved your player and the right one shot lasers in rapid-fire succession. The brilliance of the design was that you could fire in a completely independent direction while moving.

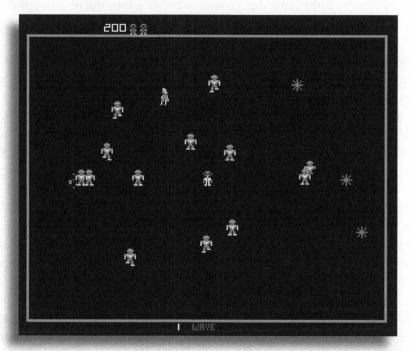

Figure 5.11: Perhaps Eugene Jarvis's greatest masterpiece, *Robotron: 2084* introduced the world to the twin-stick shooter, arguably the best-ever control scheme for such intense, dystopian gameplay.

In *Robotron: 2084*, you needed to, as the pace of the game was fast and relentless. The game started with stationary electrodes and large groups of Grunts, determined red robots that stalked the player. Later waves saw the introduction of the fearsome green Hulks; they were indestructible, although you could slow them down with your shots. There were also Spheroids that generated levitating Enforcers, which homed in on your player using a simple algorithm that targeted the pixels around the player in a random fashion. This led to an accurate but unpredictable travel path. Later still were Quarks that would produce robotic Tanks. Perhaps most memorable were the Brains. Every fifth wave was a Brain Wave. Brains chased the humanoids and turned them into frightening ghosts of themselves called Progs, which left a light trail behind them as they chased you at high speed. You could rack up your score in Brain Waves, as each Brain was worth a whopping 5,000 points.

The varied group of enemies, combined with the sheer number on the screen at any one point, made for a potent and challenging combination. "The philosophy of enemy design was to create a handful of AI opponents as unique as possible from one another, with unique properties of creation, motion, projectile firing, and interaction with the player," Jarvis said. "The enemies would be deployed in a wave-related fashion, with distinct themes for each wave. Some of the most interesting and deadly aspects of the enemies were bugs caused by improperly terminated boundary conditions in the algorithms. Often these bugs produced behavior far more interesting and psychotic then anything I conceived of."[29] Starting with the first Brain Wave (wave five) and then again every four Brain Waves (wave 25, 45, and so on), a bug in the code made all of the Brains target Mikey, while ignoring all of the mommies that populated this kind of Brain Wave. That means that as long as you kept Mikey alive, you could blast all of the Brains but one and collect all the human bonuses. These sorts of tricks were found in lots of coin-ops of the day and provided endless fodder for the myriad strategy guides on store bookshelves, as well as player-to-player gossip at the arcades themselves.

Despite the hardware's sluggish 1MHz 8-bit 6809 CPU and 1MHz custom image coprocessor, the graphics, sound, and animation in this game were spectacular. "The amazing thing is this slow circuit had more image processing power than PCs until the early 90s," Jarvis said. "What made it so powerful was that the image coprocessor was one the first examples of what later became known as a bit blitter—popularized by the Amiga computer…The coprocessor wrote two-dimensional objects to the bitmap with transparency, color paletting, color substitution, and other special effects."[30]

Electronic Games magazine called *Robotron: 2084* a "remarkable technical achievement," adding that "it is perhaps the fastest-moving arcade game ever created, with dozens of aliens converging on the player's surrogate as he attempts to hold back and destroy the attackers while rescuing the hapless inhabitants." Williams sold 19,000 standard-size cabinets, not counting additional cocktail and cabaret models. As veteran reviewer Bill

Kunkel wrote, "*Robotron* is a very simple game that faithfully follows the first law of coin-ops: easy to play, difficult to master." In a time of terrific coin-ops, *Robotron: 2084* was peak arcade.

Space Duel (Atari, 1982)

Combine the mechanics of *Asteroids* with the color vector graphics of *Tempest*, add a few elements, and you'd have the addictive *Space Duel*. In a single-player game, you could choose to play as a fighter ship or as a space station, the latter of which consisted of two starships (red and green) linked together with a fuse. Two players could play together, either cooperatively or competitively, making *Space Duel* the only multiplayer vector game Atari released.[31] The high score board separately tracked individual scores for one- and two-player games. The game consisted of 18 waves containing 12 different enemies, seven of which would split into smaller pieces.

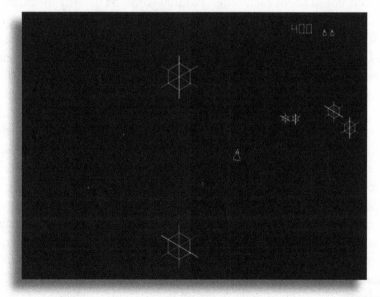

Figure 5.13: Dump *Asteroids* and *Tempest* into a blender, add some cooperative seasoning, and you get *Space Duel*, a compelling shooter that didn't quite find the audience it deserved.

According to Atari art director George Opperman, the art for *Space Duel* was some of his favorite during his tenure. The cabinet made it onto the album cover for The Who's 1982 record *It's Hard*.[32] *Space Duel*'s motherboard contained a MOS 6502 CPU and a pair of POKEY chips for audio. The controls consisted of buttons for rotate Left, rotate Right, Thrust, Shields, and Fire. As in *Asteroids*, each wave began with objects appearing at the edge of the screen. Destroy all of them and you'd move on to the next wave. Spinners took the place of asteroids; they'd even split into two, and then medium-size spinners would split into two small ones that would be destroyed when shot. As you reduced the number of targets on screen, two different alien saucers would appear, sometimes alone and sometimes both at once, firing around the board and becoming more accurate over time.

You could fire four shots at once. The shield protected you from all shots and collisions, but only lasted for a short time, and other ships could also destroy it. Space stations had more than double the strength shield. When damaged, your ship slowed down and you could only fire one shot at a time. In a space station game, a second hit would destroy one of the ships, igniting the fuse that would then blow up the other ship. In a fighter game, two players could shoot each other, but that wouldn't destroy the other ship; instead, it would disappear and reappear somewhere else on the board.

Each time a wave ended, a bonus level began with a low droning sound in the background. The game would box in the player and then send all manner of enemies into it; the goal would be to destroy them all. Run out of time or get hit, and the bonus level ended. You'd also receive a bonus ship every 10,000 points. Later levels replaced the spinners with octahedrons, cubes, pentagons, books, stars, and hexagons. Other enemies included fuzzballs that would try to collide with your ship and mines that would just become stationary and change color when hit and that would take many shots to destroy.

The vertically mounted coin door came with two separate keys, one for accessing coins and the other for servicing the coin collection system. It also had a failsafe lockout coil that would reject inserted coins if something was wrong with the motherboard or its connection. *Space Duel* did well, with some 12,000 cabinets sold between the upright and cocktail versions.[33] It sold better than *Asteroids Deluxe*, but neither coin-op was near the same level of hit as the original.

The Rise of GCC

The story behind General Computer Corporation was much more exciting than its name and had huge consequences for the arcade industry. It began at MIT, where two students named Doug Macrae and Kevin Curran set up a profitable coin-op route on campus with some 20 pinball machines. One day, they decided to add three *Missile Command* cabinets.[34] Initial revenue for the game was outstanding, at some $600 per machine in the first week, but it dropped off to just $200 per cabinet by week three as MIT students quickly became good at the game.[35] Either way, revenue plummeted. This was hard on small operators stuck with giant, outdated machines. To get around the problem, Macrae and Curran developed "PAL" boards that fit onto the circuit boards of existing machines to alter the gameplay. The boards watched the addresses in memory and would intercept Atari code with their own.

Macrae, Curran, and seven other college students developed the first board, called *Super Missile Attack*, to update the *Missile Command* cabinets and make them tougher to play. *Super Missile Attack* was faster, and it included some new enemies and color schemes. The team upgraded the three machines on campus, at a cost of about $30 per board. The operation was a success, so they took out ads in *Play Meter* and *RePlay* magazines under the name General Computer and tried selling the enhancement kits for $295 each. The ads worked, the demand was there, and they moved more than 1,000 units.[36] Atari wasn't happy about the *Missile Command* kits and sued for infringement—though the real reason was the huge threat these kits were to new Atari coin-op sales. The two sides agreed to a settlement where Atari would drop the suit and even pay them $50,000 per month to make games as long as they stopped making enhancement kits, unless given explicit permission from the original copyright holder. Atari let that last bit into the contract assuming no other company would give GCC permission.

McCrae and Curran went back to Bally-Midway and pretended they just won a suit against Atari (which they hadn't) and that they were going to build their next kit for *Pac-Man* machines, a new, less repetitive version of the game that would appeal to women.[37] They acted as if they just wanted to notify Bally-Midway in advance, when in fact they were bluffing the entire time, according to hardware designer Steve Golson.[38] It turned out Bally had no follow-up planned for *Pac-Man*, so company executives countered by suggesting they make the game a real sequel and not an add-in board.[39] In the end, Bally was pleased, as it was now off the hook for coming up with a *Pac-Man* sequel. All the company had to do was build more *Pac-Man* boards, attach a GCC kit to each one, make new cabinet graphics, and introduce the game to the world.[40] In turn, GCC hit the big time, although its name was nowhere to be found on the games.

Ms. Pac-Man (Namco, 1982)

Arguably the best in the *Pac-Man* series, *Ms. Pac-Man* had all-new graphics and sound effects, starting with the more melodious and memorable intro theme. *Ms. Pac-Man* wore a small red bow and lipstick, and the game was faster. When a monster caught *Ms. Pac-Man*, she'd spin around and die—or, rather, she "dramatically swoons and falls," as per the Midway brochure. Instead of just one maze that you played over and over, the game shifted between four separate mazes in different colors. The fruit no longer appeared in the center; it rumbled around the board for a few moments before exiting through one of the side tunnels. All of the intermissions between mazes were new; they told the story of how Pac-Man and Ms. Pac-Man met, got married, and had a baby Pac-Man.

Another difference was in the behavior and artificial intelligence controlling the ghosts. Blinky (the red one) and Pinky (guess which) incorporated some level of random movement despite their personalities. This meant you could no longer rely on learning and memorizing patterns to beat the game. The other two moved the same way as in *Pac-Man*, although the orange ghost was now named Sue; Inky was still cyan. Scoring was the same: Dots were worth 10, power dots 50, and the ghosts were worth 200, 400, 800, and 1,600. The bonus fruit started with cherries at 100 points; from there, it went to a strawberry (200 points), orange (500), pretzel (700), apple (1,000), pear (2,000), and banana (5,000). Unlike in *Pac-Man*, after the seventh fruit, each successive board would start with a random fruit worth 5,000 points. The game came in upright, cabaret, and cocktail table versions. To this day, you may find a *Ms. Pac-Man* machine that lets you move *Ms. Pac-Man* at twice her usual speed—which, if you can keep up at the controls, makes it much easier to progress further in the game and score higher.

Ms. Pac-Man was a smash hit in arcades, and the merchandising opportunities were unreal. It's estimated Midway sold 125,000 *Ms. Pac-Man* cabinets in the U.S., and the game was translated to every major home console and computer system. The most notable conversion at the time was the 2600 cartridge, which fixed everything that ailed the rushed, low-memory 2600 *Pac-Man* that broke sales records but nonetheless was a tremendous disappointment. Although nothing would capture the public imagination quite like *Pac-Man*, *Ms. Pac-Man* brought its own cultural significance with its female protagonist in a video arcade world dominated by teenage males. It also helped *Ms. Pac-Man* was a superior game.

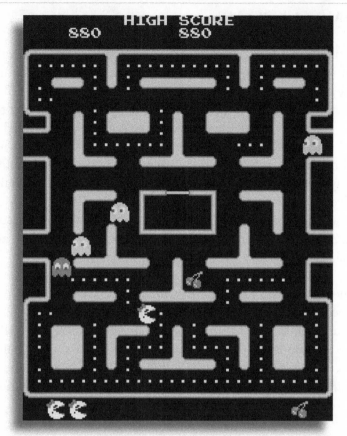

Figure 5:14 The conversion kit that launched a phenomenon, *Ms. Pac-Man* up-dated the original with multiple mazes, floating fruit, and most importantly, a female protagonist.

Random story: Back in 1998, I gave a talk at the International Computer Music Conference about video game sound, what was then becoming a new frontier in adaptive music that ebbed and flowed to how well the player was doing in the game, instead of just looping the same tunes on repeat. To set a different mood for what was a decidedly academic and research-focused audience, I began the talk with a digital audio tape (DAT) recording of about 30 seconds of *Ms. Pac-Man* gameplay, starting with the intro music and gobbling up some ghosts. The crowd began to laugh and then cheer, first at the intro theme and then more as *Ms. Pac-Man* audibly went after the ghosts. I was stunned that even the simplest game audio had such recognition in the audience. (Either that, or they were just relieved it would soon be time for lunch.)

Arcades Around the World

My own time spent in arcades was confined to the New York City area, in Brooklyn where I grew up as well as in Long Island and nearby northern New Jersey. That offered plenty of access to current machines, but the rest of the country and the world was often afforded with more luxurious arcade spaces. *Electronic Games* magazine ran a regular feature called "Arcade Spotlight" that would review a location, often with details about whatever the latest machines were as well as what old standbys were on offer. Some of the early 1980s locales were drool-worthy, such as an arcade built into a nightclub on a cruise ship in New Orleans ("The Paddlewheel," which is still around!) and one on the U.S. Aircraft Carrier Constellation (decommissioned in 2003). There was also a *Star Trek*–themed one in Mountain View, California, called Starfleet Command (now defunct).

Many of the "Arcade Spotlight" stories served to beat back the popular notion (not subscribed to by any *Electronic Games* readers, of course) that arcades were dingy, derelict places that only seedier types hung around in, smoking and talking about some form of juvenile delinquency that only existed in the minds of worried parents watching too many evening news programs. From the military installations to family centers, the arcades covered in the magazine were wholesome and cool, if both of those were possible together (maybe not, by definition).

Arcade game revenue jumped from $50 million in revenue in 1978 to an eye-watering $900 million in 1981, with $5 billion in total sales that year.[41] Bally's revenue increased from $693 million in 1980 to $880 million in 1981. Williams saw $83 million in sales the first nine months of 1980; that leapt to $126 million in 1981, and the company opened a new manufacturing plant in Illinois capable of making 600 to 700 *Defender* coin-ops per day.[42] The pinball industry stagnated as coin-op video game sales skyrocketed. By the end of 1981, just six pinball machines were sold for every 50 video games.[43]

Arcade games were all in full color and began to feature more detailed graphics as well as background music. And vector graphics games were becoming commonplace, with many releases from Cinematronics, Atari, and Sega, and the first color vector graphics coin-ops began to appear as well. Arcade game screens were incredibly sharp, not just with vector monitors but also with RGB video signals. The cables contained three colors that corresponded with the electron guns in the picture tube. Televisions, in contrast, carried RGB plus a load of other signal information over a single cable, including audio, sync, and radio frequency for broadcast.[44] Even if consoles had similar memory capacity and hardware power as arcade games—which they didn't—the picture would never look as good. Nonetheless, console production also hit an all-time high, with its market tripling in size and projected to reach $2 billion on its own by the end of 1982.[45] The Atari 2600 and Mattel Intellivision were enjoyable and gave players hours of gaming at home. But the arcade remained an unmatched social, technological, and adrenaline-pumping experience.

By all accounts, it was a terrific time for video games. No one could imagine it ever changing.

6 > Light Speed

The first two consumer magazines dedicated to video games were *Computer and Video Games* and *Electronic Games*. The first was a British publication that focused on home computer programming and reviews of commercial software games. The latter, more relevant for our purposes, covered console cartridges as well as arcade, home computer, and handheld games. The magazine was edited by Arnie Katz and Bill Kunkel, the same two folks behind "Arcade Alley" in *Video*, and included news, game reviews, tips, and roundups of new machines, with regular features on arcade locations around the world and deep dives into topics such as how arcade games were manufactured.

It was a fantastic read not just for the detailed coverage but for the insights as they evolved. For example, as part of a space game roundup in the March 1982 issue, a small section called "Multi-Phase Mayhem" covered the latest batch of titles (*Gorf, Phoenix, Pleiades, Vanguard*) that included "multi-scenario contests," which today we would just call levels. "Skilled arcaders prefer the idea of a dozen or so mini-games to repeating the same play sequence 10 or 12 times in a row," the editors wrote, in a shot at all of the single-board or even fixed-screen arcade games of the preceding 10 years.[1]

Arcades also continued to shed their seedier reputation. A 1982 *InfoWorld* article detailed the way two 12- and 13-year old friends would play coin-ops upwards of 100 times per week, and that at 25 cents a pop, it became an "expensive habit."[2] Arcade games could "amaze the senses and frustrate the faculties," and the current number one game was still *Pac-Man*, where "lines and crowds form around these screens." This was happening at a store called Gameways, a shop on Manhattan's Upper East Side that sold coin-op cabinets (at six per week on average) but that also let all the local kids play as if it were an arcade. The article concluded by saying, "The famous entertainment district around Times Square now features *Pac-Man* machines in arcades vying with girlie cinemas and Broadway theaters for consumer dollars."

Merchandising

Thanks to the wild success of arcade games such as *Pac-Man*, *Asteroids*, and *Defender*, merchandising became a profitable ancillary market for manufacturers. Vast arrays of accessories popped up that included everything from board games, T-shirts, collector pins, sweatshirts and jackets, bumper stickers, stuffed animals, and lunch boxes to bizarre ideas such as the song "Pac-Man Fever" and *Asteroids* chewing gum.[3] By the end of 1982, there were more than 600 *Pac-Man* products licensed through Midway.[4]

With the video arcade's newfound wholesome image and merchandising, it was only a matter of time before the motion picture industry took notice. Walt Disney Productions became the first major studio to release a movie about a video game. *Tron* was a science-fiction thriller about a computer expert who operated a local video arcade and who was looking for evidence to prove his former employer stole his game programs, only to find himself stuck inside a video game and sentenced to death. His former colleagues then had to help him defeat his employer. The movie employed backlight photography and exposed the live action frames through different color filters to get a unique glow effect for the circuitry, along with some computer-generated images.[5] *Tron* received an Academy Award for Technical Achievement and was nominated in several other categories, but it didn't get nominated for Best Visual Effects because the Academy considered using computer-generated images to be cheating at the time.[6] Aside from the usual merchandising, Disney also lined up agreements with three manufacturers to produce coin-ops, handhelds, and home video game cartridges of various sequences in the movie.[7]

The film itself was a disappointment, but *Tron* nonetheless became something of a pop culture phenomenon. It was also the first movie to put live actors in a computer-generated world.[8] Soon, it would be arcade gamers' turn.

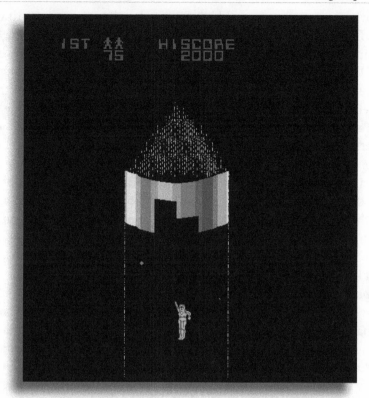

Figure 6.1: Video games hit Hollywood with *Tron*, an imaginatively designed coin-op with four minigames based on the Walt Disney motion picture.

Tron (Bally Midway, 1982)

If *Tron's* main goal as a coin-op was to capture the computer-generated world shown in the movie, then it succeeded. In the game, developed by a team led by Bill Adams, you played as Tron, a video warrior of the Electronic World. You had to defeat the tyrannical Master Control Program (MCP) and its top warrior Sark, who were doing everything they could to "derezz" you. The coin-op consisted of four minigames that mirrored scenes of energy and light from the movie: I/O Tower, Tank Maze, Light Cycle Grid, and MCP's Domain. In these minigames, you controlled either a human player or a vehicle, using a slick eight-way flight stick with firing trigger and a companion rotary dial on the left that would aim your shots. There were 12 levels, each named after programing languages. *Tron* began with RPG, and progressed through COBOL, BASIC, FORTRAN, SNOBOL, PL1, Pascal, ALGOL, Assembly, OS, JCL, and User.

Start a game and you would be presented with four maze quadrants to choose from. Each was a different color and corresponded with one of the minigames, and the locations were randomized each time. I/O Tower (for Input-Output) pitted you against a series of bugs on a grid emanating from the tower; they'd come out, grow, and multiply until they took over the entire screen. You were equipped with a light disc, and had to enter the tower to gain another disc. In Tank Maze, you drove a red tank that fired bouncing energy pellets at Sark's blue tanks; a pink diamond randomly relocated you to a different part of the maze. In the Light Cycle Grid, you rode a blue cycle using the trigger as a throttle. The point was to box in your opponents so that they ran out of room—without crossing any of the dangerous light traces the cycles laid down in their wake, and without crashing into the walls. In MCP's lair, you needed to blast a hole in the rotating color column as it descended toward you; if you shot a hole in it and managed to reach the cone of light above, you'd win the game.

Tron's graphics followed Syd Mead's set design, with vibrant electric blues, reds, and yellows (it would have made for an ideal Quadrascan X-Y game, had Atari released it). Bally Midway built some advanced operator options and diagnostics into the machine, such as a continue feature that only worked after the player completed three of the minigames, as well as nine difficulty settings. The company manufactured the game in standard upright, cabaret (increasingly called "mini"), and cocktail versions. Total sales figures are hard to come by, but the game received a tremendous amount of press in the video game magazines of the day, including a "Coin-Operated Game of the Year" award from *Electronic Games*. Even now, cabinets are prized by collectors (and not all that rare, if the classifieds are any indication).[9]

Tac/Scan (Sega, 1982)

As the fleet commander of a Tac/Scan squadron of seven ships in a distant galaxy, your objective in this fast-spaced, multiscenario Sega color vector game was to fend off a hostile armada of Annihilator and Stinger ships and escape. The Annihilators shot rockets, and the Stingers fired laser beams. In a unique twist, *Tac/Scan* let you control the use of ships as resources, instead of just burning through them sequentially until the game was over. As your ships on screen were depleted, you could press the Add Ship button— or dock with additional ships that appeared during gameplay. You could also fall back to just one ship and still have several in reserve, but if you lost that single ship, the game would end.

During play, another mechanic revealed itself. In the first wave, you'd shoot enemies from the usual top-down overhead view. In the second stage, the perspective would shift to three dimensions, with a view from behind your ship. The third stage was a twisting, eye-level, third-person view through a roller-coaster-like warp tunnel. You had to fly carefully here; crash any of your ships into the side and you'd lose it. It was like an amusement park ride, except with graphics. As with *Zaxxon*, *Tac/Scan* showed another way of achieving a three-dimensional effect that proved effective in the absence of anything such as today's graphics cards supporting the real-time rendering of zillions of simultaneous polygons.

Figure 6.2: A variation on the common space shooter, *Tac/Scan* delivered attractive color vector graphics and the first instance of a game with multiple perspective views.

Sega sold *Tac/Scan* both as a standard upright cabinet and as a "Convert-a-Game" kit that would update an existing *Space Fury*, *Eliminator*, or *Zektor* upright for less than half the cost of a new machine. The stand-alone cabinet was a garden-variety, wood-paneled affair with no side or front-panel graphics, and a marquee and bezel design that were somewhat difficult to read at a distance unless you already knew what the game was. The light-gray control panel presented a metal spinner control in the center, and a pair of red Fire and yellow Add Ship buttons on either side to accommodate one- and two-player games.

Sales figures remain a question, but it's clear *Tac/Scan* didn't gain the same worldwide recognition of other coin-ops such as *Zaxxon* and *Galaga*. That wasn't helped on the home front; the only port of the game was a mediocre 2600 cartridge that didn't do justice to the graphics and sound effects, for obvious reasons. But even more so than *Space Fury*, *Tac/Scan*'s super-smooth fast animation and gameplay, along with deep, resonating sound effects (some 1,300 variations in all) and alien explosions that sent lots of pieces in different directions, made this a shoot-'em-up unlike any other. It's worth seeking out an example of this rarer game to see in action just how good Sega's color vector graphics were—assuming the machine works. "As with all of Sega's vector games, the Electrohome color vector monitor used for this game has a notorious tendency to catch fire," according to the Killer List of Video Games. "It is unknown what to do to prevent this."[10] Maybe bring along a fire extinguisher just in case. (Come on, it'll be fine.)

Dig Dug (Namco/Atari, 1982)

The colorful maze game that became an unlikely smash hit, *Dig Dug* was everywhere in the early 1980s. As the miner Dig Dug, a blue-and-white robot, you spent most of this fixed-screen "strategic digging" game underneath a garden digging tunnels through dirt. You were equipped with a shovel and a pump. At the start of each board, which was a four-color cutaway section of the ground, Dig Dug would walk on the grass at the top of the screen until he reached the hole, which he would then descend so that the game started with him in the center of the screen. He slowed down when digging through the dirt.

There were two main monster enemies you needed to destroy to move to the next level: Pooka, a tomatolike creature wearing yellow goggles, and Fygar, a fire-breathing green dragon. The monsters, which started trapped in their own caves, soon began to chase you. You could strike back by inflating them until they popped, or by digging a tunnel underneath a rock that would drop down and crush them. You could also inflate them just one or two pumps of air worth; that would stun them so you could make your escape, even by passing by them. If either monster caught you when it was moving normally, you lost a life.

Figure 6.3: *Dig Dug* was a fun maze-digging game with colorful characters and exceptionally distinctive audio effects.

Once per level, after the second time you dropped a rock, a vegetable would appear in the tunnel where Dig Dug began the level; if you retrieved it within the 10 seconds it stayed on screen, you would score bonus points. One other detail: Although you "freed" Pooka and Fygar by digging into their caves, they could also travel through the dirt as ghosts and were impossible to inflate when in that state. They became vulnerable again once they landed back in a tunnel or cave. The last monster would always try to escape above ground; you'd lose points if he succeeded.

The rounds were indicated with flowers; one flower for Level one, two flowers for Level two, and so on. As you cleared levels, the monsters chased you a little faster and became better at avoiding falling rocks. Strategies included learning to turn around a corner earlier rather than later to gain speed and lining up monsters behind you so you could drop a rock on several at once. Destroying a monster on the bottom dirt level was also worth more points. Monsters moved faster vertically and slower on the surface grass. *Dig Dug's* PCB sported three Z80 CPUs—two for game control logic and one for sound, which drove Namco's own three-channel WSG chip responsible for the game's catchy soundtrack and 21 separate sound effects.[11]

"During the Golden Age of video games, we saw a lot of novel approaches to gaming," said Chris Lindsey, the director of the National Video Game and Coin-Op Museum in St. Louis. "'*Tempest*', for instance, required things of its players that we'd never seen in a video game before. You had to learn a whole new set of skills to further the game experience. *Dig Dug* is another game that provided a novel approach. The types of movement you had to learn, the skills you had to develop, were like none other up until that point.[12]

"And this gameplay was combined with a really engaging subject matter, which was this guy, *Dig Dug*, who digs around underground after subterranean monsters, and who explodes them with a really bizarre weapon, an air pump!" Lindsey continued. "There was just this string of interesting, engaging things for the viewer to look at and experience while dealing with this new type of game." He said the sounds in *Dig Dug* were also really distinctive. "When people hear that music start to play here at the museum, they'll laugh with recognition. It's quite funny watching people play that game."[13] *Dig Dug* became one of the most popular arcade games of 1982, with Atari selling some 22,000 cabinets. The game appeared on all of the main home computer and console systems of the day, with varying degrees of success. Like *Donkey Kong, Frogger*, and other hit coin-ops, the quality of the conversion was a subject of attention and intense debate.

Universal

Universal Entertainment Corporation began life as Aruze, a Japanese manufacturer of coin-op amusement games such as slot and pachinko machines. Among Universal's first two dozen or so video games were the influential 1980 release *Space Panic*, possibly the first platformer game with a digging (but not jumping) mechanic; *Cosmic Avenger*, a horizontal scroller with intricate backdrops depicting futuristic, *Jetsons*-like cities, with towering spires topped with inhabited glass globes; and *Lady Bug*, a nifty bug-themed maze game released in 1981 that combined *Pac-Man*–style dot eating with a series of opening and closing doors, changing the maze layout as you played. The next title we'll discuss further showed it was a gold-rush era of maze games, as *Dig Dug* wasn't even the only popular coin-op in the maze-digging subgenre.

Mr. Do! (Universal/Namco, 1982)

As the circus clown Mr. Do, you ate cherries and obliterated red monsters. Each level contained a series of passages, some earth to dig through, and multiple groups of eight cherries. The pathways were arranged in a layout that displayed "Do;" subsequent layouts looked like the corresponding level number, such as 2 or 3. You could move faster though the passages, and more slowly when you were busy digging new ones, which was necessary to reach the fruit. As you ate cherries, a musical motif would sound and rise in pitch with each one until you stopped. If you ate an entire group of eight cherries in a continuous unbroken pattern, the notes would rise through an entire musical scale and you'd receive 500 bonus points.

Meanwhile, monsters arose from a nest in the center of the board and chased *Mr. Do!* around. Pressing the button threw the ball, which would ricochet around the passages before returning to you, hopefully wiping out a monster on the way. Sometimes a monster changed into a multicolored silhouette and dug its own path, the same way *Mr. Do!* could. Another way to dispatch a monster was to drop an apple on its head by pushing it out into a passage, or as in *Dig Dug*, onto a thin piece of ground that the apple would pass through. The monsters could also do the same to you, so you had to be careful, and unlike you they could eat the apples.

Once all of the monsters were free of the nest, a cake remained in its place. If a monster then ate the cake, an "EXTRA" monster (alternately re-ferred to as the Alphamonster) appeared that held one of the letters of the word; three blue "creeps" would also materialize and chase you. The EXTRA monster also appeared every time you scored another 5,000 points. If you hit it with the ball, you'd collect that letter and it would light up at the top of the screen. Once you collected all five letters by defeating the appropri-ate EXTRA monsters, you'd get an extra life. Very rarely, a diamond would appear when an apple broke in half; if you grabbed it in time, it would give you 8,000 points and a free game, which was the biggest prize of all when it came to arcade games. In total, there were four ways to advance to the next board: eating all the cherries, eliminating all the monsters, spelling out the word EXTRA, or finding the diamond.

Designed by Kazutoshi Ueda for Universal, *Mr. Do!* proved massively popular, with 30,000 cabinets sold. It also appeared on nearly every home game console and computer, with the Atari 8-bit and the ColecoVision seeing the best conversions thanks to their greater capabilities. *Mr. Do!* didn't have much staying power after the video game crash, although it did appear on the SNES and in some 1990s game collections. But for a time, it seemed as if both *Dig Dug* and *Mr. Do!* were everywhere. People liked digging their own mazes. That the games were colorful and displayed cartoonlike graphics didn't hurt, either.

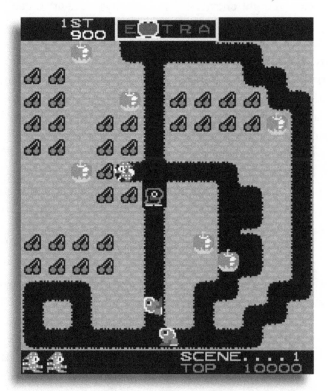

Figure 6.4: The other top-selling maze-digging video game of 1982, *Mr. Do!* introduced a shrewd but effective extra-life mechanic.

The first time I saw a *Mr. Do!* machine was at a roller rink in Sheepshead Bay, Brooklyn. The rink was called Roll-a-Palace and had opened sometime in the 1970s after the original movie theater closed down. Inside, several machines could be found in the lobby area where you rented the skates. The main rink was a sight for a sheltered 10-year-old in the early 1980s, with its pulsing strobe lights and the latest hits such as Shannon's

"Let the Music Play" and Herbie Hancock's "Rockit" blasting through tremendous towers of speakers along the perimeter. I don't want to bury this book in pop-culture references—this isn't meant to be the second coming of *Ready Player One*—but playing the games now, be it with emulators, Arcade1UP cabinets, or original hardware, can evoke wonderful memories of back when the games were new.

Coin-Op Lifecycles and Conversion Kits

Most gamers today tend to think of a video game's development as mostly software based—and rightly so, given that the hardware is a relatively fixed platform, such as a PlayStation console or a Windows PC, and stays that way for years. For arcade games, the process was much different. It involved teams of people, even back when the software development was still done solo.

After workshopping and prototyping different ideas, for example, game designers would choose from different kinds of monitors (X-Y, raster, vertical or horizontal orientation, and so on), along with color overlays of special design for the black-and-white monitors. A team of artists would draw the cabinet artwork, including the sides, the marquee, and the control panel. The hardware controls and the cabinet itself could be customized to suit the game in question. The manufacturer often tested the game on location in a couple of phases. Then the company set up the assembly line for manufacturing within the factory (and back then, U.S. games would always be assembled in the U.S.). Completed cabinets were sent to distributors, who signed contracts with establishment operators and brought the games to their locations.

Arcade coin-ops were complex, with plenty of mechanical and electronic parts. And although arcade components were built to a much tougher standard than home consumer gear, even those weren't impervious to abuse by competitive kids and adults alike. Often you'd see an "out of order" sign on a machine to let you know in advance. But sometimes you didn't, and whether you received your quarter back would be up to the kindness of the establishment's proprietor, if you could find them.

Given how these machines were treated in daily use, especially when someone was frustrated with a low score, it's surprising they didn't break down even more than they did (which was already often). Some failure examples common to the period were snapped joystick springs, loosened ground wires, crossed wires shorting out, jammed coin boxes, unresponsive buttons, blown power supply fuses, and circuit boards wiggling out of sockets.[14] Operator error was another issue; the volume may have been turned all the way down, for example, so it would seem as if the speaker was broken, or the game was inadvertently set to one life instead of three.[15] Collectors rescuing old machines today have even more problems to deal with, such as burned out (or burned in) screens, rotted cabinets from flood damage, and failing power supplies and cooling fans.

Back in the day, repairs were only so much of a problem because most coin-ops didn't last long on the arcade floor. Poor earners would barely make it to a month or two, and even the most profitable games were usually out after a year. Once it was time, the distributors picked up the machines and brought them to warehouses, for resale to private clubs, resorts, and collectors. Others would be taken back to the factory, reconditioned, and converted to new games before being sent back out again.[16] Third-party companies such as GCC and Romstar began selling conversion kits, off-the-shelf packages that let arcade owners convert an existing arcade game themselves on location for a fraction of what a new machine would cost ($500 on average, compared with the $3,000 necessary for a new upright cabinet). [17] These kits would contain a new motherboard or add-in board, new decals for cabinet graphics, and some other smaller hardware changes.[18]

Many lesser kits were simply derivative games with little staying power. Atari resisted the phenomenon, saying that the state of coin-op technology couldn't be advanced with conversion kits alone. The real reason: Their low cost and margins made it impossible for top designers to work on the games.[19] Eventually management caved, and manufacturers such as Atari, Sega, and Midway began selling kits as well. For example, Midway released *Pac-Man Plus*, an upgrade kit for *Pac-Man* cabinets that increased the speed of the ghosts, changed the board color, replaced the bonus fruits, and tweaked the appearance of the ghosts in regular and vulnerable modes. It also added randomized effects from gobbling up power pellets, such as turning the maze invisible or only turning three of the ghosts blue instead of four, making it impossible to use not just old but new patterns as well. The way it worked with *Pac-Man Plus* was that you would remove the Z-80 processor from the original board and then plug this new module's ribbon cable into that socket. The module contained a new Z-80 and other components, including replacements for the original cabinet's ROM chips, as well as a new marquee. Other conversion kits operated in a similar manner, and the concept soon became almost as common as buying or leasing new machines.

Irem Corporation

Irem started as a local store in Osaka, Japan, in 1969, founded by Kenzo Tsujimoto to sell cotton candy machines. Later, Tsujimoto branched out to pachinko coin-ops. In 1974, he established a larger company called IPM, which manufactured and installed video games in small stores. Tsujimoto's company began releasing its own video arcade games in 1978, starting with a clone of *Space Invaders* called *IPM Invader*. He soon rebranded IPM to Irem, for International Rental Electronics Machines, as indicated on a flyer for another space shooter called *Demoneye-X*.[20] Irem also manufactured and distributed coin-ops from other vendors, such as GDI's *Red Alert*, a 1981 shooter that resembled *Space Invaders*, but with an air assault and city defense theme.

Irem released its first breakout hit in 1982. It may have landed on Earth, but it was set 240,000 miles away.

Moon Patrol (Irem, 1982)

It wasn't easy exploring and defending the Moon—especially when no one else was helping you—but someone had to do it. In *Moon Patrol*, as an employee of the Luna City Police Department, you drove a six-wheeled purple moon buggy from one area of Sector Nine to the next, fighting off aliens targeting you from in front and overhead. Along the way, you navigated tough terrain that included boulders, volcanoes, land mines, and craters, and you only had a short amount of time to reach the next checkpoint. Each was denoted with a letter of the alphabet, starting at letter *A*. A gauge overhead showed you where you were on the course, which consisted of five sections: *A–E*, *F–J*, *K–O*, *P–T*, and *U–Z*. Subsequent sections introduced new obstacles, such as land mines. Complete the Beginner course and you'd move on to the more difficult Champion course, which would then repeat forever if you were good enough at the game.

Moon Patrol was known for its graphics, including what is commonly referred to as the first popular instance of parallax scrolling, where multiple levels of scenery scrolled at different speeds to add a sense of depth. Your view of the action was from the side; your buggy drove toward the right. The game depicted a rough lunar surface with a green-and-blue backdrop of mountains, hills, and space-city skyscrapers. The realism was amplified by the buggy's wheels independently traversing the bumpy terrain as it scooted across the surface. And no one could forget the bluesy, uptempo bass line that provided the audio backdrop underneath all of the sound effects.

The joystick controlled the buggy's speed. The Fire button shot missiles in front and up above, so you could take on flying enemies and stationary ground obstacles simultaneously. The missiles you shot in front traveled a short distance before vaporizing. The other button let you jump over craters, land mines, and other things in your path. Most obstacles you shot or overcame were worth from 50 to 200 points, and destroying something was worth less than jumping over it. Obliterating a UFO formation of three, four, or five ships earned you 500 to 1,000 points. Take out an alien car or space plant in later stages and you'd earn a random bonus from 300 to 1,000 points. The game also awarded bonus points for completing course sections. You earned an extra buggy at 10,000, 30,000, and 50,000 points, and you could continue from where you left off with another quarter.

Figure 6.6: Perhaps the game with the best bass line ever, *Moon Patrol* put you in a six-wheeled, weaponized lunar rover on a rocky obstacle course in an alien-infested sector.

Players learned to jump over two obstacles at once when necessary, drive faster to jump farther, and be extra careful around UFOs that dropped bombs and created new craters right in front of your buggy. No other game in the arcade was like it at the time. *Moon Patrol* received an excellent conversion on the Atari 5200 and near-perfect one on the 16-bit ST platform, and also appeared on a large variety of other systems through Atari's Atarisoft brand.

Kangaroo (Sun Electronics/Atari, 1982)

Sun Electronics launched in 1971 as an electronics equipment manufacturer and began designing and producing coin-operated arcade games in 1978, including *Arabian*, *Block Challenger*, and *Block Perfect*. It found its first hit with a platformer that Atari picked up for U.S. distribution, in one of the few cases where Atari didn't develop the coin-op game itself. *Kangaroo* was one of the first derivative platformers to land in the arcades after the runaway success of *Donkey Kong*—and one that attracted considerable scorn.

Figure 6.7: *Kangaroo* **was a good example of everything that could go wrong when a company decides to manage its way to a new video game rather than relying on its best engineers.**

You needed to rescue your "baby kangaroo," as told on the machine's instruction panel, to complete each round. You controlled the mother kangaroo, with a bounce in her step and some handy red boxing gloves. Monkeys chased you around and threw apples, which you could avoid by either jumping or ducking, and you could punch out the monkeys as well. Ringing the bell replenished the on-screen fruit. The first board was simple, with just three platforms to navigate before reaching the joey on the fourth and topmost platform. The second level added staggered platforms to jump on. The third consisted of a stack of monkeys that you either punched out or jumped over to reach your joey. The fourth was more complex, with lots of small platforms and ladders to navigate.

Kangaroo's cabinet was bright and cheerful, with white and yellow base coloring, nicely drawn kangaroos and fruit, green tree leaves, and lots of bold, blue, orange, and red lines. The control panel consisted of an eight-way joystick, although only six ways were used in the game. You could push up to jump, or diagonally up in either direction for a "super leap." Left and right bounced you along the platforms, and down would duck, handy for avoiding thrown apples. The game's intro sequence made no sense; three mother kangaroos on three different platforms would move to greet their joeys. But the top platform had a small hole in it, and for some reason your mother kangaroo fell through it. Weren't kangaroos supposed to be good at jumping?

The game exhibited some other problems. Chief among them was flicker, which seemed to affect the monkeys and your kangaroo the most. The high-pitched musical theme also annoyed; there was no reason it had to be in such a high register, and that carried over to some of the screechy sound effects and short musical motifs. Finally, the game just seemed sluggish and stiffly animated. Atari was known for fast games such as *Tempest*, *Centipede*, and *Gravitar*, so this made little sense. The sprites were large and well drawn, but each could have used a couple of extra frames. If you had just played *Donkey Kong* or *Galaga*, the lack of smoothness was noticeable.

So, what happened? The problem, as was often the case, was management. After the success of *Donkey Kong* and *Crazy Climber*, Atari executives wanted their own platform game, and fast—fast enough that the company's own engineers couldn't do it, at least to the standard they wanted to uphold. So management went out and licensed this game from an unknown company, did minimal field testing, set it up for mass production, and celebrated it internally as a fast and successful turnaround.[21] Atari engineers were having none of it—including Rich Adam, who was working on a new game called

Lunar Battle that was suddenly being shoved aside for *Kangaroo*. He wrote a memo, dated, May 4, 1982, to Atari's top executives:

> There is an epidemic raging through the Coin-Op Marketing and Engineering Management staff. The disease is called License Fever. It destroys the brain cells of its victims, crippling their thought processes. These poor souls can no longer distinguish between a product that is junk and one that has the quality the public identifies with Atari. How could a healthy, logical person make a decision to build a game of the caliber of Kangaroo based on one week's collections report? Such a decision must be the result of a severe cranial dysfunction.
>
> The impact of Kangaroo to Coin-Op's reputation is discouraging to think about. More serious however, is the impact within Engineering. The product teams that develop games here work extremely hard. For these individuals to have to compete with trash games like Kangaroo…for engineering support creates a very real morale problem. The mere consideration of these half-done games is confusing to engineers who are used to much higher standards. Result: even lower morale…[In] light of all the priority which is being given to these inferior games, I must ask myself "why am I working so hard to make a quality product?"[22]

No one in management acted on the memo. *Kangaroo* was nonetheless a sales success, with just under 10,000 cabinets sold and a bunch of home conversions that brought in additional revenue.[23] Sun Electronics went on to represent the Sunsoft brand, which developed original home console games and also ported some Sega titles for Nintendo, and the company teamed up with Acclaim Entertainment in the early 1990s for additional distribution before closing up shop in 1995. A later iteration of the company continued on developing games for platforms as diverse as the Neo Geo and the Game Boy Color. It still exists today. As for *Kangaroo*, it sees little love among collectors, and stands as a cautionary tale and an unheeded warning sign for the coin-op industry.

The Rise of Video Arcade World Records

A hallmark of the Golden Age of arcades was the desire to not just achieve the high score on the game that day, but to achieve one for all time, either locally or on a national level. News reports of the day would tell of young video game players who set records for duration of play as well as high scores, and how they would "master the game to the point that they could play them continuously until their bodies could endure no more pushing a joystick, pressing a button, and coordinating hand and eye."[24] This led to such examples as a 14-year-old in Maine playing *Asteroids* for 29 hours and 35 minutes, and a Washington State player holding defenses in *Missile Command* for 28 hours. Often a gamer would play as long as they could and would sacrifice a small portion of accumulated lives or ships in a game for bathroom breaks.

The way video games were designed also contributed to the high-score phenomenon. A difference between video games and pinball was that most of the skill you earned playing one game wouldn't necessarily transfer to the next, which would have different goals, hardware controls, rules, and strategies. With pinball, once you became good at one machine, you would just have to learn the playfield and multipliers on another and not have to relearn the rest of the skills.[25] Arcade games would always require more diverse strategies, thanks to their wildly different control schemes and in-game rules. But some common themes had developed: Focus. Don't panic. Keep your eye on your own ship and play defense; don't just shoot every-thing without ensuring you can stay alive as long as possible. Learn the rhythm of your shots and fire just the right amount, without being left for several seconds with none in reserve. If the game gives you bonus weapons, use them; don't just save them for later.[26]

Top players could spend hundreds of dollars over a few months getting good at their favorite game, and would seek out establishments that had the difficulty set low (such a granting free ships earlier or giving you more lives to start with) to get additional practice time.[27] Some gamers rose to the top of even this crowd, and the desire for championship gaming continued to grow. In 1981, Walter Day bought an arcade called Twin Galaxies in Ottum-wa, Iowa, and began to record high scores for every game in more than 100 video arcades across the country. He compiled the data and unveiled it the next February as the Twin Galaxies National Scoreboard. This became the premier target for gamers across the nation, as teams began to form on a state-by-state basis for national tournaments.

Day soon began organizing competitions across more than a dozen states to compete for high scores in *The Guinness Book of World Records*. The Gold Arcade Club launched a nationwide tournament in Colorado in 1982 with $100,000 in prizes; the competition was divided into seven age categories, and progressed from local to city, region, state, and international events.[28] The August 1982 issue of *Electronic Games* dedicated an entire page to all the new coin-op records set and the arcades across the country where existing records had tumbled, complete with photographs of the record-setters. Soon, the magazine began to run a National Vanity Board of score records for the most popular arcade coin-ops in every issue.

There were issues to work out. For example, sometimes there existed different versions of the same game, maybe with a bug fix or a tweak to the AI, and it was tough to tell which one you were playing. Another issue was the difficulty settings available to operators, usually via DIP switches or motherboard jumpers. Nonetheless, these questions were worked out over time, and to this day Twin Galaxies continues to maintain world records for arcade game scores. There's even drama, as the organization invalidated some scores Billy Mitchell achieved as shown in the 2007 documentary *The King of Kong*. After frame-by-frame examination, it was determined the records were achieved in emulation and not on a real cabinet, and the organization invalidated his records—only for *Guinness World Records* to reinstate them in June 2020.

Not all of the tournaments worked out, either. An Atari-backed tournament held in Chicago's Expo Center from October 28 to November 1, 1981, had promised $50,000 in prizes. Tournament Games, the company chosen to run the tournament, already knew billiard, foosball, air hockey, and dart competition. It promised 10,000 to 15,000 attendees, but it only managed to round up an "unbelievable" 150.[29] Among the issues were that not only did competitors have to pay for their own games, but the machines were rigged to stop after three minutes. It didn't help that the company also changed the rules and schedules mid-tournament. To cap off the disaster, Atari's prize checks to the winners all bounced. The company had to set up a toll-free support line to fix the problem for each person one by one.[30]

Tutankham (Konami, 1982)

Stern's next maze shooter, released just after the 1972–1981 exhibition of artifacts from King Tut's tomb, put you in control of a brave adventurer (grave robber?) in ancient Egypt. You explored a multitiered pyramid's tunnels to find as much treasure as you could within the allotted time. Along the way, you avoided enemies shooting at you and picked up keys to open special doors within the labyrinth. For reasons left unexplained, you had a laser pistol to defend yourself. There were also warps on each board that you could use to escape enemies by teleporting from one location to another in a straight line—or transport into even more danger, depending on what was happening on screen.

Figure 6.8: *Tutankham* capitalized on the popularity of *Raiders of the Lost Ark* with an addictive maze shooter set in Egyptian tombs.

The cabinet design evoked a medieval theme, if not quite Egyptian, with a jeweled sword to either side, a black bezel surrounding the monitor, and a fake-gold-inlay look for the marquee. Reportedly, the misspelling of the pharaoh's name was to fit it on the marquee, although there was plenty of space given the tall, thin font used in the final cabinet. The control panel consisted of a four-way joystick on the left that controlled King Tut's movements, a two-way joystick on the right that would shoot your power beam left or right, and a Flash button in the center. Using the latter, you could flash the screen and destroy all enemies once per board. A radar screen at the top showed you the entire playfield, not just the visible portion. The flash bomb and radar screen evoked *Defender*, and showed how a lot of games of this time period were mixing up elements of existing games as well as new ideas.

The game included one strange mechanic: You could only shoot left or right, even though you were in a four-way maze. In an era when color raster graphics were still limited, *Tutankham* made the most of what it had with its unique style. The sound combined space-age laser shots and exploding effects with Egyptian-themed background music and motifs. As part of its "Coin-Op Classroom" series of hints articles, *Electronic Games* ran a two-page story by monthly contributor Becky Heineman. Reading the story gave you hints, but more than that, Heineman's copy stimulated the imagination in a way that was common for the time period—by wrapping the hints in a second-person narrative reminiscent of young-adult, Choose Your Own Adventure–style books:

You enter the doorway. Walking down the corridor, you hear a crash behind you. The door behind you has sealed you in forever. You light your lantern and see an archway that fills with white smoke and a deadly cobra emerges. You shoot it quickly, but another takes its place...

This sort of thing helped make up for the lack of realistic graphics, just like the imaginative cabinet graphics on arcade coin-ops, the box art for console cartridges, and the detailed instruction manuals that were already common on computer games. Arcade coin-ops lacked instruction manuals by definition. *Tutankham* went on to see home conversions on the 2600, ColecoVision, Intellivision, and Commodore VIC-20, with several more in the works before Parker Brothers pulled the plug later on in 1983. It was one of six games featured in *Life* magazine's Twin Galaxies photo shoot of top game players on November 7, 1982. The game also inspired programmer Harry Lafnear to develop the 1985 release *Time Bandit* for the Atari ST, one of the first games to appear on the platform and a clear upgrade from what was possible on 8-bit computers.[31] Playing *Tutankham* again today, you can't help but wonder why you can't shoot up or down, but that misses the point. *Tutankham* was of its time—a desirable coin-op to play even despite the proliferation of maze shooters available then.

Joust (Williams, 1982)

One of the most original and addictive games to come out of the Golden Age of arcades, Williams' *Joust* put you, a gallant knight, atop a giant flying ostrich—the trusted steed of top-tier gallant knights the world over. The game depicted a side view of the playfield, which consisted of several rocky platforms above a thick floor surrounded by lava pits. The playfield wrapped around, so anyone flying off one side of the screen would reappear on the other heading in the same direction. You had to collide your knight and steed into enemy knights in such a way that you were at a higher elevation when your lances connected. If your lances were the same height, you would just bounce off of each other. If your lance was lower, you'd lose a life. But if you succeeded and your lance was higher, your opponent would turn into an egg that would drop to the ground. You needed to then collect the egg for bonus points before it hatched into a new knight—at which point a buzzard would come from off the side of the screen, pick up the knight, and fly into battle once more. Defeat all the enemies on the board and you'd progress to the next wave.

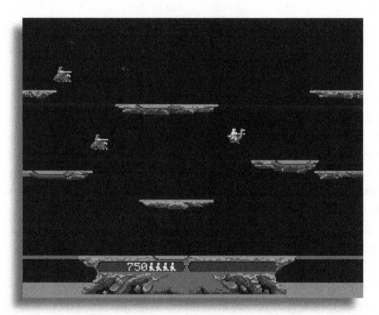

Figure 6.9: *Joust's* **original concept, well-balanced gameplay, and excellent graphics made it one of the Golden Age's greatest coin-ops.**

There were three kinds of opposing knights, each more challenging than the last. The Bounder (red) knights were the easiest. As you played further, you'd begin to encounter faster Hunter (gray) knights. The toughest to defeat were the Shadow Lords (blue), which flapped their wings incessantly and weaved up and down. If you took too long on any given wave, the dreaded, almost indestructible pterodactyl would appear and charge at you, chasing you across the screen and cawing madly. At the start of level three, the ledges over the lava pits would burn away, and starting with level four, a troll in the lava pits would reach up and grab any unsuspecting knights and mounts flying too close to the surface. Then it would attempt to pull them down under the lava, incinerating them in the process unless they could break free. (Every time my 5-year-old daughter plays "The Floor Is Lava," I think of *Joust*.) Level five was an Egg Wave, where you would fly around to different platforms collecting several dozen eggs. If you took too long, all the remaining ones would begin hatching and would soon take to the skies against you. Subsequent boards would cycle through these waves and have fewer platforms to land on.

The controls consisted of a two-way joystick and a button for each player. The button flapped the bird's wings, which controlled height. The flapping mechanic, devised by designer John Newcomer, is what gave the game its unique challenge. Moving the joystick left or right aimed the bird during flight or ran along a platform with its spindly legs moving at a high rate of speed. This meant the player had just three possible inputs to choose from: left, right, and flap. It was an ingenious design. Graphically, the game looked sharp, with a higher-than-normal 292-by-240 resolution and vibrant color. *Joust* was powered by a Motorola M6809 CPU running at 1MHz, along with a companion M6808 sound chip. Williams games also became known for their punchy, distinctive sound effects, and *Joust* was no exception—in fact, when birds materialized on their platforms, changing colors in a psychedelic fashion for a moment, the related sound effect sounded straight out of *Robotron: 2084*.

With the two sets of controls, a second player could play cooperatively with the first instead of competing. This could change on a level-by-level basis depending on the strategies employed. *Joust*'s attract mode was also interesting. By 1982, these modes had become more advanced, with plenty of fast animation, flashing color, and little tutorials on what happened in the game. It was also a distinguishing feature of arcade games compared with home console versions. Few had attract modes yet, other than the built-in routines on Atari machines, which would change the entire screen's color periodically to prevent burn-in. That was a real threat; by this time, arcade-goers had also become familiar with burn-in, as static parts of the graphics (often the text and numbers for the score, high score, the current level, and so on) would stay on all the time and burn ghost images into the monitor.

Arcade games such as *Joust*, *Tempest*, and *Moon Patrol* were successful examples of taking chances with original ideas. It's one of the things that began to diminish a bit as the industry headed further into the mid and late

1980s, where game design settled into some exciting (and even new) but nonetheless predictable ruts. Williams knew full well *Joust* was a risk, but it was one well taken. The company sold some 26,000 cabinets, making it one of the most popular arcade games ever.[32] Williams later released a unique cocktail model that put both players side by side instead of opposite each other, as well as a limited-run pinball game; both are prized by collectors today for their relative rarity (fewer than 500 units of each were made). Under the Atarisoft brand, Atari ported *Joust* to a variety of popular home consoles and computers, and the best conversion was one of the first to appear on the company's 16-bit Atari 520ST computer in 1985. It was a fixture of the arcade scene in the 1980s and one of the best games of the era.

Think about it: *Joust* was the original *Flappy Bird*. Except, you know, actually good.

Donkey Kong Junior (Nintendo, 1982)

There was no stopping the juggernaut that was *Donkey Kong*, and Nintendo knew it had a good thing on its hands. Naturally, that called for additional games. First up was the company's polished, imaginative sequel staring the big ape's offspring—complete with a diaper and pin. After defeating Donkey Kong in the first game, Mario had captured and imprisoned him in the jungle, and was standing watch outside his cage. Now Junior had to free his pop.

As before, Junior could run left and right and jump, just as Mario could in the original. But now there were new possibilities; you could jump onto a vine or chain, climb up it slowly with both hands, speed up by grabbing two vines at once, or slide down quickly. Once again there were four stages, with new stages appearing in a stacked order as you played. On the first (Vine) level, you climbed up and over a series of vines while avoiding (or dropping fruit on) the blue and red Snapjaws, each with differing behaviors, in order to get the key at the top of the screen. The Chain level included eight chains, six of which had keys you had to push up the chains and into their proper locks. Do so and he'd kick Mario off the screen, and then you started over on the first level, albeit with an extra stage added to the mix. The Jumpboard screen let you propel yourself high into the air by falling on giant springs, avoiding the purple Nitpickers and bouncing onto platforms, cables, and chains. Finally, Mario lived in the Hideout level, the most difficult one to reach. Here, you needed to avoid the sparks that moved across the platforms and cables to reach Donkey Kong.

Like its predecessor, *Donkey Kong Junior* was the brainchild of Shigeru Miyamoto; Yoshio Sakamoto helped with the graphics, and Yukio Kaneoka composed the music. The game went on to see brisk sales, if not the stratospheric success as the original (30,000 cabinets in the U.S., versus 67,000)[33], and it spawned a bevy of conversions to all of the popular home systems of the day. The ColecoVision and Atari 8-bit versions were impressive. *Donkey Kong Junior* was still popular enough to be one of the five arcade games chosen for the first video game world championship, held at Twin Galaxies in Iowa and filmed for ABC's *That's Incredible!* in January 1983.

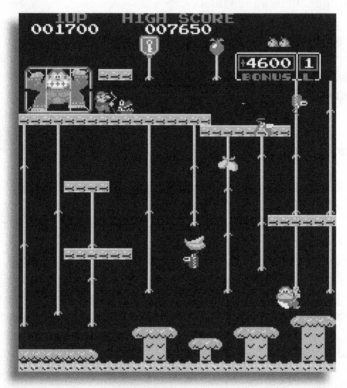

Figure 6.10: *Donkey Kong Junior* had to save his dad from the suddenly-evil Mario in this well-designed platformer.

Donkey Kong Junior didn't meet sales and revenue expectations, but its colorful graphics set a different, more cartoonish tone that was matched by the catchy, bouncing bass-note tunes that played in the background on each board. The game also was quite challenging, with plenty of ways to die, such as getting hit by a monster, falling too far from a vine, falling off the bottom of the screen, or letting the timer run down to zero.

Quest for a Hit

Atari grew large enough to maintain multiple coin-ops in various stages of development simultaneously. It would take the most promising ones and place them in a big room with one wall as a see-through mirror. The designer, project lead, and other programmers would watch players and see how they reacted to each game. They would ask them the usual survey and QA questions: Was the game time too short or just right, how were the graphics, and so on. But more important was how they played the games, as Atari's Don Osburne said in a 1983 interview:

> When I attend these sessions, I look for emotional response on the part of the player. I look for signs of anger and frustration. When a person pounds the control panel upon losing a man or a life, it's a strong indication that he or she is really involved in the game. Or the player may let out a loud groan, or shriek…When the person doesn't show any emotional reaction on losing a life, it's a tipoff that he or she doesn't care much about the game.
>
> Another way to tell…is to simply put your hand on the side of the cabinet as the game is being played. When a player is enthusiastic about a game, you can feel the energy, the vibrations, as they joystick is moved about. Players have been known to topple over games by wrenching the joystick back and forth…It's a bad sign when a youngster sits around and sips a Coke or something, and fails to pay attention when someone else is playing the game. I like to see non-players act as observers, watching what's going on.[34]

The Backlash Begins

Along with the national publicity, some troubling signs for the video game industry surfaced. Arcades were beginning to accrue a reputation for truancy. A 15-year-old named Steve Juraszek of Arlington Heights, Illinois scored 15,963,100 in a 16-hour game of *Defender*. His school banned him from leaving the grounds afterward, because it was clear he was playing hooky after seeing local coverage and his picture in *Time* magazine.[35] Several small towns pushed for laws to monitor arcades. Oakland, California, banned minors from arcades during school hours, after 10 p.m. on weeknights, and after midnight on weekends. Mesquite, Texas started a fight with the Aladdin's Castle arcade chain that went before the Supreme Court. Other states began requiring operators to apply for licenses to operate arcade games, with fees as much as $200 per game per year—bulking up city coffers and limiting the proliferation of coin-op video games.[36] Pittsburgh prohibited minors from playing games during school hours and threatened to revoke arcades' licenses if anyone was caught.[37] Ferdinand Marcos banned video games in the Philippines in 1981 and gave arcade owners two weeks to destroy them.

Movies weren't helping either. Centuri's *Pleiades* earned a place in pop culture lore as a plot device in the 1983 movie *Nightmares* with Emilio Esteves and Moon Unit Zappa, in the second vignette entitled "The Bishop of Battle." The scene also did a bang-up job in packaging up every possible arcade myth at once, including school truancy, smoking, drinking, and gambling.[38]

"Never will I let my daughter go into one of those arcades," fumed one citizen at a city council meeting in Long Beach, California, about the proposal for a new arcade. "An arcade would result in groups of adolescents and young adults loitering, littering, vandalizing, fighting, drinking, and engaging in other forms of anti-social behavior," a spokesperson for the group said at the meeting. "There's going to be trouble, trouble, trouble, right here in River City!"[39] A three-page 1982 feature in *Electronic Games* was dedicated to the debunking of myths around arcade-goers, the games they played, and what would happen to their behavior and value systems as a consequence. The backlash against arcade games was huge, with chapters of books or even entire books being written on the downsides, such as Charles Beamer's 1982 book *Video Fever: Entertainment? Education? Or Addiction?* Endless television news segments aired on whether video games were good or bad for kids.

All of this had no effect. A *Time* magazine story said Americans spent $5 billion in quarters in arcades in 1981 and that "video game addicts" spent 75,000 man-years playing the machines. The industry earned twice as much as Nevada casinos combined, twice the movie industry, and three times the MLB, NBA, and NFL. A 1982 *Play Meter* study said there were 24,000 arcades and 400,000 street locations in America, with 1.5 million machines in operation in the U.S.

In fact, arcades seemed as if they were going nowhere but up. By 1982, the top-earning game was collecting an average of $255 per week, compared with $157 per week for the top pinball game and several times what video games were bringing in just a few years prior.[40] Arnie Katz wrote in *Electronic Games* that arcading is not only "very much here to stay," but that it may not even grab as many headlines as it "becomes more fully integrated into the American lifestyle." He noted there were some "faddish happenings," such as setting long-play records—sometimes playing a game nonstop for two to three days on a single quarter—or the sudden rush of poor-quality strategy guides for this or that arcade game hitting store shelves while the game was still hot. But take those away and "what remains is the nucleus of an enduring pastime that is destined to rival all existing hobbies in popularity. Unlike recent crazes such as Rubik's Cube, these games don't have pat solutions. Even when you know the best strategies for *Tempest* or *Centipede*, playing is no less challenging and enjoyable." Katz compared arcade gaming to television, in that TV "is no longer a craze…yet the medium itself is probably 10 or 20 times as popular today as it was three decades ago. TV has simply become part of the fabric of life in this country." This did happen for video games, but maybe not in the way Katz had envisioned.[41]

7 > Race

Perhaps the most obvious indication of the arcade's ongoing popularity was *Starcade*, a quiz show that aired Monday through Friday at 3:00 p.m. on TBS from 1982 through 1984.[1] Each episode featured the host (first Mark Richards and later Geoff Edwards) asking two contestants trivia questions about video games. The contestants were mostly teenagers, but some were younger than that and a few were adults, including at least one over 65. Whichever contestant answered correctly first would then get to play one of five arcade games. In the final round, the high scorer selected one of the two remaining games and had to beat a certain score to win the grand prize: a brand new arcade game, an awesome treasure for any enthusiast at the time. In all, more than 100 *Starcade* episodes were filmed, and the show did wonders to expose dozens of popular and not-so-popular arcade games to the public. The show paved the way for future series in the 1990s and 2000s such as *Video Power*, *Nick Arcade*, and *Arena*, and foreshadowed the launch of G4, an entire pay TV network dedicated to gaming.

Starcade's fame reflected the newfound mainstream acceptance of arcade games and the profound impact it had on millions of players across the U.S.—and, increasingly, pop culture itself. If coin-op manufacturers were mindful of the backlash from some corners, it wasn't obvious in the product output. They remained laser-focused on introducing the next big thing, the next hit game that would look, feel, and sound amazing and captivate players the world over. Namco's latest coin-op nailed the formula.

Pole Position (Namco, 1982)

The arcade racing game that defined the genre, Namco's *Pole Position* put you inside a Formula One car on a track modeled after Fuji Speedway in Japan. The graphics were what Atari called a rear "perspective view," with a colorful depiction of the asphalt and a picture of your car from the back, complete with spinning tires and smooth turning to the left and right. Designed by Shinichiro Okamoto and Kazunori Sawano, each *Pole Position* cabinet included a horizontal 20-inch monitor, a steering wheel, a shifter for low and high gear, and an accelerator pedal, along with a two-speaker sound system (still in mono). The sit-down (or cockpit) cabinet added a brake pedal and upgraded to four speakers, with the other two mounted behind the seat. Even more extravagant than that hardware was what was under the hood: a pair of expensive 16-bit microprocessors that enabled the game's scaling sprites, third-person view, and full-color landscapes. Okamoto said using two 16-bit processors for an arcade game was unheard of at the time.[2]

Figure 7.1: *Pole Position*'s **stunning graphics and unmatched sense of speed made it one of the most popular arcade games of 1982.**

Pole Position consisted of two stages. In the first, you would complete a qualifying lap of the course within an allotted time limit. A blimp flew a banner across the screen that said, "Prepare to Qualify." A synthesized voice spoke the words, and a short musical motif played in the background. Starting lights blinked out the countdown until you could smash the gas pedal. Then you worked the steering wheel, accelerator pedal, and shifter to go as fast as you could, slowing down for the sharper turns and avoiding obstacles such as billboards on the sides of the road and occasional puddles on the course. Even if you missed the billboards, driving on the sides of the road slowed down your car. Other realistic touches included staying on the inside line for a faster lap and steering into a skid to retain control of the car.

Your time in the qualifying lap would determine which of eight spots you started the main race in and how many bonus points you earned at the end of the first stage. Complete the lap in under 73 seconds and you'd make it to the next stage; otherwise, you kept driving until the 90-second time limit expired. During the race, you competed against seven computer-controlled cars. At the start, the blimp would appear again, this time with a banner and synthesized voice that said, "Prepare to Race." If you completed the course before the timer ran out, you'd get extended play for up to four laps, after which you'd finish the race. This "checkpoint" model of continuing play became standard fare in video games throughout the next several decades. At the end of the game, you received a bonus of 50 points per car passed and 200 points per second remaining.

The track was surrounded by green meadows and hills and a rendering of the snow-capped Mt. Fiji. The game completed the 3D effect by moving the racetrack's vanishing point from side to side as the player turned the steering wheel. The checkered red-and-white pattern denoting the sides was smoothly animated; nothing at the time looked as good. It provided a convincing illusion of driving into the distance, much more so than *Night Driver*'s moving road pylons along the edges of the course. In *Pole Position*, the multicolor car models looked ultrarealistic compared with anything that came before it. The billboards at the side of the road functioned as in-game advertising, as in the real thing, not just a simulation of it. At the time, Atari's version displayed ads for its own games *Centipede* and *Dig Dug*, as well as 7-11 and Dentyne chewing gum. If anything, it all seemed humorous in the early 1980s, a nod to an unusually realistic depiction of driving in real life. But it turned out to be an early example of the kinds of ad-filled games we see absolutely everywhere now.

All told, *Pole Position* went on to become one of the most successful arcade games ever, with sales of 21,000 machines for $62 million,[3] and a whopping $9.5 million in weekly revenue for operators.[4] As with many of the biggest arcade games of the Golden Age, playing it on your home computer or console became of paramount importance. The Atari 8-bit and 5200 versions of the game delivered, with a simpler, blockier rendition of the cars especially when turning, but an otherwise accurate depiction of the racecourse that moved just as fast and animated just as smoothly. The 5200 version even let you control the car with the trackball, which frankly was a poor substitute for an actual steering wheel. Atari also released a surprisingly good conversion for the 2600, and under its Atarisoft brand, converted the game for play on Commodore's VIC-20 and 64, the Texas Instruments TI-99/4A, and the ZX Spectrum. A vector graphics version even showed up on the Vectrex. To follow up *Pole Position* in the arcades, in November 1983 Namco and Atari released *Pole Position II*, a sequel with additional tracks, new car colors, the addition of debris to explosions, and new music and billboards on the sides of each track.

Gravitar (Atari, 1982)

High-score competitions, such as those held by Twin Galaxies and seen on *Starcade*, wouldn't be as interesting with easy games, and making them harder wasn't always about revenue collections. Atari's next coin-op demonstrated this trend quite clearly. *Gravitar* relied heavily on the mechanic of gravity, which in video games dated back to the original *Spacewar!* and was put to devastating effect here. Similar physics guided the player's spacecraft, including thrust, rotation, and momentum, as any *Asteroids* or *Space Duel* player would recognize. Your mission was to travel to alien planets, destroy enemy bunkers, seize fuel units, and ensure the safety of solar systems for all of humanity. Designed by Mike Hally and Rich Adam, this color vector graphics game took place across multiple solar systems, universes, and all manner of board layouts. It looked beautiful, but it was so hard that today it's remembered more as frustrating rather than groundbreaking.

Each universe consisted of three solar systems of four or five planets. Fly to a planet's surface and you'd first see a zoomed-out view of the layout. Then, as you approached the ground, the game zoomed in (shades of *Lunar Lander*) and you'd end up on a landscape that scrolled to the left and right. It was here that you could shoot the bunkers and seize the fuel units with a tractor beam. Meanwhile, your fuel depleted whenever you activated the thruster or shield, which made it challenging just to navigate to the right positions on the board. Plus, the thruster was much faster to accelerate and the rotation controls twitchier than in *Asteroids*, and enemy ships soon appeared to add to the challenge.

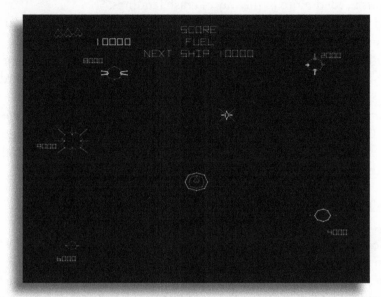

Figure 7.2: Maybe everyone didn't get it, and it was certainly extremely difficult, but *Gravitar* was a good-looking space shooter with varied mechanics and color vector graphics.

After destroying the bunkers and picking up the fuel units, it would be time to visit the next solar system. Some boards included tough caves with stalactites and stalagmites instead of just mountain ranges. The final red planet consisted of a spirallike tunnel you navigated around and around until you arrived at the center and had a clear shot at the reactor. Then you would have to escape—in just 23 seconds. A later "dark" universe had negative instead of positive gravity and would push you away from the ground. Even though there were just a few colors on the screen, the game had a *Tron*-like minimalist look to it perhaps only bested by *Tempest*'s beautiful, bursting level designs.

It may have seemed Atari made *Gravitar* hard on purpose for increased revenue collection, but that wasn't the case. "Technically, the hurdles were learning how to exploit the hardware, adapting it to this particular concept, and balancing difficulty versus fun," Adam said. "There was a lot of talk in the lab about the game being too hard. I was very hardheaded about it.

Some of the staff would tell me it was too hard, but I would shoot back that *Defender* was really hard and that this game had the same control set up as *Asteroids*...In the end, the game probably was too hard for the masses."[5] One review called *Gravitar* "The perfect game for anyone who thought that *Asteroids* needed more in the way of crash landings."[6]

To add insult to injury, *Gravitar* sold fewer cabinets than the poorly programmed *Kangaroo*—5,400 in total. To help mitigate the losses, Atari sold *Gravitar* owners an inexpensive conversion kit for its next color vector game *Black Widow*, which used the original *Gravitar* motherboard and just needed a few new chips (though *Black Widow* wasn't a hit either). Still, *Gravitar* had lasting impact, and to this day dedicated fans play the machine. Other developers picked up on the concept over time, with perhaps the most notable being 1987's *Oids* by FTL Games, one of the best titles to grace the 16-bit Atari ST computer platform.

Jungle Hunt (Taito, 1982)

Arcade coin-op manufacturers continued to look for interesting twists on proven genres. Taito's 1982 attempt at a side-scrolling platformer was *Jungle King*, a standard rescue-the-girl adventure that was just a tad too close to an existing property. Taito ran into legal trouble soon after the game's release, when the estate of *Tarzan* author Edgar Rice Burroughs noticed *Jungle King* looked almost like what you'd envision a video game about Tarzan to be and filed suit. In response, Taito renamed the game *Jungle Hunt* and changed the main character from one wearing a loincloth to an explorer wearing a safari outfit and helmet. It removed the Tarzan yell and replaced it with a musical phrase, and it replaced the swinging vines on the first board with ropes. Taito also revamped the cabinet graphics and marketing materials.

Jungle Hunt was one of the first two games to introduce parallax scrolling backgrounds (the other was *Moon Patrol*). The game started with a forest scene, where you swung from rope to rope to avoid attacking gorillas. You needed to jump far enough down the vine to get enough of an arc during the next jump, or you wouldn't make it. In Reptile River, you had to stab man-eating crocodiles and avoid air bubbles; you also had to rise to the surface to refill your oxygen levels. You could kill the crocodiles whenever their mouths were closed. The third scene was a run on dry land uphill during a rockslide—perfect for a morning cardio routine. You had to either jump over or duck rolling boulders of various sizes. The last scene showed the captured woman suspended over a flaming cauldron; you had to jump over two cannibals and avoid poison darts to rescue her. Succeed and the game would start again at a tougher difficulty level.

Figure 7.3: *Jungle Hunt*'s **newfound safari theme was a quick 90-degree turn after a lawsuit from the estate of the author of** *Tarzan.*

Scoring was based in part by how tough a task was. Jumping between ropes was 100 points per jump. Stabbing a crocodile was worth anywhere from 100 to 300 points depending on how deep in the water it was or whether its jaws were open (and therefore more dangerous). Jumping over rocks in the third scene was worth more points (200) than ducking under them (100) or running under them (50). You'd get 500 points for completing each of the first three stages and a timer bonus for rescuing the woman in the fourth stage.

In an *Electronic Games* review in February 1983, Bill Kunkel praised the game with the exception of the visuals. "[The] graphics are, especially at the start, downright hideous, looking as if they were drawn and crayon-colored by a kindergarten class. Subsequent sequences are somewhat more eye-pleasing, but this one is never going to challenge *Zaxxon*—or even *Pitfall!* for that matter—in terms of visual frills."[7] Harsh words given that *Pitfall!* wasn't even an arcade game but an Atari 2600 cartridge (albeit one of the best ever made for that system). Home conversions of *Jungle Hunt* appeared on the Apple II, Atari 2600, Atari 8-bit computers and 5200

SuperSystem, the ColecoVision, the Commodore 64 and VIC-20, and MS-DOS. *Jungle Hunt* didn't have much staying power, but it was a popular game in its day.

Gottlieb

The Chicago-based Gottlieb started as a pinball manufacturer and helped kickstart the coin-op amusement industry. It produced more than 100 flipper-based pinball tables, and later, the company branched out into bowling games, pitch-and-bat games, and other recreational toys. After Columbia Pictures acquired Gottlieb in 1976, it also began to produce arcade video games, such as licensed titles from Universal and Sigma Enterprises. Gottlieb's first original video game was *Reactor*, designed by Tim Skelly of Cinematronics fame and his first raster graphics game. *Reactor* put you in charge of cooling off an overheating nuclear reactor core. You controlled the cursor with a trackball and had to roll it against the momentum of gravity from the sun while fending off different kinds of particles that behave according to physical laws. *Reactor* was the first arcade game to display the programmer's name, something many console developers fought hard for (most famously, the four Atari employees that left to form Activision). It's also remembered for its opening music riff on the attract screen, achieved in very little memory with a synthesizer and distortion applied.

The innovative *Reactor* was a modest success. Gottlieb's second original arcade coin-op became much more than that. It was the company's only big video game hit.

*Q*bert* (Gottlieb, 1982)

The puzzle-themed action game that became a phenomenon in its time, *Q*bert* stood out for its unique orange mascot with a giant nose, colorful M.C. Escher–inspired isometric graphics, catchy sound design, and addictive gameplay. You changed the color of the tops of the cubes to a target color by hopping back and forth onto them. Meanwhile, all manner of nasties bounced around the pyramid in an attempt to thwart you. Each round, the game began by showing you a quick demo of *Q*bert* hopping onto four cubes so you could see what the start and finish colors were. You started at the top of the pyramid in each round; when you completed the entire pyramid of cubes, you'd move on to the next round, with four rounds comprising each level.

Figure 7.4: *Q*bert* **was a delightful, colorful romp on a series of pyramid-shaped boards brought to you by M.C. Escher and "pop" sound effects.**

The four-way joystick was the only method of control, as there were no buttons. The joystick moved in diagonal directions to mirror Q*bert's possible moves to adjacent cubes. Each move resulted in a "hop" sound that resembled a bubble popping, as if Q*bert's feet were two more of his noses and produced suction. Colorful rotating discs at the sides carried you back to the top if you jumped off the pyramid and onto them; otherwise, jumping off the pyramid would result in losing a life. The game started with two enemies chasing you, a red ball and a purple ball. The red ball would just fall off the bottom of the pyramid, but the purple one changed into Coily the snake at the bottom and chased you around the board. The only way to dispatch Coily was to jump onto one of the rotating discs, which inevitably led to Coily following you off the pyramid to his doom. If any of the enemies caught you, a cartoon bubble would appear showing "@!?@!" and you would hear Q*bert "curse" in some gibberish alien language, thanks to the cabinet's SC01 speech synthesizer chip.

The third round dispensed with the red ball but brought two new purple enemies: Ugg and Wrong-Way. They moved around the board more as obstacles. Sometimes a green ball would also appear, which netted bonus points and also froze the rest of the characters on the board for a few moments. Adding to the challenge were Sick and Sam, two green enemies that would undo Q*bert's work and change the colors of the cubes back to where they started. Starting with the fifth round—meaning level two—it would take more than one hop to change the cube color to the target color, with an additional color in between. Later levels alternated how many colors you needed for each cube. On level three, you couldn't hop onto a cube you "finished" anymore, because it would change back to one of the wrong colors.

All of this resulted in an addictive platformer that soon became a top draw at arcades, with 25,000 cabinets sold. The game soon heralded all manner of licensed merchandise, conversions to many home computers and consoles, and the now-requisite Saturday morning cartoon. As with many arcade successes before it, it became something of a competition amongst platform owners to see which one had the best conversion of Q*bert, no doubt helped by Parker Brothers magazine ads showing nine screens, eight of which displayed what the game looked like on various systems. It inspired plenty of imitators if not clones, such as Sierra On-Line's *Mr. Cool*, Activision's *Frostbite*, First Star Software's *Flip & Flop*, and Master Control Software's *Pharaoh's Pyramid*. Sometimes the simplest ideas, when implemented well, prove to be the best.

Perhaps in total *Q*bert* didn't achieve quite the level of success as *Pac-Man* or *Donkey Kong*. But for a brief, shining moment (or hey—terrible moment, if you didn't like the game), *Q*bert* was everywhere.

Satan's Hollow (Bally Midway, 1982)

Satan's Hollow was one of my favorite games—who could resist the devil, after all? It was a fixed shooter notable for its gothic setting and flight stick controller, the same unit as the one used in *Tron* cabinets. The Fire button was the trigger on the stick, rather than separate on the console—par for the course in some kinds of games, but unusual for a fantasy shooter. You destroyed swarming gargoyles in order to assemble the Bridge of Fire, which spanned a river of lava. Then, you confronted Satan, the master of darkness. The Dark Scrolls warned of this, or so it was told (in a 1982 Bally Midway brochure):

Figure 7.5: *Satan's Hollow* **added a bridge-building mechanic to take you to the board with the greatest evil character himself.**

He, the Prince of Darkness, reigns over an infernal underworld so abhorrent, the grotesque gargoyles who safeguard his lair cower at his cloven-hoofed approach. 'Tis he who rules supremely his domain, by twisted swirls of flame and obedient creatures so wretched, no mortal dareth traverse the Bridge of Death crossing the River of fire. Beware him. He is darkness, he is the omnipotent demon Lucifer, he is SATAN OF THE HOLLOW.

Okay, then! The object of the game, designed by Bill Adams, was to destroy swarming gargoyles. The gargoyles would attack in formation, sometimes a few at a time and sometimes more than a dozen, diving at you and attacking with fireballs and flaming eggs. You were positioned at the bottom of the screen, with the gargoyles on top. *Satan's Hollow* played and sounded a bit like a *Phoenix* clone in disguise. Your character was armed with a rocket launcher, because that's normal in a fantasy setting. In addition to your main gun, you had a protective shield that for a short time would vaporize any enemy who touched it. Gargoyles could even steal a ship from your reserves. Meanwhile, bombers tried to destroy the unfinished bridge, and for added fun, floating devil heads would breathe fire at you and grow larger the longer you took to clear each level. As you fought and destroyed the gargoyles, you'd earn bridge pieces that you could collect and bring to the right side of the screen to assemble the bridge. You had to put in one piece before another one would appear from killing a gargoyle..

Once the bridge was fully assembled, you could cross it and enter the valley to go after Satan. Occasionally, you'd fight a miniboss first, either Lucifer, Old Nick, or Beelzebub. Satan himself was no cakewalk either; he threw deadly accurate pitchforks at you. Destroy Satan and you'd start again on a more difficult setting and have to build a larger bridge, albeit with more firepower at your disposal this time around. Flags would appear on top of the castle as you played.

Bally Midway's MCR-II hardware powered *Satan's Hollow*, with a pair of Zilog Z80s controlling the action and Midway's SSIO board with two AY-3-8901A chips providing sound effects. The graphics consisted of bold reds and purples in the sky and a twisty, windy path up the right side of the screen to Satan's lair. As you advanced in the game, the sky took on ever-darker shades, making it tougher to see the gargoyles. The game came in standard upright, mini, and cocktail versions, and was a hit game for Bally Midway. *Satan's Hollow* received a Commodore 64 conversion by David Berezowski, and CBS Interactive completed Atari 400/800 and 5200 Super-System versions and even advertised them, but those were never released.

Time Pilot (Konami, 1982)

Time Pilot was a multiscrolling shooter with a new game mechanic: You were a jetfighter pilot that traveled through time, shooting enemy aircraft and rescuing other pilots trapped in the wrong eras. The first thing that would strike you about playing *Time Pilot*, designed by Yoshiki Okamoto, was the control scheme. Longtime fans became used to it, but the way the joystick worked was closer to *Rally-X* than most space games. If you pushed the joystick in a direction, the ship would rotate around and then fly in that direction. Rescuing lost parachuting pilots would earn bonus points, but contrary to the supposed plotline, you didn't have to rescue them. You'd also get bonus points for destroying formations of enemy fighters.

The game began in the year 1910, where you were dropped into the middle of a dogfight with biplanes. You needed to destroy dozens of them and then shoot the mothership seven times in order to complete the level and go through the time warp. The second level was set in 1940, where World War II–era monoplanes and bombers swarmed your ship. The bombers took for hits to destroy; an even tougher one appeared at the end of the level. Next up was 1970, which brought in helicopters and their side-winding, homing missiles. The year 1983 featured jet planes with their own breed of homing missile, along with a jet bomber miniboss. Finally, you'd travel to the future, which in 1983 meant the year 2000, where you'd find UFOs and aliens to fight. (Oh well.) The difficult last level ended with a "superfortress" UFO that took many shots to destroy. The game awarded you a free ship at 10,000 points, and then every 50,000 points thereafter. Complete all five levels and the game restarted in 1910 at a faster speed.

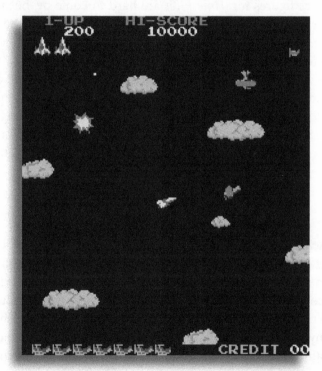

Figure 7.6: *Time Pilot* **brought you to five different eras in an effort to rescue lost pilots, from 1910 A.D. to the far future of…2000.**

According to a 1998 interview, Okamoto said his first game after Kona-mi hired him was supposed to be about earning a driver's license by driving on "crazy roads."[8] Okamoto didn't like this and proposed a flying game. His boss said no, so Okamoto wrote the game he wanted anyway while keeping a driving game on the screen whenever his boss would swing by his desk.[9] *Time Pilot* became Konami's biggest hit to date. But nothing prepared Okamoto for his boss's response. "The game I made [was] completely different from what I was supposed to do. [After it became a big hit] my boss said, 'You know, you were right to do what I told you to do. This game is doing very well.'"[10] Even worse: In the office one day later on, Okamoto passed by his boss and the president of Konami having a conversation. "My boss was talking to the president and called me to come over to them. He was telling the president that my game was successful because of the instructions he gave me. He hadn't done a thing [on the game]. I heard that and wanted to kill the guy…Instead, I agreed with my boss so he would not be disgraced. This boss was a lucky guy."[11]

True sales figures for *Time Pilot* are hard to come by, but it did well enough that Konami released a sequel called *Time Pilot '84* the following year. This one was set over alien cities and strangely removed the time-period mechanic, though it threw in a few nods to the original game with the appearance of bonus biplane squadrons. The original *Time Pilot* also saw a few home conversions; easily the most significant one was for the ColecoVision in 1983, which I personally sunk many hours into playing. Decades later, in 2018, the New Generation scene group ported the game to Atari 8-bit home computers and somehow made it play smoother and better than even a late-era NES port.

Data East

Data East achieved most of its fame as a developer of popular Nintendo Entertainment System cartridges, but it saw its first successes in the arcades. Founded in 1976 by Tetsuo Fukuda in Tokyo, Data East started releasing arcade video games in 1978 beginning with *Super Break*. It produced more than a dozen before releasing 1980's *Astro Fighter*, a fixed space shooter and the company's first breakout hit, and which Gremlin/Sega brought stateside.

That same year Data East unveiled its DECO Cassette System, the first official "platform" for arcade games that allowed operators to switch between different games as their revenues decreased. The platform consisted of a cassette tape reader and a motherboard with a pair of MOS 6502 chips for the main CPU and audio, plus two General Instrument AY8910 chips for music. The system worked by reading game data off of the cassettes— that is, it worked until the cassette wore out, which happened quickly and rendered the game useless.[12] One of the most popular DECO Cassette System games in the U.S. was *Bump 'n' Jump*, a silly and fun overhead car racing game. Most DECO titles saw mediocre sales.

THE DATA EAST MULTI CONVERSION KIT INCLUDES:

Master PC Boards   Side Panel Decals
Cassette Deck   Monitor Plex Modifications
Harnesses   Marquee Modifications
Control Panel Graphics

Figure 7.7: Data East's DECO Cassette System was the first interchangeable arcade platform and would have been successful had it been more reliable.

Instead, let's cover the best DECO Cassette System game here, because in a history of the rise and fall of video arcades, it's impossible to leave this one out. Just thinking about it now is making me hungry.

Burger Time (Data East, 1982)

In this silly platform game, you were Peter Pepper the Chef and had to assemble hamburgers using buns, lettuce, pickles, and other ingredients. Walking all the way across each part of the hamburger dislodged it from its perch and sent it down a step. Its ultimate destination was the bottom of the screen, where the parts piled up into each finished burger. You had to assemble four burgers to complete each level.

Meanwhile, runaway hot dogs, pickles, and eggs with legs chased you around the board; they were named Mr. Hot Dog, Mr. Pickle, and Mr. Egg (all singular, even though there were many of each). Whenever any of them caught you, you would lose a life, indicated by the chef's heads at the left side of the screen. Crushing them under a falling piece of a burger earned you points, and if you dropped an ingredient as an enemy was standing on it, you'd score higher and the ingredient would fall two levels for every enemy you wrapped into that single move.

You started the game with six sprays of pepper. Spraying an enemy would immobilize them so you could pass by and make a quick getaway. You could score bonus points by way of ice cream, coffee, and French fry icons that appeared periodically. Complete the first board and you'd hear victory music; the next level would look different and include an extra ingredient for the burger. There were six boards in all, each with more difficulty, enemies, and ingredients. The current level was indicated on the bottom-right side by the number of tiny hamburgers in a pile. The graphics were quite colorful even despite the black backdrop.

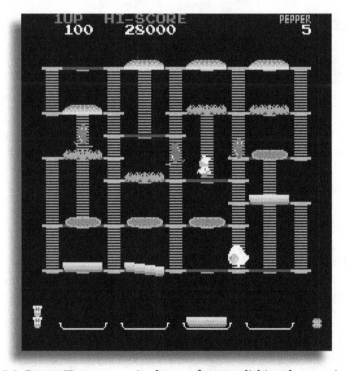

Figure 7.8: *Burger Time* **put you in charge of accomplishing the most important thing ever: making hamburgers. Everyone has to eat, right?**

The mustard-yellow upright cabinet included a white-and-orange marquee, a blue bezel around the vertically oriented monitor, a four-way joystick with a red ball, and Pepper buttons on either side of the stick for

left- and right-handed players. *Burger Time* went on to become a resound-
ing success in the arcades. Although the game initially appeared on the
DECO Cassette System, Bally Midway soon licensed it and manufactured it
as a dedicated arcade cabinet that proved much more reliable. Home conversions appeared on the Atari 2600, Apple II, IBM PC, and most famously
the Mattel Intellivision, as well as Mattel's ill-fated Aquarius computer. A
ColecoVision port arrived late, and then some more appeared throughout
the mid 1980s including one for the NES. The game also continued to appear in remixed and "Super" versions, and on game collections throughout
the 1990s and beyond. It had enough cultural impact for an appearance in
Walt Disney Pictures's 2012 motion picture *Wreck-It Ralph* (along with just
about every other game in this book).

Millipede (Atari, 1982)

Centipede was too good of a game, so it was natural Atari would want to
release a sequel. Millipede used the same trackball-plus-Fire-button control
scheme as the original coin-op and had much of the same gameplay and
pacing. This time, you were an elf with a bow and arrows. Your job was to
defend a mushroom forest from hordes of marauding giant insects, most
notably the millipede, which was faster than the centipede (presumably because it had 900 more legs?). It's reported *Centipede Deluxe* was the working
title for the game during development. Wisely, Atari moved away from the
"Deluxe" branding of sequels so as to better let the game stand alone on its
own merits.

New enemies included the mosquito, which bumped all of the mushrooms up one row when you nabbed it, and the inchworm, which when
hit slowed down everyone else temporarily. Beetles made a nifty geometric
pattern on the screen, down, across, and back up; any mushrooms they
touched would turn into invulnerable flowers. Shoot a beetle and it would
bump the playfield down a row. To balance the increased difficulty from the
new enemies, the biggest change was the introduction of four DDT canisters scattered across the playfield. When you shot one, it exploded and took
out anything surrounding it, for three times the points—including multiple
segments of a centipede unlucky enough to walk into the poison cloud before it dissipated.

Otherwise, most of the same mechanics from *Centipede* remained in
place, albeit with new graphics and some new names. Mushrooms were still
worth a point each. The millipede's head was worth more than its body, and

you could end up with multiple heads as the single creature became segmented after being shot, or after new heads started appearing once the millipede reached the bottom of the screen on a given level. The spider was also a familiar foe recurring throughout the game, and it was still worth more points depending on how close it was when you shot it, though there was a new 1,200-point award in addition to 300, 600, and 900. You could even get 1,800 for a spider if it was caught in a DDT explosion. Bees and dragonflies took the place of the flea, dropping down the screen (and zigzagging, in the case of the dragonflies) and adding new mushrooms. The earwig replaced the scorpion for poisoning mushrooms.

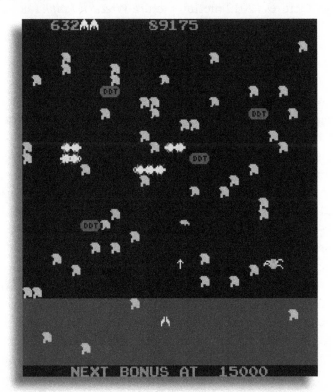

Figure 7.9: *Millipede* **took** *Centipede* **to an even more alien place with a slew of new enemies and a large helping of DDT poisoning for good measure.**

To mix things up, periodically the game would enter Bombing mode after you cleared a level. In this frenetic portion, the screen filled up with waves of bees, dragonflies, or mosquitoes bombarding you. They were worth lots of points, so picking off as many as you could was helpful and doing so would help you survive the bombardment. Lose a life and you would get five points for every damaged mushroom restored; the machine gun sound would also restore the poisoned mushrooms as well as the ones that beetles had turned into flowers. Veteran players also had the option of starting the game at a higher difficulty level, where everything was worth more points with a multiplier.

Millipede wasn't as successful as *Centipede*, but it was still sufficiently different to keep many players interested. Atari ported the game to the 2600, its 8-bit computers, and later, to the 16-bit Atari ST, but otherwise the game received fewer home conversions.

Front Line (Taito, 1982)

In *Front Line*, you had to capture the enemy's fort, which was hidden in a forest deep in enemy territory. You were equipped with a pistol and hand grenades, as were the initial barrage of enemy soldiers. You could hide behind trees, but otherwise it was an open battlefield. As you progressed, you'd encounter bombs and land mines, and further behind enemy lines, tanks that you could only destroy with the grenades. A better option was to climb into a tank and command it on your own, firing on opposing troops with the tank's machine gun. Later on, a heavy tank with a massive cannon would become available, although it was slower to pilot. Make it all the way to the brick-barricaded enemy fort and you would have to leave your tank, run, and throw a single grenade into it. Score a hit and the enemy would fly the white flag of surrender. Then the game repeated with faster troops that were worth more points to kill.

Front Line established many of the conventions of what would be called the run-and-gun genre, with its vertically scrolling playfield, ground combat, grenades, and the ability to commandeer tanks while on foot. In another first, when the tank you were driving was destroyed, you had a few seconds to exit it and escape before it exploded. The cabinet's controls were especially interesting; in addition to the eight-way joystick, there was a rotary dial that would aim and fire your gun. You would use the two together to play the game. Another button let you throw grenades and jump in or out of tanks.

In a 1985 interview, designer Tetsuya Sasaki said that he became a game developer because of *Space Invaders*.[13] To further push the game, Taito offered a trade-up program where the company would buy back older coin-op gear including arcade cabinets, pinball machines, jukeboxes, and other games in trade for a new *Front Line* game that the company said was "one of the top three earning video games for the past four months on all locations," according to a 1983 brochure to arcade owners and operators. In *Electronic Games*'s 1983 Arcade Awards, *Front Line* scored the runner-up spot just behind *Pole Position*; the editors said that "this arcade approach to the dirty business of infantry combat forces the player to keep moving and firing constantly," not unlike when playing *Robotron: 2084*, if not as fast, and that "action is non-stop in this attractive shoot 'em up."[14]

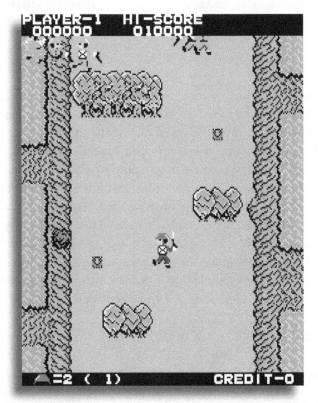

Figure 7.10: The original run-and-gun shooter, *Front Line* put you behind enemy lines in a Vietnam-style combat scenario.

Front Line didn't look particularly good, with somewhat stilted and blocky animation that was amateurish even considering the limited tools, resolution, and memory available. *Front Line* wasn't converted to many home systems, with only the ColecoVision seeing a release in the U.S. and a smattering of others overseas. It was only later that *Front Line*'s historical significance has become more apparent, even if other games such as *Ikari Warriors* and *Commando* were more polished.

Popeye (Nintendo, 1982)

It's difficult to envision now, but Popeye was an internationally known cartoon character and remained a pop-culture mainstay for decades. Nintendo's
next arcade game was another platformer based on the old comic strip character from the 1930s that was still in TV cartoon syndication at the time, not
to mention a 1980 movie starring Robin Williams. The pipe-smoking Popeye
had to save his girlfriend Olive Oyl from the evil Brutus. *Popeye* was very
much of its un-PC era, and the operator advertisements for the game repro-
duced all of it, from the references to smashed wine and beer bottles to the
"blubber face" caricature of Brutus, Olive Oyl's swooning and flirting for Popeye, and her penchant for throwing things at Popeye and thus being a "nag."

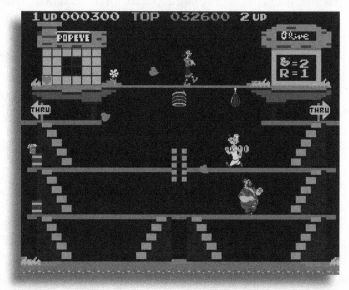

**Figure 7.11: Based on the famous spinach-loving sailor man, *Popeye* was a fun
platformer, if a thinly disguised cash-in on *Donkey Kong*'s popularity.**

The game itself was less offensive, and consisted of three stages. On the
first, which included four platforms and a series of side and center staircases,
Popeye had to catch 24 of Olive Oyl's hearts, which she threw from the top of
the screen. When he caught enough of them, he'd fill up the squares on the
side of his house. In the meantime, Brutus was busy throwing beer bottles
at him and trying to punch him into the water. If Popeye grabbed the bonus
can of spinach, he'd eat it, turn pink, and be able to punch Brutus while the
"Popeye the Sailor Man" music theme played. On the apartment building

board, Popeye had to catch 16 musical notes falling from Olive's flute to fill a musical phrase at the top of the screen. He also had to avoid the sea hag, who, like Brutus, threw bottles at him. Wimpy sat on a seesaw at the side as Swee'Pea flew above; bounce off the seesaw to reach him and you'd score bonus points. The third screen took place on a ship; Brutus held Olive Oyl prisoner at the top as she cried "Help!" Popeye had to catch 16 letters from the word while avoiding a vulture as well as Brutus and the sea hag.

The game's cartoonlike graphics and multivoice sound were well executed, if not much different from what you saw in *Donkey Kong*. The control panel presented a four-way joystick with a black ball to control Popeye's movements, either left and right on platforms or up and down staircases. A single orange button on the right let Popeye punch objects, as well as Brutus after eating spinach, or a punching bag at the top of the first board that would knock a barrel of beer loose and that could fall on Brutus's head. There was no Jump button, which already seemed unusual post *Donkey Kong*.

Popeye was one of the most successful games of the Golden Age of video arcades, with some 20,000 cabinets sold. Still, in light of *Donkey Kong*, that was considered something of a disappointment, and to be expected given the short shelf life of video games in general and especially those with similar themes one after the other.[15] Overall, *Popeye* was well liked, if not well remembered given how the coin-op and home conversions were everywhere in the early 1980s.

Warning Signs Ahead

Many of the top games to come out in 1982 were sequels, such as *Frenzy*, a cool *Berzerk* sequel with walls you could shoot and a slightly different algorithm to generate the random maps;[16] *Donkey Kong Junior*; *Millipede*; and *Super Pac-Man*, which added special power pellets that made you huge. Midway kept going, too, with *Jr. Pac-Man*, a fun and challenging derivative with much larger, scrolling playfields, and *Professor Pac-Man*, a bizarre quiz game that flopped. The sequel trend suggested the industry was beginning to become complacent.[17] Countless other coin-ops—not just *Popeye* and *Kangaroo*—were derivative if not outright clones. Some of the better ones included Data East's *Lock 'n' Chase*, a *Pac-Man* clone where you played a thief collecting gold coins before making a quick getaway. Universal's *Lady Bug* and Exidy's *Mouse Trap* were two dot-eating maze games with switchable gates that changed up the layout on each level, but that were otherwise Insect Pac-Man and Rodent Pac-Man.

The first warning signs that this complacency could be a problem for the video game industry appeared in the middle of 1982, although they were easy to miss. On the surface of it, the industry was going gangbusters, with arcade games raking in billions. Hit coin-ops such as *Space Invaders*, *Pac-Man*, and *Defender* were each pulling in hundreds of millions of dollars apiece.[18] As 1982 wore on, heavy competition between game manufacturers would begin to take its toll on the coin-op industry. So did an increasing preponderance of mediocre games and what was fast becoming a crowded consumer market.[19] But arcade owners and operators were the ones to feel it first. Indeed, the first to notice something was awry were the distributors, the ones that delivered coin-op games to restaurants, hotels, and grocery stores. Profits started to fall, causing these entrepreneurs to default on their loans to buy the games. The largest arcades that depended on thousands of customers per week to meet overhead began to fail. Smaller arcades hung on for a bit, but many of those, too, would shut their doors.[20]

Some industry pundits, seeing the trouble, began to question the entire phenomenon. Peter Nulty of *Fortune* magazine wrote in November 1982, "Can the home video game boom continue much longer? Softening prices last summer and an advertising blitz this fall are raising speculation that there's trouble ahead for game makers. If the kids are getting tired of blasting space blobs, won't the manufacturers be left blasting each other for shares in a stagnant or shrinking market?" He added, "Some observers even talk of a collapse similar to those suffered by CB radios, digital watches, and pocket calculators."

BusinessWeek ran an article in December 1982 called "Arcade Video Games Start to Flicker," saying that with the exception of the companies producing the top arcade games, coin-op manufacturers found themselves stagnating. Although sales grew tremendously from 1978 through 1981, 1982 was shaping up to be the first flat year: "Distributors are overstocked, and few operators foresee a repeat of the action in 1981, when players slid an estimated $7 billion worth of quarters into arcade game machines...A shakeout among operators, whose ranks grew by the thousands with the lure of easy money, is already underway."[21] Eddie Alum, the publisher of *Re-Play* magazine, proposed one major reason: "We know that the stuff we sell is generally called 'novelty,' and novelty is not forever; you have to constantly freshen it. We tried to freshen it, but apparently not to the point where the public would play it with the reckless abandon that they were playing before."[22] Whatever it was, something happened to the customer traffic at the arcades that year that remains murky to this day.[23]

While the arcade industry continued to rake in revenue, it had become clear to insiders that trouble was brewing. The biggest public indicator was what happened to Atari. On December 7, 1982, in a move that stunned Wall Street, the company said its sales projections were way off target, and that instead of 50 percent, it now expected just a 10 to 15 percent increase in sales in the fourth quarter of 1982. If that wasn't bad enough, Atari CEO Ray Kassar found himself at the center of an insider trading scandal after selling 5,000 shares of parent company Warner Communications stock less than half an hour before announcing the news. Shares soon plunged in value by 40 percent. Kassar settled with the SEC and resigned from Atari seven months later.

Most of the new games were coming from American companies such as Williams, Midway, and Exidy. That meant fewer distribution and licensing deals that had originated in Japan. Atari went the other way, though, and signed a new distribution deal with Namco for its Japanese games beginning with *Dig Dug*. Taito and Sega continued to make strong showings with games such as *Bosconian*, *Qix*, *Turbo*, and *Zaxxon*. Bill Kunkel noted in December 1982 that an earlier push toward 50-cent games seemed to have "fizzled," and that original ideas continued to be a source of new coin-ops as *Tempest* and *Frogger* indicated.[24] Kunkel wrote that the prior summer would be remembered as a "golden era" by arcaders: "Even though gamers spent more money in the pleasure palaces of America, the money was split among a far greater number of titles," he wrote. "This will probably result in a shakeout of the weaker sisters in the industry. In other words, we may never again see as many new titles in such a short span of time. Enjoy it while you can, fellow coin-oppers!"[25]

Nonetheless, the future still looked bright to arcade-goers—and game journalists. In a January 1983 *Electronic Games* feature story titled "A Time Trip to the Game Parlor of the Future," Rich Pearl envisioned a world in the year 2001 where "arcades [will] be constructed along the lines of big budget science fiction movie sets, with special effects [such as] chairs that rock back and forth, swing side to side, or swivel."[26] Tom Lopez of Activision pointed out how the price of computers would drop, and that it would soon be cheaper and more stimulating to play computer games than be entertained at clubs, concerns, or in packed sports arenas."[27] Pearl wrote that because arcade games were purpose-built for one specific program, they would "maintain an edge over home computers, and that wrap-around projection screens, scanning devices, thought-reading, emotion detection, and even devices that release smells would become available." (Smell-O-Vision redux?) Soon, he wrote, the "game itself will disappear—as if it melted—and you will forget you're playing a game."[28] The article also predicted the rise of large teams of people necessary to make games.

Warning signs aside, arcades still earned a record $4.3 billion in revenue in 1982, with even more hits such as Sega's *Pengo*, Data East's *Bump 'n' Jump*, and new, beautiful Atari color vector games such as *Black Widow* and *Major Havoc*. But even the non-vector games still delivered revenue with passable home conversions. All told, people kept on flocking to arcades that remained in business, and the lucky gamers with home consoles kept buying cartridges in hopes that the latest conversion of such-and-such game would be just as much fun as the arcade, even if it didn't look quite the same.

As we cover the rise and fall of the video arcade, let's kick off our discussion of 1983 with the opposite—a game based on a television show, one of the most storied and beloved of all TV franchises.

Star Trek: Strategic Operations Simulator (Sega, 1983)

This beautiful, color vector graphics coin-op, launched with a massive promotional push, made you the captain of the starship Enterprise. Your mission was to destroy threats to the United Federation of Planets. The full name of the game was *Star Trek: Strategic Operations Simulator*, but most of the advertising around the cabinet called it *Star Trek*, or even *Star Trek: The Arcade Game*. The coin-op came in both standard upright and sit-down versions, the latter of which resembled an Enterprise bridge chair. Each arm contained a weighted spinner for setting the Enterprise's heading, plus button controls for impulse power, warp drive, phasers, and photon torpedoes. On the upright model, the rotary knob and buttons were traditionally arranged across the control panel.

The in-game view was divided into three sections. The top left displayed your ship's remaining resources, including photo torpedoes, shield strength, and warp energy. The top right showed a long-range scanner of the current quadrant with your ship at the center. The bottom half of the screen displayed the view out the ship's window in three dimensions. When you started the game, it would play the first few notes of the theme song and then say, "Welcome aboard, Captain," in a clear voice that showed off Sega's prior work with synthesis dating back to *Space Fury*. You'd find yourself in a sector with nearby Klingons and Starbases. There were three kinds of Klingon battle cruisers. Red ones went after Federation Starbases, purple ones targeted the Enterprise and fired plasma energy balls, and white ones were known as "maniac Klingons" and would attempt to ram the Enterprise kamikaze-style. Multiple in-game views of the action were dramatic and effective; the targeting computer would light up and beep whenever a Klingon ship was in range and on target.

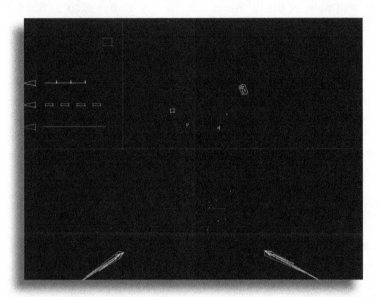

Figure 7.12: *Star Trek: Strategic Operations Simulator* **put you aboard the Starship Enterprise in a gripping, color vector graphics space battle.**

To dispatch the Klingons, you had several options. Phaser shots were unlimited and immediate. Photon torpedoes took longer to reach their targets, and you only had a few, but they could take out multiple enemies in one shot. At any point you could depress the Warp button; this would rocket you forward and render you impervious to enemy fire, but you only had a limited supply. If you were unlucky enough to have your shields depleted, from that point on enemy fire would take out the Enterprise's shield system, photon torpedoes, and warp drive, in that order. One more shot to your damaged ship would destroy it and end the game, where it would display "Simulation Complete." At this point, you urgently had to navigate to a starbase and dock with it. If successful, your ship would be repaired and all systems replenished, and you could continue playing.

Each time you eliminated all the Klingons, the game would display "Sector Secured," and you'd warp to the next sector where it would speak "Entering sector 1.2," and so on. Sometimes an antimatter saucer would appear and flit about, attempting to attach to the Enterprise to suck out its warp energy. In another round, nomad ships laid mines that could explode together in lethal chain reactions. Depending on how the game was configured, you'd earn bonus shield, photon torpedo, and warp units every 10,000 to 40,000 points.[29]

Star Trek offered smooth animation, fast action, and detailed, punchy sound effects throughout. "*Star Trek* is sure to be a top-grosser in the arcades this year," read an August 1983 *Electronic Games* article. "If you can squeeze through the crowd around the machine, you may never want to leave." Reports were that it wasn't quite the revenue generator Sega had hoped, and within a few months the company released the game as a conversion kit to juice sales.[30]

Enterprising enthusiasts have attempted to program *Star Trek* games on mainframes since the early 1970s, and by the time of this coin-op's release there had been many action games following similar templates. In most respects, the game was a coin-op incarnation of *Star Raiders*, the seminal Atari 400 and 800 title released in late 1979—and that game was a highly successful attempt to merge *Star Trek* and *Star Wars* into a video game. Yet *Star Trek* brought something new to arcades, with its sharp color vector graphics, computerized speech synthesis, and revolutionary controls that put you in the captain's chair.

Xevious (Namco/Atari, 1983)

Xevious set the template for the vertical-scrolling shooter. The story of the game, which was designed by a small team led by Masanobu Endō, was that the advanced Xevious civilization had to evacuate Earth before the Ice Age. As a Solvalou spacecraft pilot, you defended the planet from the aggressors, who were now trying to return and reclaim their heritage. You flew over hostile terrain the Xevious people had already secured, bombing ground entrenchments by targeting them with the crosshair ahead of your ship. You also fought off waves of air attacks from invading Xevious ships. There were a total of 32 enemies to destroy between land and air across 16 (unlabeled) areas, and you also had to avoid a variety of obstacles such as flying resistor shields.

Periodically, you would encounter the Andor Genesis Mother Ship, which bombarded you with explosive black spheres and other projectiles. The eventual object was to shoot its central reactor, all while fending off the worst air attacks the Xevious people had to offer. In addition, strewn about the landscape were occasional hidden structures called Sol Citadels; whenever you flew over one, your targeting sight flashed red briefly. If you dropped a bomb and it landed on the right spot, you'd uncover a silo object; this would award you 1,000 points, and then bombing the silo would give you another 1,000 points.[31]

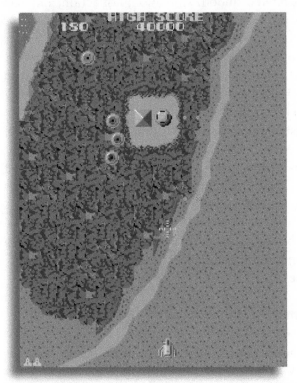

Figure 7.13: Xevious paved the way for Raptor, Tyrian, and other vertical shooters with its colorful graphics and fast pace.

Namco designed the game to run on its existing *Galaga* board, which included three Zilog Z80s and Namco's own three-channel PSG chip for audio. The control panel consisted of an eight-way joystick with a red ball on top, and two sets of buttons on either side that fired the ship's air zapper and blaster bombs. Instead of becoming more difficult as the game went on, it adapted to the player's ability and self-adjusted "moment by moment," as a brochure for the coin-op claimed. That meant no wave of alien attacks was ever the same, and the operator could also choose from four overall difficulty levels.

At the time, *Xevious* received excellent reviews for its originality, addictiveness, and graphics quality. It was a monster success in Japan, reportedly selling as many cabinets as *Space Invaders* in its first weeks of release. In 1983, it also became the killer app for the then-new Nintendo Famicom, the system that would appear a few years later in the U.S. as the Nintendo Entertainment System. The theme music from *Xevious* even appeared in *Starcade*. Atari advertised the game to operators in a unique way, too: "Get ready for devious Xevious! It's the Atari game they can't play at home." That would soon change, as in addition to the Famicom port, the game saw home versions on a large variety of 8- and 16-bit computer systems from the Apple II and the Commodore 64 to the Atari ST and Amstrad CPC. It did appear on the Atari 7800 and the Game Boy, but never saw a release on the 2600, ColecoVision, Intellivision or other common systems around the time of the coin-op's release.

Xevious's appeal was also in some ways its downfall. Self-adjusting difficulty meant that there wasn't much consistency to the gameplay, and it all felt a bit amorphous and random, with small squadrons of aliens appearing and just kind of being all over the place during the game. But the scrolling terrain was key to the game's lasting influence. You can see it in many games such as Capcom's *1942* and *Raptor: Call of the Shadows*, an MS-DOS shooter in VGA.

Sinistar (Williams, 1983)

At its core, *Sinistar* was a multiscrolling space shooter, but it was also so much more. The object of this high-intensity coin-op was to go on an intergalactic mission to the outer corners of the universe, mining the crystals your home civilization needed to sustain vital technologies that enabled life itself. An on-screen deep-space scanner showed you the current sector of the galaxy three parsecs across. Your ship had a special laser; when you fired it at a rogue planetoid, it would break apart and you could collect each crystal. You could hold down the button to fire rapidly or tap it for individual bursts.

It would all be easy, and not much of a game, if it weren't for the Sporgs. Red Sporg worker ships attempted to construct a Sinistar from the same rogue planetoids you were mining crystals from. You could find the Sinistar in progress. Meanwhile, gray warrior ships attacked you as a distraction. If the workers succeeded, the Sporgs would use the "eminently unstable" Sinistar to destroy you and your civilization. Fortunately, you also could use the crystals to make Sinibombs, which were necessary to destroy the Sinistar; you needed 20 crystals to make a Sinibomb.

When the Sinistar appeared, it said "I Live," which is one of the scariest things you've ever heard especially if it was coming from off the screen somewhere else in the playfield. The Sinistar moved fast, its eyes and mouth glowing as it tracked your location and tried to suck you in. Only the Sinibombs worked against the Sinistar; if you succeeded in destroying it, it shattered to pieces in a massive explosion and you'd move on to a new sector of the galaxy. I couldn't get enough of it. My memory of this game was playing it on our lunch periods in fifth grade; this girl in my class and I used to walk over and play it, and we'd scream every time the Sinistar showed up. Thankfully the guy at the counter thought it was funny.

Figure 7.14: Arguably the scariest space shoot-'em-up ever (and certainly at the time of its release), *Sinistar* was the end boss you watched aliens assemble in real time as you played.

Williams made the game in both upright and environmental versions, the latter a first for the company. I only played the upright back then, but the sit-down model stunned; a giant ship cockpit painted in black, with striking red and blue graphics and some red lights around back. The effect was both futuristic and vaguely demonic. Inside, a vertically oriented 19-inch CRT displayed 256 colors and an unusually rectangular 340-by-240 resolution. The control panel featured a joystick and a pair of Fire buttons and Sinibomb buttons. *Sinistar* was notable for its optical joystick control. Williams said the controller was modeled after a military aircraft joystick for both response and durability. The stick itself resembled a standard eight-way model with a metal shaft and a red ball. But inside were six opto-isolators that controlled direction and speed, with three on the x axis and three on the y axis. This design yielded a total of 49 possible positions (six speeds, eight directions, and a center "off" position). Notably, the upright model of the game lacked this mechanism; the stick looked the same, but in that case it was a simple eight-way joystick.

Sinistar ran off of a Motorola 6809E processor. The game included true stereo sound, provided by two complete sound boards with 6808 CPUs and two separate volume controls. A separate speech board (a first for Williams) contained a series of digitized voice phrases stored in ROM chips. The phrases were transmitted as digital pulses, translated into analog speech, and mixed with the sound effects before being amplified through the speakers. All told, Sinistar was one of the best arcade games from this era: fiendishly difficult, and downright frightening when the Sinistar appeared and announced his presence. Many Golden Age arcade gamers recall the title fondly.

Gyruss (Konami/Centuri, 1983)

One of the best games to reimagine the traditional fixed space shooter, *Gyruss* did so perhaps literally—by twisting the playfield to generate a three-dimensional effect, making it a tube shooter similar to *Tempest*. In this game designed by Yoshiki Okamoto, you fought your way from the edge of the solar system to Earth. There were 23 stages full of enemy fighters that spun their way into formation and then attacked your ship in smaller squadrons. Your ship faced the center of the screen, and with the joystick you spun it around to the left and right, with the movement restricted to the perimeter of a large, imaginary circle. To enhance the depth effect, stars flew toward the outer edges, making it seem as if you were flying into the center of the screen.

The game began with the message, "2 stages to Neptune." Most of the gameplay consisted of the aforementioned enemy fighters swirling about, trying to either shoot you or collide with your ship. Periodically, you'd get the chance to shoot three satellites, the round center one of which gave your ship a double shot that was a serious help. If you lost your current ship, the new one would no longer have it and you'd have to collect it again. If you already had the double gun, the next time around the three satellites would all be the same.

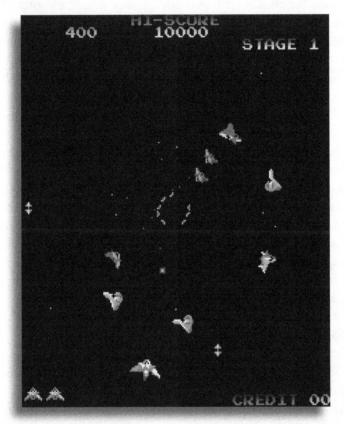

Figure 7.15: *Gyruss* **delivered 360-degree thrills and a compelling premise that spanned most of the length of our solar system swarmed by alien forces.**

Each time you completed a stage, you warped ahead to the next one. When you finished the first two, it played a victory theme and showed Neptune rendered at the center of the screen. You could even fly around and into it just for fun (although you didn't have to land or anything). A Challenge Stage would occur next, where you confronted four squadrons of 10 fighters each; if you picked off all 40, you'd get an extra bonus on top of it and another short musical theme of triumph. After that, it would be three stages to Uranus, followed by Saturn, Jupiter, Mars, and finally Earth—after which you would progress through three more stages at warp speed before returning to Neptune and starting the procession again.

The game's audio deserves special mention. First, it was in stereo, courtesy of a pair of discrete mono circuits, giving the game still more depth to go with its perspective view. The music was sped-up Bach, specifically "Toccata and Fugue in D minor," set to a stuttering electronic beat. Between the fast music, the tubelike perspective, and the constant onslaught of enemies, few games of the time were as adrenaline producing. It's impossible to imagine *Gyruss* with any other soundtrack.

Parker Brothers released a series of home conversions of *Gyruss*; the Atari 8-bit in particular captured all of the excitement of the original coinop. In the late 1980s, a Konami subsidiary brought the game to the NES with several enhancements to gameplay, as well as the addition of extra stages to reach Venus, Mercury, and the sun. After completing *Time Pilot* and *Gyruss*, two of Konami's most successful games, Okamoto asked for a raise; astoundingly, the company fired him instead. Soon he went on to the fledgling Capcom, an up-and-coming coin-op company, "because [it was] the only company that would hire me." Okamoto was only the second game designer Capcom had brought on.[32] As we'll see later in this book, it would prove a fateful move.

Star Wars: The Arcade Game (Atari, 1983)

A pinnacle of Golden Age arcade gaming, *Star Wars: The Arcade Game* was a technological and cultural milestone. Arriving on the scene alongside the motion picture *Return of the Jedi* in theaters, the game put you inside the *Star Wars* universe. As Luke Skywalker, you flew your X-wing fighter to defeat the Empire's forces and blow up the Death Star. The game, designed by Mike Hally, included several dozen unmistakable voice samples of Luke, Obi-Wan Kenobi, Darth Vader, Han Solo, and R2-D2 saying various catchphrases at the appropriate times from the three films. Throughout the game, different musical selections from the movie would play in a random order.

Key to the success of this coin-op, which was basically a first-person rail shooter, was its control yoke. You could fire lasers with either the trigger buttons or the thumb buttons on the top of the controller. To destroy the Death Star, you maneuvered through three stages of play in order to reach the exhaust port. The first was a battle in space with squadrons of TIE fighters that took off from the Death Star to defend it. The second stage took place on the surface of the Death Star, with its laser towers and bunkers.

You navigated around these and avoided surface-to-air shots, while shooting off the white tops of the yellow laser towers to destroy them. The final stage brought you into the famous trench scene. The game rendered this in green, with lines flying by to show movement. Red laser turrets fired at you throughout your approach, as well as walls in different colors that you would maneuver around. Get hit with any giant fireball shots from the TIE fighters or turrets—you could shoot the fireballs to deflect their impact—or crash into objects and your deflector shields would decrease.

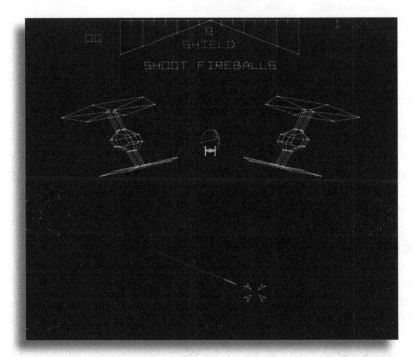

Figure 7.16: *Star Wars: The Arcade Game* **was a high-water mark in the Golden Age of arcades, successfully translating everyone's favorite space opera to the video game screen with an excellent control yoke and voice samples from all of the movie's top characters.**

Once you reached the exhaust port, you'd get a voice alert and a notice telling you it was straight ahead. You needed to shoot it; if you missed, you'd crash through the wall behind the port and lose a shield, and R2-D2 would not be happy. But if you succeeded, you'd fly away in the X-wing, far from the Death Star as it soon exploded in fantastic fashion. The game would award bonus points based on how you did and replenish some of your deflector shields. Then the proceedings repeated at a higher level of difficulty.

The attract mode displayed the title in the famous logo design floating in front of a star field. Then it switched to a scrolling text view that showed a new crawl for the game, just like in the movies.

> Obi-Wan Kenobi is gone but his presence is felt within the Force. The Empire's Death Star under the command of Darth Vader nears the rebel planet. You must join the rebellion to stop the empire. The force will be with you. Always.

Pop in a quarter (or two, as the game was often set to 50 cents), and you would enter Select-a-Death-Star mode. Here, after Luke said "Red 5 standing by," you could choose one of three Death Stars by positioning the flight yoke and pulling the laser fire trigger. Your choices were the default Easy, which awarded no bonus for destroying the first Death Star; Medium, which offered a 400,000-point bonus; and Hard, which delivered 800,000 points. In the Medium and Hard modes, the TIE fighters shot more often in the first stage, there were more surface-to-air missile installations in the second, and more trench obstacles appeared in the third. The game was powered by two Motorola 6809 CPUs, with audio courtesy of four POK-EY chips and a TI TMS5220 synthesizer. The cabinet came with special tamper-proof screws and a companion wrench the operator could use to remove them. The adjustments included four difficulty settings (separate from the three the player chose at the beginning of games), as well as a choice of starting with six, seven, eight, or nine shields.

Designer Ed Rothberg, of *Battlezone* fame, had also worked on *Dragon Riders*, an unreleased game that would have tied into Anne McCaffrey's *Dragonriders of Pern* books if Atari could have secured the license (it couldn't). Rothberg then started making a simulation game about space flight called *Warp Speed*, where you would fly in and attack a space fortress. Rothberg left Atari, so the rest of the team finished the game, and also added the new joystick yoke Rothberg had developed for the *Bradley Trainer*, the military version of *Battlezone*. In the meantime, Atari had just struck a licensing deal with George Lucas. The company decided to modify the in-game ships and fortress, added the voices to the game, and voilà.[33]

Atari made both environmental and upright versions; the former had behind-the-player speakers. *Star Wars: The Arcade Game* became one of the top-selling games of 1983, with the company moving more than 12,600 units. To this day, *Star Wars* coin-ops are coveted collector's items and are often the subject of ground-up restoration work. A cabinet in good physical condition and perfect working order can command many thousands of dollars on the market. Atari made two sequels, naturally *The Empire Strikes Back* (primarily as a conversion kit) and *Return of the Jedi*, which was a new raster game, not vector. As these were both released during and after the industry crash, they didn't do nearly as well. The game also saw many home conversions; most couldn't approach the arcade game in quality because of technical limitations, but the Atari ST, with its higher resolution and mouse control, got much closer in 1987.

In the mid 2000s, I lived in Astoria, a residential part of Queens still pretty close to Manhattan. I loved the neighborhood's Museum of the Moving Image for a lot of reasons, but one of them was a video game exhibit they ran one year. It included Golden Age arcade games such as *Missile Command* and *Space Invaders*. The crown jewel of the exhibit was a sit-down *Star Wars: The Arcade Game* cabinet in impeccable condition. As a member, I could get in for free, so I would walk over some afternoons just to sit down and play the game. I was treating the entire museum as a street location for a coin-op, as if it were 1983 once more. I no longer live near there, and the exhibit was rotated out long ago, but it was nice to create a "new" memory of playing arcade games the same way I used to back in the day.

Food Fight (Atari, 1983)

After *Ms. Pac-Man*, General Computer Corporation, now under contract with Atari, designed *Quantum*, a complex color vector game based on quantum physics that was unveiled in December 1982 to little fanfare. Three months later, Atari made a bit more of a splash with GCC's *Food Fight*. In this game, you played Charley Chuck, a blonde dude who liked ice cream. The cabinet was suitably cheery, with a white-and-blue paint job and brightly colored ice cream, fruits, and vegetables everywhere. The controls consisted of a centrally mounted analog joystick with 360-degree movement and a Throw button to either side. The button only worked when Charlie was holding a piece of food he picked up.

Your job on each board was to eat the ice cream before it melted. But standing in your way were four chefs named Oscar, Angelo, Jacques, and Zorba, who would climb out of holes on the board, chase you, and throw food at you. Strewn about each board were piles of pies, tomatoes, peas, bananas, and watermelons that Chuck could throw back at them. Whenever someone was hit with food, they briefly turned the color of the food before disappearing. Charley would not only lose a life, but all of the food on the board would fly toward him at once, making a huge mess. Charley could also lead the chefs to fall back into one of the holes. Each of the four chefs had his own AI algorithm, and each food flew differently when you threw it.

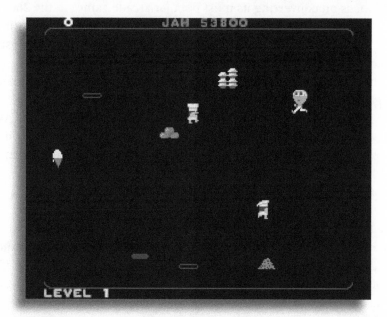

Figure 7.17: Perhaps the best thing about *Food Fight*, aside from its fun premise, was that you didn't have to clean anything up after you played.

If Chuck made it to the ice cream, his head would enlarge so that he could gulp the whole thing down in one shot. Then the game restarted on the next level of difficulty. The boards were prearranged, but it was tough to tell for newcomers because the levels were mostly a plain black background. It all looked a bit disorganized, like a free-for-fall, which I guess it was. Like some contemporary coin-ops such as *Tempest* and *Star Wars: The Arcade Game*, *Food Fight* let you choose from one of 10 levels to start from. One development was an instant replay of sorts, where if Chuck just barely missed getting hit with food, the game would pause and then show the move again in slow motion, as if it were a football or basketball game on television.

Operators could configure the game to give Charley anywhere from two to five lives, as well as choose from four difficulty settings and two bonus award options for free lives. In one of Atari's brochures, the company described *Food Fight* in the usual breathless prose about the profits an operator could make and called the game "far out fun for kids aged 5–150." (Hey, finally something I could play.)

Both *Food Fight* and *Quantum* were enjoyable, but neither sold well. Estimates were Atari sold just over 2,000 *Food Fight* cabinets and fewer than 500 of *Quantum*. After these games were completed, Atari asked GCC to instead focus on converting its most popular arcade games to the 2600 and 5200. GCC worked on several dozen 2600 cartridges that resulted in millions of sales for Atari, with many of GCC's conversions being surprisingly good considering the system's 1977 hardware. Atari soon canned an Atari 5200 SuperSystem conversion of *Food Fight* on account of the impending video game crash. Later, the company resurrected the title in two 1987 cartridges for its 7800 console and the repackaged XE Game System. As for Charley Chuck, he didn't become the hot new mascot Atari had hoped, and aside from those two later home conversions, we never saw him again.

Discs of Tron (Bally Midway, 1983)

Unlike the original *Tron* coin-op, *Discs of Tron* was a single game and not a series of minigames. In fact, it was supposed to be one of the minigames in the original, but memory requirements made it impossible to fit, so it was spun off into its own coin-op. *Discs of Tron* pitted the blue video warrior Tron against the red Sark, the defender of the Master Control Program, in what amounted to a combination of the film's jai alai and disc combat styles. *Discs of Tron* was designed for one or two players, with players alternating turns in the latter mode. The controls were the same as in the first game. These included a translucent-blue control grip with a trigger; the grip moved the player in all directions, and the trigger threw discs. A Shield button, also on the control stick, let the player deflect Sark's discs and chasers. To the left was a rotary spinner that let you position a movable target along the walls of the arena. You could employ two deflects per turn.

You confronted Sark in an enclosed arena with floating rings in various configurations. To do this, you threw *Discs of Tron*, banking shots across the various sides of the arena. You had to hit Sark twice to derezz him and advance to the next level. Each thrown disc returned to its owner, boomerang style. In turn, Sark jumped from ring to ring and tried to derezz you. You also had to mind the edges of the rings so that you didn't fall off. Both you and Sark could throw up to three discs at any one time; once three discs were in the air, you had to wait until they returned to throw another one. Sark could also send after you chaser orbs, super-chaser orbs with companion discs, and energy pellets that split into several missiles. These could all be destroyed, but the orbs took two shots to eliminate. Beginning on level seven, the rings would move up and down, adding a vertical dimension to gameplay. The spinner control would let you aim your arm up and down. There were 12 levels in all; after level 12, the game repeated seven through 12 until the player lost all of his or her lives. Barriers and scrolling walls also appeared later in the game.

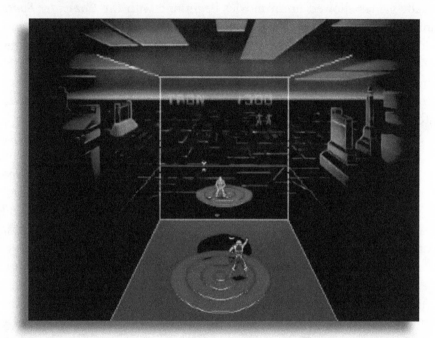

Figure 7.18: *Discs of Tron* **was notable as much for its addictive game play as its incredible environmental cockpit version.**

Discs of Tron came in a standard upright and a two-player cocktail form factor. But the game was especially notable for its environmental cockpit model, which weighed more than 700 pounds. In addition to offering sit-down play, the dimly lit environmental version sported a carpeted back, an energy disc graphic on the floor, and specially designed stereo sound, acoustics, lighting, and special effects that activated in tandem with game-play. The effect was similar to that of *Space Invaders Deluxe*, where the game projected the graphics over a realistic-looking backdrop of a computerized city to add a third dimension. "The idea is to place gamers into the arena so they feel more physically in the game," said designer Bob Dinnerman in a 1983 interview.[34] In all cases, the cabinet's purple, red, and black graphics were unmistakable, as was the *Discs of Tron* marquee in the same font used in the original game and, of course, the motion picture. The game's graphics, sound design, and Sark's synthesized speech all came in for praise, and to this day the environmental cabinet is prized by collectors.

Arcade Games in Movies and TV Shows

Arcade games showed up in movies beginning with the *Computer Space* cabinet in 1973's *Soylent Green*. Coin-op video games appeared in at least a dozen movies between then and 1983, if not more, including such films as *Midnight Madness* and *Fast Times at Ridgemont High*. By the early 1980s, movie scenes such as in *E.T.: The Extra Terrestrial* reflected arcades as they were in real life. Kids had relative autonomy from their parents compared with today, riding on their bikes and hanging out in arcades playing video games as their parents worked.[35] Video games also made appearances on TV, most notably in Saturday morning cartoons with shows based on *Pac-Man* and other hot arcade coin-ops. *Saturday Supercade*, which aired in 1983 and 1984, consisted of a series of short segments based on popular video games, including *Donkey Kong, Frogger, Q*bert, Kangaroo*, and even Pitfall Harry from the best-selling Atari 2600 cartridge. *Dragon's Lair* scored its own 13-episode series on ABC.

In addition to *Star Trek: Strategic Operations Simulator, Star Wars: The Arcade Game*, and *Discs of Tron*, we also saw television-series-themed games such as Gottlieb's *Krull*, Sega's *Buck Rogers: Planet of Zoom*, and the aforementioned *Popeye* from Nintendo. Video games continued to have an effect on major motion pictures as well. The third installment of *Star Wars, Return of the Jedi*, hit theaters that year (never mind it's now the sixth installment, somehow) and full of scenes that would find themselves in a video game within two years, just as the first two movies did. *The Last Starfighter* centered on a character who played an arcade game that was designed as a test to find someone who could fight in a real war. The biggest game-themed motion picture that year was one about a home computer, not an arcade machine: *WarGames*. The movie featured a young Matthew Broderick playing a kid who hacked into a military computer system designed to simulate potential outcomes of nuclear war, except at the time it was hooked into real nuclear weapons. Broderick's character thought it was just a game but began to set World War III in motion—tying the video game age to the Cold War at a level even *Missile Command* couldn't achieve.

To gamers, the video game age seemed to be flying high, with packed arcades still leading the way and consoles and cartridges flying off store shelves. And then it was over.

8 > Crash

In 1983, video games were as big as The Police, but just like the band, their future was suddenly in doubt. What would come to be known as the Great Video Game Crash came for everyone. The arcade industry, successful as it was, was plagued by a number of issues. Simple saturation was a top reason, and some of it wasn't on the level. Not just clones, but bootlegs of games filled arcades, as unscrupulous vendors copied successful designs and distribute them to locations at lower costs with little more than a name change and new cabinet graphics. The problem was never adequately addressed, if there even was a way to address it.

Home consoles, meanwhile, had ramped up in quality. By the end of 1982, several new machines appeared that offered higher-end specs and the promise of "just like the arcade." Perhaps the most famous of these was the ColecoVision, a console that offered 32KB cartridges instead of the 2KB to 8KB found in Atari 2600 games, as well as more on-screen colors and better sound. Coleco secured the rights for plenty of good games from Universal and Exidy, but its biggest coup was landing a superior conversion of Nintendo's *Donkey Kong* as the pack-in cartridge. Although it only offered three of the four levels of the arcade, that was one more than you could get on the 2600 and the Mattel Intellivision, and the graphics were much closer to the coin-op's. Nintendo went with Coleco in part because Coleco CEO Arnold C. Greenberg promised to do both the cartridge and a tabletop console, and Nintendo needed the exposure for its still-struggling American division.[1] Coleco paid Nintendo up front for the contract and promised royalties of $1.40 per *Donkey Kong* cartridge and $1 per tabletop machine. The console was a hit holiday gift in 1982, and six months later when the exclusivity clause ran out, Coleco began selling 2600 and Intellivision versions.[2]

Two other new consoles also arrived. The Atari 5200 SuperSystem offered much higher-quality arcade game conversions than the 2600. The 5200 also let you group the two pack-in joysticks together for *Robotron: 2084* and *Space Dungeon*, and the optional trackball console was ideal for *Missile Command* and *Centipede*. The GCE Vectrex, meanwhile, delivered arcade-quality black-and-white vector graphics on its built-in monitor, a combination no other home system offered. It played quality versions of *Berzerk*, *Star Castle*, *Scramble*, Cinematronics' *Armor Attack*, and other arcade hits, as well as original games such as *Cosmic Chasm* and *Clean Sweep*. And the pack-in *Mine Storm* was a convincing clone of *Asteroids* (which Atari wouldn't license).

Mattel released a voice synthesizer module for the Intellivision, and Magnavox did the same for its aging Odyssey 2. Fairchild launched a refreshed Channel F II, and the Bally Astrocade was rereleased as the Astrovision Astrocade. An October 24, 1982, *Newsweek* article described how a new generation of video games such as *Zaxxon*, *Smurf*, *E.T.*, and *Donkey Kong* was "gobbling its way onto toy-store shelves like so many Pac-Men. By and large, the entries are a startling leap forward…for the first time, the graphics and play action of home games are beginning to approach the quality of video-arcade games."[3]

After years of promise and futuristic looks, even vector graphics technology found itself on the chopping block. Games as varied and awesome as *Asteroids*, *Space Fury*, *Star Castle*, *Tempest*, and *Star Wars: The Arcade Game* had appeared. What changed? Raster graphics were catching up in resolution, they were already far ahead in color support, and depicted detailed, filled-in objects. Raster would only improve further as memory costs fell. Vector monitors weren't the most reliable, either. Still, nothing will ever replace the sharpness and the phosphor glow of a proper X-Y display, though it's fair to say a good portion of my brain remains forever locked in the greatness that was 1982 and 1983.

The Industry Nose-Dives

The mainstream cultural recognition of arcade games was there, but the industry was burning out. By the end of 1983, the financial damage was clear. Arcades were closing down, and machines were already being pulled out of restaurants and bars and not replaced. Profit sank 35 percent, to $2.9 billion, and industry-wide losses totaled about $1.5 billion. Although the number of arcades peaked at around 10,000 sometime between 1980 and 1982, more than 2,000 would close by the end of 1983.[4] Total arcade and home video game revenue plummeted from $3 billion at its peak to just $100 million in 1985.[5] Atari itself rang up $538 million in losses by the end of 1983, leading Warner Communications to start thinking about selling the company.[6] Retail prices also plummeted. Jack Tramiel, the CEO of Commodore, was credited with kicking off that phenomenon after he slashed the price of the popular Commodore 64 from $595 to $295. That helped spur a price war that saw the prices of home computers, game consoles, and video cartridges all tumble. Part of it was also economies of scale: Chips were becoming less expensive and production lines were increasing in size.[7]

The video game market crash was driven by a number of factors, where arcades were maybe a small part of the problem but largely collateral damage. The monstrous failure of Atari's 2600 *Pac-Man* was probably the biggest, with the mediocre *E.T.* cartridge having more of a pile-on effect than causing the crash outright. Above all, it was the glut of third-party cartridges, many of them poor quality, and the corresponding rise of much more capable home computers that drove the crash. Home video game manufacturers suffered the most, with storied companies such as Imagic, Data Age, U.S. Games, and Games by Apollo among the casualties. Mattel's electronics division lost $195 million in 1983 and almost filed Chapter 11. Coleco didn't survive the decade, despite its successful ColecoVision and the Cabbage Patch Kid craze.

If you were an arcade gamer, little of the above mattered as it was happening. But some arcade manufacturers wouldn't make it through, either; Centuri, the U.S. distributor for *Phoenix*, *Pleiades*, and *Vanguard*, closed at the end of 1983. There was less reason to go to the arcade in the first place. Home consoles became much better at reproducing existing arcade titles. Powerful game-playing home computers were available, too. Systems like the Commodore 64 and VIC-20, the Atari 400/800, the Apple II, the TI 99/4A, and others weren't limited to just arcade-style games—they also ran sophisticated role-playing games, adventures, and complex simulations, to say nothing of tons of productivity and educational software, and could connect to fledgling online networks. And although the true cost to the software industry would never be quantified, piracy also played a huge role. The temptation to copy disks and trade them with your friends was just too strong, and meant you had access to dozens of top "cracked" programs for the cost of a pack of blank disks.

One of the biggest draws of coin-ops were their industrial-strength controllers and dedicated layouts, as each game's control scheme was customized at the design stage. But third-party manufacturers began creating arcade-style controllers for home computers and consoles, neutralizing even that advantage. Wico, which began selling computer joysticks after building hardware controllers for arcade manufacturers, offered ball-top, bat-handle, and finger-grip Command Control products popular with Atari and Commodore players, as well as dedicated varieties. J.D. Home offered the Obelisk, a free-standing controller console made of wood and mica and set up to be arcade height. Suncom, Epyx, and Amiga also made arcade-style controllers, among other vendors. Even trackballs with 9-pin joystick connectors appeared, both from Atari and others.

One factor not often spoke out loud was the move toward video games as family entertainment—and, by extension, something you would do more at home, even with the existence of family-friendly establishments. Much of this went back to how, in the popular imagination, the arcade could be something threatening for teenage boys. Arcades continued to be associated with pinball, which itself was harmless but nonetheless still carried a reputation more akin to gambling and organized crime, and something that was even still banned in some cities just a few years prior.[8] The more home conversions of arcade games appeared for consoles and home computers, the less reason there was to go to an arcade. It coincided with the way home game consoles were marketed—not as toys, but as objects for the rec room or "Family Game Center," as Sears catalogs put it in the late 1970s, alongside dart boards, chess and checkers, and ping-pong tables.[9]

With things looking bleak, arcade manufacturers were prepared to try anything, as releasing endless sequels and clones of existing successful games wasn't enough. There was one bright hope on the horizon, though—not just a new game, but entirely new technology that enabled the creation of games on a level never seen before.

The Rise of Laserdisc

Disc-based video was already nothing new—the analog videodisc format had first appeared all the way back in 1964. But the late 1970s and early 1980s saw the beginnings of digital optical media. Laserdisc, introduced in 1978 and so named for the laser-based mechanism that read the data on the disc, was the first optical disc storage medium. In 1981, David Lubar wrote an Apple II program for *Creative Computing* magazine that could control a laserdisc and display scenes from a movie (1975's *Rollercoaster*), demonstrating for the first time a laserdisc could be used for video games.[10]

In contrast to raster and vector coin-ops, laserdisc games looked less like computer graphics than they did Hollywood-produced video—which is what it was. The August 1982 issue of *Electronic Games* ran a feature on upcoming "Games on Disc" that showed off a minimally interactive, photorealistic golfing simulation called *Go For the Green* that would run on laserdisc players. The article also covered more narrowly focused efforts such as Ford Motor Company's laserdisc-based interactive training for its employees. Laser's introduction in arcades came just after the well-publicized downturn in the arcades. One local news station claimed, when introducing laser, "the familiar din of the video arcade is fading out," and that "business has dropped in half over the past year, and companies like Atari claim losses of $350 million...the craze has definitely peaked. But there's something completely different that's invading the video emporium these days, because of the marriage between the laser and computer technology."[11]

The first genuine arcade coin-op based on a laserdisc to be unveiled was Sega's *Astron Belt*, a third-person space combat game. Thanks to some technical issues, a different game beat *Astron Belt* to market in the U.S. It would go on to become one of the biggest—and last—hits of the Golden Age of the video arcade.

Dragon's Lair (Cinematronics, 1983)

Dragon's Lair was the other landmark *arcade* moment in 1983, after *Star Wars: The Arcade Game*, and made it look as if the future had arrived and nothing would ever be the same. Rick Dyer, of RDI Video Systems, designed the coin-op, and it displayed animation from ex-Disney icon Don Bluth, who had directed *The Secret of NIMH* the prior year. In *Dragon's Lair*, you were the screwball knight Dirk the Daring on a quest to rescue Princess Daphne from an evil dragon inside a wizard's castle, which was filled with traps and monsters. Dirk had to travel through many passages to get to the dragon, which kept Daphne imprisoned in a magic cage.

Dyer conceived the game in the vein of a computer graphic adventure, with a text-based interface and "pseudo-artificial intelligence" (his words) inspired by *Colossal Cave* and accompanied by still photos.[12] He later reimagined it as an interactive film after seeing *Astron Belt* at AMOA in 1982.[13] Dyer approached Bluth and, with a paltry $1 million budget, had the game made. Thirteen artists hand-drew 50,000 frames of animation, which were then painted on cels and scanned to create 24fps video, the same speed as a motion picture reel. The game used the laserdisc like a hard drive—a slow one with a ton of space. This caused heavy wear and tear on the Pioneer LD players installed in the cabinets and resulted in frequent breakdowns during operation. (Two different models were used during production, with largely the same effect; conversion kits have since appeared for collectors looking to restore the cabinets or just keep them running today.)

Figure 8.1: *Dragon's Lair* **brought Hollywood-quality animation to the video game age, an incredible achievement that was ultimately let down by its on-rails gameplay and zero replay value.**

Even so, the formula worked. *Dragon's Lair* delivered amazing graphics compared with anything else on the market. There were no visible pixels, computerized graphics, on-screen text, or other obvious clues that "looked like a video game," aside from an attract mode that displayed the title while a narrator explained what was going on. Instead, the graphics was all finely drawn lines, smoothly shaded colors, and fluid, Disney-like animation that depicted heroic action sequences. Perhaps the most memorable were the dozens of amusing death scenes, where Dirk was variously strangled to death by serpents, fell screaming into pits, became a skeleton that then collapsed in a pile of bones, or was eaten alive by bats. The disc also played a full musical score for each scene, which was recorded with a live orchestra, and all of the sound effects were professionally produced and synced with the video instead of generated with low-cost synthesizer chips. The game was the first ever to look and sound like a motion picture, complete with a narrative and (hand-drawn) cinematography. It would have been impossible even with the best graphics technology of the day and unlimited ROM chips. To the arcade gamer of 1983, it seemed as if the ultimate achievement had finally been realized.

Starcade is often credited with introducing *Dragon's Lair* to the public, but soon the game was everywhere. "We're in the entertainment business and no one had really come out with anything new, a new novelty," Dyer said in a 1983 television interview. "People were sick of computer graphic games that didn't have appeal, they were tired of them. They wanted something a little more real."[14]

At 50 cents per play, *Dragon's Lair* pulled in $48 million in revenue in 1983 and remained in production through early 1984. Unlike earlier coin-ops, *Dragon's Lair* came from the factory set to 50 cents a play *without* the ability to adjust it back down to 25 cents; operators needed a special modification kit to do so. Cinematronics wanted to ensure operators recouped their investment with this high-priced cabinet, which cost more than $4,000.[15] In an industry where operators were averaging $141 in coin drop per machine in 1981 and $109 in 1982, *Dragon's Lair* was pulling in up to $1,400 per machine per week.[16] Also keeping interest high: None of the game consoles and home computer systems of the day could handle the immense storage requirements and graphics resolution necessary to translate the game. Home gamers were treated to a variety of mostly terrible ports across systems ill suited to the task.

The reality was that *Dragon's Lair* was a house of cards. It has since gained a reputation for its poor control scheme. It looked pretty simple at first, with just a joystick and a Sword button to either side. But you didn't control Dirk the Daring; instead, you controlled his reflexes, anticipating his intended movements indicated with an on-screen flash, to advance the action. If you moved incorrectly at any point, you'd see one of the many death scenes. Otherwise, the game would continue for another few seconds. For example, with swinging ropes, you needed to move to the right at just the right time for Dirk to grab the next one; otherwise, you'd sail right into the lava pit below. So, although most of the movements were at least somewhat intuitive, it was just a series of control inputs you needed to make in the correct order to complete the game. Memorizing them meant winning. Using today's terminology, *Dragon's Lair* was on rails; it was an interactive movie. The entire game consisted of dozens of scenes strung together in an order that varied slightly from game to game. Played start to finish, *Dragon's Lair* took about 12 minutes if you did everything perfectly. For a good amount of time, though—much longer than 12 minutes, at least—*Dragon's Lair* ruled the video arcades.

Crystal Castles (Atari, 1983)

Some other solid coin-ops arrived at the tail end of 1983, even as the market crash continued in earnest. *Crystal Castles* put you in control of the esteemed Bentley Bear, who had to collect gems from a variety of three-dimensional mazes while avoiding numerous baddies. An original Atari hit, the game consisted of nine levels with four castles each, and a final 10th level where you finished the game—an early example of an arcade game with a true ending, similar to the *Adventure* cartridge on the Atari 2600 and many computer role-playing games. Although the dot-clearing and maze-like pathways of *Crystal Castles* were reminiscent of *Pac-Man*, the game itself played nothing like the Midway classic.

The cabinet design was one of the nicest ever. It looked like a giant, cartoonish M.C. Escher drawing, and extended from top to bottom on the cabinet sides. More drawings covered the front, including the control panel and in a *U* shape around the coin box. The control panel contained a trackball and a Jump button; the trackball moved Bentley Bear around the mazes, and the Jump button let you leap over enemies. Each board was depicted in distinct colors and with a true sense of three dimensions thanks to its trimetric-projected rendered castle designs. Gems you collected were worth an increasing amount of points, starting with 1 and going all the way up to 99 if there were that many on the board. Some enemies also collected the gems, including Nasty Trees, Crystal Balls, and Gem Eaters, the last of which you could dispatch by running over them mid-gem-eating. This could rob you of the bonus at the end of a board, which you only scored if you were the one to grab the last gem. Dancing skeletons and a ghost also made appearances on some levels.

Each board contained either a witch's hat or a honey pot. The hat was worth 500 points and made Bentley Bear invulnerable for a few moments as an arpeggiated theme played, and it also let you defeat Berthilda the witch at the end of a level for 3,000 points. The honey pot attracted a dangerous swarm of bees until Bentley Bear picked it up for 1,000 points. The boards contained plenty of neat details, including hidden tunnels, ramps, and elevators.

One of the coolest things about *Crystal Castles* was the way it handled high scores. Let's say you landed in the high score list after completing a game and then entered your initials. The next time you (or better yet, someone else) started the game, your initials would be incorporated into the first level's design. There were also hidden warps, starting with one in the first level that took you to level five; it was around the back of the castle, where Bentley Bear would end up hidden. If you jumped in that spot, it would execute the warp. These warps were sprinkled throughout the castles and levels in the game.

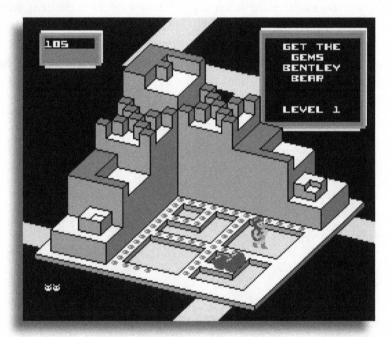

Figure 8.2: *Crystal Castles* **was equal parts M.C. Escher and…dot eating? It was an attractive and unique game, whatever its components, and largely defined by its unusual trackball-based control scheme.**

Crystal Castles was notable both for the aforementioned Easter egg and the built-in warp zones. It was ported to numerous home computer platforms but never made it to any consoles save for the Atari XE Game System. Speaking of which, two POKEY sound chips delivered audio in the *Crystal Castles* cabinet, and a 6502 controlled the game, the same as the hardware in Atari's long-running line of 8-bit computers. The audio in *Crystal Castles* consisted of snippets of several songs from classical repertoire, including Tchaikovsky's *The Nutcracker* and Listz's Mephisto Waltz no. 1. Playing the game was always memorable, and the distinctive audio marked a memorable part of the ambient sound of 1983 and 1984 in arcades.

Elevator Action (Taito, 1983)

In this innovative platform-and-shooter hybrid, you were Agent 17, a spy who had to pick up top-secret documents and remove them from a 30-story office building. Enemy spies chased you; you could either shoot them or kick them. The documents were stashed in special rooms with bright red doors. Once you had the documents, you headed for the basement, where a getaway car was waiting. The central game mechanic was the pink elevator, which transported you between floors. Enemy spies surprised Agent 17 by jumping out of random offices (drawn with dark blue doors). Either you or the enemy spies could also shoot out the lights, which would cause a temporary blackout; some floors had no lights at all.

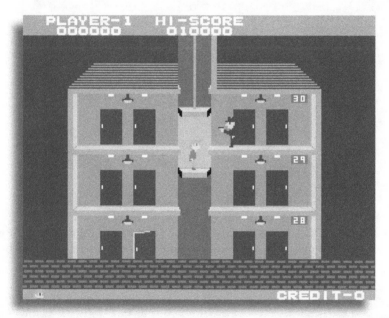

Figure 8.3: *Elevator Action* **put you in control of a spy who had to pilfer vital documents out of an office building teeming with enemy agents.**

The controls consisted of a four-way joystick, a Jump button, and a Fire button that shot up to three bullets at a time. A short introductory sequence showed Agent 17 arriving on the roof of the first building via helicopter and then taking his position down the elevator to the top floor. Agent 17 could move back and forth, jump, and duck, and whenever he was in the elevator, he could control it by pushing up or down on the joystick. He could also climb on top of the elevator and ride it, but then he couldn't control it, and when he was inside it, he couldn't duck. You'd figure out how to anticipate when enemy spies would appear in a nearby office doorway right as you arrived in the elevator. An alarm would sound and speed up the agents, and if you tried to escape in the getaway car without all the documents, you'd get sent right back up to finish the job. Successfully complete one building and you'd be brought to the next, tougher one.

The game's graphics served the action perfectly, and a background tune played the entire time. There were also some escalators at the ends of the floors; it was impossible to ride them and not think of Activision's *Keystone Kapers*, which was set in a mall. You boarded an escalator by walking onto it and pushing up or down; several small lines marked the right spot on the floor, the same as were in front of the red doors to show you how to walk in and out.

Elevator Action was made in upright and cocktail versions and was sufficiently different from other platformers, thanks to the espionage theme and your ability to shoot opponents. *Elevator Action* did receive a port to the Commodore 64 and several overseas computers like the ZX Spectrum and the MSX, and it made it to the NES and Game Boy as well, an odd lineup that probably had to do with the arcade game appearing right in the middle of the Great Video Game Crash. *Elevator Action* didn't have a lot of replay value, as the successive buildings were largely the same and the graphics and music never changed. But it was a fun, short diversion unlike anything else in arcades at the time.

Mario Bros. (Nintendo, 1983)

The original Mario and Luigi game, *Mario Bros.* pit a pair of Italian-American plumbers against a variety of creatures emerging from pipes, including Shellcreepers, Sidesteppers, and Fighter Flies. The control panel included a single two-way joystick and a Jump button for each player. The game presented a single-screen playfield bracketed by a series of pipes. You could walk off one side of the screen and appear on the other. Various creatures went after Mario and Luigi; eliminate them all and you'd advance to the next level. You dispatched the creatures by jumping up on the platform below so that you punched into the ceiling spot they were standing on. The move bent the floor upward, which stunned them and flipped them over.

You then had to go up and walk into them to "kick" them away, or else they'd soon flip back over and be angry and faster. In addition, you had to avoid Slipices and fireballs as you play. Slipices can freeze the floors, making them slippery for Mario and Luigi. You could also punch the fireballs when they hit the floor.

With two players, the game dynamic was a bit different. You could co-operate, for example, and finish the boards faster; one player punched as the other kicked from above. Or you could get in each other's way, such as by punching a stunned enemy again at just the right time to threaten your opponent. You could also punch the other player from below or push him off of a platform. Right before you completed a board, the last remaining creature would also speed up. The POW icon in the middle of the board, when punched, knocked over all the creatures simultaneously. You could only hit it three times per level, at which point it disappeared. Clear all the creatures and you'd move to the next round, or "phase," with an on-screen number indicating the current phase next to an equals sign (such as P=2).

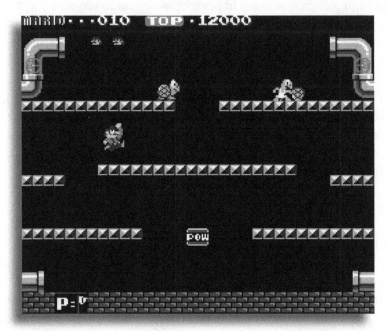

Figure 8.4: *Mario Bros.* **was the game that put Luigi on the map, along with a series of Nintendo staples such as Shellcreepers and the green pipes.**

Mario Bros. showed a middle point in the evolution of Nintendo games. It was still an action-focused arcade coin-op with the score as the primary focus. You scored higher in the game by kicking several stunned creatures in a row. Bonus points also came from the coins that emptied out of the pipes whenever an enemy was kicked. A bonus round let you run around collecting as many coins as you could before the timer ran out; if you nabbed them all, you'd also collect a bonus. At 20,000 points, you'd get an extra Mario or Luigi. When you lost all of your lives, the game would end.

Mario Bros. introduced a number of elements of future Nintendo games, including not just Luigi, but turtles, the pipes, coins, and the stun-and-kick maneuver. (The crabs became more of a callback thing; they were later known as Sidesteppers and showed up here and there in later games like the Mario Kart series.) *Mario Bros.* was both an important title not just for arcades but for video games in general.

Track & Field (Konami/Centuri, 1983)

In *Track & Field*, you competed for the gold medal in a series of six Olympic-style events. You didn't need to know how to play the actual sports so much as how to push buttons quickly. The game depicted play in a horizontal side-scrolling view, with one or two tracks at a time depending on the event, a large scoreboard on top that included world records and current runs, and a packed audience in the stands near the center of the screen. The white-and-blue cabinet looked sporty, with its American-style logo on the marquee in red, white, and blue. The control panel contained two sets of controls, with each player getting a pair of red Run buttons and a white Jump/Throw button. The game also had a mode to accommodate up to four human players, where pairs of two would alternate to use the two sets of controls on the front panel, oddly arranged for players two and four on the left and one and three on the right. The multiplayer games were the most fun; sometimes playing by yourself felt like practicing for those times, as opposed to playing a satisfying single-player game.

When you first put in a quarter, you were asked to enter your name, normally something you'd only do after achieving a high score. The game started with the 100-meter dash, where you just had to run as fast as you could with alternating Run button presses. The bottom of the screen showed your speed meter; it was tough to get it to approach the top end of the range and required fast button mashing. If you ran faster than the qualifying time, you'd progress to the next event regardless of whether you beat the other human- or computer-controlled player. Next up was the long jump, where you ran as fast as you could and then, at the exact right moment, pressed and held the Jump/Throw button just long enough so you came as close to a 42-degree angle as possible. Following was the javelin throw, where you would run and then press and hold the Jump/Throw button to achieve a 43-degree angle.

In the 110-meter hurdles, you'd have to do the same sprint as in the 100-meter dash, but also press the Jump/Throw button to jump over the hurdles. The hammer throw required a sharper 45-degree angle; in this event, the game would run your character automatically, and you pushed the Jump/Throw button at just the right time. Finally, in the high jump, you pressed the Jump/Throw button when you arrived at the bar and then kept pressing it fast to achieve additional height. Each time you didn't qualify for an event, you lost a "life." On the high score table, the game played "Chariots of Fire" from Vangelis, because what else would it play?

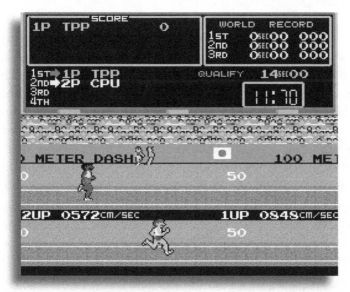

Figure 8.5: *Track & Field* **showcased excellent graphics and six Olympic events that were essentially six variations of the 100mph Button Mash.**

Konami scored an official license the following year for the 1984 Summer Olympics. Despite its simplistic button-mashing gameplay, the game became a huge success in its time, with some 38,000 cabinets sold in Japan alone and an unknown total in the U.S.[17] The game led to a long series of home conversions; clones from developers such as Activision (beginning with 1983's *The Activision Decathlon*) and Epyx (starting with 1984's *Summer Games*); and sequels, with the most recent (at the time of this writing) being *Hyper Sports R* on the Nintendo Switch. Even though the series still lives today in one form or another, it feels of its time, with most other sports games today either requiring gamepads or motion controllers instead of rapid button pushing.

Spy Hunter (Bally Midway, 1983)

One of my favorite arcade games at the time, *Spy Hunter* was everything a car nut who liked James Bond and *Knight Rider* could want: a steering wheel, spy gear, crashes, a rolling headquarters in a truck where you could get special weapons—the works. It was clear that's what Bally Midway was going for, too, if the U.K. brochure was any indication. It showed a car interior that looked suspiciously like the Knight Industries Two Thousand, complete with a flight yoke for a steering wheel, and the sit-down coin-op cabinet was shown amidst photos of a handgun, car keys, a portable video surveillance monitor, and glasses of whisky.

Bally Midway couldn't get the rights to the James Bond theme, so instead it went with Henry Mancini's iconic theme to *Peter Gunn*, the 1958–1961 private eye TV series—giving this coin-op an instant sonic signature in crowded arcades. *Spy Hunter* also included one of the earliest examples of an adaptive music soundtrack in video games, which the company called "Artificial Artist." It played AI-generated solos on top of programmed music backing tracks in the vein of the spy theme, and followed the pace of the gameplay—this was the kind of thing we'd start to see a lot more of in circa-1990-and-up MS-DOS games such as *Wing Commander*, but it was unheard of so early in a coin-op cabinet.

At its core, *Spy Hunter* was a top-down, vertical-scrolling driving game in the grand tradition of *Speed Race* and *Wheels*, but with detailed color graphics and sound effects and a vehicular combat mechanic. You played as a secret agent driving a turbocharged Interceptor car armed with special weapons. Both sit-down and standup cabinets presented a flight-yoke-style steering wheel with two triggers on each handle. The right triggers fired a machine gun with unlimited rounds and a smoke screen. The left triggers fired surface-to-air missiles and laid down oil slicks. The control panel also had a two-position gear-select lever, and a metal accelerator pedal was located on the right side near the floor.

You dispatched as many enemies in other vehicles as you could while protecting the civilian cars. The enemy cars and bomber helicopters would try and destroy you or force you off the road. Each time you started a new turn, you'd back out of the weapons van; periodically, you'd come across the truck van, which you could dock with to get a new weapon. Obliterate a civilian car and you'd stop earning points for a bit as a penalty. As you drove in the game, you'd occasionally reach a fork that led to different terrains and weather conditions. The best part: You'd even get the chance to go off-road, transform into a hydroplane, and pilot it up a river, fighting off Mad Bombers and Torpedo Cruisers.

Figure 8.6: *Spy Hunter* **played into everyone's James Bond fantasy, thanks to its vehicular combat missions and secret home base inside an 18-wheeler.**

Spy Hunter was a successful coin-op; Bally Midway tried to follow it up in 1987 with a sequel using three-dimensional graphics, but it was a major flop. The original game received conversions on many major platforms of the day and came out as a NES game a few years later. *Spy Hunter* appeared in a variety of TV shows, including *Murder, She Wrote* and *Robot Chicken*, and showed up in an Excel 2000 Easter Egg. There's also been an on-again, off-again motion picture in development since 2003, a soap opera full of details not worth reporting here.

Tapper (Bally Midway, 1983)

In *Tapper*, you played as a bartender specializing in draft beer on tap. You served as many thirsty customers as you could without missing any. The game cycled through four different levels, which included a western saloon stocked with cowboys, a sports bar full of athletes, a punk rock venue with musicians, and, naturally, an outer-space bar full of alien life-forms. (I still want to go to that bar.)

Figure 8.7: In *Tapper*, you served dozens of customers draft beer, all without spilling a drop or letting anyone's thirst go unquenched.

The cabinet resembled an actual bar, with its lustrous wood paneling and chunky brass bar rail accents. Anheuser-Busch sponsored the first run of machines, which were fitted with Budweiser-branded tap handles. (Bally Midway later switched to miniature plastic beer tap handles, albeit still with the Budweiser logo on them.) A conventional four-way joystick with a red ball, for controlling the bartender's movement, sat between the two tap handles.

Each board contained four bars of increasing lengths. The longest one was the easiest to serve. Patrons would begin filing into the establishment and making their way down the bar toward the right side where you and the kegs were. Pushing up and down on the control stick whisked you from bar to bar. You tapped three times to serve; the first filled the glass by half, the second topped it off, and the third would send it down the bar. A patron would drink the beer and then disappear, though as you played, increasingly that patron would send the glass back down for another round and pound on the bar while waiting for the next one. If there was no customer to receive the beer you poured, it would sail down the bar to the end and crash onto the floor, and you'd lose a life. The same would happen if you missed a patron and let them get to your end of the bar or if you missed catching an empty glass that was sliding back. Occasionally, a customer would leave a tip; when you ran down the bar to grab it, a reward sequence would play. For example, in the saloon, three girls would begin dancing on stage as that customer watched; meanwhile, the rest of the patrons carried on as normal. Serve all the patrons on a given board and the bartender would do something humorous, such as tossing back a round and throwing the empty glass up in the air, stubbing his toe when he tried to kick it, or somehow managing to get it stuck on his head.

After each successful round, a bonus round displayed six cans on the bar. A masked figure shook five of the cans and then pounded the bar, which shuffled them around. If you could keep track of the single unshaken can and then chose it, you'd get bonus points. Choosing any of the other five cans by mistake would lead to you getting sprayed with beer foam, and then the correct can flashed. Complete all four boards and bonus rounds and the game would repeat and become tougher.

Tapper was powered by Midway's MCR III Computer Logic System, which also drove *Spy Hunter*, *Discs of Tron*, and some other titles. Amusement industry ads for the game were full of puns such as, "Catch a mug full of fun," "Tap into profits with the street location game of 1984," and "We're serving another round of street location fun!" Bally Midway also made a "nonalcoholic" iteration called *Root Beer Tapper*, in an effort to head off accusations Bally Midway was advertising alcohol to minors. *Tapper* reportedly sold 3,300 cabinets in a declining market but was popular enough to see conversions to numerous consoles and computer platforms.[18]

Hybrid Arcade Games and Pinball Tables

One small subgenre of the video arcade was the hybrid machine, which combined elements of pinball with those of a video game. The earliest was Chicago Coin's *Super Flipper*, which integrated a vertically oriented CRT monitor into the table portion of an otherwise normal pinball machine. Later, manufacturers went in the other direction with models that looked like video arcade cabinets. The most famous model was Bally Midway's *Baby Pac-Man*, although there was also *Caveman* from the same company as well as Gottlieb's *Granny and the Gators*. These games consisted of smaller-than-usual pinball tables built into an otherwise normal standard upright arcade cabinet. The pinball table was positioned behind the control panel, with the arcade game's CRT positioned above it.

Figure 8.8: Hybrid coin-ops that combined pinball with video game graphics didn't take off. Shown here was the one that was arguably the most popular, *Baby Pac-Man*. Credit: Rob DiCaterino/Yestercades, Somerville, NJ

Hybrid games didn't survive the industry crash. But the idea was resurrected around the turn of the millennium when Williams Electronics introduced Pinball 2000, a pinball hardware platform that employed a CRT as part of the table design to display animation, scoring, and even in some cases targets. Thanks to a mirrored glass design said to be inspired by *Asteroids Deluxe*, the video portion was perceived as part of the mechanical playfield, where the physical silver ball could "hit" targets that were part of the video game. Two games appeared using this hardware platform: Bally's 1999 pinball table *Revenge From Mars*, which looked like half a video arcade cabinet was grafted onto the back portion, and Williams' *Star Wars Episode I*. At least five more were planned, but Williams Electronics shut down its venerable pinball division in the year 2000 thanks to poor sales and canned all in-progress projects in the process.

These hybrid coin-ops were unsuccessful on the distribution circuit in their day, but a certain kind of collector loves these games today and will go to serious lengths to refurbish or otherwise restore them to full operation (just like anything else, basically).

The Industry Stumbles Into 1984

As the industry crash wore on, arcade machine manufacturers continued to come up with successful ideas for games such as *Discs of Tron*, *Mr. Do's Castle*, and *Donkey Kong 3*. Exidy released *Crossbow*, a unique standard upright with a miniature crossbow as a controller to be used in tandem with an on-screen light beam. It let you choose from one of several storylines as you went. Williams released a number of cool games that didn't sell as well, such as *Inferno*, a firefighter-rescue maze game with a *Crystal Castles*–like board layout. The market was just too saturated and constricted, and with too many arcades having closed.

Even so, several coin-ops managed to rise above the pack.

Punch-Out!! (Nintendo, 1984)

The video game industry may have been in tatters, but that didn't stop Nintendo from releasing a jaw-dropping arcade game—and it wasn't made of glass. The unique, dual-screen *Punch-Out!!* presented a main CRT for the boxing ring and in-game action, and a separate screen above it showing the fighters, their position in the world championships, scoring, round number, and clock. In this game, designed by Genyo Takeda and with characters designed by Shigeru Miyamoto, you confronted six increasingly skillful boxers topping out at the champion, Mr. Sandman; defeat him and you'd win the title, only to have to then defend it. The game looked and sounded like a televised boxing match complete with all the pomp and circumstance, albeit with a just-behind-your-boxer view of the action instead of multiple camera angles.

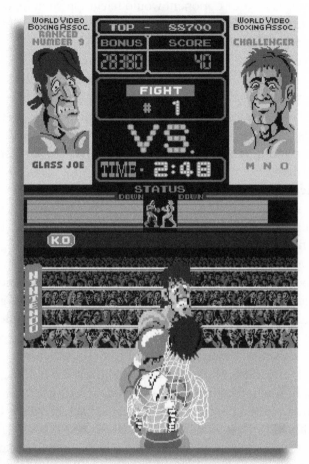

Figure 8.9: *Punch-Out!!* **was a body blow to the video game industry with its first-person perspective, you-are-there graphics and sound effects, and dual-monitor cabinet (shown here as a combined screenshot).**

The control panel consisted of a four-way joystick for guarding, dodging, and directing blows. There were two buttons for head and body blows. An on-screen status meter showed each player's relative health; the closer the meter fell to the middle of the screen, the closer that boxer was to being knocked down. As you punched, your strength would build and the power meter would increase. When the meter reached the top, it would flash "Knockout," at which point you could throw a hook or uppercut to finish off your opponent. If you didn't land a long-enough sequence of hits, then the power meter would fall back to the right side. If you ran out of time or were knocked out, the game would end. The trick became obvious: Eye twitches and color changes in your opponent would telegraph what he was about to do next. That didn't make the game easy, but it was informative and could help set you up for the next blow exchange or block.

Today, it all sounds like standard fare for a boxing game, aside from the innovative-for-1984 power-up and status bar mechanics. But it truly excelled in the graphics and overall presentation. Your character was a green, transparent wireframe silhouette that looked almost computer-generated (which it was, but style wise, too). This way, you could see through your own character and never lose sight of your opponent, aside from the solid color of your hair and your boxing trunks. The opponents all looked like cartoon caricatures and appeared larger and more colorful than the tiny sprites in so many other arcade games. Even the ring looked real, with a sold-out auditorium full of people cheering in the background. Look closely and you'd find Mario, Luigi, Donkey Kong, and Donkey Kong Junior.

The live action commentary also made the game. As you landed hits, it would say "body blow!," "left," "right," or "uppercut!" Sometimes your opponent would also taunt you, saying "come on," and tilting his glove. For a generation raised on stick-figure graphics and small invading aliens, *Punch-Out!!* looked decidedly real. And if you didn't know the game yet, hearing the commentary would pique your interest from the other side of an arcade or bowling alley. In 1987, Nintendo translated the spirit of this game, if not the graphics, to the home with its *Mike Tyson's Punch-Out!!* release for the Nintendo Entertainment System (later changed back to *Punch-Out!!* when its license with Mike Tyson's name expired). *Punch-Out!!* also marked the debut of Nintendo composer Koji Kondo, who would later gain tremendous fame as the composer for the *Super Mario Bros.* and *The Legend of Zelda* series on the NES and later consoles.

Karate Champ (Data East, 1984)

Karate Champ saw the birth of the one-on-one martial arts contest in video games. It was for one or two players; each player controlled the game with a pair of four-way joysticks that allowed for a wide variety of combo moves. Whoever won the best two out of three matches would win the tournament. It wasn't the most technically impressive game, aside from the novelty of the synthesized voices, but it was far more prescient than it appeared in 1984.

Data East fashioned the game in a black upright cabinet with blue marquee, bezel, and control panel graphics. The game started with a karateka walking to the arena, followed by a practice round where each player could practice some moves and earn some points up front. A judge sat on the far side of the arena with two assistants to either side, dressed in white and red gis. The two players in the game wore either white or red gis as well; if there was only one human player, the computer would assume control of the karateka in a red gi. When the judge said "Begin" or "Fight" in a synthesized voice, the round would start. Each player could execute any of 24 moves, thanks to the 24 possible positions of the two four-way joysticks (including leaving one joystick alone). Generally speaking, the joystick on the left controlled movement and the right one triggered skill attacks such as kicks and punches. The moves ranged from simple front and back kicks to more complex lunge punches, backward somersaults, and front foot sweeps, and you could also withdraw, block, jump, or squat in defense.

Figure 8.10: Perhaps the most calculated and strategic fighting game ever, *Karate Champ* pitted two martial arts experts against each other one tournament move at a time.

Unlike later fighting games, *Karate Champ* lacked health bars. Instead, after a single successful move, the game would pause, the judge would render the ruling on that round saying who the winner was, and then the karatekas would return to starting position for the next round. Each successful move was worth between 100 and 1,000 points, but the game was won or lost based on a traditional martial arts system where a successful hit was scored as either a full or half point. The first player to reach two points or the one with the highest score when the timer ran out would win that match. There were 12 arenas in all that served as backdrops for the matches. After each match, there would be a bonus round where you performed various tricks, such as splitting wooden boards with a single kick, avoiding flying objects and destroying others with your punches and kicks, and even fighting charging bulls.

Data East released a separate iteration called *Karate Champ: Player vs. Player* that focused on two-player-only combat with a variety of indoor and outdoor backdrops. Conversions appeared on the Apple II and Commodore 64, and a couple of years later, on the Nintendo Entertainment System. In 1986, Data East unsuccessfully sued Epyx for the similarities in its own *World Karate Championship* (known as *International Karate+* overseas). The game appeared in the movie *Bloodsport* with Jean-Claude Van Damme, and John Tobias, the cocreator of the *Mortal Kombat* series, said his primary inspiration for it was *Karate Champ*. Although few play *Karate Champ* today, it's a slower-paced, cerebral, and deliberate game compared with the Tekkens and Street Fighters of more recent decades and has value in and of itself. *Karate Champ* is where it all started, and as we'll see later, the format would hold the key to the early 1990s' arcade Renaissance.

Capcom

In 1979 Kenzo Tsujimoto, the president of Irem, also founded a separate company called I.R.M. Corporation and later established Capsule Computers as a division to sell electronic arcade video games. Tsujimoto ran both companies until he left Irem in 1983. After some more corporate shuffle-puck of various assets, the renamed Capcom (a shortened Capsule Computers) opened in June 1983—perhaps poor timing, considering the market crash. It didn't matter. The company's first title, a fixed shooter named *Vulgus*, appeared in May 1984. Soon, Capcom began releasing more arcade games—at least 20 through the end of 1986 alone.

The company's first hit came early. It was programmed by Yoshiki Okamoto, of *Time Pilot* and *Gyruss* fame, the one who had left Konami and just joined Capcom as only its second game designer. Way to make a first impression.

1942 (Capcom/Williams, 1984)

This Capcom arcade coin-op mixed things up with the usual space shooter by putting you in the cockpit of a World War II–era fighter plane, the "Super Ace," in the skies of the Pacific Theater over land and sea. The Super Ace was modeled after the Lockheed P-38 Lightning, which was unmistakable thanks to its twin "booms" on either side of a central housing that contained the cockpit and weapons. The game was a popular vertical-scrolling shooter in the vein of Atari's *Xevious* and landed Capcom on the map as a major player in the coin-op market.

Figure 8.11: Capcom made its first big splash in the video arcade with *1942*, a vertical shooter set in the Pacific Theater of World War II.

The control panel included an eight-way joystick, a Fire button, and a Roll button. The Fire button offered unlimited ammunition, and the Roll button let you perform a defensive 360-degree forward roll, otherwise known as a loop-the-loop. During the several seconds it took to complete the roll, you couldn't shoot, but enemy fire couldn't hurt you. You started the game with three rolls, marked with a red *R* at the bottom-right corner of the screen. At the beginning, your plane performed an introductory barrel roll before encountering enemy aircraft in different formations. Green planes were worth anywhere from 30 to 200 points each, and red aircraft were worth 100 points a pop.

Destroy an entire red formation and a "POW" power-up would appear that either equipped your plane with a double machine gun, a wider shot path, a smart bomb that destroyed all enemies on screen, or added two friendly fighters that flew alongside your plane and helped destroy extra aircraft. You would also get 500 or 1,000 points for shooting all enemies in a formation. Sometimes a POW would give you an extra roll or even an extra life. There were 32 different levels; a variety of other enemies appeared later on, such as larger bomber planes (worth 2,000 points and up) and a small bonus plane that, upon exploding, dropped an award worth 5,000 points. Complete a level and you'd see statistics for how many planes you shot down and your hit percentage, along with bonus points for any unused rolls before they were replenished on the next level. At the end of the fourth level, a stage boss plane would appear that was exceptionally difficult to shoot down.

Technically, the game was based on a pair of Z80s and a pair of AY8910s for sound effects, with a 256-by-224 resolution and 256 colors. The coin-op also offered a way to continue by inserting another quarter and holding down the Fire button within 10 seconds after the first game ended. Versions of *1942* made it to the Commodore 64 and most notably the NES, where it was a big seller, as well as numerous computers and consoles in the U.K. and Japan like the NEC PC-8801 and the MSX. Today, the game is largely forgotten; first-person shooters in the *Call of Duty*, *Medal of Honor*, *Battlefield*, and *Brothers in Arms* series have taken up all the air in the room and few scrolling shooters today have revisited the World War II theme. Capcom followed up *1942* three years later with *1943: The Battle of Midway*, and much more recently in 2017, a mobile conversion for iOS and Android devices that included the necessary "casual" mode to make things easier on a phone touch screen.

In addition to the original *1942* cabinet, Capcom also made conversions available through another company. Founded in Torrance, California, in 1984, Romstar was a distributor for video games, including coin-op machines from Capcom, Taito, and SNK. Its employees had a sense of humor.

For example, the manual for the *1942* Romstar kit, which let you convert an existing cabinet, included not only a helpful list of recommended tools and supplies but also what it felt were the necessary character traits for maintaining the cabinet and hardware. The manual also provided tips on increasing revenue: "Thorough research shows that two and a half minute games both satisfy players and also keep the quarters flowing. If games aren't running about two and a half minutes long, then collections probably aren't at their peak. You'll want to tailor your game to your location. The trick is to adjust a few DIP switches…It's easy!" In addition, the manual sold the idea of continues as a buy-in feature: "After completing a game, players are invited to 'buy in' or continue where they left off. Continued games are more challenging than original games. So continued games tend to involve skilled players at the level they prefer **and to increase collections**" (emphasis in the original).

Figure 8.12: Conversion kits such as the one advertised in this Romstar package let operators update existing coin-op cabinets on premises for a fraction of the cost of a new arcade game.

It's never fun to learn how the sausage is made, and this side of it was kept away from us gamers. But it's instructive to see it today from the operator's point of view back then, as opposed to ours, or even the designers and programmers in a behind-the-scenes discussion.

Demolition Derby (Bally Midway, 1984)

Demolition derbies were all the rage in the 1970s and 1980s, and it was past time for an update to Exidy's 1975 *Destruction Derby*. Bally Midway led the charge with *Demolition Derby*, a single-screen overhead racing game that implemented visible crumpled metal and damage meters for each player. Notably, you could also join a game in progress, a mechanic that soon became much more popular with games such as *Gauntlet* and *Street Fighter*; it would display "Car Entering Derby" and start again. Two main cabinet styles were available: a standard upright with two sets of controls, and a sturdy cocktail monster with four sets of controls, two per side. The game employed a pair of Z80 CPUs, a Motorola M6809, and two General Instrument AY8910 chips for sound. It also displayed at a higher-than-usual 512-by-480-pixel resolution but just 64 colors.

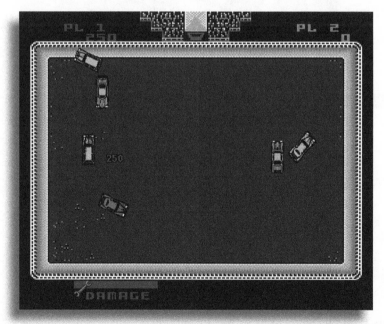

Figure 8.13: Lots of kids liked cracking up cars, and *Demolition Derby* let up to four of them do it to each other with satisfying crunch sounds and crumpled hoods.

Each player received a steering wheel and a forward/reverse throttle lever. A game started with six cars on the track, their trunks all facing away from each other; the four-player game would put eight cars on the track. The computer controlled blue cars, and each player had their own color vehicle. As soon as the game started, all the cars would back into each other. You strove to protect your own car from damage, specifically the front end where the radiator and engine were located, while reversing into other cars to try and put those out of commission.

One way to protect your own car was to keep the front end near the side walls, so that opponents would have a hard time maneuvering to hit your car's radiator. The damage meter would show how much trouble each car was in; if it depleted, that car was out of the race and an oil slick took its place. Those could spin you out; sometimes a car even ended up on fire, and wrenches and screwdrivers that appeared occasionally on the track would help you repair your car during the race. The player left at the end was the winner.

If you were a car nut who grew up on 1970s cop shows, you wanted to see cars get destroyed in video games, and it simply hadn't happened enough. *Destruction Derby*'s black-and-white graphics were too low resolution, but *Demolition Derby*'s were just right; you would not only see the corners of cars crushed in, but you'd even see hoods pop off and bumpers crumple. One unfortunate game mechanic was the "garage girl" that appeared in between each level. The further you progressed in the game, the more of her body the game would reveal on screen. I had completely forgotten about this part of the game until I began researching this book. Despite that salacious detail, *Demolition Derby* caused none of the moral panic that *Death Race* had eight years earlier. In fact, *Demolition Derby* didn't make much of an impact in the arcades at all. It would have done much better had it not been launched right in that middle period between the Great Video Game Crash and the resurgence that would soon follow beginning in 1985. Not much information is out there about it today, but I still see a machine for sale on occasion and the game has its dedicated fans. It was the perfect group game in its four-player incarnation.

Kung-Fu Master (Irem/Data East, 1984)

The grandfather of side-scrolling beat-'em-up games, *Kung-Fu Master* was cinematic in its presentation. You controlled Thomas, a warrior who had to fight through five levels of the Devil's Temple in order to reach the crime boss Mr. X and rescue his girlfriend Sylvia, who was kidnapped and tied to a chair. Designed by Takashi Nishiyama of *Moon Patrol* fame, the game opened with Thomas and Sylvia "suddenly attacked by several unknown guys." A letter addressed to Thomas notified him of the kidnapping and invited him to come to the Devil's Temple, where five "sons of the devil" would "entertain" him. Unlike most arcade games up until this point, *Kung-Fu Master* had a genuine narrative arc and a beginning, middle, and end;[19] it wasn't just about your score when you ran out of lives.

Figure 8.14: The original brawler, *Kung-Fu Master* landed a full three years before the beat-'em-up craze took off in arcades.

The controls consisted of a four-way joystick, a Punch button, and a Kick button. The joystick let you move to the left or right as well as jump or duck, and you could throw punches or kicks from any of those three positions. The game started on level one with a series of Grippers that would gang up on Thomas and grab him, draining his energy. Each time that happened, you'd shake the joystick back and forth to break free. Bandana-wearing Knife-Throwers required two hits to kill. Levels two and four added a variety of objects that would drop on Thomas, such as pots, balls, snakes, and even dragons. Levels three and five included short Tom Toms that would do somersaults to attack Thomas from surprise angles.

At the end of each level was a different son of the devil, otherwise known as a boss character. Like Thomas, the end bosses all had health meters, so the game would momentarily become a one-on-one fighter as you attempted to dispatch them. The first level had a boss with a simple wooden stick, but later bosses would prove tougher. Defeat Mr. X himself on the fifth floor and you'd rescue Sylvia and then start the game over at a higher difficulty level. Make no mistake, though; even on the first play-through, this game was hard, with a relentless barrage of enemies small, large, and inanimate from the moment you started playing.

As 1984 wore on, we began to see not just advances in color and in background music but in higher resolution displays as well. *Kung-Fu Master* presented detailed graphics, with larger-than-usual sprites for all the fighting characters, smooth animation, a fast playing speed, and a trademark, relentless bass-and-percussion backdrop to the audio. Short digital audio samples abounded, such as a painful "ooh" from being stabbed and a death cry that would echo out to the void as Thomas fell off the board.

Data East made *Kung-Fu Master* in standard upright, mini, and cocktail versions. Nintendo also released a port of the game, titled *Kung-Fu*, for its then-brand-new Nintendo Entertainment System. The graphics were simpler than in the arcade, with minimalist backgrounds and a three-color Thomas with black hair and a black-and-white shirt, instead of a blue-and-white shirt, red belt, white pants, and brown hair. But Nintendo managed to preserve all of the gameplay, and *Kung-Fu* went on to sell an astounding 3.5 million cartridges. The Atari 2600 and 7800 also saw ports of the game, neither of which was as compelling as the NES version. Most importantly, *Kung-Fu Master* went on to spawn a new arcade game genre—it would just take a couple of years before anyone realized it.

Sente and Atari Games

In 1984, in the middle of the video game industry crash, Nolan Bushnell opened a new game company called Sente. The idea was to offer kits at lower prices that would plug into a new hardware platform that wasn't cassette based like DECO with all of its downsides. After launching *Snake Pit*, a game that was welcomed more for its connection to Bushnell than its gameplay, Sente nonetheless found a buyer in Bally Midway and began pursuing licenses for hot properties such as *Trivial Pursuit* and *Name That Tune*. Sente produced nearly two dozen coin-ops, but never quite found a hit, and Bally shut it down in 1986.[20]

Also, in mid 1984, Atari split into two companies. Warner had just about had enough of Atari's sagging revenue by the start of the year. Jack Tramiel, CEO of Commodore, left after a rumored boardroom blowout with senior management. After some months of negotiations, Tramiel bought Atari Incorporated's computer and console divisions and relaunched them as a new company called Atari Corporation. Warner held on to the more profitable Coin division and rebranded it Atari Games, where it would continue to release new coin-ops uninhibited. It soon became apparent Atari Games would carry the torch of the original Atari quite well—if not at first. Atari Games division planned two new coin-ops based on the 1984 motion pictures *Cloak & Dagger* and *The Last Starfighter*. The first hit the market as a poor-selling conversion kit for earlier Williams games, and the latter was canned when the movie's box office results disappointed. Atari management also balked at the proposed design's $10,000 price tag.[21]

The company had much better luck with its next original IP, its first major release as Atari Games.

Marble Madness (Atari Games, 1984)

The object of this innovative game, designed by Mark Cerny and programmed by Cerny and Bob Flanagan, was to maneuver a red or blue marble along futuristic cubic raceways and cross the finish line within the allotted time. Along the way, numerous oddball creatures such as the Black Steelie and the green Marble Muncher would get in the way or try to destroy the marble. As you progressed down each board, the playfield scrolled upwards, revealing more of what was beneath. It was easy to accidentally fall off the track, and some of the creatures would try to bump you off as well. Even if successful, the marble would always reappear, but you'd lose several seconds that you probably needed to finish the board in time. If you did succeed, you'd get bonus points based on the amount of time remaining and then progress to a new, more difficult course; any bonus time you had remaining in the previous course was carried over to the next, so moving as fast as you could throughout the game wasn't only for the purpose of a high score.

Two players could play the game together with both marbles on the screen at once. They could choose to cooperate or to compete against each other for the highest score. The control panel held a large trackball for each player, one colored blue and the other red. The marble had considerable momentum, so it took a bit of time to react to your input; you needed to get the trackball rolling a bit earlier than you expected the marble to move in that direction. Some of the courses had multiple paths to the finish line, although not all of them would work out. If the marble fell a short distance, it would land, and little birdies would circle over its head to signal momentary disorientation. If the marble fell too far, though, it would crack and break into pieces and you'd have to wait a moment before the next one appeared.

Marble Madness excited with its colorful, quasi-three-dimensional graphics, stereo music, and accurate modeling of the ball's weight and feel relative to the playfield and its various inclines. It was noticeable not just in the obvious ramps but in the portions of the racetrack that were concave or convex surfaces. Maneuver the ball correctly and the channel would hold it in place. Mess up and the ball would balance precariously on the top line of a track, or worse, easily roll off either side of it. There were six screens in all, each with different layouts, colors, and creatures. Wave five was a "silly wave" with backward laws of gravity and the ability to strike back at the creatures, and wave six was an "ultimate wave" that was tougher than all the rest. Operators could adjust the difficulty between five different settings for the amount of allotted time in each level.

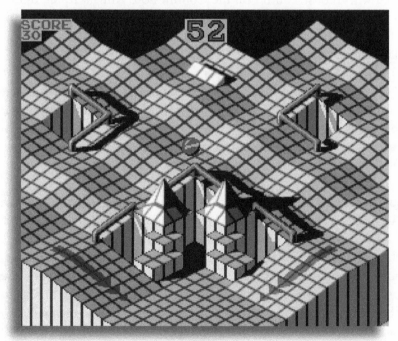

Figure 8.15: *Marble Madness*'s **astounding 3D graphics and smooth trackball physics posed a unique challenge for arcade gamers.**

Atari marketed the game to operators around the company's new System 1 board, which supported multiple game kits. Atari promised a new kit every three to four months; each would include a "pop-in game board" and attraction panel graphics, and if necessary, a new control panel and related graphics as well. The board included a 16-bit Motorola 68010 CPU, 1MB RAM, and support for hardware playfield scrolling, 56 motion objects, 256-color graphics, a 336-by-240-pixel resolution, and custom sound, music (FM synthesis, as in Yamaha's famous DX7 keyboard), and speech processors. The cabinets supported horizontal and vertical monitor orientations as well, with the included tube being a 19-inch Electrohome G07 CRT.

Marble Madness was a hit in the arcades despite its post-crash release, with rave reviews, a number one position on the weekly earnings charts, and sales of about 4,000 cabinets. It also looked more advanced than just about anything else in the arcade; no other game had *Marble Madness*'s detailed, isometric boards, with their hills, valleys, shadows, and bright colors. The game lacked staying power, though, and was too hard for casual players. After six weeks, it quickly fell off the charts. Nonetheless, *Marble Madness* lived a long life in home conversions across many platforms and did well with mouse control on the Commodore Amiga, Apple IIGS, and Atari ST, and the 16-bit graphics on those three helped as well. Other ports didn't fare as well, either from graphical issues or the lack of a trackball or similar control option.

The Atari System 1 board also served as the basis for a number of other Atari Games titles, among them 1985's humorous *Road Runner*, based on the famous Looney Tunes character, and *RoadBlasters*, an enjoyable 1987 combat car racing coin-op.

The Fall of Laserdisc

Manufacturers bet big on laserdisc interactive-movie games, with advances in read speeds enabling more sophisticated gameplay. Arcades began to stock new videodisc cabinets such as another Rick Dyer game called *Space Ace*, Mylstar's *M.A.C.H. 3* that put you in the cockpit of a fighter jet, the manga-influenced *Cliff Hanger* from Stern, and a new Midway distribution of Sega's *Astron Belt*. Many were begun in the prior year or two, so the timing could have been better. Some incorporated animation in the same manner as *Dragon's Lair*, but others employed video footage integrated with gameplay. These games were fun to experience and delivered cutting-edge thrills, but all had little staying power with the exception of *Space Ace*'s two levels of difficulty.

After *Dragon's Lair* and *Space Ace*, Dyer developed a laserdisc-based home console called Halcyon. The console launched in 1984 and proved a failure,[22] thanks in part thanks to its astronomical $2,195 entry price.[23] Once the novelty wore off, it became clear the underlying games weren't compelling enough for laser's 50-cents-a-play cost, so arcade operators balked. Console or coin-op, the biggest problem was that all laserdisc games were "on rails," with storylines that went from beginning to end and stopped, with no increasing challenge throughout. Soon, the mystery and "wow" factor of laserdisc faded. The games were Simon Says with a joystick and buttons. Once you beat one, it had zero replay value. Few players came back and the fad didn't last long.

Figure 8.16: The video game industry, for a time, threw everything it had at laserdisc, with titles such as Dragon's Lair, Space Ace, and M.A.C.H. 3 (pictured), a game that integrated real video footage of flying as a backdrop.

Worse, the disc players were unreliable; they would often overheat in the long hours arcades were open for business and would sometimes jam. At first, operators didn't mind the expense of the machine because of the promised revenue, but soon they began to rely on it and the machines didn't hold up. "To be honest, we weren't prepared for the volume of failures," Starcom president Jim Pierce said in a later interview. "We had been assured that [*Dragon's Lair's* laserdisc unit] was the absolute best disk player in the world. It was Pioneer's industrial model, it retailed for $2,499.00." To top it off, Pioneer turned out to have no parts for the player, a three-year-old model the company sold Cinematronics and other coin-op manufacturers.[24]

In the long arc of video game history, new laserdisc titles helped carry the coin-op business through a rough period. But the fall of laserdisc would consume several companies. Stern tried its hand at an over-the-top laserdisc game it licensed from a small Massachusetts company. The game was called *Atomic Castle*, and it came complete with costumed actors and Hollywood special effects, but Stern went out of business late in 1984 after building just two prototypes.[25] Game Plan then acquired the rights to make a conversion kit for *Atomic Castle* that would work in other laserdisc cabinets, and then went out of business itself in 1985 before it could get *that* off the ground.[26] Mylstar, formerly Gottlieb, also folded in late 1984, despite the success of *Q*bert* and *M.A.C.H. 3*.[27] Before long, laserdisc coin-ops that once commanded prices of $3,000 and $4,000 were "now being sold off at a thousand dollars apiece, so eager are distributors to clear out their inventory," Dan Persons wrote for *Electronic Games*. "It's not uncommon to enter an arcade nowadays and see *Space Ace* and *Firefox* standing idle, their attract modes repeating endlessly to no one in particular. Where are the players? They're crowding around such games as *TX-1* and *Punch-Out!!*, machines that feature high-res, computer-generated graphics." The technology didn't amount to much besides a dead end.[28]

Laserdiscs did foretell another important invention—multimedia CD-ROMs. Those optical discs carried on the spirit of the idea, but in a way that proved much more practical and forward looking, even without the feature-film-quality animation.

After the Crash

The number of people playing arcade-style games at home had skyrocketed, thanks to the influx of powerful, inexpensive computers and software that made it much more affordable for first-timers to buy in. At one point, every month brought at least 50 new video game cartridges, even though the average gamer was buying six per year, or one every two months. And for every good game, there were at least 10 or 20 hastily produced and not worth the money.[29] Pundits assumed the home video game console age was ending, and that the computer age was beginning. Computers could run all kinds of software, including education, productivity, and business, and they played more kinds of games, many of which with more sophistication, in-depth plots, and keyboard input. Adventure and role-playing games let you save your progress. Often unmentioned was the relative ease in pirating software, letting people trade for new games for the price of a blank floppy disk.

The coin-op industry patient, such as it were, stabilized in the second half of 1984. "With traffic in the arcades—and, consequently, sales volume—on the rise once more, it's only natural to wonder where the field will go from here," Katz wrote in September 1984. "The arcades have apparently attained something close to their full growth potential, and efforts to greatly increase the number of machines might bring back the oversupply situation that had arcade operators tearing out their hair—and cutting down on orders for the new titles."[30] He went on to predict that the next step would be the creation of new types of establishments in which coin-ops were major attraction—not just arcade discos and bar/game room combinations that had already been tried but private clubs and other more adult-themed venues that would provide a "generally lower external noise level and the presence of various amenities that go well with gaming." He predicted more sit-down simulation coin-ops that would lead to full-surround games, assuming the prices would come down from the $20,000 to $30,000 necessary to buy the more advanced sim coin-ops. Ultimately, the point was to offer gaming not yet available on microcomputers, and that in the future, there would be "fewer, more innovative titles instead of trial-ballooning a dozen potential entries to see which the operators order."[31]

The video arcade industry would never again see the revenues achieved during the Golden Age. The fall from the top was dazzling, as predictions about the proliferation and, soon, permanence of video arcades, and how going to the arcade would become as normal a pastime for Americans as baseball or watching television, all vaporized within 18 months. Even games that should have caused a stir saw few takers. Atari's *I, Robot* was a coin-op based on the popular Asimov sci-fi short story collection and designed by industry legend Dave Theurer of *Missile Command* and *Tempest* fame. It was the first arcade game to employ filled, shaded 3D polygons, and it even offered the ability to control the camera in game. It just wasn't the right time, and technology advanced too quickly to just release it again later (see also: the Atari 7800 and XE Game System). But while the Golden Age had ended, the video arcade story was far from over.

9 > Continue

For the relatively small number of arcades that remained after the industry crash, all was not lost. Chains such as Time-Out, Aladdin's Castle, Pocket Change, and Diamond Jim's continued to see plenty of foot traffic across America, as giant indoor malls became a staple of teenager hangouts. Coin-op manufacturers saw a less rosy picture because machine sales tanked; the industry went from $12 billion in sales in 1982 to a scant $100 million in 1985. The home computer industry was going gangbusters, and soon there would be a new home console war. But the kinds of video games that appeared on these platforms were different than those of arcades, with deeper stories, more complex control schemes, and much longer playtimes. Many computer adventure games took 10 hours or longer to complete.[1]

Arcade machines were in danger of losing their place at the top of the video game industry. "Coin-ops had traditionally represented the leading edge of the electronic gaming universe in terms of both technology and artistic achievement," Kunkel wrote in 1984. "Home games have generally been measured against the arcade yardstick, attaining status and success in direct correlation to their ability to ape some coin-op cousin. That era, however, is in the process of ending abruptly." He wrote that companies such as Electronic Arts, DataSoft, and Synapse began taking home games in new directions and down paths where coin-ops couldn't follow, in complexity, storyline, and the length of play during one sitting (quarter).

In 1985, the Japan Amusement Machine and Marketing Association developed a new wiring standard for arcade cabinets so that they could accept a motherboard for any JAMMA-compatible game. The standard covered the PCBs, wiring harnesses, and power supplies, most of which were custom made for specific cabinets on earlier games. Within a couple of years, most arcade games began to use this design, making it easier to convert existing cabinets in the field to new games. The standard included a 56-pin edge connector that supported 5- and 12-volt power for the game and sound; two joystick inputs with three buttons each; two Start buttons; analog RGB video output with negative composite sync; a single-speaker sound output; and coin counter, lock, service, test, and tilt inputs.[2] As the year kicked into full swing, the coin-op business was still working out what it wanted to be and what kind of changes it wanted to embrace. Fortunately, innovation—and good games—were in plentiful supply, enough to see a new Platinum Age rise from the wreckage of what was left of the video arcade industry.

Gauntlet (Atari Games, 1985)

In *Gauntlet*, perhaps the best top-down dungeon crawler ever made, from one to four players would explore dozens of mazelike levels, fighting all kinds of enemies and collecting food and treasure. Inspired by the 1983 APX game Dandy on Atari home computers (and which resulted in a threat of legal action),[3] designer Ed Logg wanted to find a way to build a hack-and-slash arcade game that was like playing Dungeons & Dragons.[4] More than any coin-op up until that point, *Gauntlet* succeeded with its riveting action and massive four-player control panel.

You played as long as you could until your health fell to zero. Each player had an eight-way joystick and Fire and Magic buttons, and could choose from four characters with various benefits: Thor the Warrior (red), the strongest in close combat; Thyra the Valkyrie (blue), with the best armor; Merlin the Wizard (yellow), possessing the most powerful magic skills; and Questor the Elf (green), who had a bow and was the fastest. Although the console displayed concise game instructions, the attract mode stepped through a game demonstration, a screen full of the objects players could find, and individual screens that showed Ghosts, Grunts, Demons, Lobbers, Sorcerers, Deaths, and Thieves, with the mechanics and scoring for each. That was in addition to the usual title screen, high score table, and increasingly common credits displaying everyone who worked on the game.

The first level of *Gauntlet* offered multiple exits that warped to other levels. You could warp from level one to four or eight, or you could ignore the warps and exit normally to level two. In *Gauntlet*, the first seven levels were always the same, but starting on level eight, you would be served from a random selection of more than 100 levels. As you played, you'd find treasure, keys to unlock gates, magic potions to cast spells that vanquished on-screen enemies or supercharged your character, and food to recharge your health. A potion was also the only way to kill the fearsome death monster. *Gauntlet* was stellar to play, with colorful graphics, fast action, and memorable sound effects, most notably the synthesized voices from the characters. "Warrior needs food, badly" is a catchphrase even today. Although you could play the game by yourself, *Gauntlet* rewarded cooperative play, as a team could get further and score multipliers of points when finding treasure. In addition, putting the Warrior and Valkyrie ahead of the Wizard and Elf was usually a stronger "marching order," just like in Dungeons & Dragons and in other role-playing games.

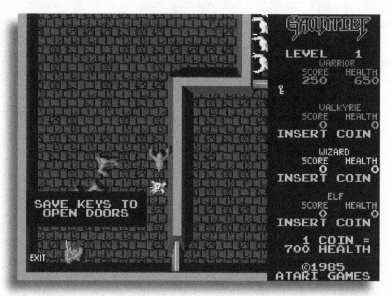

Figure 9.1: Perhaps 1985's best arcade coin-op, the four-player *Gauntlet* delivered the Dungeons & Dragons experience stripped down to its core action elements and choice of four character classes.

A pivotal *Gauntlet* innovation was the ability to continue indefinitely just by adding additional quarters. Plenty of games already offered the ability to continue from the Game Over screen. But here, you could charge up your character's health as you played. This along with four-player support meant *Gauntlet* could rake in a lot of money for its owners and operators. *Gauntlet* gave them a wide variety of ways to increase "collections," which for our purposes were just ways to make the games more challenging. These options included eight levels of difficulty (with the default at four, or "moderate"), and a couple dozen settings for the amount of additional health a player would get by inserting another coin (from just 100 through 2,000, with 600 being the default). Even an "automatic high score table reset" option was available so that a few extremely good players didn't make it impossible for anyone else to land on the list. Those were in addition to the usual option of how many quarters were necessary to begin play.

Atari Games knew the large cabinet wouldn't fit in every location, so the company also released a smaller, two-player cabinet that took up the same space as a standard upright console. In the end, the company sold 7,848 *Gauntlet* cabinets—not huge compared with the peak of the Golden Age of arcade games, but a big win given the year and especially the higher cost of the four-player machines. Atari Games went on to release a direct sequel called *Gauntlet II* both as a separate cabinet and as a conversion kit, with the main difference being that multiple players could be the same character in different colors. The new game also included new levels, voice samples, monsters (including a large dragon), ricochet shots, booby traps, secret rooms, and the ability to designate a player "it" and have all the enemies target that one player. Some players prefer the sequel to this day for its even better multiplayer gameplay.

Paperboy (Atari Games, 1985)

Your job in *Paperboy*, designed by John Salwitz, was to deliver the *Daily Sun* newspaper on bicycle to your suburban customers. The attract mode showed the front page of a newspaper with the headline: "Amazing Paperboy Delivers!" Atari Games modified its existing *Star Wars: The Arcade Game* yoke to work as a handlebar, with buttons on each side for throwing papers. The handlebar also accelerated or braked depending on whether you pushed or pulled it. At the start, you chose between Easy St., the Middle Road, or Hard Way. "He doesn't make the news; he just has to deliver it!" The game showed you a map of the houses along the street with the subscribers in color, and the non subscribers in dark gray.

The game's graphics were presented in a three-quarter perspective. During each day of the week starting with Monday, you delivered papers to subscribers in colorful houses and broke the windows of non subscribers living in dark-colored houses (hey, it was a rough business). There were a variety of obstacles to contend with, such as cars entering driveways, kids playing, pets, potholes, and having to cross a busy street with cars speeding in both directions. Each time you crashed into something, you'd either end up on the ground with a paper bag over your head, or in a tangle of bike parts if you crashed into a car. If you missed a house, that house would turn dark and cancel their subscription. You picked up newspaper bundles along the way to replenish your supply. Land all the deliveries on the welcome mats and you'd get a double bonus, plus extra points anytime you managed to throw a paper into someone's mailbox; an unsubscribed customer would also come back after such a performance. For extra points, you could hit special targets, such as a thief trying to break into someone's house. Each time you finished a day, there would be a training course where you threw papers at or jumped over obstacles.

Figure 9.2: Delivering papers was a thankless job that got many kids their start in the workforce, but somehow *Paperboy* made it fun, with an excellent handlebar control and crisp graphics.

With art by Dave Ralston, the graphics looked bright and charmingly cartoonish, and a step above games from just a couple of years earlier. *Paperboy* was an Atari System 2 game, capable of higher-resolution 512-by-384 graphics. The new hardware consisted of a DEC T-11 10MHz CPU, a MOS 6502 coprocessor, two POKEY chips for sound, a Yamaha YM2151 for stereo music, and a TI TMS5220 for speech synthesis. Despite this load-out, the game was ported to many home consoles and computers, with the Atari ST's pitch-perfect conversion leading the way. Key to the arcade game's draw were the sharp graphics and the control scheme, both of which lent it an aura of novelty. Take away the handlebars and the resolution and there wasn't a huge amount of game underneath, which many of the reviews of the time noted. Nonetheless, the game was successful enough to see a sequel in 1991 on home systems, if not in the arcade, and the original arcade game appeared in a large variety of compilations throughout the years.

Gradius / Nemesis (Konami, 1985)

Gradius, technically the sequel to 1981's *Scramble*, showcased a tremendous leap in technology in just four years, with its high-quality music, multichannel sound effects, and weapon power-ups. Most important were its beautiful quasi-biological alien graphics, a far cry from the low-resolution mountain landscapes in earlier horizontal-scrolling shooters. At the same time, it wasn't a hit by itself. *Gradius* was released in low volume as *Nemesis* in the U.S. but with otherwise identical gameplay. It was one of the first post-crash games that wasn't successful until it was converted to home consoles—notably in this case, the Nintendo Entertainment System.

The concept was that the peaceful world Gradius was under assault. Amoeboid aliens from the sub-space star cluster Bacterion swarmed in and were threatening to destroy the planet. You flew the prototype hyperspace fighter Warp Rattler in an attempt to reach the Bacterion superfortress Xaerous, securing energy capsules along the way to boost your ship's powers. There were seven stages: Volcanic, Stonehenge, Inverted Volcano, Moal, Antennoid, Amoeboid, and the superfortress. The memorable Moal stage was as if Easter Island was somehow transported to space, and of course the heads could shoot at you.

Gradius was the first shooter to incorporate a weapon bar. It included six levels: Speed Up, Missile, Double, Laser, Option, and a question mark. Whenever you shot an entire formation of aliens or some special ones (often red in color), an energy capsule would appear; when you collected it, you'd advance one level on the weapon bar and the corresponding power-up would light up. At any point, you could "cash in" with the Special Power button and activate the new power-up. Speed Up let you maneuver more quickly; Missile gave you a bomb-like attack along with your regular shots; Double let you shoot two shots at once, with the second one arcing upward; Laser converted the bullets to lasers; the powerful Option added a second, smaller doppelgänger ship that fought with you at the same time;

and the mystery *?* would wrap your ship in a force field barrier that could withstand several hits before disintegrating. The more energy capsules you collected, the more you could amp up these abilities, with the only caveat that you couldn't use Double and Laser together.

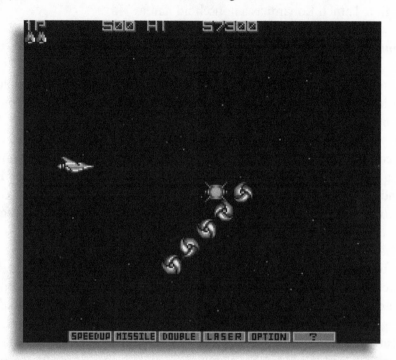

Figure 9.3: Most *Gradius* fans learned about it from the NES, but this game started life as an excellent coin-op that made every horizontal shooter before it suddenly look old.

The game was stocked with more than a dozen enemies, including flying fanlike creatures at the start of the game, anti-aircraft guns of various shapes, and Xaerous cruisers and fighters. It was a hard but rewarding play, with lots of targets to shoot and plenty of rewards in the power-ups as well as points. That last part is critical. At this point in arcade history, you could start to see the beginnings of the score losing its place as the all-important meter of how well someone did. It would take decades for that to happen and would never completely go away with some titles. But in a game like *Gradius*, you'd often talk more about what board you made it to rather than what score you achieved. This would happen more and more as time went on. In the meantime, *Gradius* launched a host of further sequels, including the superb *Salamander*, which became *Life Force* on the NES, and *Gradius*

II and *Gradius III* in the arcade, the latter of which received an ill-fated Super NES conversion as a launch title. It looked and sounded good but couldn't overcome the console's sluggish 68C516 CPU. All told, the original arcade coin-op was an important release, and the NES cartridge was enough to launch Konami as a household name.

Commando (Capcom, 1985)

In *Commando*, designed by Tokuro Fujiwara, you played a crack soldier deep in a jungle amidst fierce guerrilla warfare. Even though the movie *Commando* starring (who else?) Arnold Schwarzenegger came out that same year, the two franchises were unrelated. Nonetheless, the game capitalized on the cultural moment post-Vietnam that saw a surge in movies like that one, such as *Apocalypse Now*, *First Blood*, *Rambo: First Blood Part II*, and *Commando*, and soon after, *Platoon*, *Full Metal Jacket*, and *Good Morning, Vietnam*, Capcom's *Commando* popularized the "run-and-gun" game that *Front Line* first established.

As Super Joe on a secret mission, you fought hundreds of enemy soldiers before reaching and destroying a supposedly impregnable base. The cabinet set the tone, with a black paint job, minimal side art, and a control panel done up in camouflage. The eight-way joystick moved your soldier; the right button shot unlimited rounds in any of eight directions, and the left button threw a grenade, which you had a limited supply of and had to replenish during the game. Each grenade would fly ahead for a few seconds and then explode, killing anyone nearby eliminating obstacles.

The game started with a helicopter dropping off Super Joe in the jungle. You moved up against a scrolling background to progress in the game, though you could stop whenever you wanted to. You spent most of the time either shooting enemy soldiers or dodging enemy bullets, which travelled slow enough that you could outmaneuver them with the joystick. Along the way, you'd encounter sandbag walls, rivers, ponds, and trees, among other obstacles. Periodically, you'd encounter two soldiers escorting a prisoner; pop off the two soldiers and you'd earn bonus points. Picking up gold bars also increased your score. At the end of a level, the enemy officer would unleash more soldiers and then try to escape; you could shoot him in the back. Enemy leaders and headquarters were worth the most points, and the arch bridge was a tough obstacle that forced you to avoid attacks from above. In later rounds, jeeps and trucks would try to run you over. Extra lives were awarded at 10,000 points and every 50,000 thereafter.

Figure 9.4: *Front Line* **was first, but** *Commando* **was the game that put the run-and-gun genre on the map.**

The game's graphics did a nice job of depicting the inner parts of a jungle while offering enough clear terrain to make navigation easy. The game was largely done up in greens and browns, but the soldiers were more colorful, and some deep blue ponds and rivers broke up the scenery. The soundtrack had an appropriate marching beat to it. The game was ported to most home computers and game consoles of the day, most notably the NES and the Commodore 64, but 16-bit machines such as the Atari ST and Commodore Amiga also saw improved versions that nearly matched the arcade in graphics and color. The 8-bit NES cartridge, also developed by Capcom, wasn't quite a facsimile of the arcade game but was excellent in its own right and a huge seller.

The second half of the 1980s saw plenty of other run-and-gun games with war themes. Konami's side-scrolling *Rush'n Attack*, which sounded like something else when it was said aloud, delivered smooth combat, albeit with a more disturbing and specific Cold War theme and a gratuitous introduction sequence that showed the cold-blooded murder of four help-less POWs. It was toned down a bit for the NES conversion. More run-and-gun games followed, such 1986's *Ikari Warriors* and 1987's *Contra*, another Konami title with a fun cooperative two-player mode that soon became one of the best NES cartridges ever released. (We'll get to *Ikari Warriors* a bit later in this chapter for a specific reason.) But *Commando* still holds its own and provides satisfying, challenging action. Capcom followed it up in 1990 with *Mercs*, another run-and-gun shooter with vastly improved graphics.

Hang-On (Sega, 1985)

Hang-On, the motorcycle racing game with simulated three-dimensional ef-fects (known as "2.5D"), was responsible for multiple firsts: ushering in the 16-bit coin-op era; running at a steady 60fps; and employing scaled sprites, which allowed for a convincing (if not real) three-dimensional effect at high frame rates, thanks to Sega's new Super Scaler board. More of a simulator than a game, the top-end "ride-on" cabinet was a full-size model of a racing bike (or "crotch rocket," as it was sometimes derogatorily called). There were five stages, each with different scenery: Alps, Grand Canyon, City Night, Seaside, and the Circuit. During each stage, you would race and pass by competitors in order to reach each checkpoint before the clock ran out.

The in-game screen adopted most of the conventions established in Namco's *Pole Position*, with a first-person view albeit just behind your biker and various race stats and specs floating across the top of the screen. As you shifted your weight to the side to bank the motorcycle, the entire bike would lean over the same way a real one would. It also took the view with it, as the monitor was mounted on the front of the motorcycle. Of course, you couldn't bump another racer, or worse, ride off the course and crash. On the handlebar controller, turning the right-hand grip toward you increased your speed; turning it back toward its original position slowed it down. A separate lever attached to the right grip braked. For audio, the deluxe cabi-net had four stereo speakers that projected your motorcycle's exhaust sound and, dramatically, the roar of passing competitors' motorcycles. Nothing else in the arcade played or even sounded like this game.

It wasn't always a given that there was enough room for one. The ride-on cabinet was tremendous, measuring 78 by 63 by 52 inches and weighing a massive 529 pounds, in part thanks to the separate platform to the left of the bike and ashtray-like coin box mount. Sega also produced two lower-cost versions that would fit in smaller arcade spaces. One was a standard 253-pound upright, and the other was a sit-down model that was basically a lowered upright with a small bench attached; this one weighed 269 pounds. Without the ride-on effect, these versions were not as groundbreaking, but the game still held up thanks to the fast frame rate, stereo sound, and well-designed handlebars that just turned a bit more like a regular bicycle would have, but still otherwise had the accelerator and brake in the right-hand grip as before. The manual was full of technical advice on how to calibrate the steering, the accelerator, and the brake—the kinds of things that would fall out of adjustment over time or be knocked around in the initial shipment. As was often the case, buying an arcade machine was rarely just a matter of unpacking it and plugging it into the wall.

Figure 9.5: Sega's awe-inspiring *Hang-On* was the first racing game since *Pole Position* to make arcade goers drop their jaws in amazement.

Hang-On was a milestone moment in arcade game history. A 1985 *Computer and Video Games* review said *Hang-On* was "the most realistic arcade game to hit the arcades for a long while," and called out the way you tilted the "life-size" motorcycle and the placement of the throttle and brake controls mirroring that of a real one.[5] *Hang-On* is one of the coin-ops credited with bringing gamers back to the arcades after the industry crash. It paved the way for more advances from Sega, as we'll soon see.

Indiana Jones and the Temple of Doom (Atari Games, 1985)

Released shortly after the 1984 motion picture, this coin-op put you in control of Indiana Jones—who everyone wanted to be at the time. The object of the game, directed by Mike Hally and produced by Peter Lipson, was to recover the Sankara stone that protected the ancient remote Indian village of Mayapore. Most important, you needed to rescue missing children enslaved by a death cult in Pankot Palace and forced to excavate gems from nearby Thuggee mines. The controls consisted of an eight-way joystick and an action button that activated Indy's whip, which basically did everything in the game from attacking foes to opening cages and swinging across platforms.

Figure 9.6: More than a quick cash-in, *Indiana Jones and the Temple of Doom* was an innovative coin-op with several minigames and excellent graphics.

At the start, you could choose from easy, medium, and hard difficulty levels via an introductory, bug-infested room with three different tunnels. The game itself consisted of three waves. In the first, Indy had to traverse the various cavern passages, ladders, chutes, and conveyer belts. Indy had to fend off the Thuggee guards with his whip and some explosive gas cans strewn about and open the cages the kids were held in; a bonus would be awarded if Indy freed all of the captive children. If Indy took too long, Mola Ram would appear and throw fireballs. Indy had some freedom of movement on the platforms, and he could also fall a short distance without dying.

The second wave put Indy in control of a mine car; the game switched to a three-quarters-perspective racing mode, where you navigated around broken tracks with missing rails, pulled off successful jumps, and steered clear of various denizens of the mines. The joystick controlled the speed and the direction the mine car would travel. Thuggee guards rode in other mine cars, and would try to ram Indy or collide with him from a side track. Indy could also use dynamite sticks or gas cans to derail the other cars. A Thuggee Giant and some invasive bats would also get in the way. The final wave took place in the Temple of Doom, the sacrificial chamber that held the Sankara stone. Indy had to grab the stone, located past a floor trap in front of the statue of Kali, the four-armed goddess of death. If Indy made it out alive, the game repeated until Indy recovered three of the stones, at which point he had to make a hasty exit on a dangerous rope bridge.

Operators could choose from eight different coin-and-number-of-lives configurations. As some games of the period did, the system would reset every 2,000 games to ensure that high scores remained achievable. The game also came with sophisticated statistics tracking, including a histogram that would map out how long the average game lasted, with the ideal range being between 90 and 150 seconds. If too many games ran less than 90 or more than 180, the manual recommended adjusting the difficulty settings. Additional stats were provided for games that cost 25 cents or 50 cents, with the suggestion that a 50-cent game should last from 180 to 240 seconds to give the player more time for the extra cost.

As an Atari System 1 game like *Marble Madness*, *Indiana Jones and the Temple of Doom* presented high-resolution color graphics and played multivoice arrangements of John Williams's famous score. It was also Atari's first System 1 game to employ digital speech samples. Hearing short phrases such as "We'll walk from here" and "I'm not leaving without those stones" was always a fun diversion. Atari Games moved some 2,800 units of the game between cabinets and conversion kits—not bad for 1985, if indicative of how far the coin-op industry had fallen and how quickly,[6] given that by most accounts the game was considered a success.

Ghosts 'n Goblins (Capcom, 1985)

Arcade games had already become more difficult for several years, but for many players it was extremely tough to beat *Ghosts 'n Goblins*. In fact, you were lucky if you lasted a minute or two. The interesting thing about this fantasy-themed side-scroller is that the home conversions all preserved this difficulty level, and given that cartridges were so much smaller and lighter, it was much easier to throw one against the wall or out the window in frustration. I never did this.

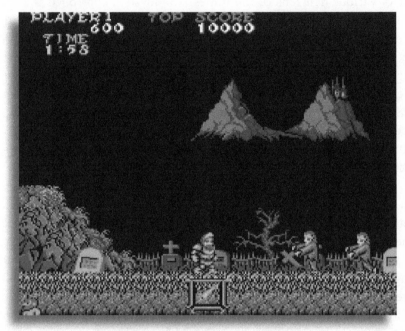

Figure 9.7: *Ghosts 'n Goblins* **combined a fantasy theme and charming, whimsical graphics with extremely difficult gameplay.**

Designed by Tokuro Fujiwara, the same person who made *Commando*, *Ghosts 'n Goblins* put you in control of a knight on a mission to rescue a princess from a demon (the character names differed depending on the region). You started the game equipped with flying swords and a suit of plate mail. Get hit once, and you'd lose not only the armor but your clothes, leaving you standing there in underwear. Get hit a second time and you'd lose a life and have to start either at the beginning of that level or halfway through, if you made it to the checkpoint. Along the way, you'd encounter all manner of zombies, demons, ogres, and other monsters, as well as new weapons and extra suits of armor. Available weapons included an axe, lance, cross, dagger, and flames.

When you first started a game, you would see the knight and princess together, sitting on the grass having a picnic; the demon would then swoop in and kidnap the princess right in front of you and fly away. The game map displayed each time you started a new level or lost a life. There were seven levels: Graveyard and Forest, Town, Caves, Bridge, Castle Lower Level, Castle Upper Level, and the Final Boss. Along the way, smaller "boss" monsters such as other demons and a dragon would appear and have to be defeated. The game had a comic touch, not just with the underwear gag but in the way the knight ran and the fact that he would collapse into a pile of bones upon his death.[7]

The game's graphics and sound design were top notch. Although the resolution wasn't there yet to pull off comedy with the main character and monsters, the presentation was nonetheless colorful, and the background music composed by Ayako Mori stuck in your head for days. Along the way, you would discover tricks to stay alive, such as from what position to defeat certain monsters and whether you should pick up every weapon or hold on to certain ones for specific situations. Or you would just die all the time, if you were me. Many side-scrollers were tough, but *Ghosts 'n Goblins* was especially so because enemies seemed to come from all directions—even under your feet, often with other enemies ahead and in the sky.[8]

Ghosts 'n Goblins saw its biggest success in home conversions, where it appeared on the NES, Commodore 64 (in a more limited form) and Amiga, and Atari ST, among other platforms. Capcom released numerous sequels, including *Ghouls 'n Ghosts*, *Super Ghouls 'n Ghosts* (which appeared on the Super NES), and spin-off series such as *Maximo* and *Gargoyle's Quest*. It's an example of the kind of crossover we'll begin to see more and more often, where a game finds its largest audience not in the arcade but in the home.

Space Harrier (Sega, 1985)

Space Harrier showcased a distinctive third-person view set behind a jet-propelled human character in a fantasy world full of alien creatures. In this second game to use Sega's new Super Scaler board (after *Hang-On*), you played a space war veteran on a mission to save the Dragon Land, an alien planet occupied by supernatural and barbaric creatures. There were 18 scenes in all, and Sega designed the game to be full of surprises, such as a giant dragon that turned out to be friendly and even rideable. At its core, *Space Harrier* was a rail shooter, but it captivated with its 3D presentation, checkerboard ground mapping, sheer speed, and colorful graphics. It was unlike anything else in arcades.

The game came in a rolling deluxe cabinet with a fighter-jet-style seat as well as a standard upright and a smaller sit-down model. An analog flight stick moved the warrior backward, forward, horizontally, and diagonally;

when playing the rolling type, the entire cabinet moved along with the joystick. Redundant Fire buttons on the flight stick and to either side of it shot unlimited bullets. The only thing you couldn't do was change your speed; the trick to staying alive was to keep moving all around the screen so that you were never a stationary target.

Figure 9.8: The quintessential rail shooter on shrooms. *Space Harrier*'s **psychedelic color palette and sprite scaling was an experience like none other.**

Sega claimed the game was the first with a 1.2MB "graphics capacity," with support for more than 32,000 colors thanks to the use of pastel shades. The game's vibrant, psychedelic palette—and it became progressively nuttier as you advanced from scene to scene—had an interesting story behind it. The color of the sky came from a bug during development, as designer Yu Suzuki said in a 2015 interview:

At the time, we had worked up a pretty sky background with nice color gradations…and, well, this is a little bit of a digression, but President Nakayama used to visit our office from time to time. The thing with Nakayama was, if he saw that the graphics were complete in your game, he would tell you it was done and it was time to release it. Nevertheless, we couldn't just hide the game from him and show him nothing when he came by.

So I rigged up a little switch underneath my desk. When I pressed that switch, it would wipe the color RAM. You could wipe the color RAM, and it wouldn't affect the rest of the game—everything would keep running, just the colors would get all glitched. To a layperson, it would look like the game wasn't complete yet. Well, one time we did this, and randomly, the colors of the sky looked extremely striking. Then I used our development tool ICE to stop the CPU and extract the color RAM data, and those became the colors we used for Space Harrier.

The game also included a distinctive stereo soundtrack by Hiroshi Kawaguchi, thanks to Yamaha's YM2233 sound chip controlled by a Z80, as well as digitized audio and speech samples via Sega's own PCM chip. Even the title screen looked special, with its animated gold plate inscribed with the title and fantastical combination of a woolly mammoth next to a futuristic mecha warrior with three red circular lights for eyes. Home conversions of the game were all over the board, with the 16-bit Atari ST and Commodore Amiga faring well and their mice acting as decent stand-ins for the analog flight stick. Sega's own Master System and even Genesis couldn't handle it as well—all the more reason to head to the arcade and play the real thing.

The NES Launches

By this point, Nintendo had stopped making arcade coin-ops in lieu of its new Family Computer game console, unveiled in Japan in 1983 and launched as the Nintendo Entertainment System in America—first in a limited New York City–focused trial run for the holidays in late 1985, and then nationally in 1986. The NES brought back the U.S. home video game market, with massive sales of not just consoles but cartridges from Nintendo, Konami, Capcom, and Tengen throughout the rest of the 1980s. The ColecoVision, Atari 5200, and Vectrex each brought convincing facsimiles of the arcade home in their own ways in 1982 and 1983. But after the market crash, the NES pushed the bar even higher, not just in conversions but also allowing for much more in-depth play with games such as *Super Mario Bros.* and *The Legend of Zelda*. Nintendo's success was so huge that Atari Corporation scrambled to restart production of its 7800 and revamped 2600 consoles after having shelved them two years earlier amid company turmoil.

The NES, although still an 8-bit console, was good enough that, arguably for the first time, it would take more than that to bring people into arcades. Coin-ops would always have to be a step ahead of game consoles.

But the NES marked the point where, even if the graphics quality wasn't identical, the distinction between arcade games and home games began to blur. By the mid 1990s, that distinction would almost disappear.

SNK

SNK was founded in 1978 by Eikichi Kawasaki as Shin Nihon Kikaku. The company started producing arcade video games in 1979, beginning with *Ozma Wars* and *Safari Rally*. Its first major hit was in distributing Tose's 1981 coin-op *Vanguard* in Japan and Germany, the game Centuri distributed in the U.S. That success prompted Kikaku to open a U.S. branch called SNK Electronics Corporation. SNK kept producing arcade games, including the *Pleiades*-like *Satan of Saturn* (1981) and *Main Event* (1984), a side-view boxing game. The year 1986 saw SNK's biggest hit to date and its breakthrough coin-op for the U.S. market.

Ikari Warriors (SNK/Tradewest, 1986)

Capcom's *Commando* being the hit it was, other manufacturers looked to broaden the run-and-gun shooter genre. The object of *Ikari Warriors*, designed by Keiko Iju, was to penetrate enemy defenses deep inside a jungle in order to reach the village of Ikari. The game put you in control of a shirtless, bandana-wearing soldier in the vein of *Rambo: First Blood Part II*, which had hit theaters the year before. Either alone or cooperatively with a friend, you pushed forward to dispatch all manner of enemy soldiers, helicopters, armored bunkers, tanks, and amphibious vehicles. To get to Ikari, five gates served as checkpoints. Reach and destroy a gate and you'd progress to the next stage. Along the way, you could climb into tanks to increase your firepower and run over enemy soldiers. The tanks were impervious to enemy shots but had a limited fuel supply and would become vulnerable to damage from nearby explosions. When this happened, you had to jump out of the tank before it exploded.

 Ikari Warriors pioneered rotary-style joysticks. They moved in eight directions like other joysticks, but the handles also rotated, letting players aim their gun independently of the direction of movement. In addition, each player had two buttons, one for firing the rifle or tank cannon and the other for lobbing grenades or entering and exiting tanks. The vertical-scrolling playfield took up most of the screen, with enemies coming at you fast and furious as you moved forward. The numbers of bullets and grenades, and the amount of tank fuel you had remaining, were tracked on screen, and you could pick up POW icons and gas cans to replenish your supplies.

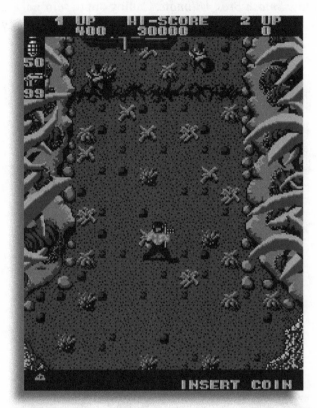

Figure 9.9: *Ikari Warriors* added rotary joysticks with sophisticated aiming capability to an otherwise standard-issue run-and-gun game.

Operators could configure DIP switches for four difficulty levels and whether friendly fire was possible with bullets or a grenade. Many players preferred *Ikari Warriors* over *Commando* not just for the extra power-ups and improved graphics but for the unique rotary joysticks. (I still preferred the kind of straight dual-joystick setup used in *Robotron: 2084*, but that's me.) Home conversions varied in quality, with many platforms (especially the NES) suffering in speed and animation smoothness compared with the original coin-op, although the NES added the ability to board helicopters in addition to tanks. *Front Line* may have kick-started this subgenre of game, and served as part inspiration here given the former's tank mechanic and ability to aim the gun separately, but *Ikari Warriors* was arguably the genre's peak. The two main characters, Colonel Ralf (the red one) and Second Lieutenant Clark (blue), made additional appearances in future games, most notably in the 1990s *The King of Fighters* and *Metal Slug* series, and as cameos in *Super Smash Bros. Ultimate.* Calling out to seminal arcade games of the 1970s and 1980s has become a bit of a tradition in many of today's console titles.

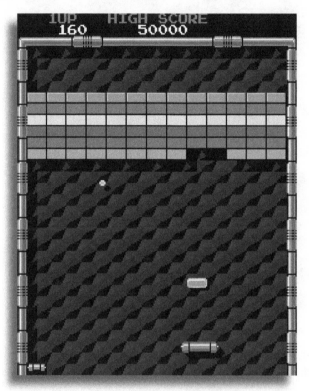

Figure 9.10: *Arkanoid* **was the first brick-breaker game since** *Super Breakout* **to improve the genre, with its capsule-based power-ups, crisp color graphics, and dozens of imaginative board layouts.**

Arkanoid (Taito/Romstar, 1986)

Breakout clones were common, but *Arkanoid* was a true improvement that gave the entire genre a shot in the arm. Taito designers Akira Fujita and Hiroshi Tsujino set the *Tron*-inspired game in space. You controlled the Vaus, a ship in the shape of a paddle, which escaped from a doomed mothership at the start of each game. You shattered successive walls of bricks by bouncing an energy ball toward them. In this way, it was the same as *Breakout*: You needed to clear all of the bricks before you could move on to the next level, and *Super Breakout* had introduced different wall designs in 1978. But *Arkanoid* was much more creative about it, with not just fresh brick formations but beautifully varied backdrops. It included three kinds of wall sections instead of one: normal ones that disappeared when hit with the ball, tougher ones that required multiple hits, and indestructible bricks. Some screens also introduced roving enemy ships of various types that would descend in kamikaze-like attacks.

The varying board designs, crisp neon-like graphics, and metallic sound effects drew players in, but the power-ups made the game what it was. Rotating capsules would drift down from the wall that, when caught, powered up the Vaus or otherwise changed the play dynamic. There were seven available: *S* (Slow), which slowed down the energy ball; *C* (Catch), which let you catch the ball with the paddle and then release it when you wanted to; *E* (Expand), which doubled the size of the Vaus; *D* (Disrupt), which split the ball into three; *L* (Laser), which gave the Vaus unlimited laser shots and was the most valuable of them all; *B* (Break), which advanced you to the next board; and *P* (Player), which gave you an extra life. Strategically capturing the power-ups you needed or wanted proved to be smart strategy. If you managed to clear 32 stages, the 33rd contained the end boss Doh, a statue-like giant alien brain. Whether you dispatched it or not, the game ended after this battle. Even the high score table echoed the space combat theme; it read, "The following are the records of the bravest fighters of *Arkanoid*."

Arkanoid was ported to nearly every home computer and game console available. The speed in which this happened diminished the arcade game's appeal, as machines such as the Atari ST and the PC were able to deliver not only a pitch-perfect conversion but also provided a passable control substitution with a mouse. This story happened more and more as time went on, and it's tough to separate how much of *Arkanoid*'s enduring popularity was from the home versions as opposed to memories of playing the original arcade game. Recognizing success when it saw it, Taito turned *Arkanoid* into a franchise and released many games, starting with *Tournament Arkanoid*, which contained a new pack of levels; *Revenge of Doh*, with its level warps and other new game mechanics; and several new home-console-only versions of the game.

Bubble Bobble (Taito/Romstar, August 1986)

It's tough to find a game that exhibited the ideal Nintendo Entertainment System title as closely as *Bubble Bobble*. But it was an arcade game first and foremost, and was one of the most popular coin-ops of the year. This plat-former from Taito starred Bub and Bob, two tiny dragons. You entered the Cave of Monsters and played through 100 levels of Baron von Bubba's min-ions to rescue their two kidnapped girlfriends and then get turned back into human form. Each level was a fixed playfield with borders at the edges. Levels contained a series of platforms designed in different ways, some-times with portals at the bottom of the screen that would teleport you to the top, and with distinctive color schemes. You controlled Bub or Bob with the joystick, moving them left or right, jumping to higher platforms or over gaps, or and dropping down to lower platforms. You entrapped enemies by blowing them into bubbles, which then began floating up the screen. Crashing into the bubbles popped them, yielding you bonus fruit, and you'd earn more points for knocking off several enemies in succession.

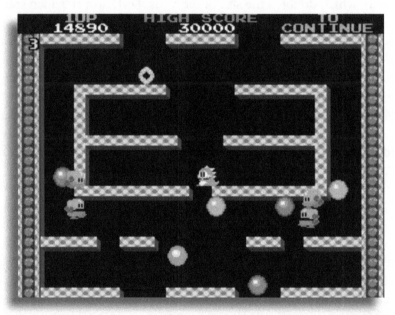

Figure 9.11: Bubble Bobble was a fun single-player game but a downright excel-lent cooperative one, with cute graphics and sound effects masking surprisingly satisfying gameplay.

The game had numerous ways of increasing the challenge. Leaving an enemy floating in a bubble for too long would cause the bubble to pop on its own. The enemy would then turn red and move faster; and boy, he was pissed! It was also easy to lose a life not just by colliding with an enemy not in a bubble but with any of the fireballs, rocks, or other items they threw at you. If you spent too long on the same board, an invincible enemy would appear and chase you around, and the last enemy left would also turn red and become angry. You could also ride bubbles containing enemies to reach other parts of the board. Occasionally, you'd come across magic items that gave you special abilities, as well as a series of bubbles with the letters E, X, T, N, and D in them; spell "EXTEND" and you'd get an extra life and warp to the next level.

Make it to level 100, and you'd reach a final boss. The game was one of the first to feature multiple endings; winning by yourself would only get the message to "come here with your friend." But if two players won together, they would transform back into their human forms and be reunited with their girlfriends, and the game would then give you a super code that could be used to play a more difficult game. *Bubble Bobble* played fluidly on its own, but where the game truly shone was in its cooperative play—a top design goal of creator Fukio Mitsuji. Mitsuji wanted to create a game that appealed to women as well as men, and couples who would visit an arcade and play the game together. The game was ported to many different consoles of the era and landed on a number of "best of all time" lists of popular arcade games. It did make a good NES game, too—enough so that it appeared as one of the 30 bundled games with the popular NES Classic Edition Nintendo released in 2016.

Out Run (Sega, 1986)

Out Run defined the modern, three-dimensional "arcade-style" racing game. It consisted of various highway scenarios through locales such as France, the Alps, and a winding road around the edge of a cliff. The game also included uphill and downhill terrain and opposing cars that changed lanes. You drove a convertible Ferrari Testarossa, an Italian supercar that didn't exist in real life without a roof. You had to drive as far as you could in the time allotted, passing checkpoints along the way. Sega manufactured *Out Run* in four versions. The top of the line was a massive, 770-pound deluxe moving cabinet; it was a sit-down model with a 26-inch CRT, a car seat with two rear wheels, and a hydraulics system to move the seat around. There was also a regular sit-down model with a stationary car seat, but without the wheels and hydraulics system; this one still weighed 660 pounds. Then there was a standard upright, which still included a "crash" simulation that moved the steering wheel from side to side when you go off road or crash. Finally, there was a miniature upright with a smaller 20-inch monitor. The control panel consisted of a small steering wheel, a gear shift on the right that selected between low and high, an accelerator pedal, and a brake pedal.

Like *Pole Position*, *Out Run* delivered realistic driving with its selectable gears and two pedals, and you'd even see the brake lights activate when pressing the left pedal. As you played the game, you'd periodically get the chance to take a left or right at a fork in the road; each would take you on a different path, to a different set of scenes, each more difficult than the last. When you ran out of time, the game would show you a course map depicting which turnoffs you took; there were 15 scenes, five stages, and five destinations in all, arranged in a fanning-out pattern from a single starting point on the left to destinations *A* through *E* on the right.

Figure 9.12: Sega's *Out Run* defined the arcade racing game, with its force-feedback steering wheel, colorful scenes, and tunable car stereo.

Thanks to System 16, a board based on Sega's second-generation Super Scaler architecture, *Out Run*'s graphics were a leap beyond anything released pre-crash. They depicted a wide variety of scenery on the sides of the road and over the horizon, including trees, rock formations, and even overhead trusses for a tunnellike effect. The view was from behind, with a third-person perspective and the camera situated near the road. Sega was able to render the opposing car graphics with enough detail that you could easily make out Porsche 911s, BMW 325i convertibles, Volkswagen Beetles, and Corvette Stingrays. The steering wheel delivered an impressive, realistic turn-in feel. Even outside of simulation-style games, accuracy counts. The catchy stereo soundtrack may well have been the defining feature of the game. You could choose between "Passing Breeze," "Magical Sound Shower," and "Splash Wave," as if tuning the car's radio. When the game ended, it played a fourth track called "Last Wave" for the high score board.

The game saw home conversions on the Sega Master System and Genesis, Commodore Amiga, Atari ST, the ZX Spectrum, and the Amstrad, with most from a company called U.S. Gold; some came with an extra music cassette containing the songs from the arcade game. Sega brought some of *Out Run*'s innovation to its 1987 *Super Hang-On*, an update of the motorcycle racer with additional racetracks around the world, new backdrops, and a choice of four background tunes in the same vein as *Out Run*. Sega released several sequels, such as *Out Run 3-D*, *Turbo Out Run*, and *Out Run Europa*, and even spawned a subgenre of "synthwave" music based on how the game sounded. In 2015, IGN listed the game in fourth place in "The Top 10 Most Influential Racing Games Ever," behind *Pole Position*, *Gran Turismo*, and *Virtua Racing*.[9]

Rampage (Bally Midway, 1986)

Sometimes the most fun you can possibly have is when breaking things apart. Bally Midway took the idea to its logical conclusion: Why not make a game where you get to be a giant monster destroying a city? In the humorous *Rampage*, you climbed each skyscraper in a city and punched, kicked, and otherwise destroyed enough of it so that it would collapse into rubble. When all the buildings on the screen were destroyed, you'd advance to the next city.

Naturally, the populace wasn't thrilled about you coming in and destroying the buildings, so there were a variety of hazards to contend with, such as bullets from troops or airborne helicopters, random sticks of dynamite, and even lightning strikes. As you destroyed buildings, you needed to eat food to survive. You could punch open windows to find food items, or—why not?—gobble up National Guard and police forces attacking you from windows. You could also pick up a person who was walking along the sidewalk below and eat them, too. Each time a building began to collapse, you had to jump off or you'd get caught in the implosion and take damage. If someone with a camera popped out of a building, you'd have to eat them before they snapped a picture and the flash made you fall off the side.

Jeff Nauman programmed the game for Bally Midway, with Brian Colin handling the art and Michael Bartlow as sound designer. When you started the game, you and up to two other players could choose from three monsters in a newspaper-like interface that showed pictures of each monster and the person they were originally. Each monster had his own story. George transformed into a King Kong–like ape after taking an experimental vitamin. Lizzie became a lizard after stepping into a radioactive lake. Eating a recalled food additive turned Ralph into a wolf. In real life, the people depicted were Colin, his wife, and Nauman as George, Lizzie, and Ralph, respectively.

Figure 9.13: *Rampage* **gave every comic-book-reading kid their dream: the ability to play as a giant monster destroying skyscrapers and eating people. That was every kid's dream, right?**

During play, you could save people leaning out of windows yelling for help. Each monster had its own rescue target; George saved women, Lizzie saved men, and Ralph saved businessmen in suits. Some items were too hazardous to eat, such as cacti, bombs, bottles of poison, or toasters. Grab a TV (hopefully it was off first!), a flowerpot, or a money bag, and you'd get bonus points. When your health bar reached zero, you would revert back into a naked human and walk off the screen sideways, covering the important parts with your hands. If you made it, you'd mutate back into the monster, but another monster could eat you when you were human.

Another player could drop into a game in progress—literally, as you would come flying in and then fall to the ground. More quarters added health, letting you play as long as you wanted, and not necessarily because you were "killed," as in most arcade games. The game was a success, defying expectation from some in Bally Midway management, and soon was ported to many home computers and consoles of the day; I was fond of the Atari 520ST conversion. But what few expected—least of all Colin, as he said in a 2018 interview—was that the game would be made into a motion picture starring someone who would become one of the most famous actors on the planet, Dwayne Johnson.

"I loved *King Kong*; as an animator, I loved Willis O'Brien and Ray Harryhausen's stop-motion," Colin explained in the interview. "Godzilla made me so annoyed as a kid because it was a guy in a suit—don't hate me, Godzilla fans, I'm sorry. When we were talking about the third character, I did the math and realized we didn't have enough [data] for a whole third character, so we switched palettes and all I had to do is change his head. Jeff Nauman, the programmer, said, 'Let's make him a wolf,' and he named him Ralph." The $120 million movie went on to do well at the box office, grossing more than $400 million in combined revenue in the U.S. and overseas. Not bad.

Rastan (Taito, 1987)

This side-scroller pitted a medieval warrior against variety of mythical fantasy creatures in an effort to find and slay a dragon. Enemies included Graton warriors with iron tridents; three-headed, fire-breathing Chimairas (the spelling in the game); and Gigas who were encased in plated armor and wielded wooden clubs. Designed by Toshiyuki Nishimura and produced by Yoshinori Kobayashi, *Rastan* was heavily influenced by Robert E. Howard's *Conan the Barbarian*, from the main character to the storyline and, as Hardcore Gaming 101 pointed out, even in the attract mode shot of the aging king sitting on a throne, which echoed the final scene of the 1982 movie.[10]

The controls included an eight-way joystick, a Jump button, and a Sword button for attacking. Holding the Jump button down longer would give you additional height, and attacking using the joystick would let you execute specific moves such as leaping into the air and then thrusting downward. *Rastan* included six stages, each with three areas to explore and clear out. These areas included an outdoor portion, a castle's interior where the action became more difficult, and a throne room where you would find an end boss. The six end bosses were a skeletal warrior with a halberd, a winged demon with a sword, a wizard, a dragon-king, a five-headed hydra, and the final dragon. Along the way, Rastan would find power-ups that could increase his strength and power. These included an axe, a mace, and a fire sword that shot fireballs; new body armor, a mantle, and a shield to improve your defenses; and various jewels that just provided bonus points. Once equipped, each of the power-ups lasted a limited time before disappearing and returning your abilities to normal. An interesting addition was the energy bar at the top of the screen. Each time you were hit, you would lose some health. Run out of health and you'd lose a life. You'd also die immediately if you fell into water or fire, or if you were crushed by a ceiling or impaled by spears jutting out of the ground. It was as much fun as it sounds!

Figure 9.14: *Rastan* **polished off** *Ghost 'n Goblins's* **rough edges and delivered a smoother, less frustrating game with a** *Conan the Barbarian* **sensibility.**

Rastan's graphics were colorful, and the programming team made clever use of objects with different coloring and positions to distinguish the backgrounds between levels. The game also displayed convincing time-of-day and weather changes, something rarely seen at the time.[11] The in-game music, composed by Naoto Yagishita and Masahiko Takaki, evoked elements of Basil Poledouris's score for *Conan the Barbarian* while still managing to sound like a 1987 action platformer. Even the sound of Rastan's heartbeat is modeled, and the rate increased as you ran out of health, adding a sense of urgency to the proceedings.

Rastan successfully combined elements of run-and-gun, hack-and-slash, horizontal-scrolling, and platforming games. The colorful graphics and digitized sampled effects evoked a look and feel that typified late-1980s 16-bit video games, both in the arcade and on next-generation home consoles that would appear a couple of years later. *Rastan* was sold in a standard upright form factor and as a conversion kit. Notable home conversions included quality ones on the Apple IIGS and PC, good Sega Master system and MSX ports, and inferior Commodore 64 and ZX Spectrum versions. Although *Rastan* wasn't terribly innovative, it succeeded in being one of the best games of its era—something that consoles would soon take over for good.

R-Type (Irem/Nintendo, 1987)

R-Type expanded on the *Gradius* and *Salamander* formula, a horizontal-scrolling space shooter with multiple levels of cosmic parallax landscapes, alien creatures, power crystals, and boosted sound effects. Aside from improved graphics and larger sprites, *R-Type* employed a weapons-switching system that deviated from *Gradius*'s power-up accumulation. The object was to use the R-9 interstellar ship to defeat the Bydo, an alien race bent on destroying humanity, before it could destroy you with its serpentine creatures, space bugs, walking cyborgs, and huge warships. The developers of *R-Type* reportedly drew from *Gradius*, the movie *Aliens*, and H.R. Giger's biomechanical human-machines.

Your ship's main gun fired repeated shots; holding down the Fire button charged up the wave cannon for a huge burst of firepower. Perhaps the biggest difference in *R-Type* was the Force, a floating orb you could acquire that also shot enemies in tandem and protected you from their shots. You could attach the orb to either the front or back of your R-9 Arrowhead, or you could let it fly freely by shooting it away. When attached, it provided one of three special weapons in addition to the main gun and the wave cannon. Otherwise, the game tracked the usual shooter template, including a series of levels that each had a powerful, often screen-filling end boss. Irem's 16-bit M72 hardware powered *R-Type*, the first game to use it. The main board consisted of a V30 CPU running at 8MHz, a Z80 for sound processing, and a Yamaha YM2151 synthesizer, the same music chip Sega used.[12] *R-Type*'s legendary soundtrack was one of the best video game scores of its time.

R-Type made it to many different home computers and game consoles. The conversions included a quality Commodore Amiga port and what is commonly thought of as the best arcade space shooter for the

TurboGrafx-16. The Atari ST's port suffered from its choppier animation thanks to the lack of hardware scrolling (which was remedied later on with the STE's blitter chip). In one of the stranger bits of video game history, there was one notable absence: *R-Type* never made it to the Nintendo Entertainment System, even though Nintendo was *R-Type*'s North American distributor. A game called *Super R-Type* did arrive on the SNES, but it was a mishmash of *R-Type II* levels and some original ones. As with *Gradius III*, that one was also known for serious slowdowns when many enemies were on the screen at once.

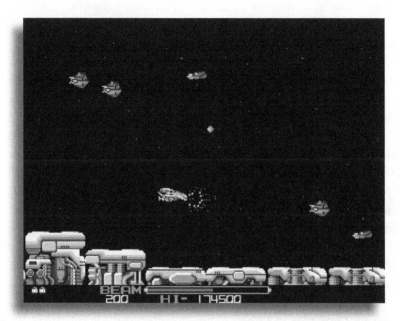

Figure 9.15: *R-Type* **built on** *Gradius* **and** *Salamander* **with its unique weapons scheme and oversized sprites that amped up the bio-alien motif.**

Regardless of the various conversion issues, the arcade *R-Type* and its sequels were some of the defining space shooters of the late 1980s. Factor in the *Gradius* and console-only *Thunder Force* series, and it was a golden age for shoot-'em-up fans that liked their games difficult, with detailed graphics and memorable electronic music soundtracks. In 2015, *R-Type* made IGN's list of "The Top 10 Toughest Games to Beat," thanks to the trial-and-error-and-die system required to get any good at the game and how slow your ship was to maneuver around the intricate level layouts. Yet even an article like that was full of praise for *R-Type*: "Luckily, the clever level design and awesome boss fights made all the frustration worth it."

After Burner (Sega, 1987)

After Burner strapped you in—literally—to an F-14 "Thunder Cat" fighter jet, or at least a model of one. The game included large sprites, fast animation, a frenetic soundtrack, and sampled drums and sound effects. It attempted to simulate the sensation of flying at speeds faster than Mach 2. At the time, *After Burner* seemed more advanced than anything else in the arcades. The enemy wanted to conquer the free world and had mapped it out in a two-part plan. You shot down supersonic enemy fighters with your jet's machine gun and heat-seeking missiles to battle your way to the locations of the two plans. The game itself was on rails, and you'd refuel the jet in the air at predetermined milestones. The machine gun had unlimited ammunition but a set number of missiles. The controls included a flight stick with integrated missile and cannon triggers, and a separate hand throttle that moved up and down to adjust your flight speed. If you bumped the stick left or right and then immediately again in the opposite direction, the plane would perform a 360-degree roll.

Figure 9.16: Everyone got to pretend they were in *Top Gun* with *After Burner*, Sega's air combat game that moved *Hang-On* and *Space Harrier* scaling tech to the skies.

Designed by Yu Suzuki, the game came in a beautiful cockpit cabinet that moved physically to simulate the G-forces building as you pitched forward, banked left or right, or pulled back to climb. The entire cabinet would rotate side to side, and the seat could tilt forward and backward. Two stereo speakers sat at head level, and the cockpit even included seat belts to hold the player in place as the cabinet moved around. A standard upright was also available, and a smaller sit-down model called the Commander cabinet was made for overseas markets; it lacked the rolling motion when pitching down and climbing, but it still moved left and right.[13]

After Burner contained from 18 to 23 stages, depending on the cabinet and time of release. At 5 million and 15 million points, you'd score an extra fighter jet. On the PCB were two Motorola 68000 CPUs and a Z80 CPU, plus two Yamaha synthesizer chips and one Sega PCM digital audio chip. The game displayed at 320-by-224 resolution, and it used the Sega X platform's scaling effects to simulate high speeds in three dimensions. A small radar map at the top-right corner of the screen showed enemy locations and current banking angle. *After Burner* was a huge hit thanks to its sophistication and gameplay, and the popularity of the movie *Top Gun*, which had arrived in theaters the previous year. You even took off from an aircraft carrier called the Sega Enterprise at the start of the game.

After Burner and its successors were top draws in arcades. They were also some of the last hit coin-op titles that weren't about fighting or racing. Sega ensured its Master System console received a quality port, and it also appeared on a wide variety of home computer platforms (sometimes with mixed results). In the U.K., it was also bundled into the starter packs that came with the 16-bit Atari ST computer system along with some other Sega games. Fans of the motion picture *Terminator 2: Judgment Day* will remember John Connor playing the game in the Galleria as the T-1000 searched for him.

Sega unveiled a revamped model called *After Burner II* later that same year and carried the theme forward with new titles such as *Strike Fighter* and *Sky Target*. The series culminated in 1990's *G-LOC: Air Battle*, another mildly updated iteration of *After Burner*. It came in a deluxe R-360 cabinet that rotated the player a full 360 degrees during combat. It resembled a space-age Ferris wheel in the place of a driving or flying cockpit. *G-LOC: Air Battle* is remembered mostly for the R-360 version and that players often lost their lunch—which, given how G-LOC stood for "G-force–induced Loss Of Consciousness," only seemed appropriate.

Galaga '88 (Namco/Atari Games, 1987)

There have been plenty of remakes of popular games over the past several decades, and they've been all over the board in quality. Namco had already iterated on *Galaga* with *Gaplus* in 1984, but *Galaga '88* was one of the first remakes to show everyone how it was done post-crash. *Galaga '88* included improved graphics and sound effects, new background music, and extra polish in the animation and controls. It's as if Namco created a sequel by shoving *Galaga* and *Gyruss* together.

Figure 9.17: Namco showed everyone how to update a classic with Galaga '88, an addictive return to form with powered-up graphics and stereo sound.

In *Galaga '88*, you confronted enemies in each of 29 progressively more difficult sectors of the galaxy. At the start of the game, you could select between single and dual firepower, and you could continue where you left off by inserting another quarter. *Galaga '88* added the ability to get a "triple ship," by waiting for your double ship to get picked up by a tractor beam and then freeing it. New in-game warps meant you didn't always have to start from the beginning, and four new kinds of enemies offered different weapons and defenses. By shooting certain enemies, you could score items; get two and you'd get a new warp. There were also new Challenge Rounds, where you shot galagas for bonus points as different tunes played in the background.

The mere existence of *Galaga '88* was enough to attracted dedicated space shoot-'em-up fans. It's remembered today not just for its quality, but also for its TurboGrafx-16 port, which was considered one of the best of that era and one of the console's top cartridges overall. The fact that *Galaga '88* didn't see many other conversions in the U.S. helped preserve its appeal in the arcades. It was a good complement to the bounty of beat-'em-up and fighting games that were beginning to crowd the market. It didn't sell nearly as well as its predecessor, but it remained an important game in the evolution of the video arcade. *Galaga '88* showed that just because there were too many space shooters in 1983 and 1984, it didn't mean they were dead forever.

After the game industry crash and the continued popularity of home computers, it was natural to wonder whether gamers would return to the arcades. A reader letter in the April 1985 issue of *Electronic Games* summed up the feelings of many arcade-goers at the time:

> Back when people had to stand in line to play arcade game machines, it made sense (and dollars) for the arcade owners to set up the machines with a minimum number of lives and a high difficulty level so that the maximum number of quarters were snatched up. Now, most machines stand idle waiting for a customer...The super-skilled players, having mastered the games at high difficulty levels, are bored and are finding other uses for their quarters. The rest of us, who would love to reach advanced levels in games, have just faced the fact that it would take too many quarters and have just given up.

The editors responded, "You've just put your finger on one of the reasons why people are switching to computer games. Once you lay out the money for the game, you can play as much as you like."[14] Arcades still offered several advantages. They provided a social setting for gamers to congregate and play with strangers away from their parents, as well as video game tournaments, and the arcades themselves maintained a lineup of state-of-the-art games.[15] Some manufacturers joined the industry late. Jaleco was founded in 1974 as Japan Leisure and produced amusement park and arcade equipment but didn't begin producing its own coin-op video games until 1982, mostly for the Japanese market. The company was known for its NES cartridges, such as *Bases Loaded*, but it produced more than 100 coin-ops between 1982 and 2000.

The industry also took another stab at sports games in a way it hadn't since the days of paddle ball and *Pong* clones. This kicked off with Konami's *Track & Field* and progressed to Taito's *10-Yard Fight*, Stern's *Goal to Go*, and of course Nintendo's *Punch-Out!!*. Arriving on the heels of those games was *Tekhan World Cup*, an overhead soccer coin-op with a tabletop cabinet and trackball controllers in the vein of Atari's *Football*, albeit with much better graphics and sound. Martial arts games were popularized by *Karate Champ* and *Kung-Fu Master*, and Atari's 650-pound behemoth *TX-1* spread out a *Pole Position*–type racing game onto three monitors. In addition to the above games, Atari's System 2 hardware also served as the basis for 1986's *720°*, Atari Games' skateboarding coin-op, as well as *APB*, a 1987 police chase game, and *Super Sprint* and *Championship Sprint*, both nicely updated versions of Atari Inc.'s *Sprint 2* with much more colorful graphics and a variety of tracks to race on. This racer style remained popular, culminating in Leland's 1989 coin-op *Ivan 'Ironman' Stewart's Super Off Road*, a monster truck racer stuffed with hilly, indoor dirt tracks to bounce around on. It also came in a three-person cabinet, complete with three steering wheels and pedals arranged in a half-hexagon configuration.

It would take some serious innovation to give people a reason to go to the arcades again, with all of the games appearing on home computers. Fortunately, the next several years brought even more hit titles to bear.

Fighting games had their roots in the beginnings of the industry. Opposing players have shot at each other since Atari's *Tank* and Midway's *Gun Fight*, and the first true one-on-one fighting game was *Warrior* from Cinematronics. As the 1980s wore on, several major titles brought the battle out of the arena and onto dilapidated city streets. Their resulting popularity signaled the possibility that arcades, much like that guy in the cart in *Monty Python and the Holy Grail*, weren't dead yet.

Double Dragon (Taito, 1987)

Kung-Fu Master was the first, and 1986 saw the release of *Renegade*, a very 1980s brawler with lots of big hair and bandanas, which pit you against four different gangs. But *Double Dragon*, originally released in Japan before making it over to the states, is credited with launching the beat-'em-up craze that gave arcades new life. As twin martial arts experts Billy and Jimmy Lee (nicknamed Spike and Hammer), you and a friend had to rescue Marian from a street gang. The two brothers practiced Sōsetsuken, a form of martial arts that combined karate, tai chi, and Shorinji Kempo. You could play by yourself or cooperate with a second player, a novel addition that became part of the template for the genre, and you could continue with extra quarters whenever you wanted. At a time when karate movies were all the rage, featuring stars such as Jackie Chan, Jean-Claude Van Damme, and Steven Seagal, *Double Dragon* soon found its audience.

Figure 10.1: The brawler that put the genre on the map for real, *Double Dragon* was a dose of 1980s gang movies you could actually play.

The game was set in a post-apocalyptic New York and started off with a short introduction sequence. The basic idea was that you'd walk through the stages and beat up anyone you came across. The game progressed through street, factory, forest, and castle stages, and was filled with '80s-tastic colorful outfits and scenery. The presentation was vaguely in three dimensions, a horizontal-scroller but with the ability to move up and down within the streets as you walked. Each board progressed from left to right in a series of scenes; you had to dispatch all of the bad guys in each one before a bell sounded and you could move forward. If both players reached the end of the game, they would fight over the girl and the survivor would "win" her affections.

The controls for each player consisted of an eight-way joystick and Punch, Kick, and Jump buttons; pressing Punch or Kick together with Jump executed the move in the air. Moving the joystick twice in the same direction executed a head butt; pushing into an enemy and pressing Jump would throw them. The Jump button could also break a hold, and you could push away from an enemy while jumping to do an elbow smash or back kick. This arrangement became commonplace and extended to include additional moves as more arcade games adopted the format. You could also steal knives, clubs, dynamite, and other weapons to use against enemies, or pick up crates and oil drums to throw at them. The gang members—who went by the names Williams, Rowper, Linda, Abobo, Jick, Jeff, and Willy, and each had their own proficiencies in fighting moves and weapons—could perform many of the same maneuvers against you.

Part of *Double Dragon*'s success lay with the hardware, which employed several parallel 8-bit Hitachi HD6309 processors and Yamaha's YM2151 FM synthesis chip. This game was very much of its time, and not just because of the outfits. That's a shorthand way of saying that its graphics and occasional slowdowns haven't aged well. It also had a balance issue: The elbow smash was powerful enough to make the game easy to defeat once you became proficient with it, at the expense of all other moves. At the time, the game was a success; it spawned several sequels, conversions to all the popular game console and computer platforms of the day, a six-issue series by Marvel Comics, a 26-episode animated TV series, and character appearances in manga and many video games throughout the next few decades. In the early 1990s, *Double Dragon* was even made into a terrible motion picture. No further description of that one is necessary.

Street Fighter (Capcom, 1987)

Capcom's original one-on-one fighting game, *Street Fighter* introduced the world to the characters Ryu and Ken, as well as Sagat as the end boss. It also introduced some of the conventions we've come to know and expect in the genre. *Street Fighter* took place across five countries, each with two enemies to fight. The game featured a series of one-on-one martial arts matches where each fighter tried to knock out the other. If that didn't happen before the timer ran out, then whoever had the most health remaining would win. It took two out of three matches to advance or to lose the game. Meanwhile, a second player could join in at any time by inserting a quarter; that would end the one-player match against the computer and restart in a two-player mode. You could also continue one-player games with additional quarters if you were hell-bent on reaching Sagat.

The original deluxe cabinet offered eight-way joysticks for left-right movement, jumps, flips, and ducks; when the two fighters swapped positions on the screen, some of the moves would switch to the other side (such as pushing up and to the left for a backward flip, instead of up and to the right). Two pressure-sensitive pads delivered punches and kicks. The harder you pushed a pad, the stronger and slower the attack. The pneumatic pads were connected to air hoses inside the cabinet; the system proved difficult to maintain and broke down often.[1] Early in the first production run, Capcom switched to a new six-button layout, with light, medium, and hard options for punches and kicks, a design that soon became a staple of the genre.

Figure 10.2: The prototype for the one-on-one fighting genre, *Street Fighter* introduced Ryu, Ken, and the basic game mechanics, but lacked the control scheme and overall polish its successor would exhibit.

Graphically the game was impressive, with large player sprites and colorful, multilayered backdrops. *Street Fighter* became known for its hidden combo moves that took some practice to figure out and gain proficiency in. Three hidden moves were available: Psycho Fire (Hadōken, or "Surge Fist"), Hurricane Kick (Tatsumaki Senpū Kyaku, "Tornado Whirlwind Kick"), and the famous Dragon Punch (Shoryūken, "Rising Dragon Fist"). The last one was unbalanced; if you landed it close to your opponent, it would trigger two or even three times, and three was enough for a knockout even if your opponent was full up on health. Interspersed between the matches in different countries were two bonus rounds, one with breaking bricks and another with smashing a table.

Street Fighter was designed by Takashi Nishiyama and Hiroshi Matsumoto; they took inspiration from 1984's *Karate Champ*, the European 1985 coin-op *Yie-Ar Kung Fu*, and the 1973 Bruce Lee motion picture *Enter the Dragon*. The game was a success in its time, with most of the reviews calling out the attractive graphics and innovative control scheme (at least before it developed a reputation for unreliability). This is another game that didn't age well. Despite its speed, there's no getting around how stiffly it played, though aside from choppy animation each time you walked onto the board, the actual fighting graphics were smooth. The real problem was in executing the moves; they were too quick to recede, so you had to get the timing just right. Coming from *Karate Champ*, some stiffness was to be expected, but between that and the unbalanced hidden moves, it didn't hold up in the long haul.

Both *Double Dragon* and *Street Fighter* set the stage for new genres. Each game's concept and design was so strong, it didn't matter that their execution had some flaws.

Altered Beast (Sega, 1988)

This game has been immortalized as the original, pack-in cartridge for the 16-bit Sega Genesis game console (known overseas as the Mega Drive) launched in 1989, not to mention its trademark digitized voices. But it was an arcade game first, and impressive—if a little bizarre. Originally designed by Makoto Uchida, *Altered Beast* was a fantasy-themed brawler in the vein of *Double Dragon*, but with a distinctive graphics style and backstory. The game was set in Ancient Greece; the disjointed plot was that Zeus resurrected two Centurions, the Altered Beast and Beast King, to rescue his daughter Athena from Neff, god of the underworld. A cooperative two-player mode let each player take on one role. The game consisted of five levels stuffed with Neff's minions, which comprised hordes of undead beasts and other monsters. At the end of each level, Neff would appear in different forms as a boss character, saying "Welcome to your doom!" Why Athena, supreme goddess of war, wisdom, and crafts, needed rescuing from a pair of magically reanimated dudes was never explained.

The cabinet featured an unmistakable marquee with the game's title flanked by a blue humanlike eye on the left and a red reptilian eye on the right. A scaly skin texture faded in down the bezel and control panel, which presented an eight-way joystick and Punch, Kick, and Jump buttons arranged in a triangle for each player. If you've played *Altered Beast*, you can probably already hear this in your head, but at the start of the game Zeus bellowed "Rise from your grave." You then saw an animation of your hero character doing just that, right as you were given the controls. Aside from the now-standard array of cooperative fighting moves, the central game mechanic was the glowing orbs labeled "Get It" that appeared during fights. These orbs would build your character's strength gradually until he transformed into one of several more powerful creatures, depending on which level you were currently on. The wolf could run super-fast and shoot balls of energy. The dragon breathed fire and could electrify its body. The bear could somersault, destroying all nearby enemies. The tiger could launch new vertical attacks. Finally, on the last level, you could transform into a golden wolf even stronger than the first.

Figure 10.3: The wild, wacky *Altered Beast* smushed together Greek mythology and science fiction, and wrapped them inside a brawler.

Altered Beast, which ran on Sega's System 16 hardware, oozed style, with detailed depictions of ruins, well-animated creature sprites, and large end bosses. The whooshes that accompanied your Centurion's moves as he increased in power were exceptionally divine. On the audio side, the sampled speech combined well with a soundtrack brimming with late-1980s beats known for inspiring a subgenre of musical acts. Destroying enemies resulted in explosions of giant, bloody body parts. But aside from its batty storyline and bright visuals and audio, *Altered Beast* is best remembered for its insane difficulty. You had to time your hits just so, the techniques required for dispatching each enemy were different and had to be learned, and the monsters came at you at a fast pace. You only had three health segments before dying, and with the wrong button push you could easily lose all three within a few seconds. The game was frustrating to the point where many players developed an irrational hatred for the thing.

That criticism was probably misplaced, even if some of it was thanks to the watered-down home versions that didn't quite make up for the difficulty with enough graphics and sound punch. "These days, games aren't about beating them," said Jeff Gamon, one of the programmers who worked on Activision's Atari ST conversion of *Altered Beast* as well as Sega's *After Burner*. "They're about entertainment. Those days, they were about being satisfying, but being difficult enough to keep putting money in. That attitude translated from arcades to home computers. The difficulty was of their time."[2] That's true of a lot of the games we've covered in this book. And it's true of this pile-up of necromancy, Greek mythology, and testosterone-infused jump kicks. Nonetheless, *Altered Beast* deserves to be remembered, even if you don't want to play it again today.

Splatterhouse (Namco, 1988)

Splatterhouse spawned a subgenre of horror game that sprouted in multiple directions, from the *Resident Evil* adventure series to first-person shooters such as *Left for Dead*, which picked up speed after the zombie movie revival of the 2000s. There was an old mansion where a legendary "parapsychologist" named Dr. West lived and conducted strange experiments to create gruesome creatures. Rick and Jennifer, boyfriend and girlfriend parapsychology majors in college, visited Dr. West for a school project. But shortly after they entered the mansion, it went dark, she screamed and disappeared, and Rick was murdered—only to wake up wearing a white hockey mask and still covered in his own blood. The mask evoked Jason Voorhees from *Friday the 13th*. As Rick, you needed to find Jennifer inside the mansion and rescue her.

The controls consisted of an eight-way joystick and two buttons for attacking and jumping. Pushing down would not only duck but could also be used to pick up items. Pushing up would turn Rick away and also look at items above. The game included seven stages of play, starting with an underground dungeon full of an array of monsters and some chained zombies on the far wall. Next were the sewers, which had rotted corpses falling from the ceiling. Out in the forest, you fought monsters in the rain, only to enter a Forbidden Room that contained a spinning blade and hall of mirrors. The game concluded with a romp through a level full of demons, a subterranean cave, and finally the end scene, where you dispatched a demon causing all of the mischief. Win the game and you'd lose the hockey mask and return to normal life with Jennifer.

Getting new weapons was the most fun part of the game. Without one, you would just punch enemies, or you could kick them if jumping in the air or ducking. But you could pick up a two-by-four, which you would swing like a baseball bat; a meat cleaver, which neatly lopped off monster heads; and a shotgun for blowing their brains out. Some items you could just throw once, such as a rock, a monkey wrench, and a spear.

Figure 10.4: The original parental advisory game, *Splatterhouse* offered blood-soaked beat-'em-up action and the ability to use a variety of gross slasher-flick weapon staples.

Splatterhouse employed a checkpoint system where the player would pass milestones and then return to one of those each time he or she died. That proved frustrating for some, but the point was to discourage feeding in additional quarters and therefore making the game genuinely more challenging instead of just something you could overcome with more money and time. This made perfect sense from a gameplay point of view and was where the home video game industry headed over time, as players became more and more frustrated when they couldn't save their progress or otherwise continue in some way. That phenomenon is precisely what put off arcade rats of the 1970s and 1980s, who preferred their games tough and reflex driven. But giving people less reason to put in quarters was what arcade owners and operators *didn't* want; the whole point of the arcade cabinet was to generate revenue. This would explain why *Splatterhouse* was such an outlier, as new arcade games going forward did not adopt the milestone mechanic even as the home video game industry flocked to it.

Splatterhouse wasn't the first blood-and-gore arcade game. That "award" would go to Exidy's terrible *Chiller*, a 1986 light-gun coin-op known for its senseless depictions of violence and torture that set off another wave of public revulsion a decade after *Death Race*. *Splatterhouse* proved much better and more successful. Namco soon converted *Splatterhouse* to the TurboGrafx-16, FM Towns, and the PC, though the company reduced the amount of blood and gore in the Japanese versions. For America, Namco changed the white hockey mask to a different color to stave off potential copyright infringement, and the company also replaced images of an altar and the cross throughout the game with other horror movie staples.

Notably, the TurboGrafx-16 port came with a Parental Advisory warning, similar to what began to appear on music album releases and the first time a home video game received the "distinction." Many more would follow; Eugene Jarvis, of *Defender* and *Robotron: 2084* fame, designed *Narc*, a December 1988 run-and-gun coin-op where you went after drug dealers, junkies, and underground kingpins with a machine gun and a missile launcher. Parents didn't love this one, either. *Narc* was also the first coin-op with a 32-bit CPU, a TMS34010 running at 6MHz. The topic of video game violence would get plenty of press and the attention of Congress in the early 1990s, leading to the formation of the Entertainment Software Rating Board in 1994. That said, this first warning on *Splatterhouse*'s box was tongue-in-cheek: "The horrifying theme of this game may be inappropriate for young children…and cowards."

Hard Drivin' (Atari Games, 1989)

In a world of two-dimensional race car games, *Hard Drivin'* was the first popular arcade racer in the U.S. with three-dimensional polygon graphics. *Hard Drivin'*'s sit-down cockpit, three pedals (including a clutch), and four-speed gearshift made it feel like a real car. It did to me, and by the time I had played one of these in college a couple of years later, I already had a car with a stick, so I had a genuine reference point. I loved the game, even though it cost $1 per play. Atari Games sold it in two versions. The environmental cockpit was shaped like a red-and-black sports car, complete with gold "wheels" and a contoured, adjustable driver's seat. The upright cabinet was smaller, but it still included a small platform and bench-style seat. Every version of the game needed a seat because there was no way to operate a clutch pedal without sitting down.

Figure 10.5: *Hard Drivin'* introduced the world to three-dimensional polygon graphics, and its excellent clutch-and-shifter controls added a dose of realism.

Sitting with the wheel and shifter in your hand and your feet by the pedals, the first-person view was through the car's windshield, with a smaller dashboard-like array of gauges, scoring, and other in-game info displayed. The steering wheel included centering and force feedback, so you would get pushback as the pavement surface changed, or if you caught air and then landed again. If you botched a shift, you could stall the car and have to start again, just like in real life (but without someone blowing their horn behind you). Part of the reason the game drove so well is that Atari Games hired Doug Milliken, a leading expert in car modeling and the son of famed aircraft engineer William Milliken, to help fine-tune the game's engine, transmission, suspension, and handling.[3] The game included a stunt course with a vertical loop, drawbridge, and other kinds of ramps. You raced either one or two laps around the track, sometimes against a computer-controlled "Phantom Photon" car.

You could crash by colliding with another car, landing too hard from an airborne stunt, or driving too far off the track. When you crashed, the game would display a short instant replay of the accident, complete with an aerial view of the player's car and its surroundings and a nice fireball after the crash occurred. Then you would return to the last checkpoint you had passed, though the checkpoints themselves were invisible except at the end of the game when they were shown as flags on the on-screen map. Inside the cabinet was a 16/32-bit Motorola 68010 CPU, two TMS34010 32-bit GPUs, and a new digital signal processing chip for 3D math. Home conversions of the game were much less impressive, as no contemporary system had hardware nearly as powerful. But the next year saw the introduction of two similar MS-DOS games called *Stunts* and *Stunt Driver*, both of which played nicely on a higher-end 386 PC.

Hard Drivin' wasn't the first 3D polygon racer—that honor went to Namco's *Winning Run*, a Formula One racing game released in Japan and Europe just two months prior. Nor was it Atari's first attempt; back in 1985, the company canceled *Air Race*, which would have been the first 3D polygon racer by several years, on account of how expensive the finished coin-op would have been.[4] The (unverified) story goes that *Hard Drivin'* was finished in late 1988, but that a vice president at Atari Games once again held up the game's release, saying that its projected price point of $10,000 per unit was out of step with what the market would accept. After a few weeks of research, management decided to go ahead anyway. Ultimately, Atari Games sold 3,300 cabinets, a good number for such a top-dollar coin-op.

Some of the best environmental cabinets of the prior two decades, such as *Discs of Tron* and *Star Wars: The Arcade Game*, showed how technology could envelop and enthrall the player, and concepts such as Atari's *TX-1* previewed the use of peripheral vision with multiple monitors. With its accurate manual transmission and three-dimensional rendered polygons, *Hard Drivin'* showed not just how future games would look and feel, but how arcades could thrive again by bringing an "amusement park" vibe to the cabinets in a way that was impossible in the home. The cabinet was more expensive to buy, and depending on the cabinet, trickier to maintain thanks to all the mechanical parts. But it was a way forward.

Atari Games used the hardware from *Hard Drivin'* to develop a similar sequel called *Race Drivin'*, as well as the more impressive *S.T.U.N. Runner*, a futuristic racing game released in September of the same year. It consisted of cars travelling in excess of 900 mph through twisting tunnels as well as exposed raceways.

Golden Axe (Sega, 1989)

Golden Axe was another side-scrolling, fantasy-themed beat-'em-up game on the same System 16 hardware as *Altered Beast*, but it played more smoothly. This one pit you against the evil Death Adder, an oppressor who's murdered thousands in villages. He kidnapped the king and his daughter and had stolen the Golden Axe. Your job was to go after Death Adder, either by yourself or cooperatively with another player. You could choose from three characters to play: Ax-Battler the Barbarian, who had the most strength as well as volcano magic; Tyris-Flare the Amazon, with her sword and fire magic; and Gilius-Thunderhead the Dwarf, with his axe, acrobatics, and lightning magic. The attract mode displayed nicely done, pencil-style drawings that depicted each character; by the time *Golden Axe* was released, graphics were getting good enough to break out into distinct styles of art. The attract mode also hilariously described each character by which of their family members Death Adder had killed. The backstories seemed so real, it was as if we had known them personally...

Figure 10.6: Sega's *Golden Axe* was a beat-'em-up scroller disguised as a fantasy adventure that let you choose from three characters.

The full game took five "days" and was shown on a map as you progressed. You'd start in the woods, and push ahead through various battle scenes including Turtle Village, a crossing to the mainland, Eagle Island, the road to the palace, before its gates, in the dungeon, and the final battle with Death Adder; each scene had unique enemies. As with *Double Dragon*, the boards were mainly in 2D, but with an extra component that simulated a third dimension of depth; in other words, you could move farther in and out as well as left and right. The controls for each player consisted of a joystick and three buttons for Magic, Attack, and Jump. The buttons all did what they said on the tin, but the game also included combo attacks;

for example, you could press Attack and Jump together for a special attack, or Jump and Attack for a downward slash. Tapping the joystick left or right twice would make your character run, which was useful in combat, especially because you could also body slam, headbutt, or kick an opponent mid-run, as well as jump farther than normal. You could press the Attack button multiple times rapidly to trigger stronger attacks, beat an enemy with the handle of your weapon, or grab them and throw them down.

During combat, sometimes enemies would fall down only to get up again a bit later. You could also lure them into falling off of cliffs. When one died for real, it emitted a distinctive digitized sound somewhere between a yell and a howl. As you cleared an area of enemies, arrows would appear to show you when to move on. The on-screen indicators showed your health, lives remaining, and magic power level. The last was determined by the number of magic pots you'd collected; depending on which character you were playing, you could max out at anywhere from four to nine levels. A single use of the power would reset the count to zero.

Periodically, small elves would come scurrying out; you could bump or kick them, and they'd drop more magic pots and strength bars. If they came by as you slept at night, they could steal your stuff. Another fun detail were the Bizarrians, giant-tailed beasts under the control of Death Adder that various baddies rode into battle with you. If you knocked off an enemy, you could mount one yourself and use its skills, similar to the way you could climb into a tank in a run-and-gun game. Depending on the creature, you could swing its tail, spit fire, or shoot fireballs. These were always worth riding, both for the extra power and the comic relief. All told, *Golden Axe* was a fun diversion, especially if you could get another player on board. You had to steer clear of each other, though, because unlike many co-op games, you could hurt each other in battle.

Teenage Mutant Ninja Turtles (Konami, 1989)

The success of *Double Dragon* kicked off a rush of beat-'em-up games with different themes. One of the first and most successful derivative coin-ops was based on the biggest animated television series of the late 1980s. *Teenage Mutant Ninja Turtles* adopted a similar style as *Double Dragon* and *Golden Axe*—namely a small, scrolling playfield that went from left to right, restricted only until you dispatched a group of enemies, at which point the game signaled you to move further. But *TMNT* picked up the pace of play, with 10 levels to plow through, more responsive controls, faster movement, and a simpler two-button control scheme. And with support for up to four simultaneous human players—with each one choosing their favorite turtle—it was a fun party arcade game.

The four famous turtles helped clean up a crime-infested New York City (hey, that was a thing in the 1980s) by crushing the evil Shredder in the back of a garbage truck. But somehow, he survived. He soon hired Tora and Shogun, two bounty hunters from another world, to take out our favorite half-shell heroes—and trained a new army of Foot Soldiers that knew Taekwondo. And of course, Shredder re-kidnapped (is that a word?) April O'Neil as bait along with Splinter, the turtles' mentor. Each hero had his own specialty. Leonardo was famous for his Katana blades, Raphael preferred a pair of sai, Michelangelo wielded nunchucks, and the tech-minded Donatello had his famed bō staff. Scoring was much simpler than usual; each turtle earned a point every time he knocked off someone, and that was it.

Figure 10.7: *Teenage Mutant Ninja Turtles* **amped up the common brawler with a cinematic presentation that felt like a video game version of the popular cartoon.**

The control panel stuck out past the sides of the monitor bezel, a form factor that would become more common in the 1990s. It contained an eight-way joystick and two buttons for each player. The Jump and Attack buttons performed the expected actions; the trick was that you could press both at once for a special attack, or Jump and then Attack to kick in any direction you chose. The turtles could also launch off of the walls and use objects strewn about each level as weapons. The game took the turtles through

April's Midtown loft, Times Square, the SoHo sewers, Central Park in the winter, Vinnie's Valet Parking Garage, 7th Avenue near Madison Square Garden, the "Rock-a-Fella" Expressway (don't ask me, and I'm a native New Yorker), the Stone Warriors' lair, House of Shogun, and the final Technodrome. Through these levels you'd fight the aforementioned Foot Soldiers, plus stone warriors, Frosty the Hit Man (loved that one at Christmastime), Blackhawk helicopters, the robotic Roadkill Rodney, the velociraptor-like Mousers, and Shogun's minions Venom, Blade, and Vincent Van Growl. Some of the enemies could hold on to you and drain your energy as others continued attacking you. On top of all of these, a series of end bosses capped off with the two intergalactic bounty hunters and Shredder himself.

The game played as if you were sucked into the cartoon, with comic-book-style graphics, animation, and cut scenes showing the real characters you played and not just stylized versions. The fast-paced, high-energy soundtrack also helped. The game saw a popular 8-bit NES conversion and some less successful conversions for 16-bit home computers with improved graphics but jerky animation. In 1991, Konami released a superior sequel called *Teenage Mutant Ninja Turtles: Turtles in Time*. The new coin-op added the ability to power attack after a series of blows and knock Foot Soldiers into other enemies, along with a set of new levels and end bosses to deal with. The *Teenage Mutant Ninja Turtles* phenomenon lasted well into the 1990s, with 10 seasons of the show, a major motion picture, and toys and other merchandising efforts packing the shelves of toy and clothing retailers across the country. Heroes on the half-shell, indeed.

Final Fight (Capcom, 1989)

At first glance, *Final Fight* resembled a bigger, better *Double Dragon*. Designed by Yoshiki Okamoto (of *Time Pilot*, *Gyruss*, and *1942* fame), this side-scrolling game even had a similar premise. It was set in a fictional city in the near future (the 1990s!), and the object was to defeat the leader of a street gang to rescue a girl. The attract mode went into this in some detail, with comic-book-like still shots and suitably cheesy prose between the leader of the Mad Gear gang and our bulky protagonist Mike Haggar, a former street fighter and wrestler and the new mayor of Metro City. Despite the promise of a monthly bribe to keep quiet, Haggar no longer tolerated Mad Gear's criminal activity, so he recruited his two friends, ninja fighter Guy and karate expert Cody, to go after Mad Gear and rescue Haggar's kidnapped daughter Jessica.

Metro City included a variety of scenarios, which were just backdrops for the fighting. They included subways, streets, warehouses, mansions, and even wrestling rings. You went up against a motley cast of characters including gang members, "cops gone bad," and Samurai swordsmen. The game included the usual assortment of punch, kick, and jump attacks, and it also let you throw knives and even Molotov cocktails. Throughout the game, you could kick or throw objects such as oil drums. Enemies sometimes surprised you by bursting through wooden doors.

Figure 10.8: Upon its introduction, *Final Fight* immediately made *Double Dragon* feel old, with its larger sprites, more powerful sound effects, and more attractive overall design.

When you started the game, you chose from three characters, each of which had their own mix of pros and cons. Haggar was strong but slow; Cody was good with close combat and knife attacks; Guy rocked with the katana. One player could play through the game, and the two-player mode was cooperative. The control panel featured an eight-way joystick, an Attack button, and a Jump button for each player. The game's prominent vitality bars looked a lot like those of *Street Fighter*; as you played, occasionally you'd find food to replenish them. There was also a 360-degree "Death Blow" you performed by pressing the Attack and Jump buttons together, at the expense of some vitality.

The graphics consisted of bold paint and lines for the colorful characters, and detailed backgrounds that looked dilapidated but never drab. Audio was a mishmash of gritty-sounding stereo music beats and digitized audio samples of punches, fist whooshes, howls of pain, and the Mad Gear leader's laugh. Most importantly, the gameplay was as fluid as it came, with easy-to-execute combos, gradually building difficulty, and a rhythm of play that rarely felt stilted. Bonus stages had you destroying random cars on the street, which was strangely gratifying if horrific from a "what message does this send?" angle—only topped by the part where you sent a man in a wheelchair through an office window.[5]

Final Fight bridged the gap between scrolling beat-'em-up and fighting games at a crucial time in arcade history. The story goes that Okamoto, in a kind of friendly competition with Capcom's other top designer Tokuro Fujiwara, became worried about his job. But after playing Taito's *Double Dragon II*, he realized he could design a better game with Capcom's latest technology.[6] It was originally conceived as a *Street Fighter* sequel, but Capcom pivoted after Taito's success with *Double Dragon*. You can see it in the size of the *Final Fight* sprites—significantly larger than *Double Dragon's*, and close to what *Street Fighter II* would soon bring in a couple of years. Today, *Final Fight* remains eminently playable, unlike *Double Dragon*. As a 2014 Eurogamer article put it, "it's a model for the genre: its sprites bold and beautifully drawn, its collision detection boasting a tautness of unmatched precedent. Competing developers turned out copycat software in droves, but none could match *Final Fight's* inimitable snap: the feel of its punch volleys and the raw discord expelled from the CPS1's guttural sound chip."[7]

Smash TV (Williams, 1990)

In this spiritual sequel to *Robotron: 2084*, you defeated hordes of mutants and drones. Designed by Eugene Jarvis and Mark Turmell, the game included the same twin-stick control setup and eight-direction moving and firing as Jarvis's earlier huge hit. *Smash TV* was set in the faraway future of…1999. (Notice a theme yet?) The concept was that television had adapted to the violent nature of humans, and as the most popular kind of broadcast was the game show, the one with the biggest ratings was called *Smash TV*. Two contestants competed for prizes and cash in a closed arena, fighting tons of enemies with powerful weapons in front of a live studio audience and broadcast worldwide.

This multidirectional shooter had a lot more graphics detail than *Robotron: 2084*, though. It included smoother and more complex animation, massive serpents and robo-human end bosses, digitized speech, a variety of weapon power-ups, and a crisper 410-by-256-resolution with 32-bit graphics. When you started the game, you'd run out from behind the set to the cheers of the crowd. Within moments, the first of many hordes of mutants and drones would burst forth from the doorways in the room, as opposed to seeing most of the layout right at the beginning as in *Robotron: 2084*. After you finished the first board, you'd see a map appear only that one time, showing you where the end boss was located and the passages necessary to reach them; then you'd decide which passage to exit the current room from based on where you wanted to go. Each room had a theme, such as "mutant man," and it would display the theme in yellow letters right before you started that wave.

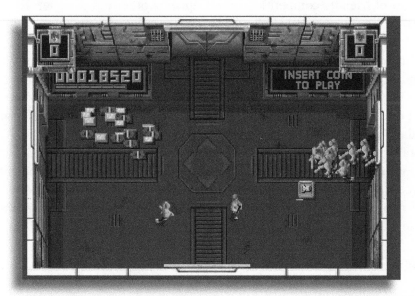

Figure 10.9: *Smash TV* **was Eugene Jarvis's attempt to bring** *Robotron***-style gameplay into the 1990s, with its futuristic TV game show theme dressing up a dystopian battle-to-the-death, all live in front of a studio audience.**

Each board was stocked with all manner of power-ups and prizes. The former category consisted of things like rotating spheres that acted as a shield, a spray gun that shot many bullets at once fanning out in different directions, a rocket launcher, and more. The latter group came mostly gift wrapped and contained fantastical items such as a 2,600-inch TV and, well, a toaster, because it was a game show, and someone had to win the consolation prize. There were also piles of cash and silver and gold bars to pick up.

Occasionally you'd find a key; collect 10 of them and you'd visit the Pleasure Dome bonus stage. Periodically, an announcer in a loud plaid suit with two scantily clad women in his arms popped up in the bottom-left corner saying cheesy catch-phrases such as "Big money! Big prizes! I love it!," "Total Carnage! I love it!," or in a sly reference to a fictional comedian in 1987's *Robocop*, "I'd buy that for a dollar!"

Smash TV was a smashing success, both in the arcades and in a pitch-perfect conversion on the Super Nintendo Entertainment System released the following year. The home cartridge was called *Super Smash TV* and also appeared on the Sega Genesis, Commodore 64 and Amiga, Atari ST, and several other systems. Midway Games released a follow-up game in 1992 called *Total Carnage*, which played well but didn't find much of an audience, as it was just more of the same with a different storyline and setting. Glory soon awaited Turmell, though.

Neo Geo Multi Video System (SNK, 1990)

SNK evolved its M68000 hardware platform through the late 1980s, taking it past *Ikari Warriors* and through such coin-ops as *Time Soldiers* and *Prisoners of War*. But its next platform became something of a 1990s standard for arcade games.[8] The Neo Geo Multi Video System, or MVS, launched in Japan in April 1990 and in the U.S. that August. It was a cartridge-based system that allowed arcade owners and operators to insert up to six games in one cabinet. The operator could also swap out an older cartridge and insert a newer game. Interchangeable "platform-style" systems had been available since the cassette-based DECO a decade earlier; some popular ones of the late 1980s included Nintendo's PlayChoice-10 and Capcom's CP System 1, with the obvious caveat being that the cabinet graphics were usually nondescript unless operators changed out the artwork each time. MVS became the most popular arcade platform of all and had an outsize effect on game development in the 1990s.

MVS cabinets were instantly recognizable thanks to their bright red coloring. There were two exceptions: a wood-paneled "gold" cabinet and a white *Samurai Shodown II*. Cabinets came in versions that supported one, two, four, or six cartridges installed simultaneously, letting operators pack a lot of arcade action into a small floor footprint. The CPU at the heart of MVS was a 16-bit Motorola 68000 running at 12MHz and a Z80 to control audio. Much more important was SNK's custom video chipset, which had a 24-bit bus and could field up to 380 sprites, sized from 16 to 512 pixels tall. The sprites were powerful enough that the system didn't need hardware playfield scrolling; programmers could draw sprites over a fixed tilemap layer to simulate background movement. The system supported 64MB ROM cartridges and display 4,096 colors from a palette of 65,536. It could play 13 channels of audio simultaneously, including five synthesized, seven digitally sampled, and one for noise, and every game supported stereo sound. Cabinets contained a pair of stereo headphone jacks so two people could play in private.

Figure 10.10: SNK's Neo Geo was a powerful, brilliantly designed arcade platform that spawned more than 140 games and an extravagantly priced home console that really was just like the arcade.

SNK also made a home console called the Neo Geo Advanced Entertainment System (AES). It was marketed first as a rental system in Japan, but SNK decided to sell it as a luxury console. SNK also sold the model in America beginning in July 1991 at $649, an astronomical price for the time, albeit including two arcade-quality joysticks and the pack-in game *Magician Lord*, an attractive but frustrating side-scroller. Even more eye-watering was the price of the additional cartridges, at $200 to $300 a pop. The Neo Geo was also the first system to include a memory card slot for saved games; before that, only disk-based computer games and the occasional cartridge with a battery backup, most famously *The Legend of Zelda* on the NES, could save your game in the progress. As Neo Geo games soon became known for their insane difficulty, saved games were all the more welcome.

Although launch titles such as *Baseball Stars Professional*, *Ninja Combat*, and the Vietnam shooter *SNK-1975* were popular out of the starting gate, MVS came into its own a bit later in the 1990s. For a time, the cabinets were seemingly everywhere. None of the 158 games that were released in all became a tremendous hit, but many were good and are highly prized today by collectors, especially the AES versions that are shaped differently and came with retail boxes and manuals. Although many MVS and some AES and CDs are relatively common, others command upwards of five and six figures and inauthentic copies are a major issue.[9]

At the time, there existed a large gulf between what could be done on the Sega Genesis or TurboGrafx-16 (the two most powerful consoles in 1990) and what the Neo Geo was capable of. Ultimately, the platform launched at a crucial time in video game history. Aside from their other virtues, Neo Geo games were notable for achieving the thing that no other home console could, despite nearly 20 years of promises—the games played identically to the arcade, because they were the arcade. The Neo Geo console was too expensive for most people to buy in, but this arcade-perfect milestone was yet another sign of the trouble ahead for the coin-op market.

11 > Fight

As time wore on, the arcade industry continued to consolidate. By 1988, with Nintendo out of the coin-op market, the biggest remaining players in arcade games were Sega, Taito, Namco, Atari Games, Midway, and Capcom. In 1990, the U.S. Supreme Court decided companies could no longer import less expensive boards of popular games from firms that weren't licensed to sell them in the country, which hurt local manufacturers.[1] Beat-'em-up games proved to be a savior for arcades, or at least help soften the landing, with those leading other popular run-and-gun and cockpit-style titles for a combined $6.4 billion in revenue in 1988.[2] Slight variations on the theme, such as *Ghosts 'n Goblins* and its sequel *Ghouls 'n Ghosts*, *Rastan*, Sega's ninja brawler *Shinobi*, and Capcom shooters *Section Z* and *Forgotten Worlds* all brought in decent revenue for operators. Later games did even better, as we began to see themed fighting cabinets for popular media properties of the day. These games didn't necessarily innovate in any way, but they were popular and remain so even today with collectors. Console games also carried the beat-'em-up torch at the time, with perhaps the most notable being the revered *Streets of Rage* series that launched on the Sega Genesis. Movie theaters were packed with major motion pictures with fighting as the core plot mechanic. It seemed there would be no end to the appetite the public had for video games that followed suit.

Throughout the 1980s, arcades never left the collective conscious, and many saw sustained business even post crash. Coin-ops continued to appear in movies as props or set pieces, with films as diverse as *Ferris Bueller's*

Day Off, The Goonies, Can't Buy Me Love, Bloodsport, and *Back to the Future Part II* all featuring at least one scene with a coin-op, if not a set in an actual arcade. The trade publication *Vending Times* said that in 1988, there were approximately 1,000,000 arcade coin-ops in use in the U.S., but by 2000 that number would shrink to just 450,000. Nothing would stop the decline of arcades throughout the 1990s—except for one singular coin-op title in 1991. It heralded the arrival of true one-on-one fighting games, ending the Platinum Age and igniting an arcade Renaissance, the fourth and final age we'll discuss in this book.

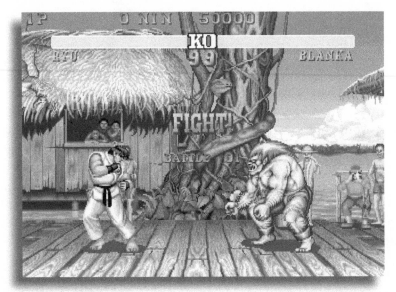

Figure 11.1: *Street Fighter II: The World Warrior* **single-handedly brought back the video arcade and launched the one-on-one fighting genre that remains popular to this day.**

Street Fighter II: The World Warrior (Capcom, 1991)

After *Final Fight,* Yoshiki Okamoto's next game for Capcom would be a sequel to *Street Fighter.* His team started with the first game's two main characters, Ryu and Ken, as well as the secret move that let them throw fireballs.[3] *Street Fighter II* used the first game's basic template but polished off all of the rough edges. It opened up the full roster of eight characters to each player instead of restricting most to the computer's control. Stepping through the selections was like perusing a greatest-hits collection of character design and game balance; each character had its own set of combos, fighting style, and secret moves. Chun Li was fast and lithe in her martial arts. Dhalsim was the Plastic Man of India, with absurdly stretchable limbs and yoga-inspired moves. Guile was straight out of U.S. military special ops. Blanka was a mutant creature from the jungles of Brazil. The rail-thin Vega was a Spanish bullfighter with ninjutsu and a claw for a hand. Letting players select their own characters guaranteed tons of replay value, as everyone who played *Street Fighter II* wanted to try out all of the characters.

As in the first game, you needed to defeat your opponent in one-on-one-style combat before the timer ran out; whoever took the best two out of three rounds would win the match. As each match began, large graphics of the two characters would appear set against a map of the world. The game ran on a 10MHz Motorola 68000 processor with a companion Z80, with MSM6295 and YM2151 sound chips delivering the game's ample audio punch, with catchy stereo music motifs and impactful, sampled attacks dominating the sonic landscape during the game. The best part: The fighting was as refined and well balanced as ballet. Honing your skills with your favorite characters and combos was a rewarding way to spend an evening. The control panel may have looked imposing to newcomers, but the six buttons soon felt like extensions of your fingertips. Even the dozens of special moves and combos were challenges in and of themselves that you could discover and practice, like woodshedding with a musical instrument, developing your technique in anticipation of your next bout with a friend (or foe). The responsive controls were intentional; engineered into the software was a joystick- and button-scanning routine that sensed the moves each player was about to make and responded with the correct choices.[4]

The combo mechanic wasn't even intentional. "The concept of combinations, linked attacks that can't be blocked when they're timed correctly, came about more or less by accident," IGN reported in 2014. "*Street Fighter II*'s designers didn't quite mean for it to happen, but players of the original game found out that certain moves naturally flowed into other ones."[5] The game marked another turning point in the arcade's evolution from achieving a high score to two players fighting against each other to determine who was better.[6] And in a flip of the script, it was the sequel, not the original, that brought accolades to Capcom. It's tough to convey on paper the dramatic improvement in graphics quality and gameplay between the first and second games.

The *Street Fighter* series went on to sell more than 200,000 cabinets across its many titles, and the SNES conversion alone sold a whopping 6.3 million copies.[7] As of 2017, the coin-op series was reported to have grossed $10.6 billion. In the annals of arcade history, that puts *Street Fighter II* behind only *Space Invaders* and *Pac-Man*.[8] Plenty of one-on-one fighting games preceded it, but *Street Fighter II* made them a genre that to this day remains one of the most popular in the world. Hundreds of "versus" games would soon blanket arcades and successive generations of home consoles. Many added to the formula and offered increasingly realistic graphics, however fantastical some of the settings were (*Injustice: Gods Among Us* comes to mind). With its focus on revisions and additional characters, Capcom paved the way for the current model of console games with downloadable content.[9]

Just like that, arcades were back—and in a big way. Much as *Space Invaders* kick-started the Golden Age, *Street Fighter II: The World Warrior* ensured arcades would not just stick around, but have a genuine second act. SNK soon pivoted with its still-new Neo Geo platform and launched several major one-on-one fighting series, beginning with *Fatal Fury* in 1993 and continuing on to *Samurai Shodown*, *The King of Fighters*, and *Art of Fighting*. Some of these saw sequels well into the next decade.

The Simpsons (Konami, 1991)

This glorious romp of a side-scrolling brawler in the vein of *Double Dragon* and *Teenage Mutant Ninja Turtles* put you in control of Marge, Homer, Bart, and Lisa. It was the first video game to be based on the *Simpsons* franchise. There was a break-in at the Springfield Jeweler's shop, orchestrated by Mr. Burns. In the game's intro, Waylon Smithers busted out of the shop and ran right into Homer Simpson and his family, who were just walking down the street minding their own business. The resulting collision sent a giant stolen diamond up into the air and then right back down into the mouth of Maggie, who began sucking on it as if it were a pacifier. With no time to lose, the robbers grabbed Maggie and the diamond and escaped.

You chased down and beat up the robbers while fending off thugs, corrupt executives, ghosts, zombies, and all sorts of other marauding denizens of Springfield. The game took place across eight stages: Downtown Springfield, Krustyland, the Springfield Discount Cemetery, Moe's Tavern, Springfield Butte, Dreamland, the Channel 6 news studio, and finally, the Springfield Nuclear Power Plant, where you fought Smithers and then Mr. Burns.

Each character had a health meter and their own attack styles, as was customary for the genre. Homer punched and kicked, Marge swung a vacuum cleaner, Bart used his skateboard as a weapon, and Lisa fought with her jump rope. One innovation was that two characters could combine moves; for example, Homer could toss Lisa on his shoulders and then attack at two different heights. Objects were strewn about the game that could be picked up and used as weapons, such as bowling balls, slingshots, and hammers. Occasionally a word balloon would appear over a character, reminding you of such things as how to wiggle out of an enemy's grip. Each character earned a point every time they knocked off someone, as in *Teenage Mutant Ninja Turtles*. There were two bonus stages as well, where the game helpfully told you to "hit buttons" in order to win. Food replenished lost energy when picked up, and you could pump quarters into the game to keep continuing where you left off. Many players did just that.

Figure 11.2: Konami milked the beat-'em-up genre for all it was worth, but that actually sells *The Simpsons* short, as it was super fun to play.

The four-player cabinet was finished in light blue, with character graphics on the left and right sides and "The Simpsons" in yellow, whereas the marquee presented the name of the game in orange. The wide control panel, also light blue, stuck out from the sides of the monitor and bezel. It consisted of four sets of controls, with each containing an eight-way joystick and Attack and Jump buttons. A two-player standard upright was also produced.

The Simpsons was soon ported to MS-DOS and the Commodore 64 (as *The Simpsons Arcade Game*). The coin-op came out after just one full season of the show and most of the well-known characters had yet to be introduced, which made it doubly significant that the arcade game captured the feel so well.[10] As with *Teenage Mutant Ninja Turtles*, Konami wasn't earning critical acclaim with these retreads of the *Double Dragon* concept. But they earned plenty of revenue for arcade owners and operators and became a beloved part of many gamers' childhoods. The formula worked.

Terminator 2: Judgment Day (Midway, 1991)

If early-1990s pop culture were to fuse with the arcade and become one, it would have happened with this gun game. *Terminator 2: Judgment Day* let players become the character they could only dream of. Released in tandem with the blockbuster motion picture starring Arnold Schwarzenegger, the game took place in the year 2029 after a horrible nuclear war that had occurred on August 29th, 1997, known in the storyline as "Judgment Day," when three billion human lives were lost. Now, the human resistance had to face Skynet's machines, including Endoskeletons and flying Hunter Killers. You played as a reprogrammed T-800 cyborg. In support of Sgt. John Connor, the leader of the human resistance, your goal in the first four stages was to destroy as many machines as you could, infiltrate Skynet Headquarters, and assume control of the Time Field Generator. Once that happened, you were sent back in time to the early 1990s. There, you would play through three additional stages. You destroyed equipment in the Cyberdyne research lab while fighting SWAT teams; protected John and Sarah Connor from the T-1000 Skynet sent to destroy them both; and at the steel mill, shot up a tanker to douse the T-1000 in liquid nitrogen before knocking it into a vat of molten steel.

Terminator 2: Judgment Day employed digitized images, a concept that started with Bally Midway's 1983 coin-op *Journey* (for foreground sprites) and continued in 1989 with Gottlieb's *Exterminator* (for the backgrounds). The idea caught fire in the early 1990s with the advent of low-cost CD-ROM drives in home computers. *Terminator 2* was one of the first arcade coin-ops to put it to good effect; Schwarzenegger, Edward Furlong, and Robert Patrick all reprised their roles from the movie for the arcade game, though a substitute actor was used for Linda Hamilton's Sarah Connor. Throughout the game, you would also hear voice samples of the actors speaking lines from the movie. More important than the graphics and sound, though, was the sheer intensity. The entire cabinet became part of the game. Your primary weapon was a fully automatic machine gun that fired as long as you held the trigger. The gun vibrated violently as you did this, just as a real one would. A second button on the side fired either missiles or shotgun shells, depending on what time period you were in. You had unlimited ammo, but if you held down the trigger too long the gun would start to overheat and shoot more slowly. You blasted away as many enemies as you could, some of them filling the screen with their large size, while protecting the humans fighting on your side. Each stage ended with a bonus tally for the kinds and numbers of enemies destroyed, though in the future stages you would also lose points for any humans you killed by accident.

Figure 11.3: Few games evoked the early 1990s as much as *Terminator 2: Judgment Day*, a gun game complete with voice-overs from almost all of the movie's major characters, including Ah-nold.

The attract screen was a big part of the fun. One of the scenes showed was a parody of the screens shown before movie previews. This one read: "This game requires one credit to start," followed by an *R* rating for "Righteous." Start a game and you'd see another parody, this time a green screen that read "The following attraction has been approved for all audiences by the Motion Picture Gaming Association of America." At the time, everyone wanted to make a game so realistic that it was like playing a movie—perhaps a lesson not learned after the laserdisc gaming craze of 1983 and 1984, but an idea not without merit, either.

X-Men (Konami, 1992)

Another brawler in the vein of *Double Dragon* and its derivatives, *X-Men* showed Konami was serious about cornering the market for these kinds of games. This coin-op gave audiences something they had long clamored for—a chance to play as Marvel superheroes in the arcade. You needed to rescue Professor X and stop the evil mutants led by Magneto, who wanted to destroy mankind and rule Earth. The game, based on the storyline from a 1989 pilot called "X-Men: Pryde of the X-Men," let you play as six different characters: Cyclops, with his optical force beam; Colossus, who could change flesh to steel; Wolverine, with his adamantium skeleton and retractable claws; Storm, with her ability to control the weather; Nightcrawler, the acrobat who could also teleport; and Dazzler, who knew how to change sounds into light blasts.

Figure 11.4: *X-Men* amped up Konami's beat-'em-up formula with an even more cinematic presentation and the arcade's first taste of Marvel characters.

Each player had an eight-way joystick and three buttons this time, instead of two, for Attack, Jump, and Mutant Power. The Mutant Powers were always super effective, depending on the character, but you would lose three health points each time—a big hit when you had just 10 health meter points before you lost a life. You fought your way through six side-scrolling stages full of evil mutants, though a big draw were the end bosses that included Pyro, Blob, Wendigo, Mystique, White Queen, and Professor X's evil step-brother Juggernaut. If you made it to the end, you would battle Magneto on his home Asteroid M. *X-Men* boasted larger sprites, a bit more room to move around vertically on each board, and punchier sound effects that had more impact than they did in earlier games such as *TMNT* and *The Simpsons*. *X-Men* also added the ability to hit enemies even when they were already down, to prevent them from getting back up. The attract screen played as if it were a movie preview, with full-screen renderings of the characters in a dynamic, comic-book-style sequence.

The *X-Men* arcade game came as a two-, four-, or gargantuan six-player cabinet. The last weighed hundreds of pounds and had two monitors side by side for a wide-screen effect. It didn't have a control panel so much as a control desk. Seriously, you could set up a monitor, keyboard, and mouse on it and work in the amount of free space left over from the six sets of controls along the edges. Or, you could take the two monitors out and sell concessions from inside; that would probably work, too. At any rate, it was shaped like an octagon with five sides visible; two sets of controls were in the center, and then one on each of the other four sides (two diagonal, two 90 degrees perpendicular to the front).

All told, it was another game that didn't earn much critical praise, but that arcade gamers loved. Beat-'em-up games just worked, both when playing solo and especially when playing with friends in co-op mode. Even though the genre faded over the years, the fighting mechanics remained, and co-op features only became more important.

Virtua Racing (Sega, 1992)

If *Hard Drivin'* showed the racing game's future in three dimensions, *Virtua Racing* rocketed the concept into the mainstream.[11] Designed by Toshihiro Nagoshi and Sega's AM2 development team, *Virtua Racing* displayed much more detailed polygons and a considerably smoother frame rate than *Hard Drivin'*—the three-dimensional graphics enhanced the gameplay this time instead of just being different. *Virtua Racing* was the first the team had designed for Sega's new Model 1 hardware (designed with Lockheed Martin) and companion custom graphics engine; it could process a then-astounding 180,000 polygons per second.[12] *Virtua Racing* also included modeling of nonhuman players in the other cars as well as four player-selectable camera angles, a first for an arcade racing game. Far more than a gimmick, the game let you switch the view as appropriate, including in-car to feel more connected to the road, albeit with a restricted view out, or outside the car to see better what was coming up.

There were three varieties of cabinet: Deluxe, which had a 36-inch wide-screen (16:9) CRT—the first instance of a wide-screen monitor in a coin-op—and a motion cockpit that resembled the rear half of an F-1 car; Twin, which paired up two cabinets with 26-inch monitors and a smaller sit-down portion that seated two; and an upright cabinet that still kept a smaller sitting stool. The three cabinets weighed from 500 to 882 pounds, and up to eight *Virtua Racing* cabinets in any combination could be hooked together for competitive head-to-head racing. Sega also sold optional "live action monitors" that arcade operators could mount on top of a series of linked cabinets to broadcast coverage from certain locations on the racetrack.[13]

The Deluxe cabinet, which retailed at an astounding $25,000, wasn't just a mechanical model similar to Sega's earlier *Hang-On*. In this case, when you first approached the game, the cockpit was positioned farther back for easier entry and exit. When you sat down and inserted a coin, the Air Drive system activated, positioning the driver's seat closer with the aid of an air compressor, air solenoid, and long piston mounted inside the back cabinet.[14] The seat also contained six airbags, three on each side, that could independently inflate via the air compressor to simulate pushback in an accident, exiting the road, or contacting scenery. A seventh airbag in the seat helped generate feedback for whenever you braked the car. The cockpit included a force-feedback-equipped steering wheel as well. The sum total of the systems was to convey the feeling of being in a real race car at high speed in a way no prior arcade coin-op had accomplished.[15]

The game itself, almost an afterthought after the graphics, cabinet design, and physics modeling, was a simple racer. There were three tracks to choose from, and each race contained 16 cars in total, with anywhere from 8 to 15 controlled by the computer, depending on how many human players were available. The game employed the standard-issue checkpoint-and-timer system. You couldn't crash the car; the game would just slow you down, even in a high-speed accident, and reorient the car forward again if necessary. The AI employed a "rubber-banding" system that would improve the performance of other human players to keep them closer to the leader; the cars were supposed to be identical in performance and only differed in color.[16]

Electronic Gaming Monthly called *Virtua Racing* a "masterpiece" and "one of the most realistic games ever," praising its "lifelike racing sensations" as "extremely impressive and exciting" and saying it left "all other racing games eating its technological dust."[17] *RePlay* listed it as the number-one-earning "deluxe" coin-op in American arcades in its April 1993 and May 1993 issues. *Virtua Racing* was a landmark release that heralded not just what was to come in arcades but with the next generation of home consoles as well.

Figure 11.5: *Virtua Racing* **was the first game to deliver three-dimensional racing at 60fps and offered a level of realism unmatched in any earlier arcade game.**
Credit: 空練 CC BY-SA 3.0

Mortal Kombat (Midway, 1992)

Mortal Kombat pitted you against either another player or the computer in a global martial arts tournament. In this sense, it was derivative of the *Street Fighter* series, but it had its own look, style, and characters. Set on a secluded island, seven elite fighters from around the world came together to see who was best, before battling the four-armed mutant Goro and final opponent Shang Tsang. The fighters were Johnny Cage, Sonya Blade, Scorpion, Liu Kang, Kano, Raiden, and Sub Zero; each one had a different, invariably thin storyline attached. *Mortal Kombat* introduced the concept of the fatality into the lexicon, the idea of a gory killing blow that finished off your opponent. The realistic graphics were enough to spur the creation of a tiered, age-specific ratings system for video games. It was also the first popular fighting game to allow for "juggling," where you strike your opponent and land additional attacks while they're still airborne and defenseless.

Figure 11.6: *Mortal Kombat* was the other one-on-one fighting game to become a phenomenon, and with its fatalities mechanic attracted unwanted attention all the way up to Congress.

For the original game designed by Ed Boon and John Tobias, the black, red, and gold cabinet held two sets of controls and a 25-inch CRT. The controls for each player consisted of an eight-way joystick, two Punch buttons, two Kick buttons, and specific to *Mortal Kombat* games, a dedicated Block button. There was a core set of attacks all seven characters could perform, such as uppercuts and jump kicks. Then there were special attacks specific to each character that you would execute with some combination of joystick moves and button presses. As with the *Street Fighter* games, in *Mortal Kombat* each character had a health bar, which when depleted meant the character lost the round. If the time ran out before someone was defeated, whoever had the most health would win that round. The first player to win two out of three rounds won the match.

Single-player games meant you would go up against each of the other six characters, and then a Mirror Match where you fought a clone of yourself before continuing on to fight Goro and Shang. The game exhibited a variety of multilayered backdrops and an energetic electronic music soundtrack. Two of the DIP switch adjustments controlled whether violent moves were shown and whether blood was visible. Periodically, you'd play a "Test Your Might" minigame, which consisted of breaking apart wood, stone, steel, and other materials by pressing a button as fast as you could.

There's not much to say about the ratings system, except that the early 1990s saw a slew of games where the technology was becoming good enough to show violence in a more realistic manner than ever before. *Mortal Kombat* set off the debate, but the later introduction of *Doom*, *Night Trap*, and similarly "adult" games led to the system that we still have today. For arcades, it had little effect. Today, the original *Mortal Kombat* feels a bit dated, as the digitized character images didn't age well, and the movements were always stiffer than *Street Fighter II*'s to begin with. To follow up *Mortal Kombat*, Midway took everything that worked well in the first game and polished it to a finer sheen in *Mortal Kombat II*, released in April 1993. *MK2* introduced several new characters, smoothed out the combo system, and added some new attacks and special moves, including multiple fatalities for each character. If *Mortal Kombat II* wasn't as huge a leap as *Street Fighter II: The World Warrior* was over the 1987 original, it was close, and the one-two punch of the first two *Mortal Kombat* games was enough to permanently establish the series as one of the most successful video game franchises ever.

NBA Jam (Midway, 1993)

With its support for four players and two-on-two basketball, *NBA Jam* was the first licensed basketball coin-op and the first game to feature the actual teams and digitized representations of real-life players, created in large part from live footage. The attractive cabinet was painted on the sides to resemble a close-up of a basketball, with a giant NBA logo overlaid on top. You couldn't miss this game in the arcade if you tried. The control panel, fashioned with court graphics, held four sets of controls. Each player had a joystick, a Shoot button, a Block button, a Pass/Steal button, and a Turbo button. The buttons and sticks were arranged differently for each player, to maximize the tight real estate inherent in squeezing four people in front of a cabinet. The control panel was larger than normal and extended past the sides, but it was less deep than the control panel on Atari Games' *Gauntlet*, another four-player game.

The PCB contained a new scaling chip that helped smooth out what could have been stilted animation. The game was also capable of displaying

256 colors simultaneously. The combination resulted in the most detailed graphics yet seen in a sports game. *NBA Jam* played as a proper two-on-two street match, but with all the pomp and circumstance of a televised NBA event.

Figure 11.7: *NBA Jam* was an over-the-top, two-on-two basketball game that couldn't be more fun, launching a 25-plus-year franchise in the process.

Designed by a team led by Mark Turmell, *NBA Jam* is credited with launching a specific kind of sports game genre where the action was nonetheless exaggerated for effect, such as physics-defying jumps and insane dunks. It also left out many of the usual mechanics, such as free throws and most of the fouls, choosing only to implement goaltending and 24-second violations. This meant you were free to shove another player out of the way. Score three baskets in a row and you'd enter a turbo mode where you became "on fire" and could play even better for the next four baskets or until the other team scored once. These were all mechanics Midway could have easily made accurate, but didn't on purpose. The digitized announcer landed catch phrases such as "He's heating up!", "He's on fire," or my favorite, "Is it the shoes?" None of this was realistic, but *NBA Jam* sure was a blast to play with a couple of friends.

Virtua Fighter (Sega, 1993)

Arcade games weren't marketed with print advertising except to establishment owners and operators. If they had been marketed to consumers in this fashion, *Virtua Fighter* would have fared poorly, as static screenshots of the game looked like garbage. Yet it's tough to overstate *Virtua Fighter*'s impact on the arcade and console worlds. In this game, you played as Akira Yuki, the last remaining fighter who used a fictional fighting technique called Hakkyoku ken, or "The Eight Point Fist." You aimed to win the World Fighting Tournament by defeating seven other fighters: Sarah and Jacky (Sekken Do warriors), Lau and Pai (practitioners of Kung Fu), the Pancratium fighter Jeffrey McWild, the wrestler Wolf Hawkfield, and the ninja Kage. Once you beat them all, you'd face the end boss, Dural.

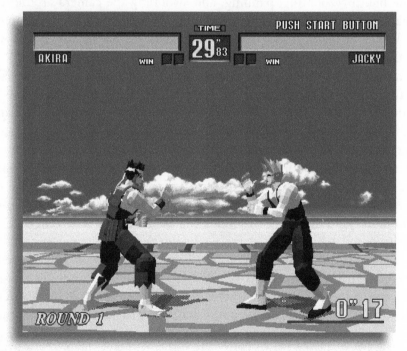

Figure 11.8: *Virtua Fighter* brought the one-on-one fighting game into the polygon age, with its fluid character animation and multiple camera angles.

Virtua Fighter was laid out in much the same way as prior one-on-one fighting games, with health bars and a timer on top and the current round and elapsed game time on the bottom. The control panel consisted of a bat-handle joystick and three buttons for each player: Defense (block),

Punch, and Kick. The fights were best-two-of-three, just as with the *Street Fighter* series. The massive difference here is that *Virtua Fighter* was the first to employ fully three-dimensional polygon graphics instead of 2D sprites. The game's fighting mechanics were detailed, refined, and polished, and for newcomers it was a bit easier to grok thanks to its use of just three buttons instead of six.

Yu Suzuki, the same mastermind behind such successful coin-ops as *Hang-On*, *Out Run*, *Space Harrier*, and *Virtua Racing*, which also ran on the Model 1 board, designed *Virtua Fighter*. The hardware was still limited enough that each character in the game had to be done with fewer than 1,200 polygons apiece, so in static shots, they looked cruder than their 2D counterparts. But the resultant fluid animation was never seen before. Of note was the camera work; the 3D engine enabled the game to show views of the fight by zooming, panning, and swooping the camera around the arena, techniques that just about every game in the genre since has adopted.

Virtua Fighter became a massive success for Sega, although it was mostly restricted to the Japanese market. In 2015, 1UP.com called *Virtua Fighter* one of the 50 most important games of all time, for single-handedly creating the 3D fighting game genre and showing what could be done with 3D polygon human characters in both animation and gameplay. The game set the stage for *Tekken*, *Killer Instinct*, *Dark Souls*, *Soul Calibur*, and many other series, all of which built upon the one-on-one fighting genre *Street Fighter II* launched and *Virtua Fighter* perfected in 3D. Many series found their own niches; for example, *Tekken*'s sophisticated hand-to-hand combat. *Killer Instinct* was notable on the technology front as the first coin-op to contain a hard drive, which sounds like asking for trouble from the perspective of today but had to be more reliable than laserdisc players.

Sega later ported the game to the Sega 32X add-on for the Genesis, as well as the Sega Saturn and Windows 95. *Virtua Fighter* had a massive effect on the home console market, but not because of any port—it inadvertently changed the trajectory of the industry. In a 2012 interview, former Sony Computer Entertainment producer Ryoji Akagawa said, "If it wasn't for *Virtua Fighter*, the PlayStation probably would have had a completely different hardware concept."[18] He said that Sony was strongly considering making the first PlayStation primarily a 2D system and not a 3D one because of budgetary constraints, but that in the wake of *Virtua Fighter*'s success, Sony reconsidered and redoubled its efforts to include high-end 3D graphics with the system, ensuring that it would see massive success and not look dated compared with the Nintendo 64 that would hit the market a year after Sony's first console.[19] Not a bad legacy for a game that drew from two pre-existing advances—*Virtua Racing*'s 3D engine and *Street Fighter II*'s gameplay—and combined them into one new thing the world had never seen before.

Ridge Racer (Namco, 1994)

Namco got plenty of mileage out of its System 21 board, first released with *Winning Run* back in 1988, but it was the follow-up board that cemented the new dominance of three-dimensional, polygon-based graphics in the arcades. The first game to debut worldwide running on Namco's new System 22 board was *Ridge Racer*, which went a long way to redefine the modern "arcade" racer, as opposed to more simulation-focused games that would follow, such as the *Gran Turismo* series. The System 22 board could process 240,000 polygons per second, more than Sega's *Virtua Racing* hardware could manage. But more importantly, *Ridge Racer* was the first coin-op to support texture mapping, which added a new level of realism to the in-game graphics—this was one of the best looking arcade games ever, and it had accurate drifting physics and a powerful audio system, too. It also helped that *Ridge Racer* was plenty of fun, and its use of production-style sports cars as opposed to F-1 racers helped gain it mass appeal in the U.S.

The game included a series of high-speed driving courses with plenty of sharp turns, including those that required you countersteer the vehicle to keep it from spinning out, making it one of the first arcade games to model oversteer. The courses included long, sweeping tunnels and mountain cliffs in addition to the usual seaside and city streets. The cabinet included a steering wheel; a three-pedal setup for the accelerator, brake, and clutch; and a six-speed manual gearbox (though you could always select Automatic when starting a game). You could also choose from six music tracks, in a nod to Sega's *Out Run*, with the nifty touch that you selected the song with the gearshift.

The game's attract mode showed off the power of the rendering engine, with its TV-style camera angles and sweeping pan shots. When starting the game, you were offered the choice of Novice (two laps with a maximum speed of 160kph), Intermediate (three laps, 200kph), Advanced (three laps, also 200kph, but on an extended track), and Time Trial (three laps, 220kph, also with an extended track). Then the camera zoomed in to the racetrack and panned around to the starting grid with the sound of the crowd cheering in the background and the announcer counting down the start. The races included 11 other opponents, and the time trial was solo (by definition). As you raced, a helicopter followed overhead, and you'd even see a jumbo jet take off over the track. The in-game narration, recorded to sound as if it was spoken through a bullhorn, egged you on as you raced and passed checkpoints. That plus the frenetic music, complete with a hyped-up slap bass, kept the energy level high throughout each game. Crashes slowed you down but didn't stop the proceedings or have any other effect. Play *Ridge Racer* today and it feels contemporary.

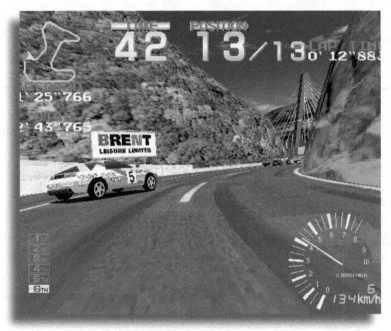

Figure 11.9: *Ridge Racer* added texture mapping to its polygon graphics and became the best arcade racer since *Out Run.*

Many gamers know *Ridge Racer* not by the arcade game but by what happened next. Namco developed a conversion of the game to serve as a top launch title for the upcoming Sony PlayStation, released in late 1994 in Japan and in September 1995 in America. The game included callouts to Namco's earlier arcade coin-ops; in the PlayStation conversion you could choose your car, and they each had names such as *Bosconian*, *Mappy*, and *Xevious*. Plus, the game let you play a miniature *Galaga* as it loaded from CD-ROM. The game proved the PlayStation's chops, showing that it was a more powerful console than the Sega Saturn and setting up a market dynamic for home consoles that persists to this day.

Sega countered *Ridge Racer* with *Daytona USA*, a 60fps racer that put you behind the wheel of a 750-horsepower NASCAR stock car capable of drifts and power slides. Like *Ridge Racer*, *Daytona USA* also supported texture mapping. But its massive 50-inch projection screen and support for linking eight players harkened back to the feel of original amusement parks. The game was a ride and in of itself. *Daytona USA* is *still* found in current arcades alongside rows of Skee-Ball machines and mechanical prize bins, and still brings in profits today, even though the average current-generation PlayStation or Xbox could blow it out of the water in graphics resolution and detail levels.

For a brief time through 1993, arcade revenues surged after hitting a low of $2.1 billion in 1991. Part of this was the cost per play; many older gamers remembered *Dragon's Lair* and its 50-cent requirement, but through the early 1990s charging two quarters per play became much more commonplace. But the biggest reason was the quality of the games themselves, both from *Street Fighter II* on to rival games such as *Mortal Kombat*, *Fatal Fury*, *Samurai Shodown*, and *The King of Fighters*, as well as the move to three-dimensional polygon games such as Sega's *Virtua* series and Namco's *Tekken*. The Neo Geo platform also continued to shine, with standouts such as the spiritual *Contra* successor *Metal Slug*, the vertical shooter *Aero Fighter 2*, and horizontal space games such as *Pulstar* and *Last Resort*. By the start of 1994, U.S. consumers were spending $7 billion in arcade games each year, $1 billion more than they spent for home consoles during the same period.[20]

But the arcade industry entered a major slump by the middle of the year, leading to another round of arcade chain closures.[21] Ultimately, arcades were unable to compete on graphics and sound quality alone. As time wore on, it was clear most people preferred the comfort and convenience of playing games at home and were happy either buying new titles at the local GameStop or CompUSA or renting them from Blockbuster. By 1999, arcade industry revenue had fallen to just $1.3 billion, and smaller arcade venues, such as those found in malls, began to disappear.[22] There was little reason to hit the arcade in lieu of buying a game for your home console. Add extra gamepads, get a couple of friends together, and you could play the copy you now owned forever.

The nail in the coffin for pure arcade games was probably the 32-bit home console lineup. It included the Sega Saturn in 1994, the original Sony PlayStation in 1995, and the Nintendo 64 in 1996, with the latter two seeing tremendous levels of success. New "multimedia" CD-ROM games on PCs in the early 1990s delivered yet another venue for new kinds of gaming unavailable in arcades, and the quality of even 16-bit arcade ports such as *Street Fighter II* for the Super NES and *Golden Axe* for the Sega Genesis was good enough to stand in for the real thing. The Neo Geo's stratospheric pricing and $300 game cartridges put it well out of reach of most console gamers. But in 1999, Sega unveiled the Dreamcast, the first of the next (fifth) generation of platforms that for all intents and purposes was an arcade machine, as anyone who played *Soul Calibur* would tell you. The Sony PlayStation 2 and Microsoft's original Xbox arrived, Sega dropped away, and the Sony-Microsoft-Nintendo triumvirate would persist for the next 20 years.

Even then, in the face of declining revenues, the video arcade still wasn't "dead." It just had to reinvent itself one last time. As to how this would unfold, *Daytona USA* offered everyone a big clue.

> Epilogue

From a critical standpoint and after the Renaissance, the video arcade became a shadow of its former self in the mid 1990s. By this point, consoles and home computers were pushing the video game industry forward, so there was little reason to leave the house and pay per play. In an effort to survive, the arcade returned to its roots, with a focus on what was fun in a public amusement environment—never mind whether the games were innovative. This new incarnation of the video arcade wasn't necessarily a bad thing.

Three of the most popular games of this era collectively illustrated the phenomenon. *Cruis'n USA*, directed by Eugene Jarvis, landed in November 1994, with city street and seaside courses and your choice of music from the in-game radio. "While less graphically impressive than its rivals, *Cruis'n USA* is the *Out Run* sequel Sega should have done, and is our pick for the driving crown," *Next Generation* wrote in its review. That game, along with its sequel *Cruis'n World*, soon became ubiquitous in movie theater lobbies around the New York and New Jersey area. Atari Games was near bankruptcy around this time, and as a last-ditch play it released *Area 51*, an alien-blasting light gun game. *Area 51* received mostly mixed to poor reviews from critics, but that didn't matter. It went on to become a major hit, selling some 20,000 cabinets at a time when that number of sales was virtually unheard of. It gave arcade gamers what they wanted. *Golden Tee Golf* was a 1990 coin-op that delivered a surprisingly realistic golf simulation and spawned endless sequels. It became known as the quintessential bar video game, beating even Video Poker. Sports bars seemed to have as many *Golden Tee* machines as they did pool tables and dart boards.

"In the years to come, when people talk about arcade games," editor of *Play Meter* Valerie Cognevich said in a *Chicago Tribune* interview in 2003, "*Pac-Man* and *Golden Tee* will be in the same paragraph."[1]

Figure E.1: Games such as *Area 51* helped return arcades to their roots as a form of amusement you couldn't get easily at home, in a world of increasingly powerful consoles that would have otherwise rendered arcades irrelevant.

Successful coin-ops such as these seemed to bridge the decline of the arcade's influence on the video game industry with the arcade's "new" role: full of amusement and novelty machines. In other words, the arcade was coming full circle, and became similar to the first arcades from the turn of the 20th century. Coin-operated games were perfect for passing time with the family or while waiting for a movie to start. New machines included environmental designs, tremendous displays, and motion controls that were impossible to get in a console. The offerings were as varied as the game genres they represented and included multiseat racing games, fighter cockpits, motorcycle mounts, and dance platforms for "rhythm games." Sega's *Top Skater* arrived in 1997 with a "skateboard interface" that somehow did not lead to broken necks and lawsuits. Games such as this were nothing more than a video arcade evolution of a Skee-Ball machine. It was something you expected to see in certain places, but you weren't necessarily surprised or delighted by its presence any more than you would be by finding a claw machine near the restrooms or a video poker machine in a bar.

Arcade innovation wasn't dead, either. Sega's *Time Traveler* wasn't the first game to portray realistic digitized characters; that honor went to 1983's *Journey*, the game that featured the five members of the real-life rock band, and that unlike the band, wasn't successful. *Time Traveler* took "wasn't successful" a step further with full-motion video that looked like convincing three-dimensional holograms. The effect worked well, thanks to a curved mirror inside the cabinet. But the game itself was lacking, something arcade-goers figured out the moment they moved on from the impressive visuals. Another company by the name of Virtuality released proto-VR arcade coin-ops such as *Dactyl Nightmare* and *Grid Busters*, games that required the player to sit inside the cabinet and wear a headset, immersing him or her in the graphics.

The most obvious successful example of more recent video arcade innovation was probably the 1998 introduction of *Dance Dance Revolution* (*DDR*). The game came with a platform consisting of four arrows that corresponded to dance moves that players had to match with their feet at the appropriate times. The better each player matched the correct moves, the higher their percentage score; if it was high enough, they'd progress to the next song. *DDR* spawned the rhythm-and-dance genre and soon led to additional "performance" games such as the *Guitar Hero* and *Rock Band* series. Another milestone was 1998's *Gauntlet Legends*, in which Atari Games added more role-playing-game elements to its successful *Gauntlet* franchise. For the first time, players could level-up their characters, gaining experience that led to increased strength, speed, armor, and magic attributes.

These genre-busting games were few and far between, though. While these and other coin-ops such as *Star Wars Trilogy*, *Virtua Cop 2*, *Time Crisis 3*, and the oodles of fighting game sequels all gave arcade-goers something to enjoy, the video arcade as a destination for innovation was now firmly in its rearview mirror.

The New Arcades

In response to declining foot traffic and a lack of innovative new games, the arcade industry began shifting into "experiences." Venues began to evolve into family-friendly establishments that were modern takes on Chuck E. Cheese, with newer chains as well as independently owned amusement parks around the U.S. and the world. This allowed owners additional revenue streams from food and drinks—similar to the Chuck E. Cheese model but purely for the revenue itself and not to showcase new arcade games. (In

Japan, the situation was different, as arcades never wavered in popularity from the 1970s onward.)

In 1996, Steven Spielberg's DreamWorks, along with Sega Enterprises and Universal Studios, launched GameWorks, a chain of giant entertainment complexes with initial locations in Seattle, Columbus, and Chicago. Disney opened DisneyQuests, virtual theme parks, in Chicago and Orlando, with arcade games that focused on Disney properties. Dave & Buster's launched in 1982, but unlike most of its peers it survived and gained steam.[2] The giant entertainment center that combined food, arcade games, and "experiences" would prove vital to keeping arcades alive, even if the changes were painful for longtime arcade fans. GameWorks even tried to stick with what were now becoming "classic" arcade games by putting in two rows of them in each location. But it became apparent these were attracting more young male gamers than they had wanted, ones that were interested in the video games but not much else.[3] GameWorks management soon began refining the formula, and this portion of the floor was "one of the first casualties."[4]

Arcades Go "Retro"

Redemption games such as Skee-Ball made a comeback starting in the late 1990s.[5] In these games, you earned tickets or tokens depending on how well you did and then could exchange them at the counter for prizes. Some games, such as the claw-drop variety, would award you the prizes. These were always fun diversions but were pushed aside for video games in the 1980s and 1990s, so their return wasn't a surprise. They began to coexist with arcade video games in a much more synergistic manner, fitting in nicely with the newfound focus on amusement instead of innovation. That also opened the door for the return of some now-retro video games as well, with games such as *Asteroids* and *Space Invaders* now welcome sights again. Around the turn of the millennium, Namco's 20th Anniversary *Galaga/Ms. Pac-Man* revival cabinet was a big seller. Really, anything family oriented with a bizarre-but-cool control scheme—be it tank controls, periscopes, what have you—would work in an arcade context when paired with a solid game concept. "North American arcades rebounded from a 2003 low of 2,500 game venues to 3,500 in 2008."[6] This was despite how most internal arcade game hardware was the same as what was found in home consoles of the day. In Japan, the arcades shifted to a model with an online component for running massively multiplayer online role-playing games (MMORPGs).

Figure E.2: Arcades Go Retro: Franchises such as Barcade (pictured) combined the Golden Age of arcade games with either craft beer or a family-friendly atmosphere, both of which are perceived today as safer and more wholesome than the arcades of the late 1970s and early 1980s. Credit: Thesandworm / CC BY-SA 4.0

In the 21st century, we also began to see an uptick in retro-themed bars that refocused on Golden Age arcade games, this time around paired with craft beers. The excellent Barcade chain in the tri-state New York/New Jersey/Connecticut area is often credited with kicking off this trend, although variations on the theme can now be found around the country. Some massive spots opened up around the U.S. with arcade cabinet collections numbering in the hundreds, often joined by rows of classic and modern pinball tables. Museums across the nation began to feature video game history exhibitions, such as periodic appearances at the Museum of the Moving Image in Astoria, New York, and the Living Computer Museum in Seattle. One common theme in the larger arcade establishments is the ability to pay for a day pass, where you get in and then can play any of the games for an unlimited number of times until the day ends—or until you get tired of standing, which is more likely if you're closer to my age. The formula seems to be working.

"Some of the most memorable times I had was with my brothers and my friends playing games throughout the Golden Age of the video game era, the late '70s, '80s and '90s," said Jerold Colonna, the founder of New Jersey Gamer Con and proprietor of Colonial Soldier Arcade in the Deptford Mall in Deptford Township, New Jersey. "Growing up we always had arcades in the mall…a place to put up a high score, compete or play with your friends or family."[7] Arcade games have also returned to the corners of larger entertainment complexes, such as the lobbies of movie theaters and alongside miniature golf courses.

It may seem strange to pay per play for video games today, given the quality of console titles. But then you run into modern-day limitations, such as hour-long tutorials just to get started, loot boxes, in-app purchases, annoying narration, in-game elements that act more as dopamine triggers than actual challenges, and persistent multiplayer components that introduce their own social mechanic. There's something to be said for pure hand-eye coordination and unbroken concentration, as anyone who has gamed on vintage arcade machines can attest. Perhaps the best thing about video arcade games—and, indeed, the march of technological progress in general—is that all the old stuff is still out there, still being maintained and showcased decades after it launched and supposedly had fallen out of favor. The games have become part of pop culture and a firm nostalgia industry has taken hold. Besides, the games themselves not only influenced the developers of today's console titles but they also continue to influence the latest group of students and game designers, as they feature in game history textbooks and university classes the world over.

In the end, the game was the thing—even back in 1982. "Nobody cares about Eugene Jarvis," Jarvis said in an interview that year. "Nobody cares about Atari. It's the substance that matters…why do people play?

"People are bored with TV. They're not participating, just constantly watching someone else do something. Games let you take part, allow you to not just escape into another reality, but be the star. You can be a hero for a quarter. That's what it's about."[8]

It's just as true now as it was then.

> Acknowledgements

Plenty of people made this book possible. First and foremost is Matthew Murray, my tireless editor whose pun is quicker than his sword, although maybe that's not saying much. His careful, smart, and detailed edits and queries have helped make me a better writer and editor myself, and for that I am eternally grateful. My wife and daughter, who are not only understanding of my various quirks but somehow put up with the several dozen "vintage" systems and accompanying games, accessories, and wires that make up most of my "home office," where I ostensibly do "work" each day. My parents, who brought me to way too many arcades when I was a kid, gave me piles of quarters to play games with, and, at least in the early days, carried a milk crate around so I could stand on it and reach the control panels.

I would also like to thank plenty of friends who either assisted me directly with this book or otherwise provided inspiration for persisting in writing it. These include such illustrious persons as Dean Notarnicola, Peter Fletcher, Leonard Herman, Josh Malone, Jeremy Lechtzin, Kay Savetz, Bill Kendrick, Joe Decuir, Nolan Bushnell, Benj Edwards, Curt Vendel, Eric Nelson, Mark Howlett, Michael Whalen, Jeffrey Wilson, Jason H. Moore, Mike Mika, Van Burnham, Retroist, Cathryn Mataga, David L. Craddock, and Steven Hugg. Special thanks to Bill Lange, Steve Fulton, and Jeff Fulton for their valuable insight and support.

This book also wouldn't have been possible without dedicated enthusiasts working to preserve arcade history. In the Bibliography section that follows, I list many important books, newspaper and magazine articles, and other sources for this book, but I also want to call out a few easily accessible online resources. In 1990, coin-op collectors opened the online Video Arcade Preservation Society, which persists to this day. The group maintains the Killer List of Video Games (KLOV), a database of collective coin-op knowledge that began on local BBSes in the 1980s and that many others have contributed to over the past three decades. It contains cabinet, marquee, control panel, and other vital info, along with screenshots and trivia, for about 5,000 coin-ops released since 1971, and there's a comprehensive forum for arcade enthusiasts there as well. Today, KLOV is a division of the International Arcade Museum, and can be found at www.arcade-museum. com. This was an invaluable resource when writing this book. In addition, I can't say enough good things about the Internet Archive (archive.org), The Arcade Blogger (arcadeblogger.com), Gaming History (arcade-history. com), Arcade Heroes (arcadeheroes.com), and Keith Smith's The Golden Age Arcade Historian (allincolorforaquarter.blogspot.com),.

Speaking of which, we've sadly lost several arcade industry heroes recently. Vector graphics icon Tim Skelly, of Cinematronics fame, died in 2019 at the young age of 51. Ted Dabney, Atari cofounder and instrumental in the hardware design of *Computer Space* and *Pong*, died in 2018 at the age of 81. Exidy founder Pete Kauffman, who remained with the company for 23 years and long past its video-arcade heyday, passed away in October 2015, but not before releasing Exidy game ROMs for free, something few other big-name developers from the era have done.[9] Kazuhisa Hashimoto worked on the hardware for early Konami games such as *Scramble* and *Super Cobra*, and was most famous for the "Konami Code" sequence that gave you 30 lives in *Contra* on the NES and that has since become a cultural touchstone; he died in February 2020 at the age of 61. Masaya Nakamura, the founder of Namco and long-running company chairman and president, passed away in January 2020. He was 91 years old. Finally, Curt Vendel, an industry icon in his own right for preserving every last aspect of Atari history, died unexpectedly at just 53, just before this book went to press. May they all rest in power.

> Bibliography

"15 Most Influential Games of All Time." GameSpot. https://web.archive.org/web/20100412225953/http://www.gamespot.com/gamespot/features/video/15influential/p13_01.html

"59 Developers, 20 Questions." *Beep!*, October 1985 via http://shmuplations.com/20questions1985/

Agnello, Anthony John. "How Ghosts 'N Goblins helped video games find comedy in failure." AV Club, April 19, 2017. https://games.avclub.com/how-ghosts-n-goblins-helped-video-games-find-comedy-in-1798260872

Alcorn, Allan. "First-Hand: The Development of Pong: Early Days of Atari and the Video Game Industry." Engineering and Technology History Wiki. https://ethw.org/First-Hand:The_Development_of_Pong:_Early_Days_of_Atari_and_the_Video_Game_Industry

"Arcade Action," *Computer and Video Games*, February 1982, 26.

"Arcade Action." *Computer and Video Games*. December 1985, 89.

"Arcade Video Games Start to Flicker." *BusinessWeek*, Dec. 6, 1982, 39-40.

Arkush, William. *The Textbook of Video Game Logic, Volume I*. Campbell, CA: Kush 'n' Stuff Amusement Electronics, 1976.

Armstrong, Larry. "Raiders Of The Video Arcade." *Bloomberg*, October 16, 1994. https://www.bloomberg.com/news/articles/1994-10-16/raiders-of-the-video-arcade

"Atari: From Boom to Bust and Back Again," *Next Generation*, April 1995, 37.

Aycock, John. *Retrogame Archaeology: Exploring Old Computer Games*. Switzerland: Springer, 2016.

Bang, Derrick. "Beating the Classics." *Softline*. May-June 1983, 43.

Barton, Matt. *Vintage Games 2.0: An Insider Look at the Most Influential Games of All Time*. Boca Raton, FL: CRC Press, 2016.

"Beastie Boys 30 Year Tribute: To The 5 Boroughs Essays." Nada Mucho. March 12, 2017. https://www.nadamucho.com/beastie-boys-30-year-tribute-to-the-5-boroughs-essays/

Bloom, Steve. *Video Invaders*. New York: Arco Publishing, 1982.

Brookhaven National Laboratory. "The First Video Game?" https://www.bnl.gov/about/history/firstvideo.php

Brooks, B. David, Ph. D. "Exploding the Arcade Myths: A Scientist Evaluates the Coin-Op Gaming Scene." *Electronic Games*, August 1982, 35.

Brother Bill. "The Bishop of Battle (Nightmares, 1983)." The Haunted Closet, April 24, 2010. http://the-haunted-closet.blogspot.com/2010/04/bishop-of-battle-nightmares-1983.html

Bueschel, Richard M. *Pinball 1: Illustrated Historical Guide to Pinball Machines*. Wheat Ridge, CO: Hoflin Publishing, 1988.

Bueschel, Richard M. *Encyclopedia of Pinball Volume 1: Whiffle to Rocket 1930–1933*. LaGrangeville, NY: Silverball Amusements, 1996.

Burnham, Van, ed. *Supercade: A Visual History of the Videogame Age 1971-1984*. Cambridge, MA: The MIT Press, 2001.

"Can Asteroids Conquer Space Invaders?" *Electronic Games*, Winter 1981, 31-33.

Capcom IR Investor Relations Code Number: 9697 via Wayback Machine. https://web.archive.org/web/20150208030840/http://www.capcom.co.jp/ir/english/business/million.html

Carter, Lance. "History of Racing Games." June 13, 2007. https://historyofracing-games.wordpress.com/installment-one/

Cass, Stephen. "Al Alcorn, Creator of Pong, Explains How Early Home Computers Owe Their Color Graphics to This One Cheap, Sleazy Trick." *IEEE Spectrum*, April 21, 2020. https://spectrum.ieee.org/tech-talk/tech-history/silicon-revolution/al-alcorn-creator-of-pong-explains-how-early-home-computers-owe-their-color-to-this-one-cheap-sleazy-trick

Cifaldi, Frank. "The Connection is Made: Developer Highlights from Game Connection 2006 (Part Two)." Gamasutra, April 20, 2006. https://www.gamasutra.com/view/feature/131077/the_connection_is_made_developer_.php

"Classic GI: Space Invaders." *Game Informer*, January 2008, 108–109.

Cohen, D. S. "Cathode-Ray Tube Amusement Device: The First Electronic Game." Updated March 14, 2019. https://www.lifewire.com/cathode-ray-tube-amusement-device-729579

Cohen, Henry. "Test Lab: Getting Into Direct Video." *Electronic Games*, September 1982, 20.

Consumer Guide's *How To Win At Video Games*. New York: Pocket Books, 1982.

Coogan, Dan. "Interview with Mike Hally and Rich Adam, designers of Gravitar." Coogan Photo, March 12, 2004 (Updated December 30, 2006). http://www.coogan-photo.com/gravitar/interview.html#interview

"The Cosmic Quarter-Snatchers Cometh." *Electronic Games*, March 1982, 44.

Costrel, France, creator. *High Score*. New York City: Great Big Story/Netflix, 2020, video stream.

Crawford, Chris. "Design Techniques and Ideas for Computer Games." *Byte*, December 1982, 96.

Current, Michael. "A History of Syzygy/Atari." Updated July 1, 2020. https://mcurrent.name/atarihistory/syzygy.html

DBG. "Harry Lafnear." Atari Legend, September 5, 2003. https://www.atarilegend.com/interviews/interviews_detail.php?selected_interview_id=4

Dear, Brian. *The Friendly Orange Glow: The Untold Story of the PLATO System and the Dawn of Cyberculture*. New York: Pantheon Books, 2017.

Defanti, Thomas A. "The Mass Impact of Videogame Technology." *Advances in Computers, Volume 23*. Cambridge, MA: Academic Press, 1984.

DeSpira, Cat. "Dying To Play: The Berzerk Curse -Fact or Fiction?" Retro Bitch. November 4, 2015. https://retrobitch.wordpress.com/2015/11/04/dying-to-play-the-berzerk-curse-fact-or-fiction/

Digital Eclipse. "Midway Arcade Treasures." PC CD-ROM, 2004.

"Digital Video Game Firsts — Michigan Pool (1954)." mass:werk, June 23, 2019. https://www.masswerk.at/nowgobang/2019/michigan-pool

Dillon, Roberto. *The Golden Age of Video Games*. Boca Raton, FL: CRC Press, 2011.

Dvorchak, Robert. "NEC Out to Dazzle Nintendo Fans." *Associated Press*, Jul. 30, 1989.

"Early Arcade Classics: 1985-1987 Developer Interviews." *Beep!*, 1985 via http://shmuplations.com/20questions1985/

"Electronic Games Hotline." *Electronic Games*. March 1982, 28-29.

"Electronic Games Hotline," *Electronic Games*, July 1982, 8-11.

Feit, Daniel. "How Virtua Fighter Saved PlayStation's Bacon." *Wired*, September 5, 2012. https://www.wired.com/2012/09/how-virtua-fighter-saved-playstations-bacon/

"The First Pinball Machines." Pinball History. http://www.pinballhistory.com/pinfirsts.html

Fisher, Adam. *Valley of Genius: The Uncensored History of Silicon Valley*. New York: Twelve, 2018.

Forman, Tracie. "Insert Coin Here." *Electronic Games*, August 1983, 100.

Forman, Tracie. "Insert Coin Here." *Electronic Games*, December 1983, 106.

Formichella, Lucien. "14 groundbreaking movies that took special effects to new levels." Insider, January 11, 2020. https://www.insider.com/most-groundbreaking-cgi-movies-ever-created-2020-1

Fries, Ed. "Fixing Gran Trak 10." Ed Fries: The Game Is Not Over, June 14, 2017. https://edfries.wordpress.com/2017/06/14/fixing-gran-trak-10/

Fujihara, Mary, "Inter Office Memo" at Atari dated November 2, 1983.

Fulton, Steve. "The Dead Lexicon Of Classic Video Games (Ver. 1.1)." Into the Vertical Blank, Dec. 28, 2014. https://intotheverticalblank.com/2014/12/28/the-dead-lexicon-of-classic-video-games-part-1/

Fulton, Steve. "The History of Atari, 1971-1977." Gamasutra, November 6, 2007.

https://www.gamasutra.com/view/feature/2000/the_history_of_atari_19711977.php

Fulton, Steve. "Willy Higinbotham, Video Game Pioneer Speaks (sort of)." Into the Vertical Blank, September 24, 2008. https://intotheverticalblank.com/2008/09/24/willy-higinbotham-video-game-pioneer-speaks-sort-of/

The Game Doctor. "Q&A." *Electronic Games*, September 1982, 17.

"GameSpy's Top 50 Arcade Games of All-Time." *GameSpy*. February 25, 2011, via Wayback Machine. https://web.archive.org/web/20110426003920/www.gamespy.com/articles/115/1151159p3.html

Goldberg, Marty, and Vendel, Curt. *Atari, Inc.: Business Is Fun*. Carmel, NY: Syzygy Company Press, 2012.

Grammer, Charlie. "Gamebusters myth 7: Berzerk." GotGame. December 27, 2013. https://gotgame.com/2013/12/27/gamebusters-myth-7-berzerk/

Hague, James. *Halcyon Days: Interviews With Classic Computer and Video Game Programmers*. Online-only publication, 1997. https://dadgum.com/halcyon/index.html

Harmetz, Aljean. "Movie Themes Come To Video Games." *Wilmington Morning Star,* July 3, 1982, 6C.

Henry, Lydia. "Skee-Ball Mania." *Reading Eagle*, Arp. 26, 2001, 19.

"Here Come the Convertibles." *Electronic Games*, August 1983, 92-93.

Herman, Leonard. *Phoenix IV: The History of the Videogame Industry*. Springfield, NJ: Rolenta Press, 2016.

Horowitz, Ken. *The Sega Arcade Revolution: A History in 62 games*. Jefferson, NC: McFarland & Company, 2018.

Horowitz, Ken. "Feature: The History Of Virtua Racing, One Of The Most Influential Coin-Ops Of All Time." NintendoLife, May 6, 2019. https://www.nintendolife.com/news/2019/05/feature_the_history_of_virtua_racing_one_of_the_most_influential_coin-ops_of_all_time

Hugg, Steven. *Making 8-Bit Arcade Games in C*. Puzzling Plans, 2017.

Hurley, Oliver. "Game on again for coin-operated arcade titles." *The Guardian*, February 6, 2008. https://www.theguardian.com/technology/2008/feb/07/games.it

"IGN's Top 100 Games of All Time." IGN, 2007 via https://web.archive.org/web/20110830043153/http://top100.ign.com/2007/ign_top_game_24.html

Jackson, Matthew. "Little-known sci-fi fact: Why Tron's FX got snubbed for an Oscar." Syfy Wire, March 1, 2013. https://www.syfy.com/syfywire/little-known-sci-fi-fact-why-trons-fx-got-snubbed-oscar

June, Laura. "For Amusement Only: the life and death of the American arcade." The Verge, January 16, 2013. https://www.theverge.com/2013/1/16/3740422/the-life-and-death-of-the-american-arcade-for-amusement-only

Katz, Arnie. "The Decline and Fall…of Prices." *Electronic Games*, October 1983, 6.

Katz, Arnie. "Switch On." *Electronic Games*, May 1982, 6.

Katz, Arnie. "Switch On." *Electronic Games*, July 1982, 6.

Katz, Arnie. "Switch On: The Future of Coin-Op Videogames." *Electronic Games*, September 1984, 6.

Katz, Arnie, and Kunkel, Bill. "The Arcade Awards." Electronic Games, January 1983, 22-37.

Kent, Steven. "VideoGameSpot's Interview with Yoshiki Okamoto." VideoGameSpot, December 7, 1998 via Wayback Machine. https://web.archive.org/web/19981207033331/http://www.videogames.com/features/universal/okamoto/ok-time.html

Kent, Steven L. *The Ultimate History of Video Games: From Pong to Pokémon and Beyond—The Story Behind the Craze That Touched Our Lives and Changed the World*. New York: Three Rivers Press, 2001.

Kohler, Chris. *Power-Up: How Japanese Video Games Gave the World an Extra Life*. Mineola, NY: Dover, 2016.

Kubey, Craig. *The Winners' Book of Video Games*. New York: Warner Books, 1982.

Kunkel, Bill, and Katz, Arnie. "Arcade Alley: Zaxxon, Turbo, and Two for Apple II." *Video*, April 1983, 26-29.

Kunkel, Bill, and Katz, Arnie. "The 1983 Arcade Awards." *Electronic Games*, January 1983, 36.

Kunkel, Bill, and Katz, Arnie. "The 1984 Arcade Awards." *Electronic Games*, January 1984, 78.

Kunkel, Bill. "Insert Coin Here: What's New In the Arcades." *Electronic Games*, Winter 1981, 64.

Kunkel, Bill. "Insert Coin Here: What's New In the Arcades." *Electronic Games*, May 1982, 26-28.

Kunkel, Bill. "Insert Coin Here." *Electronic Games*, February 1983, 62.

Kunkel, Bill. "1982—The Year in Coin-Ops." *Electronic Games*, December 1982, 64-66.

Kunkel, Bill, and Katz, Arnie. "Arcade Alley: Wintertime Winners." *Video*, November 1983, 38-39.

Kurtz, Bill. *The Encyclopedia of Arcade Video Games*. Atglen, PA: Schiffer Publishing, 2004.

La Brecque, Eric. "Technician of Suspended Disbelief: Rick Dyer, Shadoan and the Frontier of Animated CD Entertainment." *Animation World Network*, 1996. Retrieved via the Wayback Machine: https://web.archive.org/web/20090804024201/http://www.awn.com/mag/issue1.1/articles/dyer.html

Lapetino, Tim. *Art of Atari*. Mt. Laurel, NJ: Dynamite Entertainment, 2016.

Leack, Jonathan. "World of Warcraft Leads Industry With Nearly $10 Billion In Revenue." GameRevolution, January 26, 2017. https://www.gamerevolution.com/features/13510-world-of-warcraft-leads-industry-with-nearly-10-billion-in-revenue

"Leading Edge." *Electronic Gaming Monthly*, November 1992, 54-56.

Levy, Steven. *Hackers: Heroes of the Computer Revolution*. Sebastopol, CA: O'Reilly, 2010.

Lewis, Alexander. "Free play arcade to open in Deptford." *Courier News and Home News Tribune*, October 30, 2018. https://www.mycentraljersey.com/story/news/2018/10/30/free-play-arcade-colonial-soldier-arcade-opens-deptford/1676021002/

Lipscombe, Daniel. "Insane difficulty and joke endings - looking back at Altered Beast, 30 years later." GamesRadar, August 1, 2018. https://www.gamesradar.com/insane-difficulty-and-joke-endings-looking-back-at-altered-beast-30-years-later/

Logg, Ed. "Gauntlet Postmortem." 2012 Game Developers Conference.

Lustig, David. "The Big Shake-Out?" *Electronic Games*, Mar 1984, 23.

Margolin, Jed. "Schematics For Hard Drivin'/Race Drivin' ADSP, Motor Amplifier, and DSK Boards." March 9, 2002. http://jmargolin.com/schem/schems.htm

Massey, Tom. "Final Fight retrospective." Eurogamer, May 26, 2014. https://www.eurogamer.net/articles/2014-05-25-final-fight-retrospective

McCarthy, Rebecca. "Video Games Are an Exercise In Annihilation." *The Atlanta Journal-Constitution*, May 30, 1989, D/1.

Montfort, Nick, and Ian Bogost. *Racing the Beam: The Atari Video Computer System*. Cambridge, MA: The MIT Press, 2009.

Mott, Tony, ed. *1001 Games You Must Play Before You Die*. New York: Universe, 2011.

Moyse, Chris. "'80s Tomy toy turned into mini Out Run arcade cab." Destructoid, Aug. 31, 2017. https://www.destructoid.com/-80s-tomy-toy-turned-into-mini-out-run-arcade-cab-458189.phtml

Nasaw, David. *Going Out: The Rise and Fall of Public Amusements*. Cambridge, MA: Harvard University Press, 1999.

Newman, Michael Z. *Atari Age: The Emergence of Video Games in America*. Cambridge, MA: The MIT Press, 2017.

Omigari, Toshi, and Muroga, Kiyonori. *Arcade Game Typography: The Art of Pixel Type*. London: Thames & Hudson, 2019.

Parkin, Simon. "The Unexpectedly High-Stakes World of Neo Geo Collecting." *The New Yorker*, January 24, 2017. https://www.newyorker.com/tech/annals-of-technology/the-unexpectedly-high-stakes-world-of-neo-geo-collecting

Patterson, Eric. "The 5 Most Influential Japanese Games Day Four: Street Fighter II." *Electronic Gaming Monthly*, November 3, 2011 via Wayback Machine, https://web.archive.org/web/20170314064721/http://www.egmnow.com/articles/news/egm-featurethe-5-most-influential-japanese-gamesday-four-street-fighter-ii/

Pearl, Rich. "A Time Trip to the Game Parlor of the Future." *Electronic Games*, January 1983, 62-63.

Pearl, Rich. "Closet Classics." *Electronic Games*, June 1983, 82.

Petrusich, Amanda. "The Forgotten Greatness of Air Hockey." *The New Yorker*, August 9, 2016. https://www.newyorker.com/culture/culture-desk/the-forgotten-greatness-of-air-hockey

Persons, Dan. "Laser's Last Stand." *Electronic Games*, January 1985, 78-81.

Pierce, David. "'The Simpsons Arcade Game' was the best game ever based on a TV show." The Verge, August 26, 2014. https://www.theverge.com/2014/8/26/6067425/the-simpsons-arcade-game-made-me-love-the-show

Pittman, Jamey. "The Pac-Man Dossier." Gamasutra, February 23, 2009. https://www.gamasutra.com/view/feature/132330/the_pacman_dossier.php

Pitts, Bill. "The Galaxy Game." October 29, 1997. http://infolab.stanford.edu/pub/voy/museum/galaxy.html

Plunkett, Luke. "Death Race, the World's First Scandalous Video Game." Kotaku, Feb. 28, 2012. https://kotaku.com/death-race-the-worlds-first-scandalous-video-game-5889166

Rasa, Chris. "Rastan." HG101, October 4, 2017. http://www.hardcoregaming101.net/rastan/

"Reader Replay." *Electronic Games*, April 1985, 12.

Redgrave, M. "Improvements in Bagatelle." United States of America, Patent #115357, 1871.

Reilly, Luke. "The Top 10 Most Influential Racing Games." IGN, April 3, 2015, Updated May 2, 2017. https://www.ign.com/articles/2015/04/03/the-top-10-most-influential-racing-games-ever

Richardson, Willy. "The Making of an Arcade Game." *Electronic Games*, March 1982, 32-33.

Richardson, Willy. "Own Your Own Arcade Game." *Electronic Games*, Winter 1981, 70-71.

Robley, Les Paul. "An Exciting Preview of Disney's Videogame Movie." *Electronic Games*, July 1982, 34-36.

Robley, Les Paul. "Confessions of an Arcade Technician." *Electronic Games*, May 1983. 54-56.

Rose, Gary and Marcia. "Gameline." *Softline,* November 1982, 19.

Rothman, Joshua. "Mirror World." *The New Yorker*, December 16, 2019.

Rousse, Thomas H. "Reconstructing WARRIOR: Vectorbeams, Natural Magick

& Business Intrigue." *Kinephanos*, June 2015. https://www.kinephanos.ca/2015/recon-structing-warrior/

SaraAB87. "Happy 30th Birthday to Sega's After Burner! 1987-2017." Arcade Heroes, July 1, 2017. https://arcadeheroes.com/2017/07/01/happy-30th-birthday-se-gas-burner-1987-2017/

Sellers, John. *Arcade Fever: The Fan's Guide to the Golden Age of Video Games*. Philadelphia: Running Press, 2001.

Shaggy. "A History of Star Trek at the Arcades." Arcade Heroes, April 2, 2009, updated September 8, 2018. https://arcadeheroes.com/2009/04/02/a-history-of-star-trek-at-the-arcades/

Sharpe, Roger. "The History of the Arcade." *Electronic Games*, July 1982, 26-28.

Shea, Tom. "Shrinking Pac-Man Leads Game-Wristwatch Market." *InfoWorld*, Dec. 20, 1982, 44.

Siegel, Alan. "How Golden Tee became the best bar game in America." *USA To-day*, June 24, 2015. https://ftw.usatoday.com/2015/06/golden-tee-the-history-of-a-beer-soaked-american-pastime

Smith, Alexander. *They Create Worlds: The Story of the People and Companies That Shaped the Video Game Industry, Vol. I: 1971-1982*. Abingdon, UK: Routledge, 2020.

Smith, Keith. "A Literary History of the Golden Age of Video Games - Golden Age Video Game Books Part 8." The Golden Age Arcade Historian, October 18, 2014. http://allincolorforaquarter.blogspot.com/2014/10/a-literary-history-of-golden-age-of_18.html

Smith, Keith. "Galaxy Game." The Golden Age Arcade Historian, March 14, 2013. http://allincolorforaquarter.blogspot.com/2013/03/galaxy-game.html

Smith, Keith. "The Ultimate (So Far) History of Allied Leisure/Centuri - Part 3." The Golden Age Arcade Historian, October 11, 2013. http://allincolorforaquarter.blogspot.com/2013/10/the-ultimate-so-far-history-of-allied.html

Smith, Keith. "Video Game Myth Busters - The Space Invaders Yen Shortage." The Golden Age Arcade Historian, November 13, 2013. http://allincolorforaquarter.blogspot.com/2013/11/video-game-myth-busters-space-invaders.html

"Space Invaders vs. Star Wars." *Executive*, Vol. 24, Southam Business Publications, 1982, 9.

"Space Wars and Cinematronics - Vector Plots." The Dot Eaters: Video Game History 101. http://thedoteaters.com/?bitstory=bitstory-article-2/space-wars-and-cinematronics

Sponsel, Sebastian. "History of: Virtua Fighter." Sega-16, February 3, 2010. https://www.sega-16.com/2010/02/history-of-virtua-fighter/

St. Clair, John. *Project Arcade: Build Your Own Arcade Machine*. Indianapolis: Wiley Publishing, 2004.

"Stern Production Numbers and More CCI Photos." https://tokensonly.com/2012/05/01/stern-production-numbers-and-more-cci-photos/

"Steve Hanawa's Tech Talk." Sega8bit, October 31, 2008. http://www.smstributes.co.uk/view_article.asp?articleid=45

Stilphen, Scott. "DP Interviews...Howard Delman." Digital Press. http://www.digitpress.com/library/interviews/interview_howard_delman.html

Sullivan, George. *Screen Play: The Story of Video Games*. New York: Frederick Warne, 1983.

United States v. Korpan. 237 F. 2d 676, Court of Appeals, 7th Circuit, 1956.

Temple, Tony. "Atari Kangaroo: The elephant in the arcade." Arcade Blogger, November 11, 2017. https://arcadeblogger.com/2017/11/10/atari-kangaroo-the-elephant-in-the-arcade/

Temple, Tony. "Death Race: Exidy's Video Arcade Nasty." Arcade Blogger, August 26, 2019. https://arcadeblogger.com/2019/08/26/death-race-exidys-video-nasty/

Temple, Tony. "Time-Out Arcade: Amazing Classic Arcade Pictures." Arcade Blogger, August 18, 2017. https://arcadeblogger.com/2017/08/18/time-out-arcade-amazing-classic-arcade-pictures/

"The 30 Defining Moments in Video Gaming," *Edge*, August 14, 2007.

Thomsen, Michael. "Fond Memories: Kung-Fu Master." IGN, February 13, 2008, updated May 12, 2012. https://www.ign.com/articles/2008/02/13/fond-memories-kung-fu-master

Tkacik, Maureen. "Back to Bingo: Arcade Firm Shrugs Off High-Tech Flash—GameWorks Thinks It Has a Winner With Classics Like Bowling and Skee-Ball." *The Wall Street Journal*, July 23, 2001.

"Top 100 Games of All Time," *Next Generation*, September 1996, 56.

"Upcoming Coin-Ops: Fewer But Better." *Electronic Games*, August 1983, 90-91.

"Video Games Are Blitzing the World." *Time*, Jan. 18, 1982.

"Videogame Outlook…1982: Here Comes the Video Game Explosion." *Electronic Games*, May 1982, 22-23.

Wardyga, Brian J. *The Video Games Textbook: History • Business • Technology*. Boca Raton, FL: CRC Press, 2019.

Webb, Marcus. "Arcadia." *Next Generation*, February 1996, 29.

Wise, Deborah. "Video arcades rival Broadway theater and girlie shows in NY." *InfoWorld*, April 12, 1983, 15.

Wolf, Mark J. P., ed. *Before the Crash: Early Video Game History*. Detroit: Wayne State University Press, 2012.

Wolf, Mark J. P., ed. *The Video Game Explosion: A History from PONG to PlayStation and Beyond*. Westport, CT: Greenwood Press, 2008.

Wolf, Mark J. P., ed. *The Encyclopedia of Video Games: The Culture, Technology, and Art of Gaming* (2 volumes). Westport, CT: Greenwood Press, 2012.

Wong, Alistair. "Chasing Down Memories Of Making Arcade Racers With Namco Veteran Sho Osugi." *Siliconera*. March 11, 2019. https://www.siliconera.com/chasing-down-memories-of-making-arcade-racers-with-namco-veteran-sho-osugi/

Wozniak, Steve, with Smith, Gina. *iWoz: How I Invented the Personal Computer, Co- Founded Apple, and Had Fun Doing It*. New York: W. W. Norton & Company, 2006.

Zeidman, Bob. *The Software IP Detective's Handbook: Measurement, Comparison, and Infringement Detection*. Upper Saddle River, NJ: Prentice Hall, 2011.

> Notes

Introduction

1   Newman, Michael Z. *Atari Age: The Emergence of Video Games in America* (Cambridge, MA: The MIT Press, 2017), 19.
2   Newman, 20.

Chapter 1

1   Redgrave, M., "Improvements in Bagatelle," United States of America, Patent #115357, 1871.
2   Smith, A., 81.
3   "The First Pinball Machines," Pinball History, http://www.pinballhistory.com/pinfirsts.html
4   Kent, Steven L. *The Ultimate History of Video Games: From Pong to Pokémon and Beyond—The Story Behind the Craze That Touched Our Lives and Changed the World* (New York: Three Rivers Press, 2001), 3.
5   Bueschel, Richard M., *Encyclopedia of Pinball Volume 1: Whiffle to Rocket 1930–1933* (LaGrangeville, NY: Silverball Amusements, 1996), 19-20.
6   Kent. 4.
7   https://www.ipdb.org/machine.cgi?id=209
8   Smith, A., 84.
9   Wolf, Mark J. P. ed, *The Encyclopedia of Video Games: The Culture, Technology, and Art of Gaming, Volume 1* (Westport, CT: Greenwood Press, 2012), 36.
10 Sharpe, Roger, "The History of the Arcade," *Electronic Games*, July 1982, 28.
11 *United States v. Korpan*, 237 F. 2d 676, Court of Appeals, 7th Circuit, 1956.
12 Sharpe, Roger C. "The History of the Arcade." EG July 1982, p. 29.
13 Newman, 21.
14 Carter, Lance, "History of Racing Games," June 13, 2007. https://historyofracing-

games.wordpress.com/installment-one/

15 Kent, 102.

16 Petrusich, Amanda, "The Forgotten Greatness of Air Hockey," *The New Yorker*, August 9, 2016. https://www.newyorker.com/culture/culture-desk/the-forgotten-greatness-of-air-hockey

17 Sharpe, Roger, "The History of the Arcade," *Electronic Games*, July 1982, 26.

18 Wolf, *Encyclopedia of Video Games Volume 1*, 34.

19 Ibid.

20 Sharpe, Roger, "The History of the Arcade," *Electronic Games*, July 1982, 26.

21 Nasaw, David, *Going Out: The Rise and Fall of Public Amusements* (Cambridge, MA: Harvard University Press, 1999), 154.

22 Newman, 23.

23 Sharpe, Roger, "The History of the Arcade," *Electronic Games*, July 1982, 27.

24 Bueschel, Richard M., *Pinball 1: Illustrated Historical Guide to Pinball Machines* (Wheat Ridge, CO: Hoflin Publishing, 1988), 72.

25 Kent, 10.

26 Kent, 9.

27 Kent, 13.

28 Brookhaven National Laboratory, "The First Video Game?" https://www.bnl.gov/about/history/firstvideo.php

29 Dillon, Roberto. *The Golden Age of Video Games* (Boca Raton, FL: CRC Press, 2011), 4.

30 Herman, Leonard. *Phoenix IV: The History of the Videogame Industry* (Springfield, NJ: Rolenta Press, 2016), 1.

31 Cohen, D. S., "Cathode-Ray Tube Amusement Device: The First Electronic Game," Updated March 14, 2019. https://www.lifewire.com/cathode-ray-tube-amusement-device-729579

32 Herman, 1.

33 "Digital Video Game Firsts — Michigan Pool (1954)," mass:werk, June 23, 2019. https://www.masswerk.at/nowgobang/2019/michigan-pool

34 Fulton, Steve. "Willy Higinbotham, "Video Game" Pioneer Speaks (sort of)," Into the Vertical Blank, September 24, 2008. https://intotheverticalblank.com/2008/09/24/willy-higinbotham-video-game-pioneer-speaks-sort-of/

35 Herman, 1.

36 Smith, Alexander. *They Create Worlds: The Story of the People and Companies That Shaped the Video Game Industry, Vol. I: 1971-1982* (Abingdon, UK: Routledge, 2020), 42.

37 Levy, Steven. *Hackers: Heroes of the Computer Revolution* (Sebastopol, CA: O'Reilly, 2010), 43.

38 Levy, 29-30.

39 Levy, 34.

40 "Spacewar!" mass:werk. https://www.masswerk.at/spacewar/

41 Dear, Brian, *The Friendly Orange Glow: The Untold Story of the PLATO System and the Dawn of Cyberculture* (New York: Pantheon Books, 2017), 227-228.

42 Kurtz, Bill, *The Encyclopedia of Arcade Video Games* (Atglen, PA: Schiffer Pub-

lishing, 2004), 5.

43   Burnham, Van, ed. *Supercade: A Visual History of the Videogame Age 1971-1984* (Cambridge, MA: The MIT Press, 2001), 66.

44   Ibid.

45   Ibid.

46   Fulton, Steve, "The History of Atari, 1971-1977," Gamasutra, November 6, 2007. https://www.gamasutra.com/view/feature/2000/the_history_of_atari_19711977.php

47   Ibid.

48   Burnham, 66.

49   Current, Michael, "A History of Syzygy/Atari," Updated July 1, 2020. https://mcurrent.name/atarihistory/syzygy.html

50   Burnham, 67.

51   Ibid.

52   Pitts, Bill, "The Galaxy Game," October 29, 1997. http://infolab.stanford.edu/pub/voy/museum/galaxy.html

53   Ibid.

54   Ibid.

55   Ibid.

56   Smith, Keith, "Galaxy Game," The Golden Age Arcade Historian, March 14, 2013. http://allincolorforaquarter.blogspot.com/2013/03/galaxy-game.html

57   Pitts, Bill, "The Galaxy Game," October 29, 1997. http://infolab.stanford.edu/pub/voy/museum/galaxy.html

58   Alcorn, Allan, "First-Hand:The Development of Pong: Early Days of Atari and the Video Game Industry," Engineering and Technology History Wiki. https://ethw.org/First-Hand:The_Development_of_Pong:_Early_Days_of_Atari_and_the_Video_Game_Industry

59   Wardyga, Brian J. *The Video Games Textbook: History • Business • Technology* (Boca Raton, FL: CRC Press, 2019), 10.

60   Cass, Stephen, "Al Alcorn, Creator of Pong, Explains How Early Home Computers Owe Their Color Graphics to This One Cheap, Sleazy Trick," *IEEE Spectrum*, April 21, 2020. https://spectrum.ieee.org/tech-talk/tech-history/silicon-revolution/al-alcorn-creator-of-pong-explains-how-early-home-computers-owe-their-color-to-this-one-cheap-sleazy-trick

61   Herman, 10.

62   Kent, 42.

63   Alcorn, 2009.

64   Kent, 44.

65   Herman, 11.

66   Wardyga, 12.

67   Herman, 13, and Goldberg and Vendel, ch. 3.

68   Kurtz, 6.

69   Smith, A., 172-173.

70   Herman, 13.

71   Goldberg, Marty, and Vendel, Curt, *Atari, Inc.: Business Is Fun* (Carmel, NY:

Syzygy Company Press, 2012), 98.

72 https://www.arcade-museum.com/game_detail.php?game_id=9681

73 Wolf, Mark J. P. ed., *The Video Game Explosion: A History from PONG to Playstation and Beyond* (Westport, CT: Greenwood Press, 2008), 37.

74 Smith, Keith, "What Was The Best-Selling U.S. Arcade Video Game Prior to Space Invaders?," with numbers provided by Ralph Baer. https://allincolorforaquarter.blogspot.com/2012/08/what-was-best-selling-us-arcade-video.html

75 "Annotated Atari Depositions, Part 4," January 1976. http://allincolorforaquarter.blogspot.com/2015/02/annotated-atari-depositions-part-4.html

76 Burnham, 92.

77 Smith, Keith, "For-Play Manufacturing," http://allincolorforaquarter.blogspot.com/2013/07/for-play-manufacturing.html

78 Smith, A., 173.

79 Ibid.

80 "Atari: From Boom to Bust and Back Again," *Next Generation*, April 1995, 37.

81 Montfort, Nick, and Ian Bogost, *Racing the Beam: The Atari Video Computer System* (Cambridge, MA: The MIT Press, 2009), 19-21.

82 Fries, Ed. "Fixing Gran Trak 10," Ed Fries: The Game Is Not Over, June 14, 2017. https://edfries.wordpress.com/2017/06/14/fixing-gran-trak-10/

83 Ibid.

84 Goldberg and Vendel, 250.

85 Herman, 16.

86 Montfort and Bogost, 20.

87 https://www.arcade-museum.com/game_detail.php?game_id=12989

88 Smith, A., 194.

89 https://www.arcade-museum.com/game_detail.php?game_id=8190

90 Herman, 22.

91 Ibid.

92 Newman, 37.

93 Kent, 64.

94 Ibid.

95 Hugg, Steven. *Making 8-Bit Arcade Games in C* (Self-published, 2017), 74.

96 Hugg, 74.

97 Smith, A., 273.

98 Arkush, William, *The Textbook of Video Game Logic, Volume I* (Campbell, CA: Kush 'n' Stuff Amusement Electronics, 1976), 46

99 Kohler, Chris, *Power-Up: How Japanese Video Games Gave the World an Extra Life* (Mineola, NY: Dover, 2016), 17.

100 Lapetino, Tim, *Art of Atari* (Mt. Laurel, NJ: Dynamite Entertainment, 2016), 39.

101 Ibid.

102 Lapetino, 190.

103 Lapetino, 45.

104 Herman, 18.

105 Kurtz, 8-9.

106 Kurtz, 9.

Chapter 2

1   Wozniak, Steve, with Smith, Gina, "*iWoz: How I Invented the Personal Computer, Co- Founded Apple, and Had Fun Doing It.* " (New York: W. W. Norton & Company, 2006), 144-147.

2   Kent, 74-77.

3   https://www.arcade-museum.com/game_detail.php?game_id=7743

4   Wong, Alistair, "Chasing Down Memories Of Making Arcade Racers With Namco Veteran Sho Osugi," *Siliconera*, March 11, 2019. https://www.siliconera.com/chasing-down-memories-of-making-arcade-racers-with-namco-veteran-sho-osugi/

5   Barton, Matt, *Vintage Games 2.0: An Insider Look at the Most Influential Games of All Time* (Boca Raton, FL: CRC Press, 2016), 72.

6   Ibid.

7   Moyse, Chris, "'80s Tomy toy turned into mini OutRun arcade cab," Destructoid, Aug. 31, 2017. https://www.destructoid.com/-80s-tomy-toy-turned-into-mini-outrun-arcade-cab-458189.phtml

8   Barton, 73.

9   Smith, A., 201.

10 Temple, Tony, "Death Race: Exidy's Video Arcade Nasty," Arcade Blogger, August 26, 2019. https://arcadeblogger.com/2019/08/26/death-race-exidys-video-nasty/

11 Ibid.

12 Plunkett, Luke, "Death Race, the World's First Scandalous Video Game," Kotaku, Feb. 28, 2012. https://kotaku.com/death-race-the-worlds-first-scandalous-video-game-5889166

13 Ibid.

14 Young, Larry. "Local Safety Authorities Denounce Game." *The Spokesman-Review*, Dec. 29, 1976, 10.

15 Ibid.

16 https://www.arcade-museum.com/game_detail.php?game_id=7541

17 Omigari, Toshi, and Muroga, Kiyonori, *Arcade Game Typography: The Art of Pixel Type* (London: Thames & Hudson, 2019), 44.

18 Omigari and Muroga, 44.

19 Kent, 101.

20 Kent, 102.

21 Skelly, Tim, ed. Mark J. P. Wolf, *Before the Crash: Early Video Game History* (Detroit: Wayne State University Press, 2012), 141.

22 Ibid.

23 Ibid.

24 "Space Wars and Cinematronics - Vector Plots," The Dot Eaters: Video Game History 101. http://thedoteaters.com/?bitstory=bitstory-article-2/space-wars-and-cinematronics

25 Skelly, 141.

26 Skelly, 143.

27 Skelly, 145.

28 Wolf, *Encyclopedia of Video Games, Volume 1*, 110.

29 Wolf, *Video Game Explosion*, 68.

30 Dillon, 4.

31 Kent, 119.

32 Newman, 38.

33 Smith, A., 301.

Chapter 3

1 Newman, 39.

2 Ibid.

3 Burnham, 162.

4 Hugg, 75.

5 "Can Asteroids Conquer Space Invaders?" *Electronic Games*, Winter 1981, 31.

6 Smith, Keith, "Video Game Myth Busters - The Space Invaders Yen Shortage," The Golden Age Arcade Historian, Nov. 13, 2013. http://allincolorforaquarter. blogspot.com/2013/11/video-game-myth-busters-space-invaders.html

7 Kent, 116-117.

8 https://www.giantbomb.com/space-invaders/3030-5099/

9 Collins, Karen, Mark J. P. Wolf, ed. *Before the Crash: Early Video Game History* (Detroit: Wayne State University Press, 2012), 131.

10 Kurtz, 47.

11 "Classic GI: Space Invaders," *Game Informer* #177, January 2008, 108–109.

12 Newman, 40.

13 Smith, Keith, "A Literary History of the Golden Age of Video Games - Golden Age Video Game Books Part 8," The Golden Age Arcade Historian, Oct. 18, 2014. http://allincolorforaquarter.blogspot.com/2014/10/a-literary-history-of-golden-age-of_18.html

14 Kohler, 17.

15 "Space Invaders vs. Star Wars," *Executive*, Vol. 24, Southam Business Publications, 1982, 9.

16 Wolf, *Encyclopedia of Video Games Volume 1*, 68

17 "Hall of Fame," *Electronic Games*, March 1983, 22.

18 https://www.mamedev.org/roms/starfire/

19 Pearl, Rich, "Closet Classics," *Electronic Games*, June 1983, 82.

20 Herman, 44.

21 Kent, 120.

22 Sullivan, George, *Screen Play: The Story of Video Games* (New York: Frederick Warne, 1983), 37.

23 Kent, 106.

24 Horowitz, Ken, *The Sega Arcade Revolution: A History in 62 games* (Jefferson, NC: McFarland & Company, 2018), 14-16.

25 Hugg, x.

26 https://www.arcade-history.com/?n=head-on-model-822-0001&page=detail&id=1103

27 Rousse, Thomas H. "Reconstructing WARRIOR: Vectorbeams, Natural Magick & Business Intrigue." *Kinephanos*, June 2015. https://www.kinephanos.ca/2015/reconstructing-warrior/

28 Ibid.

29 https://www.arcade-museum.com/game_detail.php?game_id=10408

30 Hugg, 9-10.

31 Kent, 137.

32 St. Clair, John, *Project Arcade: Build Your Own Arcade Machine* (Indianapolis: Wiley, 2004), 273.

33 Atarigames.com, n.d. "atarinumbers90s.pdf." http://www.atarigames.com/atari-numbers90s.pdf.

34 Kent, 131.

35 Kent, 131.

36 Wolf, *Video Game Explosion*, 68.

37 "Can Asteroids Conquer Space Invaders?," *Electronic Games*, Winter 1981, 33.

38 "Top 100 Games of All Time," *Next Generation*, September 1996, 56.

39 Horowitz, 28.

40 Ibid.

41 Ibid.

42 Kubey, ??.

43 https://dadgum.com/halcyon/book/skelly.htm

44 Ibid.

45 Kent, 139.

46 Kent, 140.

47 Rothman, Joshua, "Mirror World," *The New Yorker*, December 16, 2019.

48 Herman, 69.

49 "The 30 Defining Moments in Video Gaming," *Edge*, August 14, 2007.

Chapter 4

1 Pittman, Jamey, "The Pac-Man Dossier," Gamasutra, February 23, 2009. https://www.gamasutra.com/view/feature/132330/the_pacman_dossier.php?page=2

2 Kurtz, 81.

3 Sullivan, 44.

4 Kurtz, 81.

5 Kent, 143.

6 Kubey, Craig, *The Winners' Book of Video Games* (New York: Warner Books, 1982), 33.

7 Hugg, xi.

8 Ibid.

9 Bang, Derrick, "Beating the Classics," *Softline*, May-June 1983, 43.

10 Kent, 147.

11 Ibid.

12 Zeidman, Bob, *The Software IP Detective's Handbook: Measurement, Comparison, and Infringement Detection* (Upper Saddle River, NJ: Prentice Hall, 2011), 64.

13 Consumer Guide's *How To Win At Video Games* (New York: Pocket Books, 1982), 86.

14 Kent, 148.

15 Kent, 154.

16 Bloom, Steve, *Video Invaders* (New York: Arco Publishing, 1982), 41.

17 https://www.arcade-museum.com/game_detail.php?game_id=7096

18 Grammer, Charlie, "Gamebusters myth 7: Berzerk," GotGame, December 27, 2013. https://gotgame.com/2013/12/27/gamebusters-myth-7-berzerk/

19 DeSpira, Cat, "Dying To Play: The Berzerk Curse -Fact or Fiction?" Retro Bitch, November 4, 2015. https://retrobitch.wordpress.com/2015/11/04/dying-to-play-the-berzerk-curse-fact-or-fiction/

20 https://www.arcade-museum.com/game_detail.php?game_id=7096

21 https://www.arcade-museum.com/game_detail.php?game_id=7426

22 http://www.classicarcadegaming.com/forums/index.php?topic=3129.0

23 Bloom, 62.

24 Smith, Keith, "The Ultimate (So Far) History of Allied Leisure/Centuri - Part 3," The Golden Age Arcade Historian, October 11, 2013. http://allincolorforaquarter.blogspot.com/2013/10/the-ultimate-so-far-history-of-allied.html

25 Smith, Keith, "The Ultimate (So Far) History of Allied Leisure/Centuri - Part 5," The Golden Age Arcade Historian, December 14, 2013. http://allincolorforaquarter.blogspot.com/2013/12/the-ultimate-so-far-history-of-allied.html

26 Dahlen, Chris, Mott, Tony, ed., *1001 Games You Must Play Before You Die* (New York: Universe, 2011), 40.

27 "GameSpy's Top 50 Arcade Games of All-Time," GameSpy, February 25, 2011, via Wayback Machine. https://web.archive.org/web/20110426003920/www.gamespy.com/articles/115/1151159p3.html

28 "GameSpy's Top 50 Arcade Games of All-Time," GameSpy, February 25, 2011, via Wayback Machine. https://web.archive.org/web/20110426003920/www.gamespy.com/articles/115/1151159p3.html

29 "Arcade Action," *Computer and Video Games*, February 1982, 26.

30 www.arcade-history.com/?n=asteroids-deluxe&page=detail&id=127

31 Kent, 176.

32 "Stern Production Numbers and More CCI Photos," https://tokensonly.com/2012/05/01/stern-production-numbers-and-more-cci-photos/

33 Kunkel, Bill, "Insert Coin Here: What's New In the Arcades," *Electronic Games*, Winter 1981, 64.

34 Richardson, Willy, "Own Your Own Arcade Game," *Electronic Games*, Winter 1981, 70-71.

Chapter 5

1 Wolf, *Video Game Explosion*, 103.

2 Kubey, xiv.

3 Ibid.

4 Kubey, xv.

5   Kubey, xvi-xvii.

6   Kent, 157.

7   Kunkel, Bill, "Insert Coin Here: What's New In the Arcades," *Electronic Games*, May 1982, 27.

8   Wardyga, 43.

9   Kunkel, Bill, and Katz, Arnie, "Arcade Alley: Wintertime Winners," *Video*, November 1983, 38-39.

10 Pearl, Rick, "Closet Classics," *Electronic Games*, June 1983, 82.

11 Collins, 132.

12 Rose, Gary and Marcia, "Gameline," *Softline*, November 1982, 19.

13 Kunkel, Bill,"Insert Coin Here," *Electronic Games*, May 1982, 26-28.

14 Cifaldi, Frank, "The Connection is Made: Developer Highlights from Game Connection 2006 (Part Two)," Gamasutra, April 20, 2006. https://www.gamasutra.com/view/feature/131077/the_connection_is_made_developer_.php

15 "Steve Hanawa's Tech Talk," Sega8bit, October 31, 2008. http://www.smstributes.co.uk/view_article.asp?articleid=45

16 Crawford, Chris, "Design Techniques and Ideas for Computer Games," *Byte*, December 1982, 96.

17 "Electronic Games Hotline," *Electronic Games*, July 1982, 9.

18 Kunkel, Bill, and Katz, Arnie, "The 1983 Arcade Awards," *Electronic Games*, January 1983, 36.

19 Fujihara, Mary, "Inter Office Memo" at Atari dated November 2, 1983.

20 Katz, Arnie, "Switch On," *Electronic Games*, May 1982, 6.

21 "Videogame Outlook…1982: Here Comes the Video Game Explosion," *Electronic Games*, May 1982, 22-23.

22 Kent, 237.

23 Sharpe, Roger, "The History of the Arcade," *Electronic Games*, July 1982, 29.

24 The Game Doctor, "Q&A," *Electronic Games*, September 1982, 17.

25 Kunkel, Bill, and Katz, Arnie, "Arcade Alley: Zaxxon, Turbo, and Two for Apple II," *Video*, April 1983, 26-29.

26 Sellers, John. *Arcade Fever: The Fan's Guide to the Golden Age of Video Games* (Philadelphia: Running Press, 2001), 121.

27 Harmetz, Aljean, "Movie Themes Come To Video Games," *Wilmington Morning Star*, July 3, 1982, 6C.

28 Kent, 222-224.

29 https://dadgum.com/halcyon/book/jarvis.htm

30 Ibid.

31 Lapetino, 190.

32 Ibid.

33 https://www.arcade-history.com/?page=detail&id=2525

34 Costrel, France, creator. *High Score* (New York City: Great Big Story/Netflix, 2020), interview with Doug Macrae.

35 Ibid.

36 Kent, 167-169.

37 Costrel, France, creator. *High Score* (New York City: Great Big Story/Netflix,

2020), interview with Doug Macrae.

38 Costrel, France, creator. *High Score* (New York City: Great Big Story/Netflix, 2020), interview with Steve Golson.

39 Kent, 169-172.

40 Kent, 172.

41 "Video Games Are Blitzing the World," *Time*, Jan. 18, 1982.

42 Ibid.

43 Bloom, 138.

44 Cohen, Henry, "Test Lab: Getting Into Direct Video," *Electronic Games*, September 1982, 20.

45 Wolf, *Video Game Explosion*, 103.

Chapter 6

1 "The Cosmic Quarter-Snatchers Cometh," *Electronic Games*, March 1982, 44.

2 Wise, Deborah, "Video arcades rival Broadway theater and girlie shows in NY," *InfoWorld*, April 12, 1983, 15.

3 Robley, Les Paul, "An Exciting Preview of Disney's Videogame Movie," *Electronic Games*, July 1982, 34.

4 Shea, Tom, "Shrinking Pac-Man Leads Game-Wristwatch Market," *InfoWorld*, Dec. 20, 1982, 44.

5 Robley, Les Paul, "An Exciting Preview of Disney's Videogame Movie," *Electronic Games*, July 1982, 34.

6 Jackson, Matthew, "Little-known sci-fi fact: Why Tron's FX got snubbed for an Oscar," Syfy Wire, March 1, 2013. https://www.syfy.com/syfywire/little-known-sci-fi-fact-why-trons-fx-got-snubbed-oscar

7 Robley, Les Paul, "An Exciting Preview of Disney's Videogame Movie," *Electronic Games*, July 1982, 36.

8 Formichella, Lucien, "14 groundbreaking movies that took special effects to new levels," Insider, January 11, 2020. https://www.insider.com/most-groundbreaking-cgi-movies-ever-created-2020-1

9 Katz, Arnie, and Kunkel, Bill. "The Arcade Awards." *Electronic Games*, January 1983, 35.

10 https://www.arcade-museum.com/game_detail.php?game_id=10007

11 https://www.arcade-history.com/?n=dig-dug&page=detail&id=637

12 Ibid.

13 Ibid.

14 Robley, Les Paul, "Confessions of an Arcade Technician," *Electronic Games*, May 1983, 54-56.

15 Ibid.

16 Richardson, Willy, "The Making of an Arcade Game," *Electronic Games*, March 1982, 32-33.

17 "Here Come the Convertibles," *Electronic Games,* August 1983, 92-93.

18 "Upcoming Coin-Ops: Fewer But Better," *Electronic Games*, August 1983, 90.

19 Ibid.

20 https://flyers.arcade-museum.com/?page=flyer&db=videodb&id=4071&image=2

21 Temple, Tony. "Atari Kangaroo: The elephant in the arcade." Arcade Blogger. November 11, 2017. https://arcadeblogger.com/2017/11/10/atari-kangaroo-the-elephant-in-the-arcade/

22 Ibid.

23 Ibid.

24 Newman, 41.

25 Newman, 41-42.

26 Kubey, 5-8.

27 Kubey, 9-10.

28 "Electronic Games Hotline," *Electronic Games*, July 1982, 8.

29 "Electronic Games Hotline," *Electronic Games*, March 1982, 28-29.

30 Ibid.

31 DBG, "Harry Lafnear," Atari Legend, September 5, 2003. https://www.atarilegend.com/interviews/interviews_detail.php?selected_interview_id=4

32 Digital Eclipse, "Midway Arcade Treasures," PC CD-ROM, 2004.

33 Kent, 352.

34 Sullivan, 61.

35 Kent, 152.

36 Kurtz, 82.

37 Kent, 152.

38 Brother Bill, "The Bishop of Battle (Nightmares, 1983)," The Haunted Closet, April 24, 2010. http://the-haunted-closet.blogspot.com/2010/04/bishop-of-battle-nightmares-1983.html

39 Brooks, B. David, Ph. D., "Exploding the Arcade Myths: A Scientist Evaluates the Coin-Op Gaming Scene," *Electronic Games*, August 1982, 35.

40 Newman, 41.

41 Katz, Arnie, "Switch On," *Electronic Games*, July 1982, 6.

Chapter 7

1 Kurtz, 82-83.

2 "Early Arcade Classics: 1985-1987 Developer Interviews." *Beep!*, 1985 via http://shmuplations.com/20questions1985/

3 Fujihara, Mary, "Inter Office Memo" at Atari dated November 2, 1983.

4 Defanti, Thomas A., "The Mass Impact of Videogame Technology," *Advances in Computers*, Volume 23 (Cambridge, MA: Academic Press, 1984), 105.

5 Coogan, Dan, "Interview with Mike Hally and Rich Adam, designers of Gravitar," Coogan Photo, March 12, 2004 (Updated December 30, 2006). http://www.cooganphoto.com/gravitar/interview.html#interview

6 Dahlen and Mott, 49.

7 Kunkel, Bill, "Insert Coin Here," *Electronic Games*, February 1983, 62.

8 Kent, Steven. "VideoGameSpot's Interview with Yoshiki Okamoto." VideoGameSpot, December 7, 1998 via Wayback Machine. https://web.archive.org/web/19981207033331/http://www.videogames.com/features/universal/okamoto/

oktime.html

9   Ibid.

10 Ibid.

11 Ibid.

12 https://www.arcade-history.com/?n=burger-time&page=detail&id=355

13 "59 Developers, 20 Questions." *Beep!*, October 1985 via http://shmuplations.com/20questions1985/

14 Kunkel, Bill, and Katz, Arnie, "The 1984 Arcade Awards," *Electronic Games*, January 1984, 78.

15 Kent, 352.

16 Aycock, 116-119.

17 Wolf, *Encyclopedia of Arcade Games, Volume 2*, 30.

18 Wolf, *Video Game Explosion*, 104.

19 Katz, Arnie, "Switch On," *Electronic Games*, July 1982, 6.

20 Kent, 176.

21 "Arcade Video Games Start to Flicker," *BusinessWeek*, Dec. 6, 1982, 39-40.

22 Kent, 176.

23 Kent, 176-177.

24 Kunkel, Bill, "1982—The Year in Coin-Ops," *Electronic Games*, December 1982, 65-66.

25 Kunkel, Bill. "1982—The Year in Coin-Ops," *Electronic Games*, December 1982, 64.

26 Pearl, Rich, "A Time Trip to the Game Parlor of the Future," *Electronic Games*, January 1983, 62-63.

27 Ibid.

28 Ibid.

29 Forman, Tracie, "Insert Coin Here," *Electronic Games*, August 1983, 100.

30 Kurtz, 150.

31 https://www.arcade-museum.com/game_detail.php?game_id=10505

32 Kent, 444.

33 Kent, 154-155.

34 Forman, Tracie, "Insert Coin Here," *Electronic Games*, December 1983, 106.

35 June, Laura, "For Amusement Only: the life and death of the American arcade," The Verge, January 16, 2013. https://www.theverge.com/2013/1/16/3740422/the-life-and-death-of-the-american-arcade-for-amusement-only

Chapter 8

1   Kent, 203-210.

2   Kent, 203-210.

3   Kent, 234.

4   Wolf, *Video Game Explosion*, 105.

5   Dvorchak, Robert, "NEC Out to Dazzle Nintendo Fans," *Associated Press*, Jul. 30, 1989.

6   Kent, 240.

7   Katz, Arnie, "The Decline and Fall…of Prices," *Electronic Games*, October 1983, 6.

8   Newman, 75.

9   Newman, 93.

10   Wolf, *Video Game Explosion*, 99.

11   "Dragon's Lair Historical 1983 News Reel," YouTube. https://www.youtube.com/watch?v=LM7DRYScacU&list=PLywcJMkS3J8eM5mU7PObpIedDw8ATL-6n0&index=53

12   La Brecque, Eric, "Technician of Suspended Disbelief: Rick Dyer, Shadoan and the Frontier of Animated CD Entertainment," *Animation World Network*, 1996. Retrieved via the Wayback Machine: https://web.archive.org/web/20090804024201/http://www.awn.com/mag/issue1.1/articles/dyer.html

13   Wolf, *Video Game Explosion*, 99-100.

14   "Dragon's Lair Historical 1983 News Reel," YouTube. https://www.youtube.com/watch?v=LM7DRYScacU&list=PLywcJMkS3J8eM5mU7PObpIedDw8ATL-6n0&index=53

15   Kurtz, 150.

16   Wolf, *Video Game Explosion*, 100.

17   https://historian159.rssing.com/chan-12531872/all_p4.html, citing *RePlay*, January 1984.

18   https://www.arcade-museum.com/game_detail.php?game_id=12839

19   Thomsen, Michael, "Fond Memories: Kung-Fu Master," IGN, February 13, 2008, updated May 12, 2012. https://www.ign.com/articles/2008/02/13/fond-memories-kung-fu-master

20   Kurtz, 153.

21   https://www.arcade-history.com/?n=the-last-starfighter&page=detail&id=4815

22   Wolf, *Video Game Explosion*, 105.

23   Persons, Dan, "Laser's Last Stand," *Electronic Games*, January 1985, 81.

24   Persons, Dan, "Laser's Last Stand," *Electronic Games*, January 1985, 79-80.

25   Kurtz, 152.

26   Ibid.

27   Ibid.

28   Persons, Dan, "Laser's Last Stand," *Electronic Games*, January 1985, 79-80.

29   Lustig, David, "The Big Shake-Out?" *Electronic Games*, Mar 1984, 23.

30   Katz, Arnie, "Switch On: The Future of Coin-Op Videogames," *Electronic Games*, September 1984, 6.

31   Ibid.

Chapter 9

1   Wardyga, 109.

2   https://www.arcade-museum.com/pinouts-class/JAMMA.html

3   http://www.atariprotos.com/7800/software/darkchambers/darkchambers.htm

4   Logg, Ed, "Gauntlet Postmortem," 2012 Game Developers Conference.

5   "Arcade Action," *Computer and Video Games*, December 1985, 89.

6   https://www.arcade-history.com/?n=indiana-jones-and-the-temple-of-doom&page=detail&id=1185

7   Agnello, Anthony John, "How Ghosts 'n Goblins helped video games find comedy in failure," AV Club, April 19, 2017. https://games.avclub.com/how-ghosts-n-goblins-helped-video-games-find-comedy-in-1798260872

8   Harris, Duncan and Mott, 96.

9   Reilly, Luke, "The Top 10 Most Influential Racing Games," IGN, April 3, 2015, Updated May 2, 2017. https://www.ign.com/articles/2015/04/03/the-top-10-most-influential-racing-games-ever

10 Rasa, Chris, "Rastan," HG101, October 4, 2017. http://www.hardcoregaming101.net/rastan/

11 Ibid.

12 https://www.system16.com/hardware.php?id=738

13 SaraAB87, "Happy 30th Birthday to Sega's After Burner! 1987-2017," Arcade Heroes, July 1, 2017. https://arcadeheroes.com/2017/07/01/happy-30th-birthday-segas-burner-1987-2017/

14 "Reader Replay," Electronic Games, April 1985, 12.

15 Wolf, Encyclopedia of Video Games, Volume 1, 36.

Chapter 10

1   https://www.arcade-museum.com/game_detail.php?game_id=9803

2   Lipscombe, Daniel, "Insane difficulty and joke endings - looking back at Altered Beast, 30 years later," GamesRadar, August 1, 2018. https://www.gamesradar.com/insane-difficulty-and-joke-endings-looking-back-at-altered-beast-30-years-later/

3   Margolin, Jed, "Schematics For Hard Drivin'/Race Drivin' ADSP, Motor Amplifier, and DSK Boards," March 9, 2002. http://jmargolin.com/schem/schems.htm

4   https://www.arcade-history.com/?n=air-race&page=detail&id=35309

5   Massey, Tom, "Final Fight retrospective," Eurogamer, May 26, 2014. https://www.eurogamer.net/articles/2014-05-25-final-fight-retrospective

6   Kent, 444.

7   Massey, Tom, "Final Fight retrospective," Eurogamer, May 26, 2014. https://www.eurogamer.net/articles/2014-05-25-final-fight-retrospective

8   Herman, 207.

9   Parkin, Simon, "The Unexpectedly High-Stakes World of Neo Geo Collecting," The New Yorker, January 24, 2017. https://www.newyorker.com/tech/annals-of-technology/the-unexpectedly-high-stakes-world-of-neo-geo-collecting

Chapter 11

1   "They Create Worlds" Twitter feed, January 16, 2020. https://twitter.com/tcw-podcast/status/1217824203711356928

2   McCarthy, Rebecca, "Video Games Are an Exercise In Annihilation," The Atlanta

Journal-Constitution, May 30, 1989, D/1.

3   Kent, 445.

4   Herman, 233.

5   "IGN's Top 100 Games of All Time," IGN, 2007 via https://web.archive.org/web/20110830043153/http://top100.ign.com/2007/ign_top_game_24.html

6   Patterson, Eric, "The 5 Most Influential Japanese Games Day Four: Street Fighter II," *Electronic Gaming Monthly*, November 3, 2011 via Wayback Machine, https://web.archive.org/web/20170314064721/http://www.egmnow.com/articles/news/egm-featurethe-5-most-influential-japanese-gamesday-four-street-fighter-ii/

7   Capcom IR Investor Relations Code Number: 9697 via Wayback Machine. https://web.archive.org/web/20150208030840/http://www.capcom.co.jp/ir/english/business/million.html

8   Leack, Jonathan, "World of Warcraft Leads Industry With Nearly $10 Billion In Revenue," GameRevolution, January 26, 2017. https://www.gamerevolution.com/features/13510-world-of-warcraft-leads-industry-with-nearly-10-billion-in-revenue

9   Patterson, Eric, "The 5 Most Influential Japanese Games Day Four: Street Fighter II," *Electronic Gaming Monthly*, November 3, 2011 via Wayback Machine, https://web.archive.org/web/20170314064721/http://www.egmnow.com/articles/news/egm-featurethe-5-most-influential-japanese-gamesday-four-street-fighter-ii/

10 Pierce, David, "'The Simpsons Arcade Game' was the best game ever based on a TV show," The Verge, August 26, 2014. https://www.theverge.com/2014/8/26/6067425/the-simpsons-arcade-game-made-me-love-the-show

11 "15 Most Influential Games of All Time," GameSpot via Wayback Machine, https://web.archive.org/web/20100412225953/http://www.gamespot.com/gamespot/features/video/15influential/p13_01.html

12 Sponsel, Sebastian, "History of: Virtua Fighter," Sega-16, February 3, 2010. https://www.sega-16.com/2010/02/history-of-virtua-fighter/

13 Horowitz, Ken, "Feature: The History Of Virtua Racing, One Of The Most Influential Coin-Ops Of All Time," NintendoLife, May 6, 2019. https://www.nintendolife.com/news/2019/05/feature_the_history_of_virtua_racing_one_of_the_most_influential_coin-ops_of_all_time

14 Ibid.

15 Ibid.

16 https://segaretro.org/Virtua_Racing

17 "Leading Edge," *Electronic Gaming Monthly*, November 1992, 54.

18 Feit, Daniel, "How Virtua Fighter Saved PlayStation's Bacon," *Wired*, September 5, 2012. https://www.wired.com/2012/09/how-virtua-fighter-saved-playstations-bacon/

19 Ibid.

20 Armstrong, Larry, "Raiders Of The Video Arcade," *Bloomberg*, October 17, 1994. https://www.bloomberg.com/news/articles/1994-10-16/raiders-of-the-video-arcade

21 Webb, Marcus, "Arcadia," *Next Generation*, February 1996, 29.

22 Henry, Lydia, "Skee-Ball Mania," *Reading Eagle*, Arp. 26, 2001, 19.

Epilogue

1 Siegel, Alan, "How Golden Tee became the best bar game in America," *USA Today*, June 24, 2015. https://ftw.usatoday.com/2015/06/golden-tee-the-history-of-a-beer-soaked-american-pastime

2 Kent, 528-529.

3 Tkacik, Maureen, "Back to Bingo: Arcade Firm Shrugs Off High-Tech Flash— GameWorks Thinks It Has a Winner With Classics Like Bowling and Skee-Ball," *The Wall Street Journal*, July 23, 2001.

4 Kent, 529.

5 Wardyga, 243.

6 Hurley, Oliver, "Game on again for coin-operated arcade titles," *The Guardian*, February 6, 2008. https://www.theguardian.com/technology/2008/feb/07/games.it

7 Lewis, Alexander, "Free play arcade to open in Deptford," *Courier News and Home News Tribune*, October 30, 2018. https://www.mycentraljersey.com/story/news/2018/10/30/free-play-arcade-colonial-soldier-arcade-opens-deptford/1676021002/

8 Bloom, 61.

9 https://www.gamasutra.com/view/news/247873/Obituary_Exidy_founder_Pete_Kauffman.php

> Index

> About the Author

Jamie Lendino is an author, editor, mix engineer, and technology enthusiast. In addition to his books about vintage computers and video games (*Breakout: How Atari 8-Bit Computers Defined a Generation*, *Adventure: The Atari 2600 at the Dawn of Console Gaming*, and *Faster Than Light: The Atari ST and the 16-Bit Revolution*), he has written for ExtremeTech, *PC Magazine*, *Popular Science*, *Electronic Musician*, *Consumer Reports*, *Sound and Vision*, and CNET. Jamie has also appeared on NPR's *All Things Considered* and other television and radio programs across the United States. He lives with his wife, daughter, and two bonkers cats in Collingswood, New Jersey.